TABLE OF CONTENTS

REVISED AND UPDATED

Friendly Divorce Guidebook for Connecticut

Planning, Negotiating, and Filing Your Divorce

By
Barbara Kahn Stark, MLA, JD

LawFirst Publishing, New Britain, CT

PLEASE READ

This book, the *Friendly Divorce Guidebook for Connecticut*, is intended to provide general information with regard to the subject matter covered. It is not meant to provide legal opinions or offer legal advice, or to serve as a substitute for advice by licensed, legal professionals. It is sold with the understanding that Bradford Publishing Company and LawFirst Publishing are not engaged in rendering legal or other professional services.

Bradford Publishing Company and LawFirst Publishing do not warrant that the information herein is complete or accurate, and do not assume and hereby disclaim any liability to any person for any loss or damage caused by errors, inaccuracies or omissions, or usage of this book or its forms.

Laws, and interpretations of those laws, change frequently and the subject matter of this book contains important legal consequences. It is the responsibility of the user of this book to know if the information contained in it is applicable to his or her situation, and if necessary, to consult legal, tax, or other counsel.

This edition of the *Friendly Divorce Guidebook for Connecticut* is published by LawFirst Publishing, a division of the Connecticut Bar Association, under license from Bradford Publishing Company.

LawFirst Publishing, New Britain, CT 06050

© 1998, 2003 by Bradford Publishing Company
All rights reserved. First edition 1998
Second edition 2003

ISBN 0-9740069-3-9 (Previously 1-883726-06-9)

To Cecelia Clark Flagg
and Harry Samuel Allen

PREFACE

The initial impetus for this guidebook originated with the publication of the *Friendly Divorce Guidebook for Colorado* in 1995 by my friends and professional colleagues, S.W. Whicher and M. Arden Hauer. I used much of their original text where applicable in Connecticut, and I wrote the rest to reflect Connecticut law and practice and my own views. I want to acknowledge Wendy and Arden's significant roles in this book, including the general and sidebar format, the use of icons, and Bunky. Without their excellent work I would never have had the structure and guidance that helped me so much in completing the first edition.

Finally, this book would never have become a reality without the support of my husband, Attorney Gerald H. Kahn of New Haven, Connecticut. In his heart, he may doubt that there can be a "friendly" divorce (although all of the divorces he settles qualify under my broad definition), but I work to continue to persuade him, and others, that there is a better way to help people through their divorce process.

INTRODUCTION

No matter who makes the choice to end a marriage, both spouses have options about how to handle the divorce process. This guidebook will help you to end your marriage in a cooperative, efficient way. You can work to make your divorce as positive as possible so that it provides a sound foundation for you and your children for the future.

My intention in writing this guidebook is to give basic information to help couples settle the issues that confront them in divorce. I hope that it will help people working with lawyers or mediators or on their own through the divorce process. It offers approaches to and techniques for cooperation rather than strategies for obtaining advantage in a court battle. Used cover to cover, this guidebook will lead you through the legal and personal aspects of working together to complete your divorce. It will help you gather all the data you need to consider, and it will help you organize it so that you can make informed decisions. It will help you develop an agreement that makes optimal sense of your situation now and into the future. Even if you feel some hostility, anger, or reservations about each other, you can still negotiate a "friendly" divorce that keeps you out of court.

In her most recent book, *The Argument Culture: Moving from Debate to Dialogue*, Deborah Tannen asserts that our entire society has evolved into a combative, argument culture that manifests itself in the hostility and violence that permeate our daily lives. Battlefield metaphors are used in business, politics, and social interaction. The divorce process, an experience faced by thousands of couples and their children, is a particularly revealing cultural phenomenon.

Families faced with this traumatic event turn to the legal system to resolve their problems and redirect their lives. But according to Dr. Marsha Kline Pruett and Dr. Kyle Pruett in their recent study, "Divorce in Legal Context: Outcomes for Children," most parents interviewed wanted the divorce to be "cleaner and more predictable" with the direction of the process to remain, in some way, more in their control. The children the doctors studied consistently and poignantly spoke about how the court system made it impossible for their parents to "remain friends." Of particular concern is the finding that parents (and children) perceive the adversarial system as "an unpredictable, caustic parent, capable of great harm and embarrassment."

Involvement with the legal system seems inevitably to lead to escalating emotions and fears with the divorce becoming a war

"From pro's and con's they fell to a warmer way of disputing."

Miguel de Cervantes, *Don Quixote*

"There is truly a magical quality about conflict which can call out the best in us, that which is not summoned under ordinary circumstances."

Thomas F. Crum, *The Magic of Conflict*

"When they [people] no longer trust themselves, they begin to depend upon authority."

Lao-Tzu, *Tao Te Ching*

between the spouses. This culture of argument leaves the couple's sense of self worth, their financial stability, and their children among the victims of the conflict.

It doesn't have to be this way. There are other options for couples who share the goal of ending their marriage in a constructive way, minimizing hostility and damage for all family members. There are three paths to divorce: the conventional adversarial process, a mediated settlement, and a collaborative approach. The conventional route is the one currently used by most couples. According to Tannen, divorce is perceived as a fight and emphasizes competition, winners, and losers while suppressing any cooperative impulses. Lawyers are seen as "jousting gladiators" rather than participants seeking a solution to a family's problems.

Mediation offers an alternative route to divorce. In mediation, a neutral party meets with the couple in a confidential setting. Mediation provides an environment where the spouses can discuss the issues they need to resolve before they can begin their new lives as single people and co-parents. The mediator gives no legal advice but is instrumental in sharing parenting and financial information to help the couple explore settlement options and reach an agreement.

For those couples who value and want to protect their emotional health as much as their financial state, divorce mediation offers many advantages over the adversarial process including maintaining control over the process, providing cost savings, offering privacy, producing a base for client-generated solutions, and allowing improved future communications and parenting. Mediation does not exclude legal advice, although lawyers are generally not present in the sessions. In fact, each spouse in the mediation process should consider obtaining the advice of an attorney before and during mediation sessions and before signing the final settlement agreement.

Another alternative is available for divorcing couples who want to settle their cases cooperatively but would prefer to have attorneys present while they meet to explore their options. "Collaborative law" is new to many areas, but it has grown in popularity in California and is now in high demand. Collaborative law is a negotiation process where each party is represented by an attorney at a series of four-way meetings. At these meetings, with lawyers and clients present, all parties collaborate together to identify and agree on solutions. This process is different from traditional settlement negotiations in that all four participants formally agree not to go to court or threaten litigation in the process. They jointly retain any expert needed, such as psychologists or accountants. The parties share a commitment to the family and honest, respectful, and productive problem-solving. The lawyers remain advocates and legal counselors to their clients with the shared goal of settling the case out of court. This pledge of the attorneys is sealed by the commitment to withdraw from representing the clients in the event that either party resorts to the conventional divorce litigation process.

Mediation and collaboration, while not viable alternatives for every couple, offer the promise of ending the adversarial nature of divorce for families. No matter the road taken, people do have a choice about how to reduce hostility and the loss of control, and they can eliminate the public expression of shame and blame that comes with a courtroom battle. It's time for spouses to challenge what Tannen calls "the pre-patterned, unthinking use of fighting to accomplish goals that do not necessarily require it." The welfare of children and the long-term health of family members after divorce requires nothing less.

This guidebook's format combines a complete discussion of each topic with illustrative examples, charts, checklists, questionnaires, resources, and full-size sample forms. In addition, this guidebook also uses icons:

 indicates tax information

 indicates a caution, or something of particular importance that should not be overlooked

 warns about something with dire consequences

 indicates the definition of a legal term

 points out an Internet resource

 shows a common opinion or belief that is, in whole, not quite accurate. Some are more fiction than fact. Bunkies abound in the area of marital difficulty and divorce. These widespread inaccuracies can really cause harm, thus, this guidebook aims to debunk them and clarify what is true.

"My spouse won't give me a divorce"

You don't need each other's permission to get a legal divorce. If either of you declares to the court in a written petition that the marriage is irretrievably broken, you have established sufficient legal grounds for the divorce process to begin. This does not prevent you from working together to complete it.

 "This guidebook is the only help you will need with your divorce."

This is not true. In addition to the information provided in this guidebook, you may need to consult with an attorney, a counselor or therapist, an accountant, an appraiser, a pastor, and your family and friends to be able to make clear choices.

 This guidebook is not a substitute for a lawyer's advice about your particular situation. Remember, you are legally responsible for whatever assumptions and agreements you make in your divorce. Be sure to obtain all of the legal, financial, tax, and/or psychological advice and information you need to be secure in your choices. Having a "friendly" divorce does not mean that you can ignore the legalities of the process. Take responsibility for yourself by making sure that you have all the information and professional advice that you need to make final settlement decisions you will not later question and regret. People who say, "I don't care, you take everything—I just want out," are setting themselves up for later resentment, hurt, and even rage.

CHAPTER 1

THE INITIAL DECISION

How Do You Know If You Should Get a Divorce?

Every marriage ends in either death or divorce.

Violence and Abuse

If you are experiencing physical or serious emotional abuse or threats it is important to get physicially separated as soon as possible—regardless of what you are deciding about legal separation and divorce.

If you need help confronting the issue of domestic violence or abuse, call 2-1-1 Infoline by dialing 211. You can also go to court to get a restraining order.

For Procedures for Relief From Abuse Process go to **www.jud.state.ct.us/forms/ fm142p.pdf**.

Marriage Counseling Checklist

Directions: Check or initial what is true.

☐ We have already tried it.

☐ We will give it a try.

☐ One of us is not interested.

☐ Neither of us is interested.

THE INITIAL DECISION

How Do You Know If You Should Get a Divorce?

When we marry, most of us say "Till death us do part" and mean it. The prospect of divorce is as unsettling and threatening as an earthquake for some of us, the welcome end of an intolerable situation for others, and somewhere between these two extremes for most. For everyone, divorce is both an ending and a beginning, a sunset and a new dawn. Throughout this critical time, both what you do and especially how you do it are important to the present and future wellbeing of yourself and of everyone in your family.

Options for the Marriage in Difficulty

When a couple begins to experience serious difficulty in their marriage, it sometimes seems impossible to step back and take a serious and rational look at the possible alternatives. It may be helpful to review the available options:

- Marriage counseling and the possibility of reconciling (staying together and working on the relationship)

- Physical separation (often called trial separation)

- Dissolution of marriage (divorce)

- Legal separation

- Annulment

Following is a short discussion of each of these.

Marriage Counseling

Every spouse thinks about separation and divorce once in awhile. Is the cause of your current marital discord a single incident? Do you both acknowledge and understand your problems? Do you both want to stay married if you can resolve the difficulty? If you answered "yes" to these questions, then you might want to hold off on any legal filing and seek marriage counseling.

Some common marital problems marriage counseling may help are:

- Situation stress: loss of job, death of a loved one, major illness or injury of a family member, new child, disabled child or elderly relative in the home, child at difficult age, or sudden major expenses

- Ongoing quarrels over money or budgeting difficulty

- Sexual dissatisfaction or dysfunction (If this is the type of problem you are experiencing, ask specifically about expertise in this area during your first contact with any professional you are considering.)

Whether or not either of you is thinking of ending the marriage, you must satisfy yourself that you have explored all reasonable possibilities for continuing the marriage—to avoid being plagued with guilt later for not having done your best. Marriage counseling can be of help with this, regardless of whether you decide to continue the marriage.

Physical Separation (Trial Separation)

Most people use this term to mean getting physically—especially sexually—away from each other. In most cases, one spouse moves out. Some people separate within the same house by one of them moving to the finished basement, to another bedroom, or to the mother-in-law apartment. Working out a schedule of different kitchen and laundry room times can help create a feeling of separateness and is a way to avoid difficult surprises. Many people need to be further apart than this and cannot simply separate within the same building.

The question of whether to physically separate ultimately comes down to whether one or both of you is so uncomfortable being around the other that he or she feels paralyzed or cannot function. Sometimes physical separation brings with it the insight needed to work on resolving serious differences and prompts a renewed commitment to the marriage. Other times, however, it awakens the realization that you really want the marital relationship to end.

PHYSICAL SEPARATION HAS BOTH LEGAL AND TAX CONSEQUENCES

Unless you agree otherwise, the legal consequences of your marriage continue after you separate. The law provides that the judge has the power to give your spouse any property either of you

---

How to Find a Marriage Counselor

- Get a referral from a friend you trust who can make a recommendation based on personal experience.

- Ask your pastor, social worker, lawyer, or mediator to make a recommendation.

- Look in the Yellow Pages or Smartpages.com under the following headings:
    Marriage, Family, Child, and
        Individual Counselors
    Psychotherapists
    Psychologists
    Social Workers
    Physicians – Psychiatrists

- Inquire at your neighborhood or town mental health center.

Physical / Trial Separation Checklist

Check or initial what is true:

____ We are physically separated now.

____ We plan to physically separate on

_____ (date).

_____ will move out.

____ We have no plans right now to physically separate.

____ We will separate within our home.

____ We have written down our agreement about separating. (See Chapter 5 for some ideas about how to do this.)

Dissolution of Marriage: The Connecticut term for divorce.

Divorce: The legal process which ends a marriage; dissolution of marriage.

"You're automatically divorced if your spouse has been gone for seven years."

This is not true. There is no "automatic" divorce, even if your spouse has disappeared.

accumulates after your separation. You could also be liable for the post-separation debts of your spouse.

The date of your physical separation may affect your tax filing status. See Chapter 10. To avoid this, do not allow the separation to drag on too long before reaching a final settlement.

For many reasons, it is often a very good idea to write out in detail the agreements you make with each other about your physical separation. This is what makes a physical separation into a trial separation—it is a time to try out your ideas about custody, support, and meeting your other marital obligations. See Chapters 3 and 5 for how to plan your separation so you both control the consequences.

Dissolution of Marriage (Divorce)

Court action is the only way to obtain a dissolution of marriage, more commonly known as divorce. The court will grant you a divorce once you meet all the requirements. The first step is that you say, right at the start, that your marriage has "broken down irretrievably."

The marriage dissolves—ends—when the judge verbally enters the judgment of dissolution of marriage. The judgment ends the mutual obligation spouses have to support each other—to provide the necessities of food, shelter, and clothing—and ends "conjugal rights" (sex), although you may continue a sexual relationship if you wish. The divorce also ends a person's right to any part of his or her spouse's estate at death. The moment a divorce judgment is entered, the spouses are each free to marry again.

Before the court can enter the divorce judgment, you or the court must divide the property and debts, establish custody of the children, and set child support and/or alimony (spousal support). This guidebook is about how to work together to reach these decisions yourselves with the assistance of appropriate professionals.

Common Law Marriage in Connecticut

Connecticut law does not recognize common law marriage from living together only in Connecticut. However, you may have a common law marriage that Connecticut will recognize if:

1) You have lived together (cohabited) in a state that recognizes common law marriage. You

must also have "held yourselves out" as married, meaning that you acted as though you were married. Typical proof of this is that you introduced each other as wife and husband, had the same last name, or filed married/joint income tax returns; and

2) Neither of you was still married to someone else.

If you think that you can claim a common law marriage, you should obtain legal advice before initiating a divorce in Connecticut.

Legal Separation

A legal separation judgment obtained from the court is the same as a dissolution of marriage, except that neither party is free to remarry and the right to inherit remains. All of the procedures for obtaining a divorce apply to a legal separation. See Chapter 6.

A judgment of legal separation declares that you and your spouse, as well as your financial assets and obligations, are legally separate. The judgment requires everyone, including creditors and financial and other institutions, to treat the two of you as separate persons. You can no longer file your income taxes as married taxpayers, either jointly or separately. After the court enters a judgment of legal separation, you are no longer responsible for each other's debts or actions and no longer entitled to each other's earnings or property. You are also no longer obligated to support each other except as provided in your separation agreement. (A judgment of dissolution of marriage does all this, too.)

Before the court can enter a judgment of legal separation, you or the court must divide your property and debts and decide about custody and family support, just as you must do for a divorce. In practice, the procedure and timing in court for a legal separation is the same as for a dissolution.

WHY WOULD YOU WANT A LEGAL SEPARATION?

Some couples aren't sure they want to divorce. A legal separation is a way to separate, to divide property, to end mutual responsibility for each other's support and debts except as agreed, and to take a good look at the relationship—while making divorce one additional step away.

Common Law Marriage: A marriage in which the parties did not obtain a license or go through a recognized ceremony but lived together as married.

"We don't need to go through court for our divorce, we're just common law married."

There is no such thing as common law divorce. If you are common law married in another state and you want a divorce or legal separation, you can only obtain it from the court.

"Once you are physically separated you are legally separated."

This assumption is incorrect and can be very costly. You are legally separated only if you receive a signed judgment of legal separation from a court. **Physical separation is not legal separation.**

Legal Separation: The court judgment that declares marriage partners to be separate persons not responsible for each other but still legally married.

"Possession is nine-tenths of the law."

Not true. You do not give up your rights to ownership in your home or other property by moving out. You don't lose your interest by letting the other spouse use or occupy it. By moving out you may, however, impact parenting issues and/or moving back in.

Some religions forbid or frown on divorce. Legal separation permits you to lead separate lives without divorcing.

There may be some kinds of health insurance, and some survivor benefits connected with retirement plans, which continue to cover or benefit legally separated people but not divorced people.

Social Security benefits can be based on a former spouse's earnings instead of one's own if the marriage lasted ten or more years. If you are close, it might be good planning to have a legal separation until you reach ten years of marriage and then convert to a divorce.

If you are unsure of whether to get a legal separation or a divorce, one place to start to ask questions is the benefits and/or personnel office where each of you works. Find out which benefits, if any, apply to the non-employee spouse after either a legal separation or a divorce. Find out what your respective Social Security benefits are currently and what they are projected to be. Some careful research and advice from a lawyer now may save you thousands of dollars in benefits later.

CHANGING FROM LEGAL SEPARATION TO DIVORCE

After you begin a court action for legal separation, either or both of you may change your request to one for dissolution of marriage any time before the court enters the final judgment. After the judgment of legal separation is entered, either spouse may petition the court to convert it to a divorce. The other spouse need not agree and cannot stop the conversion unless he or she alleges and proves that marital relations have resumed, requiring a new divorce action. If neither of you ever asks to have your legal separation converted to a divorce, you can remain legally separated for life.

When the judgment of legal separation converts to one of divorce, the terms of your legal separation agreement—about property, debts, custody, support, alimony—stay the same. If you and your spouse agree, changes can be made to the terms of the agreement when converting to divorce. If only one of you wants to change the agreement, the court may change the agreement if it finds that, due to dramatically changed circumstances, the agreement is no longer fair and equitable.

Annulment

If your marriage was not valid right from the start, you may ask the court to annul your marriage. In this procedure, you are asking the court to declare that your marriage never happened. You may ask for an annulment because one of you was already married, you are siblings or close relatives, you were underage, or there was serious fraud, force, duress, or "gross misrepresentation."

Annulment is a legal action that requires "grounds" that must be proved—unlike a dissolution of marriage. Consult with a lawyer if you think this procedure is what you need.

Your Other Divorces

The ending of a marriage is much more than a legal event. It is the letting go of dreams. It is the dissolution of a financial partnership. It is the forming of a new relationship with the other parent of your children—even if that is the last thing you want to do. A divorce is both an ending and a beginning.

One kind of divorce is the internal emotional divorce. It is a grief process with recognized stages. See Chapter 4.

Another kind of divorce is the relationship divorce from your partner. You accomplish this divorce by letting go of the negative or destructive parts of the relationship while preserving some of the healthy and positive aspects. See Chapter 3.

The legal divorce, no matter how final that process is, may do little or nothing toward taking care of your other divorces. Some people wake up the morning after the final judgment has been entered to find they don't feel divorced at all.

Working through this guidebook from the first to the last page is a good way to ensure that all your divorces happen together.

Annulment: The legal process which declares that a marriage never existed.

The Circle of Your Divorces

Legal/Financial Divorce

Social Divorce

Emotional Divorce

Directions: Fill in a circle, and ask your spouse to do the same, to show what you each think is the relative size of your three divorces.

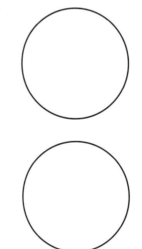

CHAPTER 2

DIVORCE AND THE LEGAL SYSTEM

Call the Connecticut Coalition Against Domestic Violence, (860)524-5890, to obtain a free copy of their pamphlet *A Guide to Connecticut's Family Violence Laws.* This pamphlet includes clear and useful information about laws designed to protect victims of abuse, including civil and criminal court remedies. It has information about how to apply for restraining orders without an attorney and a comprehensive list of state and community-based assistance programs.

DIVORCE AND THE LEGAL SYSTEM

How Do You Want to Conduct Your Divorce?

Most people want to end their marriage as efficiently as possible and do not want to make difficult matters worse than they already are. At a time when there may not be enough money to support a family in two homes, no one wants to make unnecessary payments to custody evaluators, lawyers, appraisers, tax accountants, career counselors, business consultants, or mediators. However, to get divorced requires taking the steps necessary for making sure your children will be loved and well-parented by both of you, for dividing up your current financial assets and, in many cases, for providing for future support payments. Also, even if you have a completely "friendly" divorce, the only way to divorce is to file a divorce action with the court and comply with the bureaucratic rules and regulations imposed before a judge will "grant" you a divorce.

No matter how long you have been married, whether you have children or not, whether you are amicable or fighting, all divorces require that you go through the following stages:

1. Information and Education

To make decisions about your children and your finances, you need to have information available to you so that you feel comfortable and informed. When you settle your divorce case your decisions will be final, so you want to feel you have enough information to make good decisions. Chapter 7, Gathering Information and Preparing Financial Affidavits, will help you to understand what information you need to make your divorce decisions.

There are also two different ways to get the information you need. The "formal" approach involves requiring the other spouse and/or third parties to provide information and documents under oath using interrogatories, requests for production of documents, and/or depositions. Litigated and adversarial cases usually use these formal approaches. The "informal" approach involves the informal sharing of information. You should consult with an attorney to determine which approach is best for you. No matter what approach you use, Chapter 7 will provide you with an understanding of the type of information you should consider having to make informed decisions.

Once you have all the information you need, however, your work has just begun. To interpret the information and use it to make informed decisions, you will need education so that you can understand your widest range of choices on all the decisions you need to reach. In identifying your choices and assessing their possible outcomes, you can use professionals to test out your own ideas, consider a myriad of real world considerations, and/or get advice about predictions of what a judge might decide in your case. See Chapters 8 through 12 for more information on these matters. When supplemented by professional advice, all of this information and education will help you to make the best decisions you can for yourself and for your family.

2. Making the Deal

All divorce cases are as different as each family member. Once you have all of your information and feel like you understand the issues and your options, it's time to look at your settlement alternatives. No one can look up in a book and tell you how to "solve" the issues in divorce. The standard is whether or not the financial settlement is "equitable" and the parenting provisions are in your children's "best interest." A lawyer will give you legal advice about what he or she thinks a judge might do and what he or she considers a "reasonable range" of settlement options given your unique facts and circumstances. But in settling your case and planning the future for your family, you can consider alternatives that a judge might not and apply your own personal and family values.

You and your spouse may have different views of what is "equitable," "fair," and/or "best." That is why when you assess the various settlement alternatives, you need to consider your spouse's goals. About ninety-five percent of divorcing couples reach a settlement—this means that while they have to go to court for the judge to approve the agreement they have reached, they do not need to have a trial for the judge to "decide" what is fair.

When you settle the case, the judge has the final say at the divorce hearing to accept or reject your agreement. This is one of the reasons why adequate legal advice is so crucial before you go to court for your final divorce. You can be creative in your settlement but only a lawyer will be able to identify whether or not what you are doing (or more importantly how you are writing it down) will be likely to pass the test of the judge.

No matter how "simple" your divorce is, there are many hoops to jump through to get from beginning to end. This book helps you to understand all the different components, but only legal advice and other professional assistance will insure that you are not going off on a wrong direction.

How to Win in Court—Not!

Since this guidebook is about friendly and cooperative divorce, it offers no advice or tips about how to "win" in court. If you and your spouse can't reach agreements, get legal advice and/or assistance from the court on how to obtain temporary and/or permanent orders.

3. Implement the Agreement

Once you come to terms on your settlement, you are not done with the process. All of the terms of your agreement must be put in writing in a legal document known as a Divorce Agreement, Separation Agreement, or Settlement Agreement. It is important that you get adequate legal advice before signing the final agreement as it is absolutely final in most instances and there is no looking back. The court has many forms and procedures to follow to actually get divorced, including a court hearing that you must attend in person. Chapter 6 describes all of these procedures.

Finally, to the extent that you and you spouse have a "marital economy" (commonly owned property, joint bank accounts, joint credit cards, etc.) you have to separate these things out (changing car titles, insurance beneficiaries, etc.) so you can each go on with your individual single lives. Chapter 13 will help you to understand the various things that you need to get done.

To go through these steps, most people need professional assistance. The problem is determining the level of assistance appropriate to your needs and the procedures you want to follow to go through the divorce stages. How do you want to conduct your divorce? Here are some examples of how a divorce can be done, from the simple to the complex, from the friendly to the more adversarial, as well as from the less expensive to the costly.

DIVORCE PROCESS OPTIONS

1. Do-It-Yourself Divorce

Some couples are able to sit down together and work out all of the details of their divorce. These "kitchen table" conversations may be the most attractive to you, but you should be cautious. First, as you will learn by reading this book, the various issues you need to address are complex. You may want to simply talk directly with your spouse about these issues without paying for professional assistance; however, you may find yourself bogged down in the process or in need of someone to structure your conversations and give you information about how your decisions connect together. The emotional and communication issues that are causing the divorce may also be an impediment to handling the divorce yourself. Some of these issues may make it difficult to have productive face-to-face conversations despite your best intentions. At its core, divorce is not "friendly" and you may find that you need professional help to make sure that your interpersonal issues don't sabotage your mutual desire to resolve the case in a nonadversarial manner.

You must also negotiate and prepare a divorce agreement for the court to review at the time of your divorce hearing. If you have no children and little property or debts, you may have a divorce agreement of only a few lines or paragraphs that you can include on the Divorce Agreement Form (JD-FM-172). See Chapter 6 for cautions on using this form without legal advice.

There are some legal services offices that provide free legal divorce assistance if you qualify. (http://www.larcc.org/common/network. htm). Other-wise, you need to find a private attorney who will help you to fill out the forms and/or review your agreement to see that it is complete and in a form acceptable to the court. Generally, these fees include consultation with you and preparation and filing of the forms but not the negotiation of your agreement.

2. Divorce Mediation

You can hire a divorce mediator to work with both of you as a neutral third party right from the beginning of your decision to separate. The divorce mediator can help you decide what process is appropriate for you both, help you work out all the issues surrounding your separation and divorce, and summarize those decisions in a written outline or agreement.

Divorce mediation is a process where the mediator facilitates the spouses working with each other to promote their voluntary agreements, sometimes called "self determination." Divorce mediation allows you to make your own decisions rather than having decisions imposed on your family by a judge. The mediator facilitates communication, promotes understanding, focuses the family members on the interests of all the members—including the children—and helps spouses arrive at creative solutions to financial and parenting issues. Successful divorce mediation requires that each spouse consider the position of the other, be willing to compromise, and not expect a win-or-lose outcome.

The mediator may suggest ways of resolving disputes but does not impose his or her own judgment. The mediator uses legal, financial, and emotional knowledge, supplemented by mediation skills, to help the spouses identify areas of agreement and disagreement. It is not the mediator's role to serve as a therapist or marital counselor or to give legal or financial advice. The mediator does not act as an advocate, representative, or lawyer for either party. The mediator does not act as a judge or arbitrator or in any way impose a settlement in the case.

Working together with a mediator allows you both to have direct participation in all of the stages of your divorce as opposed to having someone else "handle" it for you. To feel that you have an agreement uniquely suited to you and your family to which you

There is a list of all the forms you might need in Chapter 6. You can pick up the forms at the clerk's office at the Superior Court or find them on the Web at **www.jud.state.ct.us/external/super/forms.htm#family**. You must fill the forms out correctly, file them in the correct sequence, and pay the correct filing fee.

Mediation: Mediation is a process in which an impartial third party—a mediator—facilitates the resolution of a dispute by promoting voluntary agreement (or "self determination") by the parties to the dispute. A mediator facilitates communications, promotes understanding, focuses the parties on their interests, and seeks creative problem solving to enable the parties to reach their own agreement.

"If we don't work everything out in mediation, the mediator will decide for us."

A mediator does not make any decisions for you. Rather, he or she works with both of you to help you come to agreement. You keep your power to decide in mediation. You do not have to settle for anything you do not agree to.

will commit with your whole heart, you must feel that YOU negotiated it. Satisfaction with your agreement—as well as with yourself—and compliance with it are more likely if you BOTH walk through each stage and negotiate each issue.

A trained, skilled mediator can help to keep conflict from escalating out of control—allowing you to make good decisions in moments of stress. Working with a mediator right from the beginning increases the likelihood of the evolution of a communication process that you will use long after the entry of the divorce judgment.

Mediation allows all professionals involved in the case—lawyers, therapists, and CPAs—to serve clients in an efficient, nonadversarial atmosphere. This results in a greater degree of client satisfaction, a stronger commitment to follow through on the terms of the agreement, and much less emotional and financial strain on the parties.

Mediation can be a win-win situation for *everyone*.

Factor	Mediation	Litigation	Mediation Advantages
Time	Short	Lengthy	*Avoids delays* *Participants can "get on with their lives"*
Cost	Inexpensive	Expensive	*Higher degree of satisfaction* *Less financial stress on participants*
Confidentiality	Confidential	Public record	*Avoids negative publicity*
Decision-making	In the hands of the participants	Left to the courts	*Greater commitment to follow-through* *Greater sense of "fairness" by participants*
Communication	Direct	Primarily through attorneys	*Greater clarity* *May actually improve long-term relationship*
Agenda	Set by parties	Set by court	*Participants feel* *greater sense of control*
Emotional needs	Considered	Often ignored	*Greater satisfaction with result*
Control of process	By participants	By attorneys and the court	*Participants may end mediation at any time* *Participants feel empowered*
Decree compliance	High	Unknown	*Less chance of relitigation*

Chart courtesy of Attorney Ingrid Slezak, Portland, Oregon

A professional mediator will help you reach and/or write your own settlement based on your unique needs. A mediator can help you identify issues and options, give your ideas form and context, assist you in resolving differences, and help you and your spouse to learn to bargain collaboratively.

There are several different kinds of mediators with different kinds of backgrounds. As you choose your mediator, think about who you are and what you want to accomplish in your process.

- A divorce mediator can help you decide how you are going to approach and process your separation and divorce.

- A divorce mediator who is an experienced divorce lawyer can give you legal information to help you understand various settlement options and help coordinate the divorce process.

- A divorce mediator can help you resolve specific issues for your divorce agreement.

- A divorce mediator can help you throughout your process to develop a cooperative bargaining process that you can use well into the future. The basis of this guidebook is this mediation model. It focuses on problem solving.

- Some mediation styles have more structure. They focus more on reaching specific agreements rather than on problem solving. This type of mediation often begins by asking what solutions you want for specific problems.

- Some divorce mediation models focus on reaching an agreement based on what might happen if your case went to court, i.e., the case law or possible legal outcomes of your particular problem. This is called "evaluative" mediation and is usually used when people have been unable to settle and are looking for professional assistance to break their impasse.

- The mediator is not an expert to tell you the "right" answer or give you legal advice. There are probably a number of possible solutions, many of which would work for both of you, and the mediator can help you identify your options.

There are many styles of divorce mediation. You need to be very clear about which approach will work for you. Select a mediator who has experience in the areas which you are discussing, such as the law of property division, alimony, parenting plans and their relation to child development, divorce taxation, financial plan-

"What is great about the mediation approach, aside from its effectiveness in dealing with the immediate issues at hand, is that it teaches couples a cooperative process. They'll be able to use what they learn to cope with the new issues that will, in the future, inevitably arise."

Dr. Constance Ahrons,
The Good Divorce, 1994

Family Services Office:
The office in the courthouse that helps spouses settle disputes through mediation. If the parties can't agree, the judge may direct the family relations officer to do a custody/visitation study and make a recommendation.

ning, and business or pension valuation and division. The more expertise the mediator has in the areas you are negotiating—especially those areas where you are unsure—the more efficient and less expensive your mediation is likely to be.

Working with a mediator does not preclude legal advice from or representation by a lawyer. In fact, mediators recommend legal advice as a part of the mediation process and many judges are skeptical of agreements not reviewed by individual lawyers for each spouse.

Although mediation is about cooperating to work out financial and parenting issues in an efficient, nonadversarial manner, each spouse has individual concerns, legal rights, and responsibilities. Mediators are neutral parties and do not give legal advice to either spouse. All mediators recommend (or *should* recommend) that you get your own individual legal advice as part of the divorce mediation process. You may ask why this is necessary since you perhaps are mediating your divorce, in part, to "avoid divorce lawyers."

Working with your own attorney protects you and achieves your mediation goals by:

- Helping you to understand the law and identify legal issues

- Providing a private place to discuss your concerns and weigh your options

- Getting support from a legal professional who is "in your corner"

- Helping you anticipate how much information is necessary for settlement decisions

- Giving practical feedback on your settlement ideas and offering creative suggestions about difficult issues

- Providing review of the final settlement before you sign it

Despite what many people believe, mediation is not just for "friendly" divorces. Most divorcing couples experience extreme emotional distress. Yet, angry, fighting, emotional people can still share common goals: to avoid the adversarial process and insulate their children from the conflict. The more grounded you are with private legal information and advice, the less likely you will be to question your final settlement, no matter how friendly or hostile you and your spouse are. Consider work with your

attorney as an investment in some of the most important decisions you will make in your life.

When Should I Work With My Attorney?

Imagine that you are the coach of a baseball team. But, instead of
being in the ballpark watching the action and working with the
players, you are sitting in the parking lot on the team bus. Players
run out to the bus, describe and discuss the action, get your
coaching tips, then run back to the field to tell the players what
the coach said and try to act accordingly. Not only would this be
incredibly inefficient, but you would have to rely on what the player told you (rather than your own observation) and trust that the
player understood and could execute your recommendations—not
the best way of working with the members of your team!

Your attorney may feel this way as he or she helps you mediate
your divorce. Attorneys for each spouse generally are not present
during mediation sessions. They rely on clients to explain what
developed during each session and hope that the client can implement their advice at an upcoming session. Although this "floating
lawyer" concept can be a problem, it is not insurmountable. Too
often mediators and spouses view attorneys as enemies of the
process. But, the right lawyer can integrate into the process to
preserve the control you want while increasing efficiency.

Working With Your Attorney Through the Stages of Mediation

An attorney who works with a mediating spouse is commonly
called "review counsel." This reflects the fact that many spouses
hire attorneys at the end of the mediation for the limited purpose
of reviewing the final written agreement. However, delaying attorney involvement too late in the process can result in significant
problems. By the end of the mediation spouses can be so financially and emotionally invested in the agreement that they may
not listen to their attorneys' objections. In some cases, when the
attorney points out problems with the agreement at this late
stage, the result can be the collapse of the entire agreement. The
attorneys' roles should be broader than simply reviewing the
agreement. Early attorney involvement may prevent a last minute
crisis over an unraveling settlement agreement. For this reason,
"consulting counsel" is a better label for the attorney, reflecting
input at all stages of the mediation—the earlier the better!

Working with an attorney before beginning the mediation may
prevent difficulties during the process. Your decisions must be
based on informed consent, which requires information and education. Consulting counsel is your best teacher, answering ques-

tions, addressing concerns, and providing a solid foundation before you begin. Consulting counsel can also help you gather and analyze information and documentation. In some marriages, spouses share financial information whereas in others, only one spouse manages the money.

If you are the less financially knowledgeable spouse, your consulting counsel will tell you what you need to know and make sure you understand information when you get it. Financial documents can be complex. Your attorney may recommend hiring a divorce financial planner to help in the process.

If you have managed the marital money, you probably have a thorough understanding of your family's finances. Be proactive. Rather than waiting for your spouse and/or the mediator to ask for information, put together a complete picture of the family finances. An easy-to-follow notebook of financial summaries with comprehensive backup material demonstrates a commitment to full and complete informal disclosure, and you will jump start the process. A divorce financial planner can help you and your attorney put this package together.

Involving your attorney is critical as you consider options and make settlement decisions in mediation. Your attorney can help you to put together a comprehensive settlement proposal and analyze your spouse's proposal.

Critics of divorce mediation believe that the "less empowered spouse" is at a disadvantage in mediation. Although mediation is not right for everyone, power imbalance can be an issue in any divorce, whether in mediation or the adversarial process. The adversarial process offers the protections of formal discovery, court enforcement, and legal advocacy. But the adversarial process can also involve personal intimidation, fear of the court system, lack of control over the process and unpredictability of the outcome, and a significant drain of the family's finances and emotions. Most adversarial cases settle, but too often those settlements are "on the courthouse steps" before trial—a terrible position for an unempowered spouse. The answer to a serious power imbalance is not necessarily to reject mediation. A competent divorce mediator specially trained to work with power imbalance issues can be the best option for the less empowered spouse. The mediator may slow the process to give that person time to digest the information and negotiate from an improved power position. The success of this strategy hinges on the support and advice of consulting counsel with time for reflection and supportive decision making.

Reaching an impasse (the failure to settle one or more issues) rarely means that the spouses call it quits and go to trial. Mediators use a variety of techniques to get past an impasse. Most involve integrating consulting counsel into the process:

- If you don't have a consulting counsel at this point, you need to hire one. Straight talk from an attorney frequently will provide enough legal information, advice, and just plain brainstorming to help you settle.

- The mediator may convene a session that includes consulting counsel. If necessary, he or she can meet with the attorneys to discuss the impasse.

- The mediator may also use "shuttle diplomacy" which involves the mediator moving back and forth between meetings with each spouse and his or her individual consulting counsel.

- The mediator may recommend an experienced divorce attorney to serve as co-mediator or expert consultant. This attorney can evaluate the unresolved issues and make settlement recommendations. Integrating consulting counsel usually makes this approach more efficient.

Occasionally, an impasse cannot be overcome and mediation comes to an end. If this happens, keep in mind that a divorce settlement is like a mosaic of lots of small agreements that build to a comprehensive settlement of all issues. Most impasses come on the heels of substantial agreement on a number of issues. Although all issues are interrelated, it is a waste of mediation resources (financial and emotional) for your trial attorneys to start over from the beginning "reinventing the wheel." Even when you are headed for trial on your unsettled issues, you may be able to arrive at a negotiated settlement. If you can't settle a few remaining issues, a "limited" trial will allow a judge to accept the agreements you do have and decide the remaining issues.

Issues to Discuss With a Prospective Divorce Mediator

Ask the following questions of any mediator you are considering:

- Are you trained and experienced in family matters? How many family cases have you handled? How long have you been a mediator?

- How much do you charge? Do you charge per couple, per hour, or a flat fee? Do you meet with the parties together or

For more information about mediation in Connecticut visit the Web site of the Connecticut Council for Divorce Mediation at **www.ctmediators.org**.

How to Find a Divorce Mediator

- Ask friends or professionals whom you trust for a personal recommendation or referral.

- Look in the Yellow Pages under "Mediation Services" and "Divorce Lawyers"

Should I Hire an Attorney?

In Connecticut, whether and how you use a lawyer in your divorce is up to you. The law allows you to conduct your divorce *pro se*—the Latin phrase for "for yourself."

The question of whether to hire an attorney is not, in and of itself, the same as whether you are going to be friendly or adversarial or whether you are going to keep control through the divorce process. These are determined by which lawyer you hire and what you ask your lawyer to do for you. For example:

- You can work out an agreement on your own or in mediation and hire an attorney to do the paperwork. This may or may not include translating your agreement into legal language.

- You can do the paperwork yourselves, including your agreement, and run it by a lawyer before you finalize it.

- You can also hire a lawyer to direct operations right from the beginning and to conduct negotiations for you.

separately? How long does the average divorce mediation take in your practice?

- How available are you? How long does it take to schedule an appointment?

- Do you mediate within the legal context of the outcome in court? How important is it to you that the results in mediation be similar to the probable results in court?

3. Adversarial/Conventional Representation by an Attorney

You can hire an attorney to handle your divorce right from the beginning or at any time that you feel you need legal assistance. An attorney can relieve you of having to meet face to face with your soon-to-be-ex, work to legally protect you if you feel you need it, and/or handle the contested trial if there is no settlement and you need the judge to decide your parenting and/or financial issues.

The information you learn in this book about divorce agreements and procedures will help you help your attorney work for you. Having basic, general knowledge about many of the issues in advance will save your attorney time in explaining things to you, and that will save money on hourly fees. Many times you can't reach the best agreement because one of the parties does not understand it. Thoroughly reviewing the chapters in this guidebook can put you in a position to understand and contribute to the negotiations.

There are many different ways to use a lawyer in your divorce case. Here are some of the things he or she can do:

- Give you legal advice about the issues in your divorce

- Explain the procedures for getting a divorce

- Help you fill out your own court documents

- Prepare court documents, file them for you, and go with you to court for the final hearing

- Help you negotiate a fair settlement

- Negotiate for you

- Give you opinions about the likely outcome of the issues in your divorce if a judge decides your issues

- Draft your divorce agreement

- Litigate, as your advocate, for your rights and interests and maximize your outcome if you are unable to negotiate an agreement

You can classify these different ways to use a lawyer into two fundamental categories: lawyer as consultant and lawyer as representative. In mediation and do-it-yourself-divorce, your lawyer is your consultant, giving you information, education, and opinions on the terms of your divorce settlement—whether it is sound, legal, fair, and equitable or whether you could do better—and providing suggestions and advice about the likely outcome if you ask the court to decide. As your representative, your lawyer will speak to your spouse's lawyer on your behalf, prepare and sign court documents, and even argue in court on your behalf. Not all lawyers are willing to act in a "limited consulting" function so you need to be clear what level of legal advice and representation you want and/or need.

Which functions do you want your lawyer to fill for you? How much control do you want to have over your divorce and your role in it? Before you begin interviewing attorneys, clarify what you want and expect from a legal professional. Also, be aware that most divorce attorneys charge for all of their consulting time, including the initial appointment.

Issues to Discuss With a Prospective Lawyer

Ask the following questions of any lawyer you are considering:

- Are you trained and experienced in family law? How many family law cases have you handled? How long have you been a lawyer?

- How much do you charge? Is it hourly? Do you charge a retainer? Is there an additional rate for paralegal, associate, or clerical staff?

- How available are you? How long does it take to schedule an appointment?

- How adversarial or non-adversarial are you? Are you supportive of the mediation process? How much experience do you have assisting clients in finding solutions in a non-adversarial way?

**How to Find a Lawyer
for a Family Matter**

- Ask everybody you know who has hired a family law lawyer recently if they recommend anyone. The best recommendation is still word of mouth from a person you trust.

- Ask your marriage counselor, mediator, therapist, or pastor to make a recommendation.

- In the Yellow Pages look under "Attorneys." At the end of the "Attorneys" section is the "Guide for Attorneys." Here you will find a subheading: "Divorce and Family Law."

- You may qualify for free legal services if you meet income requirements. Call Statewide Legal Services at (800)453-3320.

- Are you willing to work with me as a consultant rather than a representative? Will you represent me if I want to negotiate directly with my spouse? Will you support our efforts to develop our own agreement?

4. Collaborative Divorce

"That's just my lawyer talking."

Don't kid yourself. If you hire an attorney, he or she becomes your representative. You are responsible for the conduct of your divorce, including what your lawyer says and how, when, and where it is said. Your lawyer works for you; this is your life.

Another alternative approach to divorce is known as "collaborative law" or "collaborative divorce." In collaborative law, each spouse retains a trained collaborative lawyer for legal advice and assistance in negotiating an agreement on all issues. You may also work collaboratively with a divorce financial planning professional and/or a mental health professional to help you with parenting and/or communication issues.

The collaborative process includes:

1. Four-way settlement meetings (both spouses with their respective lawyers) as the primary format for communication and negotiation

2. Disqualification of all lawyers and experts from participation in any legal proceeding between the parties outside of the collaborative process

3. Avoidance of litigation techniques and even the threat of litigation

4. Full, voluntary, and early disclosure of all relevant information

5. The use of joint experts (financial professionals, mental health professionals, CPAs, appraisers, etc.)

6. Settlement as the lawyers' and spouses' primary goal

7. Economy of efficiency

8. Respectful and fully participatory process

In the collaborative process, if the lawyers do not help the clients to resolve the issues, the lawyers are out of a job and can't represent their clients in the adversarial process. Everyone in a collaborative process (lawyers, spouses, and other experts) work together in good faith and honesty to work toward a "win-win" solution that meets the legitimate needs of the family.

While there are many similarities between mediation and collaborative law, there are significant differences. Instead of a neutral mediator who cannot give legal advice or help to advocate a position, collaborative lawyers are present during all joint discussions and meet privately with their clients. While two collaborative lawyers working together are not technically co-mediators, many of the advantages of co-mediation are replicated in the collaborative process. The playing field, if it has the potential to be unbalanced in mediation, is leveled as collaborative lawyers participate in the full process with spouses who lack negotiating skill, financial understanding, or are emotionally upset or angry. By involving attorneys in the process, you can eliminate some of the problems encountered in mediation when lawyers are outside the process and/or brought in too late.

An experienced collaborative attorney will be able to explain to you that there is a significant difference between a settlement negotiated in an adversarial setting and one negotiated in a collaborative process with no threat of court. It is an irony of divorce cases that most handled through the adversarial or conventional process settle—and usually very late in a very emotionally and financially expensive process. These settlements are often reached under conditions of substantial tension and anxiety and are oriented almost exclusively to predictions of "what the judge would do."

 For more information about the collaborative process, visit the Web site of the International Academy of Collaborative Professionals at **www.collabgroup.com**.

A successful collaborative case is much different. From the first day, settlement is the goal, and respectful problem solving is the process. It is generally quicker, less costly, less stressful, and more satisfying than the conventional process. In the collaborative process, two lawyers are in the same room pulling in the same direction with both spouses working on the same list of issues. They explore with their clients solutions to the issues that will be satisfactory to both spouses.

Other Approaches, Services, and Consultants

Whatever process you choose to achieve your divorce, there are a number of services you can use to help make the final result more complete and workable. Some of these services may help you with the process of coming to an agreement. They range from those who work with you both to develop your own solutions to those who decide some of the outcome for you. You may or may not need any of them, but read through the entire list to see if they might be helpful to you.

PARENTING CONSULTANTS

There are many resources and services available to help you with issues concerning your children. The following are some things you can do, as well as kinds of professionals and resources concerning children:

ADR, or Alternative Dispute Resolution: The title the legal profession has given to cover all methods of resolving conflicts outside of court. It includes mediation, arbitration, collaboration, negotiation, shuttle diplomacy, even flipping a coin.

You can divorce a spouse, but you cannot divorce a child.

- Attend parenting education class as soon as possible (*see* Chapter 8).

- See the bibliography at the end of this guidebook. There are a number of excellent books which will help both you and your children.

- Speak to the school psychologist about how your children are doing. Also ask about the kinds of difficulties which many children experience when their parents separate.

- Find a divorce recovery group for your children through your school, church, community center, local mental health center, or one of the services—public or private—which specializes in assisting children when their parents divorce.

- Hire a mental health professional to work with you and/or your children to mediate a parenting plan now and to serve as a resource for help in dealing with problems in the future.

- Hire a custody evaluator to advise you and your spouse, your lawyer, or the court about what kind of parenting plan is best for your family.

- Hire, or ask the court to appoint, an attorney for your children to represent their interests—especially if those interests are contrary to your own. This is an extreme action which might strain the fabric of your family and comes into play if you are fighting over custody.

Decide what you want from a professional. Do you want advice about your children to go directly to you? To the children? To your attorney? To the court? Do you want a professional to help you make your decision(s), or do you want someone to decide for you?

DIVORCE FINANCIAL PROFESSIONALS

This category includes various experts who can help you unravel your money issues and plan for your financial future. You can locate financial consultants by asking for recommendations from friends, lawyers, mediators, or other financial consultants; in the Yellow Pages; or on the Internet. Make sure that the financial consultant you use is familiar with and has experience working with divorce issues.

- Certified Financial Planner. A CFP can analyze any settlement you are considering to give you an idea of your earnings and net worth years from now. This is especially useful for those who have income-producing assets which one or both of you plan to live on or if you have a long-term debt to pay after the divorce.

- Certified Public Accountant. A CPA experienced in divorce taxation issues can be a tremendous help in planning your settlement and helping you to plan for and file your tax returns. Having an experienced CPA may well save you money in the future by avoiding tax errors or inadequate tax planning.

Some financial professionals receive specialized training and develop extensive expertise in the area of the financial aspects of divorce. You should ask a prospective divorce financial professional what their training and experience is and also determine whether or not they have received credentials for specialized divorce planning. A divorce financial planner can help you with short- and long-term issues related to the financial impact of proposed divorce settlements. Settlement terms that may look equitable now may need to be adjusted when the financial professional analyzes the long-term financial consequences.

Some divorce financial professionals are trained as mediators and can meet and work with both spouses to facilitate the resolution of financial issues. An experienced divorce financial professional can also be an important team member in working with your attorney (whether adversarial, conventional, or collaborative) by preparing financial affidavits, meeting with you to collect and explain financial data, providing a financial understanding of different kinds of assets, planning for insurance, planning for college, and helping you look at settlement alternatives from a financial perspective.

ASSET EVALUATORS

- Real Estate Appraisal. Real estate appraisers determine the value of your home or other real estate based on current construction costs as well as comparable properties that have sold recently. An appraiser adjusts the sold values of comparable properties by using certain industry standards, for example, a certain amount for the fact that there is no garage, so much for brick versus wood, etc. Real estate appraisers have certain specialties, such as residential, commercial, or agricultural.

Real Estate Market Analysis. A real estate salesperson or broker provides this service. He or she will review the properties sold recently in the same area and compare your property with them in a less formal and technical manner than the appraiser. The market analysis is usually much less expensive than an appraisal and is often free.

- Personal Property Appraisers. These are specialists who will appraise anything from antiques to fine art, beer can collections and beer steins, juke boxes and pin ball machines, or pedigreed livestock.

- Pension Plan Evaluators. These services are necessary only if you need to know the present value of a future income stream. For example: what is the present value of a pension which will pay only when you retire or after you reach a certain age? See Chapter 10 for a more complete discussion of the division of future assets such as retirements, pensions, and annuities as well as more about property and valuation.

As you can see, there is a great range of choices for how you can conduct your divorce and whom you can select to help. The choices you make now will determine cost, duration, and the overall tone of your transition to single lives. Keep all these options in mind as you work through your own situation.

COURT-SPONSORED MEDIATION

The court system offers four mediation services at no charge. The first is the Court-Annexed Mediation Program. Senior judges and judge trial referees facilitate settlement discussions and assist the parties in crafting an agreement. This program is most frequently used where each party has a lawyer and the lawyers have been unable to settle the case on their own. You can get more information about this program from the clerk's office at the superior court or on the Web at http://www.jud.state.ct.us/external/super/altdisp.htm#Mediation.

The second are the mediation services offered by the Family Services office in each courthouse. If you appear in court for a judge to hear any motions you file before your case is final, Family Services officers will attempt to mediate whatever issues the motions present. If you need help resolving your parenting and/or financial issues, you may be able to schedule a mediation with the Family Services office.

The third program is only offered in some courthouses and is know as the Special Masters program. Volunteer divorce lawyers serve in teams of two lawyers (a man and a woman) and meet with the attorneys and both spouses.

If you request a market value analysis on any of your properties, consider asking for three values:

- High sales value (also often the recommended listing price in real estate)—the most you can get if you are willing to wait for just the right buyer.

- Fair market value—the probable value of your property if you and a willing buyer are able to compromise.

- Fire sale value—the quick sale price.

Another settlement intervention offered in most courthouses is a judicial settlement conference where a judge meets with the attorneys and spouses and attempts to settle the case. Both the Special Masters program and this program are offered only in adversarial cases where they are the last step before the scheduling of a trial.

MED/ARB AND ARBITRATION

Some private mediators offer a hybrid process called "med/arb." Initially, you work with the professional as a mediator then, if you do not reach agreement on any given issue, the mediator becomes an arbitrator and makes that decision for you. An arbitrator can decide your whole divorce for you or can work on any single issue on which you get stuck.

Not all couples reach agreement by negotiating directly with each other or through mediation. The inability to settle usually means that the judge will have to decide. Med/arb and arbitration are alternative methods for resolving disputes without having to fight it out in court.

Med/arb is infrequently used in Connecticut but is quite accepted in other states. It is useful in high conflict cases because parties can resolve their disputes in a private setting and generally get results more quickly than going through court. If you are considering med/arb or arbitration, it is important that you consult with a lawyer about the procedure before you start. The courts have ultimate jurisdiction over family matters, particularly issues involving children. A lawyer can explain the legal alternatives available for incorporating med/arb and arbitration into your process.

The Court Aspect of Divorce—An Overview

To change your legal status from "married" to "single," you must file a case with the court. This chapter will give you an overview of the divorce process, options for how you can choose to handle your divorce (on your own or with a lawyer), and information about other professionals who are available to help you through the process.

In Connecticut, the law calls a divorce a *dissolution of marriage,* and it becomes final when you and your spouse attend a final hearing before the judge who will enter what is known as a *judgment of dissolution of marriage.* In this book, we will usually call this final order a *divorce judgment* or *divorce* since these are the more common terms for the final order dissolving your marriage.

The following is the general outline of the process for divorce in Connecticut:

- One party, the *plaintiff*, prepares the Summons and Divorce Complaint.

- The Summons and Divorce Complaint are served on the other party, the *defendant*.

- The plaintiff files the Summons and Divorce Complaint with the superior court along with the docket fee (presently $225).

- The court assigns the case a *docket number*, which is the number that is used on all of the papers filed in the case.

- The parties may agree to, or have the court enter orders for, *temporary orders* which will apply to the parties and the children until the case is finalized.

- The parties negotiate a permanent agreement for child custody, child support, property division, debt division, alimony, and any other issues, and that agreement is written up in the form of a *divorce agreement* that is submitted to the court at the final divorce hearing for approval.

- If the parties cannot negotiate an agreement on all or part of their final issues, a trial will be held and the judge will enter the final permanent orders and judgment of dissolution of marriage.

Because Connecticut is a *no-fault* state, you do not have to prove to the court that one or the other of you is at fault in the demise of your marriage to get a divorce. However, if you are unable to settle your differences on financial and custody matters, the judge will decide for you, and he or she is permitted by law to consider fault, among many other factors, as more fully explained in later chapters of this book.

The law requires a waiting period, or cooling off time, of ninety days before the judge has the power to grant a divorce. This waiting period is meant to make sure that marriages do not end without time for serious thought and consideration of the consequences of such an important and permanent action.

The ninety-day period starts with the return date. This date is more fully explained in Chapter 6. The return date is the Tuesday selected by the plaintiff and inserted in the portion of the Summons and Divorce Complaint called the caption. The

Temporary: The period between the filing of your complaint and the final judgment or divorce, also known as *pendente lite.*

caption is the same for all papers filed with the court and includes the names of the parties, the docket number, the court location, and date.

If you and your spouse permanently settle your financial and child-related issues during this waiting period, you will be able to get divorced fairly soon after the expiration of the ninety-day period. However, some couples take longer to reach a final settlement and in those instances the case will continue as long as it takes for the parties to reach agreement. While you are free to move at your own pace in finalizing your case, later chapters in this book will explain that, to a certain extent, the court system monitors your progress and a lack of action may ultimately result in a dismissal of the case you started.

Some couples are unable to resolve their financial and/or child-related issues and need to have a judge decide for them. In some judicial districts, this inability to settle and need to resort to the judge can substantially prolong the finalization of the divorce. Most court dockets are filled with cases and you will have to wait to have your day in court.

DIVORCE AGREEMENT

Couples usually use most of the ninety-day waiting period to work out their final divorce plan which, when written, is called the divorce agreement (or settlement agreement). Whether you are seeking a judgment of dissolution or a judgment of legal separation, you still call the final agreement a divorce or settlement agreement. Chapters 8 through 12 discuss all the necessary elements for negotiating and preparing your divorce agreement.

Although there is a court form to use for doing your own agreement, lawyers draft most divorce agreements to insure that the many complex issues are covered properly. Your divorce agreement should cover all the following: property division (real estate, cars, household goods, art, sporting equipment and other personal property, investments, businesses, retirement plans and pensions, and the like), payment of debts, alimony, custody and support of children, taxes, and medical and life insurance.

Your divorce agreement may also include a detailed plan for sharing time with the children, payments agreed to now but to be paid later, future higher education costs for each other or for your children, career plans or goals for each or either of you, and financial planning for the future. Your divorce agreement may also anticipate the unexpected—such as one parent losing a job or leaving the state or the death or prolonged illness of a family member.

"The court will automatically grant our divorce on day ninety-one."

Nothing occurs automatically at the end of ninety days. You have to take action to request that the court finalize your divorce.

Return Date: The date, selected by the plaintiff (always a Tuesday) to file the complaint that starts the ninety-day waiting period before the final judgment of divorce may be obtained. See Chapter 6. No one appears in court on the return date.

Dismissal for Failure to Take Action

Some courts will dismiss your divorce or legal separation case if you fail to take action to finalize it. The court may mail you a dormancy calendar. This requires that you appear in court to explain the delay in completing your case. If you don't appear or the judge does not give you extra time, your case will be dismissed.

No-Fault Divorce: No one needs to prove that the husband or wife caused the marriage to end.

Divorce Agreement: The written (typed) document you file with the court at the time the divorce judgment is entered that spells out how the parties are dividing property and debts, planning to parent their children, and paying support and alimony, as well as any other agreement between them that they want the court to approve. Also known as a "stipulation" or "settlement agreement."

Preparing your own divorce agreement may seem like a good way to save time and lawyer's fees. However, once the agreement is signed and court-approved it is very difficult (often impossible) to change. Any divorce agreement you sign, no matter who prepares it, should be reviewed by an attorney who represents you and is looking out for your legal interests.

It's up to you when you negotiate and sign your divorce agreement. Some people prefer to work everything out, write it up, and even sign it before they file the complaint. Most people file the complaint first and then use the waiting period to work things out. Use your ninety days wisely. Provisions and agreements that are acceptable when couples are separating may not work ninety days later. It is much harder (and with property division, usually impossible) to change your agreement after the court approves it. You may therefore want to make tentative agreements at the beginning of the case and then try living with them to "get the bugs out." In fact, you can usually take the time you need to be sure about your agreements. But you must submit the signed divorce agreement to the court for approval at the time you ask for your final judgment of divorce.

WHAT FORMS DO WE NEED?

You will need some, but not necessarily all, of the forms on the following list. Read the entire list and check off the ones you think you will need. Your attorneys can prepare all of these papers for you if you hire them for this purpose. This is true whether they negotiate all the terms of the agreement for you or you negotiate by yourselves or with a mediator and tell your attorneys of your agreements. You can prepare all or some of these papers by yourself if you are representing yourself. There are sample copies printed in Chapter 6, unless otherwise indicated, with line-by-line instructions for completing the forms yourself. Some mediators may be willing to prepare some of these documents as part of the mediation process.

Summons: The paper that notifies your spouse of the start of the divorce case. Everyone needs this to start a case.

Divorce Complaint: The legal paper that starts the case. Everyone needs this to start a case.

Notice of Automatic Orders: Court orders that go into effect when the case starts. These orders are attached to every Divorce Complaint.

Affidavit Concerning Children: It is the goal of the law to try to have litigation about children coordinated between courts and even between states. To advise the court about any other court actions involving your children everyone who has minor children must use this form.

Motion and Order of Notice by Publication or Mail in Family Cases: You will need these if you are serving your spouse out of state or by certified or registered mail or by publication.

Appearance: The defendant may file this document after receiving the Summons and Divorce Complaint. Once filed with the court, the defendant will receive copies of documents filed in the case and notice of any action that the court may take. By filing the appearance the defendant consents to the court's power (jurisdiction) to enter financial and custody orders.

Cross Complaint and/or Answer: The defendant need not file these documents after receiving the Summons and Divorce Complaint. However the defendant can use the Cross Complaint to go on record to disagree with any of the statements in the Divorce Complaint or to ask for categories of results different from what is in the plaintiff's complaint. The filing of a Cross Complaint and/or Answer will also insure that the plaintiff cannot dismiss the case without the agreement of the defendant.

Application for Waiver of Fees: You may use this form if you cannot afford to pay the filing fee, sheriff's costs, and some other required costs. If the judge grants this request, you will also need the Invoice Voucher.

Motions for Orders Before Judgment (also known as "Temporary" or *Pendente Lite* Motions): After filing the case and while you are waiting for the final divorce, you may need to request court assistance for the judge to enter temporary orders about child support, alimony, child custody, and other temporary issues. Many people settle their temporary issues. To put your temporary agreements into writing, file a Motion for Order asking the court to approve your agreement and to make it an order of court.

Divorce Agreement: If you have reached a final agreement on property division, debt division, alimony, child support, and child custody it is reduced to a written form and is submitted to the court for approval at the final hearing.

Case Management Agreement: Everyone needs this form to track and schedule the final divorce judgment hearing.

Dissolution of Marriage Report: The state of Connecticut keeps statistics about people who are divorced. This form must be completed in every case and be filed with the court when you appear for your divorce hearing.

Advisement of Rights: Unless the parties agree otherwise, child support and alimony will be paid automatically by withholding the support from the payor's pay. This form advises both parties of their rights and provides a place where the parties can waive wage withholding and agree that the payment will be made directly between the parties.

Affidavit Concerning Military Service: If the defendant does not file an Appearance and/or an Answer, the plaintiff must file this affidavit stating that the defendant is not serving in the military, if that is the case. In cases where the plaintiff or anyone else has not spoken to the defendant in the thirty days before the divorce and cannot swear to the fact that he or she is not in the military, the plaintiff must contact the branches of the military services and obtain military certificates to submit to the court at the final divorce hearing.

Parenting Education Program (Order, Certificate, and Results): Unless the court excuses you, if you have children you must attend parenting education classes. The approved classes are for six hours and cost no more than $100 per person. This form certifies to the court that you complied with this requirement.

Financial Affidavit: Each party must file this document disclosing his or her income, expenses, debts, and assets. The purpose of the Financial Affidavit is to tell the court enough about your individual financial situation to allow the judge to determine if your agreement is fair and to insure full financial disclosure by both parties under oath. If you do not settle your temporary or permanent issues, the judge will use the Financial Affidavit to enter financial orders. The Financial Affidavit form is in Chapter 7.

Child Support Worksheet: If your combined net weekly income is $2,500 or less, you must submit a child support guideline calculation for temporary and/or permanent child support whether you have reached an agreement or not. If you agree to an amount of child support that is different than the guideline amount, the form provides room for you to explain to the court why you have deviated. The child support worksheet form is in Chapter 9.

Withholding Order for Support: If the alimony or child support will be paid by wage withholding, this is the form that is sent to the employer and gives instructions about how to implement the withholding.

Qualified Domestic Relations Order: This document is signed by the judge and then given to the plan administrator of your company to divide most pension and profitsharing plans.

Judgment File: The permanent court record of the final divorce.

To get a divorce in Connecticut you must appear at court for a final hearing. At that proceeding the judge reviews your individual Financial Affidavits (sworn statements) detailing the financial circumstances of each of you at the moment of your final judgment. These affidavits provide the basis for the court to find your divorce agreement to be fair and to enter a judgment of dissolution of marriage or legal separation.

The court retains continuing jurisdiction over your children (custody, parenting time, child support) after your divorce or legal separation. The court also keeps jurisdiction over any future payments and promises, such as a payment due when the house sells or open-ended or modifiable alimony. Even if one or both of you moves out of the state, the original court keeps jurisdiction unless the court in another state formally takes over. The court will generally not interfere in your personal family matters and make decisions for you unless one of you asks it to. If you can cooperate with each other and be reliable—keeping all your agreements, in spirit and letter—neither of you will have to ask the court to do anything but approve your agreement, which it does in the vast majority of cases.

A Word About the Law

According to the divorce statute (Connecticut General Statutes Title 46b), if you want a divorce you must go through the court system. There is no other way to obtain a divorce.

The divorce statute lists the factors that the judge must consider when dividing property and debts, setting child support and alimony, and awarding custody. The statute does not say that you must consider all of the factors when you decide these issues yourselves. For example, the statute does not define or distinguish between marital and separate property. You may agree to define these terms in your own way for your property or ignore the distinctions as the statute does. For another example, the statute tells the court the factors it must weigh in awarding custody. You may consider these same factors or decide for yourselves what factors are important to you.

Continuing Jurisdiction: The ongoing power of the court where you filed your divorce to hear requests to enforce or change its orders made at the time of the judgment.

The court system relies on a second part of the law called case law or precedent. One or both parties may be unhappy with the judge's decision after a trial (juries are not used in family law matters in Connecticut). If so, and if they can financially afford it, either may appeal to the Connecticut Appellate Court. If either dis-

"But to live outside the law you must be honest...."

Bob Dylan, "Absolutely Sweet Marie"

"The notion that most people want black-robed judges, well-dressed lawyers and fine-paneled courtrooms as the setting to resolve their disputes is not correct. People with problems, like people with pains, want relief, and they want it as quickly and inexpensively as possible."

Warren E. Burger, Chief Justice, United States Supreme Court

"The human animal needs a freedom seldom mentioned, freedom from intrusion. He needs a little privacy quite as much as he wants understanding or vitamins or exercise or praise."

Phyllis McGinley, "A Lost Privilege," *The Province of the Heart*

agrees with the results from the appellate court, he or she may further appeal to the Connecticut Supreme Court. The appellate court must hear and decide all cases appealed to it. The Supreme Court can pick and choose and will usually decline to hear appeals in family cases already determined by the appellate court.

The appeal process reviews only the transcript of the trial proceedings and weighs written and oral arguments by the lawyers as to the relevant law. The appellate court then decides whether the trial court made a clear error of law or has abused its discretion. This means that the trial judge wandered too far beyond the boundaries of other similar cases. The court, on appeal, either affirms the trial court's decision, reverses it, or sends it back (remands) for retrial. The Supreme Court and appellate court publish their rulings as printed opinions.

While legal definitions and procedures are important, the purpose of this guidebook is to help do-it-yourself divorce participants, parties in mediation, and/or spouses working with attorneys to be thoughtful and creative in reaching agreements. By reaching agreements on your own or in a process such as mediation or collaboration controlled by you, you gain the advantage of using your own criteria when resolving important issues such as custody and division of property.

Privacy

The United States conducts its legal business in public. All courts are open to the public except juvenile court and those cases which are closed due to especially sensitive testimony. Some trials are broadcast live on television but not the ordinary divorce case! To close the courtroom to third parties during your divorce requires compliance with technical rules and is rarely granted. There is a legal presumption that courtroom proceedings are open to the public. However, the court does seal sworn financial affidavits in divorce cases that are seen only by the judges, appropriate court personnel, and involved parties and their attorneys. There is a procedure for others to attempt to "unseal" the financial affidavits.

CHAPTER 3

HOW TO NEGOTIATE
WITH YOUR SOON-TO-BE-EX

HOW TO NEGOTIATE
WITH YOUR SOON-TO-BE-EX

The second chapter of this book discussed the options available to couples experiencing difficulty in their marriage.

- Kitchen table discussions and do it yourself divorce

- Kitchen table discussions and uncontested divorce with attorneys

- Collaborative divorce

- Divorce mediation

- Cooperative divorce with attorneys

- Adversarial litigation

Assuming you have now made some preliminary decisions about what you want to do and how you want to do it, you are ready to put your first plans into action. To do this, you should try to talk and negotiate with your spouse. If the very idea turns your blood to ice water, this chapter will help you warm to the task.

Committing to Amicable Negotiation

The first step toward negotiating with your soon-to-be-ex spouse is to decide that you yourself want to do it. This is very important and quite distinct from asking your spouse if he or she wants to negotiate. Make your own decision to negotiate apart from your spouse's. You may have to hold to it for some time until your spouse comes around.

The second step is to tell your spouse that you want to work out your separation and/or divorce together. Ask your spouse to join you in a cooperative effort by choosing one of the methods described in Chapter 2. Just as it takes two to have a marriage, it takes two to negotiate an amicable divorce.

If the initial response is "no" and your spouse initiates an adversarial process, you may still keep the door open. Some people do not even consider negotiating directly with a spouse until they have a confrontation in court and experience the full effect of the adversarial process. If you are having difficulty getting your nego-

Divorce is not an event, it's a process.

The greatest discovery of my generation is that a human being can alter his life by altering his "attitudes of mind."

William James

"Let us never negotiate out of fear, but let us never fear to negotiate."

John F. Kennedy, Inaugural Address

Our Statement of Purpose

Directions: Write down your purpose in your own words. State exactly what you both want to accomplish, then add your initials and the date.

_____   _____   _____
Initials   Initials   Date

tiations started, try seeing a mediator together. Sometimes just one session with a mediator is all it takes to open communication.

Once you agree to negotiate and have selected the process and the professionals who will assist you, begin by clarifying the purposes of your negotiation. For example, how do you want to feel about your divorce when it's over? The answer to that question is probably your purpose. Here are some examples of purposes from actual cases:

- To find ways to get along as best we can in the best interests of our children

- To do our divorce in such a way that we can be friends afterward

- To do our divorce as amicably as possible in order to save time and money

- To hold our heads up afterward and not feel that anyone has won or lost

- To do a divorce we can both be proud of, regardless of what anyone else thinks

- To discuss our need to separate without hurting each other anymore

- To reach a financial agreement that is fair to both of us

Stating your purpose in advance will begin to direct your choices in negotiating and will help to pull you through difficulties in your negotiations later on.

Now, separately or together, commit to your written purpose. Commitment is not just talking about it or saying you're going to do it. It's marshalling your energy and power, inner and outer, to accomplish the purpose you envision. Never underestimate the power of commitment. You might memorialize your commitment by signing your written statement of purpose.

Goals

Goals are more specific than a purpose; goals assist you in carrying out your purpose. For example, what do you want to accomplish in your divorce? What are your intentions? As you write

---

Goals for Our Divorce Negotiations

Directions: Write your own goals in your own words, then add your initials and the date.

1.

2.

3.

4.

5.

_____ _____ _____
Initials   Initials   Date

them, keep your purpose in mind. Here are some examples of goals from actual cases:

- To separate financially and emotionally to our mutual satisfaction by the first of the year

- To provide a reasonable amount of time (state how long, if you wish) for a spouse to become self-supporting or to obtain the education or training necessary to become self-supporting

- To support the children in a secure and reasonable way, financially and emotionally, until they graduate from high school, finish college, or some other time

- To accomplish our separation in a way that does not disrupt our work or professional lives

- To allow both of us to retire by age ____

- To remain loving, equal, and committed parents in the eyes of our children

- To allow our children to survive this break-up emotionally whole and healthy

Consider signing your written statement of goals (sidebar, previous page) to signify the depth of your commitment to them.

Should you get lost or muddled in your negotiations, remind yourselves of your purpose and your goals. It will help bring you back on course.

"Effective communication between the parties is all but impossible if each plays to the gallery."

Roger Fisher and William Ury, *Getting to Yes*

Mutual Friends: Must We "Divide" Them?

Many times friends of divorcing spouses don't know what to do. Tell them how they can most help you. You can arrange with them to invite only one of you to social functions for the time being so that either of you can attend without the nagging fear of running into the other.

Sometimes friends may try too hard to protect you and give you a lot of "friendly" advice. You will have to be forthright with them. They mean well. Explain why a nonadversarial process is appropriate for you and that while you appreciate their concern, you would prefer them to be supportive friends while you rely on divorce professionals to give you advice. The two of you can turn to friends together and ask them, "Please don't take sides. We have made the decision to do this in harmony. Please stay friends with both of us. We will need you." Sometimes a joint letter to your closest friends is helpful to everyone.

You may want to decide between you who among your friends will be a confidant for each of you. If you do this, be sure you ask these friends if they agree to be "divided" this way, at least at the beginning.

From Conflict to Cooperation

Studies have shown that agreements parties reach themselves are far more likely to be carried out than orders entered by a judge or an arbitrator. Most of us would much rather make our own choices than have someone else tell us what to do, especially in personal and family matters. The move from conflict to cooperation is, in large part, a function of building or maintaining respect, trust, and good communication.

TIPS TO ASSIST YOU IN TURNING YOUR CONFLICT INTO COOPERATION

- Consider short-term, individual mental health counseling as a plan to help you handle your emotions as you go through the divorce process.

- Start rebuilding your own life as quickly and as fully as possible after your separation: home, finances, family, friends, social life.

- Focus on helping your children through the process.

- Work hard to prevent any hurt, fear, or anger you feel from controlling your words and conduct. Consider working together with a mental health professional to improve your communication and problem-solving ability.

- Accept your fair share of the responsibility for the end of your marriage and for your current problems. Tell this to your spouse.

"There is truly a magical quality about conflict which can call out the best in us, that which is not summoned under ordinary circumstances."

Thomas F. Crum, *The Magic of Conflict*

"We know that cooperation does occur and that our civilization is based upon it. But in situations where each individual has an incentive to be selfish, how can cooperation ever develop?

"The answer each of us gives to this question has a fundamental effect on how we think and act in our social, political, and economic relations with others. And the answers that others give have a great effect on how ready they will be to cooperate with us."

Robert Axelrod, *The Evolution of Cooperation*

"Conflict is *not* contest. Conflict just is. We choose whether to make it a contest, a game in which there are winners and losers."

Thomas F. Crum, *The Magic of Conflict*

- Commit to a nonadversarial approach to resolving your divorce issues.

- Get whatever input you need from other people (friends, relatives), including professionals (lawyers, counselors, pastors) and any other sources (books, seminars), for you to be able to trust yourself to make your part of the decisions. Do whatever else you need to do to be able to trust your own judgment. Lack of trust in yourself usually turns into serious dissatisfaction with the outcome, along with blaming your spouse for it.

- Keep all agreements with your spouse. Call him or her whenever you need to make a change to an agreement or parenting schedule. Avoid unilateral action on anything that affects your areas of agreement.

- When in doubt, obtain clarification. Don't assume. Be open to clarifying your spouse's questions and assumptions, too.

- Speak as positively as possible about your ex-spouse, particularly around your children. Express your negative feelings, but do it privately and only to people you trust.

- Make every effort to live up to your financial commitments and obligations. Tell your spouse right away if there is a real impediment to your keeping your agreement.

- Be sensitive about talking about or introducing a new love interest to your ex. Sometimes there are deep wounds which take a long time to heal.

- Know when you're finished and need to end the process. Realize that a fair and workable solution, even though less than perfect, is far better than continuing the conflict and the uncertainty that accompanies it.

Turbulence

While some people may find their negotiations smooth and relatively easy, others will meet hazards and difficulties along the way. The main difficulties, real and perceived, are:

- confusion

- not enough money

"If it was so, it might be; and it if were so, it would be; but as it isn't, it ain't. That's logic."

Lewis Carroll, *Through the Looking Glass*

- the desire to fight

- feelings (fear, hurt, anger)

We will discuss the first three of these here—and the fourth later—in this chapter.

Confusion. Some common ways in which you might find yourself confused while facing divorce are:

- You may not know enough about the law and the legal process of getting divorced. The information in this guidebook will help dispel this confusion so that you under stand the legal divorce process and the paperwork that accompanies it.

- You may also be confused by the facts, data, and financial information necessary to do a good job of getting divorced. The Checklist of Things to Gather in Chapter 7 and the many practical steps in this guidebook will help you deal with this, as will the assistance and advice of divorce professionals.

- The intensity of your own feelings may confuse and overwhelm you. This chapter will get you started in dealing with this, just as individual counseling will.

This guidebook by itself is not sufficient to dispel confusion. Get whatever professional input you need—attorney, therapist, mediator (*see* Divorce and the Legal System, Chapter 2). You need to understand where you are and what your options are in order to make decisions you can live with. Second-guessing yourself later is torture, and the decisions you make now may not be changeable in the future.

Not Enough Money. The issue of inadequate money is difficult for everyone. Approaching your separation and divorce in an amicable way is a major money-saver since the cost of going to trial or even negotiating exclusively through attorneys can be enormous. The more efficiency you build into the process, the more benefit you will get from the professional fees you pay.

For many people, the matter of debt division is far more significant than asset division. An already negative cash flow is even more negative with two households to support. Almost every divorcing person faces a lifestyle less comfortable than he or she experienced during the marriage, especially immediately after

"Everything that irritates us about others can lead us to an understanding of ourselves."

Carl Jung

Temptation

For many, the desire to fight is present throughout their negotiations, tempting them every moment. For others it comes and goes intermittently, lurking just at the edge of consciousness. No matter how strong the desire to fight is in you, **you can choose not to fight.** To keep peace with yourself, acknowledge your desire to fight and then talk about it. Don't condemn yourself for it.

separating. You will find money-saving tips throughout this guidebook, including some tax-saving devices which may conserve income within the family. Worrying about money during a divorce is natural and even necessary. A successful divorce minimizes the turbulence around money through mutual divorce financial planning.

The Desire to Fight. The desire to fight with your soon-to-be-ex is very common. Usually you feel the urge to prove you're right, to teach him or her a lesson, to vindicate some principle, or to be sure you win and/or your spouse loses. It is possible to live with the temptation to fight and not do it. It is not bad or wrong to fight. It is a choice that will bring consequences different from those that follow from working in a nonadversarial way, even though the outcomes may be the same or similar. You and your spouse are already hurting. You will likely hurt each other even more if you fight. If you choose to fight, in or out of court, you must expect to hurt and get hurt. If you feel you must fight, for whatever reason, you should probably talk to an attorney right at the beginning. If you or the lawyer choose litigation as the first strategy, do not throw this book away. After the first confrontation in court, many people want to return to the nonadversarial negotiating table.

Having an agreement, some specific understandings, or rules about how you will conduct yourselves during your negotiations (no matter what nonadversarial approach you elect) can help enormously with the desire to fight. The following section provides some suggestions for navigating around and through stormy weather in your negotiations, whether you are involved in do-it-yourself divorce, mediation, or collaboration.

CHECKLIST OF OUR RULES OF THE ROAD

Directions: Discuss each of the following suggestions, and adopt or alter them, or not, as you see fit. You may initial those items you both agree to, if you wish, or just re-read them from time to time.

Initial

1. *No Unilateral Actions.* We agree not to take unilateral actions. Neither of us will spend any money, incur debt, sell or transfer, or otherwise change assets without the consent of the other, other than our usual monthly activities and expenditures that we are both familiar with.   _____   _____

2. *Intercept Interruptions.* We agree not to interrupt the other in our meetings. (Consider setting a time limit on speeches.) We agree that interrupting is a sign that we are reacting to what is being said rather than trying to understand it.   _____   _____

3. *Get it! Got it! Good!* If either of us thinks we have not heard the other, we may repeat what the other said until we are sure we've gotten it. If either of us thinks we have not been heard, we may request that the other repeat what we just said until we are sure that they've gotten it.   _____   _____

4. *Use Hard Numbers.* We will use only hard numbers. We agree that every number we rely on in reaching our final settlement will be established or proven to the satisfaction of both of us. If we are discussing a particular document (for example, a credit card account or bank account balance) we agree to bring the original and a photocopy for the other person to our meeting. Gathering the items on the checklist (Chapter 7) will make this easy to do.   _____   _____

5. *All Cards on the Table.* We agree to put ALL our cards on the table to reveal everything about our assets, liabilities, and incomes and any other facts that may be important to ourselves and the other spouse as we work out our plans. We agree to hold nothing back.   _____   _____

     An agreement based on incomplete knowledge or half-truth (even if not deliberate) is a house built on sand. It will shift, crack, and eventually collapse.

6. *Patience is a Virtue.* We agree not expect to negotiate everything in one meeting.   _____   _____

     Don't condemn yourself if your initial meetings are only a few minutes long. You need the time in between your meetings to let it all sink in and to ponder what you are doing.

7. *Take a Break.* We agree that if we get stuck, really stuck, on a particular topic, we will go on to something else and come back to the difficult topic later. However, we will give ourselves a chance to resolve a difficult topic by not giving up too soon. There are several reasons why taking a break can help resolve an issue: time to think about it, time to gather more information, time to cool off and review purpose

Initial

and goals, time to find the courage to take another run at this or a different topic, time to be creative.

——— ———   8. *Write It Down.* We agree to write down what we agree to by the end of each meeting.

Some people have difficulty remembering what goes on at a divorce negotiating session. This is not unusual. Some forget a few things, others can't remember anything. To be sure that you are on top of what's going on, post your copy of what you and your spouse write at the end of your sessions on the refrigerator or some other place where you can read and re-read it so that you stay aware of where you are, and are not, in your negotiations.

——— ———   9. *Clear as a Bell.* We will be clear with each other about which decisions are final as we make them and which are tentative and subject to revision as we go along. We will also be clear with each other about when and how we each will consult with counsel or other experts.

——— ———   10. *Interests Not Positions.* We agree to negotiate from interests rather than positions. An example of a position is "I have to have joint custody." An example of the interest behind that position is "I want to feel like a real parent." There are lots of ways to satisfy this interest, but the statement of position cuts off any discussion. Another example of a position is "I have to have $1,000 a month from you." The interest behind the position is "I need enough from you to help me meet my budget." Resist the temptation to add "and that amount has to be $1,000 per month." Find out together if $1,000 per month is the right amount.

——— ———   11. *Take Your Time.* We agree to be patient and to take whatever time we need. We acknowledge that one of us is probably on a faster track than the other.

——— ———   12. *Close to the Heart.* We agree to be responsible for our own feelings and to respect the other's feelings.

——— ———   13. *Re-think.* We agree to be willing to re-think. We understand that sometimes the solution that seemed so perfect at our last meeting may not hold up in the light of a new day.

——— ———   14. *Anything Is Possible.* We agree that there is no *right* or *wrong* answer to any single problem. There are probably a number of possible solutions, many of which will work for both of us. Two heads really are better than one. We agree to get all the expert assistance we feel we need and to be true to our own interests, separate and together.

——— ———   15. *Friends.* We agree to talk about our mutual friends and how we will relate to them during our divorce.

——— ———   16. *Agendas.* We will each write down all the items we want to talk about before a meeting. We will then merge our two lists, putting an item on the list even if only one of us wants to discuss it. This will be our agenda. When we meet, we will first see if either of us has anything to add to the list, then we will agree on which item to discuss first and a tentative order for discussing the rest.

Consider choosing the "easiest" item first to give yourselves some momentum for success. Or you may want to discuss what is causing the most pressure because settling it can make everything else easier to work on. If you can't agree on what to discuss first, you can take turns choosing an item from your agenda. Flip a coin to see who goes first. Some items won't require any agreement—it may be that one of you simply needs to say something about it and be heard.

Directions: Fill in the topics you want to discuss at your first meeting in their order of importance to you.

Wife's Agenda for Our First Meeting

a.

b.

c.

d.

e.

f.

g.

Husband's Agenda for Our First Meeting

a.

b.

c.

d.

e.

f.

g.

Feelings, Roles, and Styles of Negotiating

The last of the major causes of turbulence in divorce negotiations is emotion, specifically, those feelings that are so strong they overwhelm you. Anger, fear (of being alone, of not having enough money, of the unknown, for example), and hurt are all significant during divorce. Sometimes problems unresolved in your relationship or even from your own childhood get in the way of effective negotiating. You protect these feelings by playing roles instead of being yourself.

YOUR NEGOTIATING STYLE

The two major ingredients in a divorce negotiation are relationships and issues.

Relationships include the two of you, each of you with each of the children, and the children with each other. They may also include relationships with others outside the immediate family such as other relatives, "significant others," friends, or associates in small businesses who will be directly affected by your divorce.

Issues include things like money, the family home, cars, debts, child rearing, child support, medical insurance, and the influence of relatives and significant others.

Negotiation styles focus on the relative importance one attaches to relationships and issues. A person for whom relationships are of utmost importance and who cares much less about issues is a person who tends to accommodate the relationship by giving in on the issues. "Do what you want with the money, just don't leave me," such a person might say. An accommodator may give in to the other's wishes without even considering his or her own concerns in order to protect the relationship. The accommodator takes care of the other no matter what and makes few or no demands.

The opposite of the accommodator is the shark, the person for whom issues are of paramount importance. Such a person will forget or ignore the relationship as needed to suit the issues. The shark competes to win at all cost. The shark is at home in hearings and trials of divorce disputes. The shark is able to set aside or forget that he or she was once in love and becomes abstract, rational, and legalistic. The shark ignores the relationships that surround the issues and sees issues instead as cut and dried.

"The need to judge absolutely or to become self-righteous about our opinions will eventually do violence to ourselves."

Thomas F. Crum, *The Magic of Conflict*

Another kind of negotiator is like a turtle. This is a person who says that neither relationships nor issues are of importance. Such a person is often shy, quiet, afraid, and often in denial. Such a person avoids confrontation and pain and fears failure so much that he or she avoids any risk. Some people in divorce go into withdrawal about everything in order not to be responsible for any of it, like a turtle hiding in its shell. Some people bury themselves in withdrawal during divorce. "Wake me up when it's over," "I don't care what you do," or "You can have everything, I just want out," are the voices of turtles. They will face enormous regret and anger later on when they emerge from their shells.

The shark and the accommodator are sometimes alternating aspects of the same person. After relentlessly accommodating the partner, the accommodator finally gets angry at having given too much away. Such a person then becomes a shark, going after all that can be gotten. The shark, on the other hand, eventually feels guilty for having had excess zeal and sometimes becomes an accommodator, giving everything away. This kind of pendulum effect occurs in many marriages as well as divorces.

Amicable divorce-approaches help by balancing relationships and issues as well as concerns for self and others.

Some people negotiate and compromise. They bargain, trade, and make deals. But, their solutions can be too clever. A problem with compromise is that each individual compromise may not be related to anything else, except to a kind of "keeping score." This type of person is likely to say "I'm making all the compromises here," often not noticing all the compromises their partner has made.

Being more cooperative is collaborative. A collaborator tolerates all the feelings, all the ambiguities, long enough and non-judgmentally enough for creative solutions to emerge. To collaborate is to allow yourself to say and to listen to and to hear everything without judgment, even though you can't imagine a solution that will satisfy everyone.

Why do we so easily become accommodators, sharks, or turtles in divorce? Usually because we want to avoid being responsible for our own feelings. What we call our styles of negotiating are really our ways of dealing with strong feelings during negotiation.

In order to negotiate a divorce effectively, the turtle must become able to express and stand up for both issues and relationships. The accommodator must learn to sort out his or her genuine concerns about issues. The shark must temper his or her focus on the

"From time to time you may want to remind yourself that the first thing you are trying to win is a better way to negotiate—a way that avoids your having to choose between the satisfactions of getting what you deserve and of being decent. You can have both."

Roger Fisher and William Ury, *Getting to Yes*

issues with concern about relationships. If you feel stuck in these roles but want to emerge from them and move toward compromise and collaboration, get someone trained to help in your negotiations. This is the role of the divorce professionals described in Chapter 2.

It is important to discover and understand your negotiating style in close relationships and to recognize where you are on the various issues in your divorce. Knowing your style will help you open yourself to feelings you are avoiding so that you can get into the balance that is required for compromise and collaboration. *See* the Bibliography for more information about negotiating.

Speaking Up for Yourself

Speaking up for yourself is not selfish. It is essential to a successful negotiation. If you do not, you become a turtle or an accommodator. If you dominate with your wants, you become a shark. If you negotiate from only your own needs, you are probably still a shark.

Some people think they cannot have an amicable divorce without an attorney to negotiate for them because they feel shy, meek, or weaker than their spouse. "I'm not so good at words." "I can't even think, let alone talk, when he or she is around." Some people think these are gender differences. Actually, divorce negotiation is difficult for everyone. Take care not to overwhelm each other or to be overwhelmed. Regardless of how you see yourself, you are responsible for what you agree to.

There are many people who can help you be stronger and more clear-sighted about what is real for you, individually. Sounding out your ideas and feelings with such a person is a good beginning. A lawyer, a minister, a priest, a rabbi, or a family or mental health counselor may be a good resource for this. The next step is for you and your spouse to try out your ideas about your separation and divorce on each other. Someone skilled at hearing two voices at once can be especially helpful here, such as a pastor, therapist, or mediator.

Talking in Code

You must not only speak up for yourself, you must also speak in a language your spouse can both hear and understand. Most people speak their own private language. Each of us has favorite phrases we use a lot, and our individual choice of what to talk or keep silent about is unique. A phrase as simple as "See you later"

"It is the pressure of conflict, the interference patterns of energies caused by differences, that provides the motivation and opportunity for change."

Thomas F. Crum, *The Magic of Conflict*

at parting can mean anything from "See you some day—perhaps in this lifetime" to "See you tonight as we planned—and I can't wait." We figure out the real meaning by watching body language, and facial expressions, listening to tone of voice, and, most of all, interpreting according to past history.

People in long-term relationships evolve their own language. When their relationship begins to come apart, they start looking for new words to go with the new experiences and new feelings. When "See you later" starts to get responses like "Just what do you mean by that?" you are already beginning to change your old language.

It is important to say what you really mean at this time—no more, no less. There aren't any throw-away lines. Going back to the old couples code you spoke together will begin to feel false. Try asking your spouse to re-phrase or to find a new word when the one he or she used has run out of meaning for you. "Can you say that in a different way so I can understand what you really mean?" is a very effective way to open things up. Be ready to speak with new words yourself.

Using the insights from this chapter will increase the chances for you to participate in the divorce process with dignity and grace.

CHAPTER **4**

TAKING CARE OF YOURSELF

"It is a common tendency for us to misinterpret spiritual or relationship hunger for physical hunger. When we are 'unconscious' of the distinction, we move like robots to the refrigerator every time we feel a lack of something."

Thomas F. Crum, *The Magic of Conflict*

TAKING CARE OF YOURSELF

Keeping Yourself Together So You Can Work Together

Disconnecting a marital relationship is not easy, whether you are the initiator of it, the receiver, or even when it is mutual and simultaneous. No matter which way you do it, feelings abound: grief, hurt, fear, a sense of loss, a sense of failure, guilt, and, of course, anger. Many also feel relief, sometimes even joy, that it's over or that they can stop denying that it's over. It's not unusual to feel grief and relief or joy at the same time.

CAUTION People in divorce are much more accident prone, injury prone, and illness prone than the general population. Be careful. Feeling edgy? Don't drive. You don't even have to be drinking for driving to be dangerous for you. Avoid other potentially dangerous activities too, such as using knives and other sharp objects, heavy machinery or other heavy objects, fast skiing or cycling. This is not the time to try bungee jumping or sky diving. Be careful around alcohol, medicine, and drugs. Even your ordinary day-to-day tasks that you take for granted can become challenging, if not dangerous, as you may find yourself forgetful or easily distracted.

Take good care of yourself. Be patient with yourself. Try a relaxing warm bath, a cup of herbal tea, soothing music, a massage. Don't be afraid to ask your friends to drive and for other help until you calm down. Often you consume so much of your physical and emotional energy coping with the separation—actual or impending—that there is almost no energy left for taking care of yourself.

"When people fall in deep distress, their native sense departs."

Sophocles

Working out your own divorce plan with your spouse requires some important skills, such as the ability to focus and concentrate, to understand the issues—especially about money and property—and to learn more about them. You will also need the ability to communicate in ways that do not close off discussion. The ability to take responsibility for your participation and whatever you agree to, without creating the foundation for future anger and regret, is also important. You need these skills at a time when you may feel ready to explode with some of the most difficult and intense feelings you've ever experienced.

The information in this chapter about knowing yourself and understanding your feelings will help you to think clearly and participate effectively in your negotiations. If you base any position you take or compromise you make on anger, hurt, intimidation, revenge, or determination to be a victim, you are likely to conclude the divorce process with far more emotional baggage than you came in with. It is better to do your divorce well now so that you don't remain stuck in it for years after it's over.

Just about everyone going through divorce could use psychotherapy at least part of the time. If you answer "yes" to any of the following questions, you might consider consulting a professional:

- Am I having trouble taking adequate care of myself (bathing, buying groceries and eating, putting gas in the car, and the like)?

- Am I having trouble meeting my obligations to my family?

- Am I having trouble carrying out my responsibilities at work?

- Am I having trouble sleeping?

- Am I having trouble starting and finishing my tasks each day?

- Do I experience anger or sadness that is out of proportion to the apparent cause?

- Do I hear myself saying things that I don't believe or I know to be untrue but I can't stop myself?

- Am I taking physical chances like driving too fast, not using potholders, not wearing warm enough clothing, and the like?

- Am I drinking too much, or does using drugs sound inviting?

Whether or not you are seeing a professional therapist, consider finding someone to talk to during this time—a friend, neighbor, or a pastor, or find a divorce support group to join for awhile.

The Emotional Divorce Sequence

For most people, the emotional divorce follows a fairly typical pattern. The timing of the phases may be very different for each spouse, but everyone goes through them all.

1. First is the crisis, the critical point in time when the relationship is coming apart—one of you leaves or announces that it's

How to Find a Therapist

1. Get a referral from a friend you trust who can make a recommendation based on personal experience.

2. Ask your pastor, lawyer, EAP counselor, or mediator to make a recommendation.

3. Look in the Yellow Pages or Smart Pages.com under the following headings:

   Marriage and Family Therapists

   Psychotherapists

   Psychologists

   Physicians – Psychiatrists

   Social Workers

4. Inquire at your neighborhood or town mental health center.

over, or you both decide that it's over. One spouse may recognize this much earlier than the other.

2. The second phase is the reaction to the initial crisis, which frequently just feels "crazy." This phase usually extends over several months and has identifiable stages of its own. Knowing these stages and their sequence can help you through them. See below.

3. Then, at last, comes the recovery—the healing, the sense of peace. Now, you can get on with your life.

The middle reactionary phase has five recognized stages that are actually the stages of grief. As you read them, see if any of them describes where you are. (This information is from *Rebuilding When Your Relationship Ends* by Dr. Bruce Fisher. Dr. Fisher has found that the stages of the emotional divorce parallel the five stages of grief as outlined originally by Dr. Elizabeth Kubler-Ross, which are used here by permission.)

Grief has many faces besides full blown sorrow. It frequently appears as a feeling of loneliness, difficulty in concentrating, and a sense of being weak and helpless. Sometimes it will bubble up as a kind of anger, not so much anger at the sorrow but at the inability to "be yourself" and get things done like you usually do. When you feel unable to control your mood swings or your ability to be responsible and productive, it can be frightening.

Stage 1: The first stage of grief is emotional shock. "This isn't happening to me." "This isn't real." There is a numbness about it. We suppress the anger and hurt and act as though nothing has happened. We put on our best manners. We keep it all inside, don't tell anybody, and put up walls to protect ourselves.

The next four stages are each steps toward accepting the end and letting go.

Stage 2: Anger appears in the second stage—anger turned outward toward others. It's easy to lash out angrily and inappropriately in a variety of situations. You may express much of the anger about "how terrible it was to be married to him or her" to friends and others and not to the spouse. The anger, however, is a "Catch 22" because of fear that if we are too angry at the departing spouse (or the one we are leaving or think we should leave), there will be no getting back together. The emotional door is usually still open at this stage—there is strong ambivalence about wanting the spouse back.

"Give sorrow words; the grief that does not speak / Whispers the o'er-fraught heart and bids it break."

Shakespeare, *Macbeth*

"We cannot direct the wind but we can adjust our sails."

City of Hope

Look in the Mirror

If you feel tempted to blame your present misery on your spouse, look in the mirror and pretend you see your spouse there as your reflection. You might notice that when you think or say, "I hate it when you do that," it is really code for "I hate it when I do that, and I keep doing it."

Stage 3: The third stage is yet another attempt to prolong the relationship. We repeatedly bargain and compromise—we try to make deals with our spouse in thought if not in action. This can be a "teddy bear" stage where we are willing to accommodate almost anything in order to have the relationship continue. This can be a dangerous stage because many couples get back together at this point by agreeing to be teddy bears, yet most of us can't stay that way for very long before emerging angrier than before. Frequently people get back together at this point because they can't stand the loneliness and the unhappiness of ending the relationship—choosing the spouse again as the lesser of two evils.

Stage 4: The fourth stage is the "blahs," a kind of depression and internal questioning: "Is this all there is to life?" This is the darkness before the dawn. It's a stage of growth where we build a stronger identity and find life more meaningful, more purposeful. However, some people in this stage become suicidal when they find themselves discouraged about working so hard on this relationship that they now must let go. This stage frequently comes a long time after the actual separation—finding ourselves depressed about it all over again can be surprising. Research has found that people who are aware of this stage get through it more easily.

Stage 5: The last stage brings acceptance of the loss of the love relationship. We are finally free of the pain of grief. The end of grief is the acceptance of the end of the relationship. We find internal peace, become centered, and once again move on in our lives.

It's wise to get through all five stages of grief before entering a new relationship. You may experience them in a different order, and they may overlap. Many who work professionally with people in the divorce process say the grief process takes eighteen months to two years for most people.

Staying Sane Under Insane Conditions

Passing through the five stages of grief is like navigating your ship through a storm in the Twilight Zone. Try to recognize where you are in relation to these stages. Pay close attention to yourself throughout, and expect surprises. Here are some tips to help you along the way.

- *Fear.* This is often the trigger for doing some of the craziest or most hurtful things. It can lure you away from your deepest sense of yourself. Tell your worst fears to someone, or write them for yourself. To insure that the fears do not control your choices, examine each fear. Rate on a scale of one to ten (ten

Peggy Lee sings: "Is that all there is? If that's all there is, then let's keep dancing."

Rate Your Fears

Directions: List the fears you have relative to your separation or divorce, and rate each on a scale of 1–10.

My worst fears are: Rating

Distinguish between a good belly laugh and cynicism. Cynicism is not funny.

Whining doesn't solve anything.

being the most likely) just how realistic or likely an eventuality it is. For those fears you've rated over five, ask yourself what you can and should do to minimize the risk. For example, as a marriage ends we might harbor a deep fear of "being a bag lady or bag man." To minimize this risk, be responsible for budgeting your post-divorce lifestyle and realistically assessing how much of that you can earn.

- *Let your tears flow.* Strange as it may seem, crying is the way to deal with grief and its component feelings. Weep, wail, sob, however it is you do it, in ways that don't hurt yourself or anyone else. Strong feelings are a fundamental part of who we are. Avoiding them takes all our available energy, like trying to hold the door shut in a tornado, leaving us exhausted and depressed. Experiencing feelings is the only way to release them. You must let them pass through, just as a breeze does when you open both the front door and a window. You can maintain yourself in your job and perform better at work by allocating time before or after for expressing strong feelings. You can do this in a number of ways. Play music that helps you weep. Write a letter expressing your anger but do not send it. Write or call a close friend. Therapy can help too.

- *Find your sense of humor.* Even if you think there isn't anything in your situation to laugh about, try. Think back to the last ridiculous thing you did. If you cannot find anything to laugh about in yourself, find something out there, somewhere, that will help you have at least one good belly laugh. Find something to laugh about at least once a day. Cartoons, comedy videos, animals, pets, children—all of these can be of help.

- *Blame is a black hole.* Allow your feelings to flow without placing blame for them—especially on your spouse. Acknowledge your feelings (grief, anger, hurt, fear, etc.) without focusing on your spouse or anyone else.

- *Guilt is the desire to blame yourself.* Take responsibility for whatever you did or didn't do in your relationship without judging any of it as wrong. Figure out what you need to learn from it. Try to see your own actions and omissions in terms of their results, both in your relationship and inside yourself. This step is vital to moving on to a new relationship, one that won't be a repeat of the one that's ending.

- *Be patient.* The phases of the emotional divorce, although easily described, take time to live through. To rush through them is to try to push the river or rush the harvest. Allow each stage the time it needs.

- *Celebrate when you can.* Give yourself exactly what you want for birthdays and Christmas, Chanukkah, or Kwanzaa. Don't set yourself up to receive nothing on important occasions. Don't abandon yourself. Honor your successes, no matter how small.

- *Create your own support system.* Maintain connection with several people with whom you can discuss anything. Be sure you find people who are genuinely caring, compassionate, and not just blindly militant on your behalf.

Being a Good Parent Is Part of Taking Care of Yourself

Part of taking care of yourself is being sure that you do your very best as a parent at this difficult time. It goes without saying that children need and deserve good parenting. Your own sense of self-esteem will plummet if you feel in any way that you are neglecting or harming your children. See "How to be a Good Parent Through the Divorce Process" in Chapter 8.

How to Handle Potential Violence and Other Stressful Encounters

Fear, panic, and feeling frozen emotionally and intellectually are all results of relationships that are on the edge of violence. Both spouses may feel these, and both or only one may react with violence. Such violence, experts say, is very often a result of feeling out of control (not necessarily that someone else is controlling you, but that you aren't in control of you). Some people use violence to make their partner feel helpless in order to feel powerful.

If you feel, at any time in the course of your separation, that you or your spouse is to the point of violence or abuse, whether physical or extreme verbal assault, then do the following:

- *Physically separate.* Go to reliable friends or family. You may need to go to the nearest safehouse.

- *If there is a neutral place where your children can go, take them there.* Grandparents can be a godsend or a real curse. If they will defend the children's peace against both of you, they are the ones to go to. Neutral, mutual friends with children your children's age are often best. Sometimes, if you leave and take the children with you—especially to a secret place—that, too, can feel violent to the person left behind.

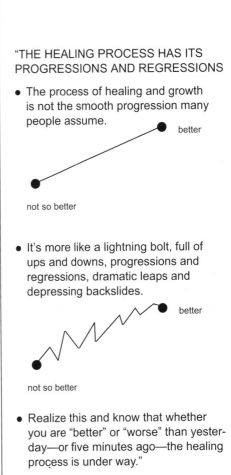

"THE HEALING PROCESS HAS ITS PROGRESSIONS AND REGRESSIONS

- The process of healing and growth is not the smooth progression many people assume.

- It's more like a lightning bolt, full of ups and downs, progressions and regressions, dramatic leaps and depressing backslides.

- Realize this and know that whether you are "better" or "worse" than yesterday—or five minutes ago—the healing process is under way."

From *How to Survive the Loss of a Love* by Melba Colgrove, PhD; Harold H. Bloomfield, MD; and Peter McWilliams, published by Prelude Press.

 www.mcwilliams.com/books/sur/srtoc.htm

You can divorce a parent, but you cannot divorce a child.

- *Do not destroy, sell, give away, or secrete any property.* Unless you must have it to survive, if the other party is likely to have an interest in it, such unilateral action often feels like violence at the receiving end and generally escalates hostility.

- *Do not try to move the divorce along too fast.* Jumping into the adversarial process or even forcing yourself into mediation or counseling when you are still hurt and fearful may only convert anger to rage and rage to more violence.

- *Establish agreements.* This will go a long way toward helping you get back in control of your individual lives: mutual agreements to stay apart, pay certain debts, preserve certain property; agreements about seeing the children without seeing each other; mutual promises of no violence or derogatory comments about each other. Try writing down what you yourself are willing to do along these lines. Make no demands about what you expect your spouse to do. Then sign it and give it to a trusted friend to give to your spouse. Such a proposal may open a door to settlement.

If none of these suggestions works, or is even possible, and you fear that violence is imminent or inevitable, then you may need to turn to the court. You should know that, in practice, a court order is just a piece of paper. Sometimes it can push someone over the edge, uncontrolled by the law. Sometimes the spouse may ignore the order.

There is a court procedure for dealing with domestic violence, whether it has already occurred or has only been threatened. You can get forms and instruction from the superior court clerk's office or from specially designated personnel who may be available in some courthouses to help you bring your petition for relief before the judge on your own. If you need more information on this subject, take care of yourself by consulting with an attorney who has expertise in the area of domestic violence and abuse.

If violence happens, call the police. Report it immediately and be willing to follow through with your charges. When it gets to this point you must seek intervention.

Spouses in marriages with actual violence may still be able to have a nonadversarial divorce. A great deal of self-knowledge and insight on the part of both spouses has to occur, however, before this is possible.

To find Procedures for Relief from Abuse Process go to **www.jud.state.ct.us/forms/fm142p.pdf**.

Restraining Order: Written action by a court which prohibits a person from doing certain acts, such as entering a certain property. Doing the prohibited act is then punishable by the court.

Beware the Eternal Return

Statistics show that without some introspection, self-reflection, and change, most of us will form a relationship with someone almost exactly like the person we just ended with. We all repeat learned patterns, especially in childhood. One of the keys to peace with yourself is knowing when you do it.

CHAPTER 5

MOVING FROM ONE HOUSEHOLD TO TWO

MOVING FROM ONE HOUSEHOLD TO TWO

If you decide to move apart—whether you are doing a trial separation, a legal separation, or a divorce—several immediate choices will face you. There will be some choices that you will want to make but shouldn't; there will be others that you will not want to face but should. This chapter will help you to choose wisely for the short term. This is a particularly important time to consult with experts (attorneys, CPAs, therapists) to get specific advice about your situation and how to handle temporary issues.

Make sure that as you separate nothing falls through the cracks. You must care for the children on a daily basis, pay your bills, and maintain your property. It is vital that at this difficult time you keep your communications open so that you can make clear agreements about all these matters.

A useful first step is to decide the time frame for each of your interim agreements. You may make an agreement about paying the bills, for example, for three or six months and an agreement about managing the children day to day for only one month or six weeks until you see how it works for everyone. Now is a good time to try different schemes to discover what does and does not work for you.

If you are planning a divorce, and will therefore be filing papers in court, the interim agreements you make using this chapter will be *temporary agreements*. You may also have your temporary agreements made into temporary orders of the court. If you and your spouse have not yet reached—or cannot reach—temporary agreements, Chapter 6 explains the procedure for filing *temporary motions* with the court. These procedures will result in the judge listening to testimony at a hearing and entering temporary orders. Most people, however, settle their differences before the scheduled hearing date.

Many couples do not need to write down their temporary agreements because their communications are clear and there is complete trust and reliability. Others want something written and filed with the court. This is your call, and consulting with an attorney will help you. There may be profitable tax planning available to you during this time, as discussed later in this chapter and more fully in Chapter 12. You may physically separate either before or after you file a complaint in court. You may even decide not to physically separate but to live "upstairs-downstairs" in the same home.

DEFINITION **Temporary Agreements:** Formal agreements, usually written, between spouses concerning use of property, payment of debts, children and their support, temporary alimony, and taxes, generally from the time of the agreement until the final divorce judgment.

DEFINITION **Temporary Orders:** Court orders that affect divorcing or legally separating spouses from the date of the order until their final decree—may be the result of a court hearing or trial, or an order approving the spouses' temporary agreement; also known as *pendente lite* orders.

"Once you are physically separated you are legally separated."
This assumption is incorrect and can be very costly. You are legally separated only if and when you receive a judgment of legal separation from a court.

You must also carefully plan your financial separation. A common problem results when, sensing an imminent separation, one spouse fears that the other will do something that will cost a lot of money. So, to "protect" the money, he or she closes the joint account and puts the money in a separate account. The other spouse then panics, matters get out of control, and the legal fees soar.

Sometimes, instead of fear, anger takes over. One spouse will angrily take the other off the health insurance policy thinking "that'll show you!" You'll hurt yourself too if you do this. Medical bills may still be joint debts, and the judge could assign them to the spouse who ended the coverage.

These and other kinds of unilateral actions, without discussion or notice—let alone agreement—usually escalate the situation from very warm to a mild simmer to a fast boil (and may violate the court's automatic orders, see page 102, if a case has been filed). Suddenly your separation is no longer a private change of life but a very expensive and public war. The more you base your early actions on joint decisions that you make ahead of time, the more chance you have of finishing your divorce in peace, if not in harmony.

Temporary Responsibility and Use, Not Permanent Ownership

Your temporary agreement does not necessarily decide who gets what permanently. It is a temporary agreement that provides for the use and upkeep of property and payment of bills until you reach a final agreement. Temporary agreements are ways for you to experiment and try out ideas. However, you should always consult with an attorney to get advice about the potential future consequences of any temporary arrangements.

Toward a Peaceful Separation

The more ground rules you specifically agree to, the better chance you have of keeping control of yourselves and the difficult process you are going through. Here is a checklist of ideas for you and your spouse to explore. Use them as a basis for developing your own ground rules for how to go about your separation.

Some of these points may seem so obvious that they go without saying. Others may not even apply in your situation. Review them carefully, together, and build your personal foundation for cooperation.

SAMPLE GROUND RULES FOR A PEACEFUL SEPARATION

Directions: Discuss the statements below and initial those to which you both agree. These are suggestions only: many of them overlap, and not all of them will apply to your situation. Feel free to alter the ones which do apply to you.

Initial

We agree that the statements below that we both initial will control our negotiations.   _____   _____

1. We agree to work out our divorce together, in a friendly nonhostile way.   _____   _____

2. We agree to jointly make any decisions that affect both of us.   _____   _____

3. We agree to decide jointly which of us will move.   _____   _____

4. We agree to cooperate and be mutually helpful to make the moving process as smooth as possible.   _____   _____

5. We agree to tell the children together about our separation and to assure them that they will always have both of us.   _____   _____

6. We agree to involve the children in the moving process and to encourage them to contribute their thoughts and ideas toward developing a second home with the parent who is moving out.   _____   _____

7. We agree to not make any disparaging remarks or statements about each other in the presence of the children.   _____   _____

8. We agree to talk, just the two of us, for a limited amount of time, _____ hours/minutes, at regular intervals, _____ times a week or _____ times a month, at least until our divorce is final.   _____   _____

9. We agree to keep our agreements with each other and to be totally reliable.   _____   _____

_____ _____ 10. We agree to notify the other immediately upon learning that we cannot keep an agreement, or part of an agreement, even if it's just that we're going to be a few minutes late.

_____ _____ 11. Each of us states that he or she will not agree to anything he or she does not intend to do.

_____ _____ 12. Each of us states that he or she will not agree to something just in hopes of winning the other back.

_____ _____ 13. We agree that we will not concede to something in anger or revenge, to prove the other wrong, or to indulge in being a victim.

_____ _____ 14. If being together before our separation becomes too difficult or causes tempers to flare, we designate _____ as a neutral and inexpensive "cooling-off" place where either of us can go for a few days, after telling the other, and then return home. If we agree one of us must go but are unable to agree who will go, we will decide the length of time and then flip a coin.

_____ _____ 15. We agree to get whatever input we need, professional and otherwise, in order to make intelligent choices and decisions we won't regret later. This includes lawyers, psychotherapists, mediators, financial planners, appraisers, accountants, real estate professionals, and the like. We agree to notify each other of any professionals we consult with and when. (This statement is about notice, not permission.)

_____ _____ 16. We agree to use only lawyers who will encourage and assist in our settlement.

_____ _____ 17. We agree that we will not consult our friends, acquaintances, and family for divorce, legal, financial, and parenting advice. We know that these people are well intentioned but that every divorce case is as different as every family, so we will rely solely on the advice of divorce professionals.

_____ _____ 18. We agree to notify each other immediately if either decides to terminate negotiations and to begin court action.

_____ _____ 19. We agree to shield our children from any hostility we feel toward each other.

_____ _____ 20. Each of us agrees not to allow our anger and hostile feelings to take over our communications and negotiations with each other.

_____ _____ 21. We agree to "check out" all the assumptions on which we are basing our agreement, especially assumptions about each other. (*e.g.*, "I assume you plan to stay in your present job." "I assume you plan to keep the house for at least five years." "I assume you want Johnny to stay in the same school.") (This statement is about being responsible for recognizing when we are making an assumption about the other and to ask about it.)

22. We agree to tell the other the truth, to put all our cards on the table, to hold no information back.   _____   _____

23. We agree to take responsibility for our own actions and their foreseeable consequences and not indulge in placing blame.   _____   _____

24. We agree to avoid exaggeration in our negotiations and communications.   _____   _____

25. We agree to acknowledge the other's feelings without "putdowns."   _____   _____

26. We agree not to attribute motives, not to second-guess, the other.   _____   _____

27. We agree to keep our own promises, even if one of us believes the other may have broken one.   _____   _____

28. We agree to avoid jumping to conclusions, especially if the conclusion is a negative one about the other spouse.   _____   _____

29. Other: (write any other ground rules you make for yourselves).   _____   _____

Once you agree on your ground rules, you will probably find that you are better able to talk about the financial and other issues of living apart.

Residence Checklist—Short Term

Fill in the property address, occupant, and the amount of the payment in the appropriate column for the person responsible for making the payment in the short term. At this point, the person who occupies a residence does not necessarily have to be the one responsible for all its expenses. Repeat for non-residential real estate, such as rentals or a vacation condo.

Address: _____

Occupant: _____

	Husband	Wife
Mortgage/ Rent	_____	_____
Mortgage (second)	_____	_____
Property Tax (if not in mortgage)	_____	_____
Insurance (if not in mortgage)	_____	_____
Homeowners' Dues	_____	_____
Repairs	_____	_____
Capital Improvements	_____	_____
Regular Upkeep & Maintenance	_____	_____
Utilities	_____	_____
Appliance & Utility Repair	_____	_____

Who Uses What and Who Pays for It

For couples to begin to live apart as satisfactorily as possible, they need a clear understanding of who will get to use what property, who will live in the home, who pays the mortgage or rent, who will drive which car, and who will be responsible for the car expenses. There are usually several major items of personal property about which you need understandings, for example: the computer, the washer and dryer, the ski condo time-share, the camping gear. Even if you are separating within the same residence, you will need to face these same questions. You are not deciding ownership at this point, only temporary use. Do not try to resolve the entire property picture right at the beginning. For now, just settle who uses what and who makes what payments.

Your plan should clearly state how long the temporary agreement will last. Having a definite cut-off point (three to six months is a likely term) helps you stay focused on finishing the final agreement. Be certain to define what circumstances will send you back to the bargaining table (loss of job, for example).

HOMES

Who will stay in the family home and who will move out? The answer to this question has serious financial consequences, both short term and long term. This chapter is about the short term. For example, one of you could stay in the family home for the short term while you think about what arrangements you will want to make for the long term.

If one or both of you wants to keep the house in the long term, test this plan for at least a month or two before committing to it. Use your temporary period to experiment. This is especially important if you're not sure whether you want to do this "for the sake of the children" or because you love the house so much.

For example, the lower-income spouse may want to stay in the house since this spouse might have difficulty qualifying for a new home loan. If the house is very large, very expensive, or difficult to keep up, the burden may not be worth it. If the spouse who wants to keep the home is not the one who usually did the repairs or tended the lawn, the amount of headache involved may be an unpleasant surprise.

How will you finance the additional expense of the new home or apartment for the other along with the expenses of the family home? Some people find they have to spend savings, sell stock, or take out a loan. If this is the case, begin thinking about who will repay the loan or whose share of your property settlement the repayment will come from. Even for the short term, be sure you list all the expenses of the family home, plus those of the new second home for the spouse who is moving.

Also consider whether either of you may have another adult living with you to help with the expenses. Are there any restrictions between you as to who this person may be? Do any of your children contribute anything toward the costs or the upkeep of either home in money or in labor?

CARS AND OTHER MOTOR VEHICLES

Make clear agreements with each other about who will drive which car for the time being. Nothing needs to be done at this point about changing the names on the title. Don't change car loans and automobile insurance, and keep payments current. You may need to talk about joint use of a single car. Think in terms of problem solving—what's going to work—and a reasonable sharing of comforts and conveniences along with burdens and inconveniences.

In the permanent property division, the spouse who gets the car ordinarily gets the loan on it too. But you do not have to do it that way in the short term. You can usually keep both cars on the same insurance policy until the date of the divorce or until the next time the premium comes due after the date of the divorce. Discuss who will be responsible for paying the premium or whether and in what proportion you will share it. You may wish to write down your agreements as you reach them.

OTHER PROPERTY AND REGULAR EXPENSES

You may wish to clarify which of you gets to use other items during this period, such as the computer, stereo, RV, microwave, camping and other sports equipment. Who has responsibility for the family pets? Make an agreement that whoever gets to use these items for now will maintain them until you reach a final decision. Remember, you are not deciding ownership, only use.

You must decide who will make your fixed payments, such as life and medical insurance, installment loans and credit cards, and student loan payments.

 It is essential at this time that you either agree not to use any credit cards except when agreed or that you each choose one or more credit cards to use and be responsi-

---

Motor Vehicle Checklist—Short Term

Directions: Fill in the vehicle year and make. Enter the amount each of you will contribute in the short term toward paying each expense. At this point, the person who has the use of a vehicle does not necessarily have to be the one responsible for its expenses. Repeat for additional vehicles.

Year & Make of Vehicle _____

	Husband	Wife
Loan/Lease Payment	_____	_____
Insurance	_____	_____
Gas & Oil	_____	_____
Maintenance	_____	_____
Other	_____	_____

Year & Make of Vehicle _____

	Husband	Wife
Loan/Lease Payment	_____	_____
Insurance	_____	_____
Gas & Oil	_____	_____
Maintenance	_____	_____
Other	_____	_____

Other Property Checklist—Short Term

Directions: List in the left hand column those items of property which are important to both of you. Then put a check in the "Husband" or "Wife" column to indicate which of you will have the use of it and be responsible for maintaining it for the time being.

Item	Husband	Wife
_____	___	___
_____	___	___
_____	___	___
_____	___	___
_____	___	___
_____	___	___
_____	___	___
_____	___	___
_____	___	___
_____	___	___
_____	___	___
_____	___	___
_____	___	___
_____	___	___

ble for their payment. For example, you may wish to retain the use of an oil company credit card for your car expenses.

Whatever your agreement about use and payment of credit cards or payment of debts, the creditor is not bound by your agreement.

FIXED PAYMENTS CHECKLIST

List your creditors in the left column. For each creditor, write the amount of the payment in the column of the spouse who will be responsible for making the payment. Be sure to indicate the time period for any payment that is not monthly.

Creditor	Husband	Wife
_____	$ _____	$ _____
_____	$ _____	$ _____
_____	$ _____	$ _____
_____	$ _____	$ _____
_____	$ _____	$ _____
_____	$ _____	$ _____
_____	$ _____	$ _____
_____	$ _____	$ _____
_____	$ _____	$ _____
_____	$ _____	$ _____
_____	$ _____	$ _____
_____	$ _____	$ _____
_____	$ _____	$ _____
_____	$ _____	$ _____
_____	$ _____	$ _____

NECESSARY PURCHASES

Some duplicate household items will be necessary when a family expands from one household to two. Such items might include: children's furniture, couch, bed, washer/dryer, towels, sheets, coffee pot, iron, tools, stereo, and TV.

 These items could easily swallow your budget. You may need to limit this list to essentials, with each household bearing some burden of doing without. You might color-code different items—red for essentials needed right away; green for things needed soon, and so on.

Consider sharing instead of duplicating. Alternate times with the washer/dryer. Use the camper on alternate weekends. Mow your lawns on different days with the same mower.

Share the burden of being without or being inconvenienced. For example, if one of you has no washer/dryer and must use the Laundromat, perhaps the other could do without the stereo. Some couples prefer to separate within the same residence in order to save for these items and not have to incur this expense right at the beginning.

Agree that neither of you will make major purchases other than those on your Duplicate Items Needed (DIN) List. This will help you build trust in one another's sense of what is necessary. Agree that neither of you will borrow any money or use any credit cards without the consent of the other.

Duplicate Items Needed (DIN) List

Directions: List in the "Item" column those things which you will want to acquire to make your two households complete. Work together on this. Under the heading "Husband" or "Wife," list the maximum cost for each item that you agree you need to duplicate for that person's household.

Category	Item	Husband	Wife
Furniture			
	_____	_____	_____
	_____	_____	_____
	_____	_____	_____
	_____	_____	_____
	_____	_____	_____
	_____	_____	_____
Linens			
	_____	_____	_____
	_____	_____	_____
	_____	_____	_____
	_____	_____	_____

Category	Item	Husband	Wife
Appliances			
	_____	_____	_____
	_____	_____	_____
	_____	_____	_____
	_____	_____	_____
Kitchen Items			
	_____	_____	_____
	_____	_____	_____
	_____	_____	_____
	_____	_____	_____
	_____	_____	_____
	_____	_____	_____
	_____	_____	_____
	_____	_____	_____
Children's Items			
	_____	_____	_____
	_____	_____	_____
	_____	_____	_____
	_____	_____	_____
Other			
	_____	_____	_____
	_____	_____	_____
	_____	_____	_____
	_____	_____	_____
	_____	_____	_____
	_____	_____	_____
Total Cost		_____	_____

YOUR CREDIT AND YOUR DIVORCE

Without credit, you can't buy a car or furniture or get a credit card. Without a credit card, you can't make hotel or travel reservations, and you don't have that margin of borrowing power for emergencies. In short, it is very important that you protect your credit in your divorce. This section is about how to emerge from a divorce with the highest possible credit ratings for each of you.

You should each immediately obtain your individual credit rating as soon as you decide to separate. This way you have ample time and the legal right to remedy any errors and to add any missing accounts for either of you. Look under "Credit Reporting Agencies" in the Yellow Pages and call at least one. A recorded message will tell you how to obtain your credit report. Be sure that you request your individual reports, not your joint report, and that you each give any previous name(s).

Credit ratings are the history of the way you pay your bills. A number of credit reporting agencies keep a credit history, and individual creditors (credit card companies, department stores, banks, credit unions) report the relative regularity and promptness of payments by those who owe them money. Marriage and divorce affect credit ratings indirectly but profoundly.

If you both applied for the debt or credit card on both your incomes, then it is a pretty good bet that it has been reported in both your names and is contributing to both your individual credit ratings. You will see the debt on both your credit reports.

If, however, one of you had the card or debt before the marriage, or you got it only on that one income, then the credit may not be reported in both names. This often happens when one spouse is the primary wage-earner. In such cases, the non-wage-earning spouse may not have a credit rating at all or may have an inadequate one that does not contain some of the major credit accounts used during the marriage. You will know this is the situation if your credit report comes back blank or without any information about jointly paid debts.

The only way an account that is in one name only will report into both your credit ratings is if the person to whom that card was issued requests in writing, before the divorce is final, that the other spouse receive credit on that account. The spouse who wants the credit cannot do this. So, if you are agreeing to finish paying off a debt or credit card as part of your settlement, be certain that particular debt or credit card is reported on your own credit rating. Otherwise, you may pay off a bill which will not establish or benefit your own credit.

"I signed all the checks to pay our bills and they were all written on our joint account, so I know I have good credit."

The correct information: Credit is reported automatically only in the name of the person who applies for the account or loan and on whose income it is based. If you did not sign the application, then this record of payments on your marital debt may not be reported in your name at all.

Credit Checklist

Directions: After you obtain your credit reports, complete the following. List the name of good credit accounts which appear on each of your credit reports.

Husband	Wife
_____	_____
_____	_____
_____	_____
_____	_____
_____	_____
_____	_____
_____	_____

Commitment: Each of you may then commit to seeing that you will report in both names any well-rated credit card or account reporting in your name only.

You may build up a credit rating for a low- or non-income spouse by making certain all the high-rated credit cards are reported in his or her name before the divorce. Then, pay off the balances on these cards at the time of the divorce. Have the low-income spouse keep at least one of the best-rated cards—with a provision that he or she will: 1) use the card for small purchases that he or she will pay off quickly 2) apply for a card in his or her own name within a certain number of months or years after the final decree and 3) then close the old joint account.

If you close any high-rated credit card accounts before the divorce or notify the issuing bank to "take my spouse off the card," you may sabotage your spouse's ability to build a satisfactory credit rating. A better arrangement is to put all the credit cards in a sealed envelope, leave it with a trusted friend or in a safe deposit box, and agree not to charge anything until you finish your agreement. Then, make clear agreements about all the cards as part of your temporary agreement.

Children

The time when parents begin living apart is one of the most stressful for children. Their worst fear is of losing a parent, so they need both of you at this time. Each parent has a clear and distinct role to play. Children can adjust to the separations and transitions involved in two-household parenting, and they adjust best when you work together to support each other's relationship with the children.

HOW TO BE A GOOD PARENT THROUGH
THE DIVORCE PROCESS

Children feel more secure when they are confident that their parents can take care of themselves. If they feel you are not doing that, they will try to take care of you, and the parent-child relationship will reverse. Therefore, taking care of yourself at this difficult time is not only good for you but it is in the best interest of your children.

Insulating children from any hostilities between the parents is critical to good parenting throughout the divorce process. This means managing your own conflict well. Work toward strengthening your children's sense of security while they navigate their own choppy waters as you separate and divorce. It's a time to be very careful about what you say and to whom you say it. Think your conduct through carefully.

Parenting Classes: Classes about the effect of divorce on children which divorcing parents are required by Connecticut law to attend. A list of state approved classes is in Appendix B.

"Divorce always hurts children." "You just can't possibly be a responsible parent and get a divorce."

The truth, shown by extensive research, is that divorce does not necessarily hurt children. What does hurt them are ongoing hostilities between their parents, whether or not there is a divorce. Research shows that children of divorcing parents who stop fighting are as well adjusted as those raised in successful marriages. The same research also shows that children of parents who stay together but continue to fight have as much trouble adjusting as children of the continually hostile divorce. So it's not the divorce that hurts the children, it's the ongoing anger and hostility that is harmful.

"Children have never been very good at listening to their elders, but they have never failed to imitate them."

James Baldwin, "Fifth Avenue, Uptown," *Nobody Knows My Name*

SAMPLE GROUND RULES FOR PARENTS

Here are some research-based ground rules for parents designed specifically for insulating the children from parental hostilities. They come from several works in the bibliography at the end of this book, especially *Sharing the Children* by Robert E. Adler.

Directions: Discuss the statements below, and initial those to which you both agree. Modify them as needed to fit your intentions. You may wish to circle or write down on a separate piece of paper any of these agreements initialed by both of you. You can refer to them if you momentarily lose your way in your negotiations about your children.

Initial

1. We agree that we value our children's relationships and the time they spend with us. _____ _____

2. We agree that we value our children's relationships and the time they spend with the other parent. _____ _____

3. We agree to make numbers 1 and 2 clear to our children. _____ _____

4. We agree to work out a fair and practical time-sharing schedule with each other, either temporary or long term, as soon as possible, and explain it to our children. If they are teenagers, we agree to get their input. _____ _____

5. We agree to make every effort to live up to the agreement that comes out of number 4. _____ _____

6. We agree to tell the other parent in advance of any necessary changes in plan. _____ _____

7. We agree to be reasonably flexible in trading off time-sharing to accommodate the other parent's needs. _____ _____

8. We agree to prepare our children, in a positive way, for each upcoming transfer to, and time with, the other parent. _____ _____

9. We agree to work out our problems with the other parent in private and not to conduct adult business in the presence of our children, including at the time we transfer them between us. _____ _____

10. We agree not to use our children as confidants, messengers, bill collectors, or spies. _____ _____

11. We agree to overcome the temptation to enlist our children on our side of any issue. _____ _____

12. We agree to listen caringly but to encourage our children to work out problems with the other parent directly. _____ _____

Temporary Legal Custody:
Designates one or both parents to be responsible for making major decisions about their children during the time between their separation and final divorce judgment—may be sole or joint.

Signing for Emergency Medical Care for Your Children

There are still a few emergency care facilities that may require both parents' signatures in joint custody situations in order to admit children for care and treatment—unless there is a written court-ordered agreement that says that either parent may sign. Not only should you have clear agreement about this but you should carry a copy of this agreement with you and give one to the children's regular pediatricians, day care providers, and schools.

WHO MAKES WHAT DECISIONS ABOUT THE CHILDREN

The two major kinds of decisions regarding children are day-to-day decisions and major decisions. The parent who has the children at the time makes day-to-day decisions—menus, schedules, bedtimes, transportation. Major decisions have a longer range, including the health, education, and general welfare of the children. The law simply provides that if you have joint custody you will have "joint decision making." It is important that the two of you evolve your own more specific list of decisions that you agree you must share during this interim period. Some examples are:

● activities of our children which will take place on both parents' time with them

● major expenses for our children which we expect the other parent to share

● major planned elective medical or dental care, but not emergency medical care

● how we will share or divide birthdays and holidays

Joint decision-making means you keep talking until you reach an agreement. You may agree that one of you will make some or all of the major decisions or categories of decisions. Even if you are agreeing that one parent alone will make particular decisions, you may list matters about which the decision-maker must consult with the other parent. This means you must discuss it beforehand, even though the decision-maker still makes the final decision. For example, one parent might make all the clothing purchases, but he or she should discuss ahead of time the limit on spending and how the clothes will be paid for.

Whatever your choices, it is vital that you both are clear, committed, and completely reliable. Being clear about who makes what decisions about your children helps them feel secure and know that you are in control.

TEMPORARY PARENTING DECISIONS LIST

Directions: List in one of the categories below the decisions concerning your children which you anticipate must be made during this interim period.

We will make the following decisions together:

1.

2.

3.

Mother will make the following decisions:

1.

2.

3.

Father will make the following decisions:

1.

2.

3.

Temporary Physical Custody: Where the children of separated parents live between the time of separation and final judgment—may be sole, shared, or split.

Temporary Residential Custody: Same as temporary physical custody.

"Children should have only one home."

Research shows that children adjust better to divorce when they continue to have stable and loving relationships with both parents. This is best done in two homes, both of which fully accommodate and welcome them.

"Children get confused when their parents' lifestyles are too different."

Not necessarily. Some experts do say that for two households to work well together, they shouldn't be too terribly far apart in value systems. For example, if one parent lives a "laid-back" hippie lifestyle and the other household uses linen napkins, the child may begin to wonder whether to be like mom and her household or dad and his. Studies show that children can make these transitions—but not rapidly and only with a great deal of support and preparation in every transition.

WHERE THE CHILDREN WILL STAY

The temporary period is an excellent time to try out various parenting plans specifying periods of "visitation," "parenting time," or "periods of residence." Put together a consistent schedule for six weeks or so, and then assess it. You may discover that some aspects of your plan do not work well for your family. Talk about it with each other, then listen to the children's input. Also, consider consulting with a mental health professional with expertise about children and divorce. Reach an agreement, and make the needed changes and adjustments. Don't expect to know right away what arrangements are going to be best for your children in the long term. Your first plan may well not be your final agreement. You will need flexibility.

Some parents want equal time-sharing when it may not be in the children's best interests. For example, infants and very young children usually are not developmentally ready for two homes on a fifty-fifty basis. Infants and toddlers are usually best served by one primary home and frequent (daily, if possible) contact with the other parent. Small children may do better by gradually expanding the overnights with the other parent. However, a younger child may do quite well in equal time-sharing if his or her connections have been quite strong with both parents and/or if there is an older sibling making the same transitions on the same schedule. Teenagers, who can do well with equal time-sharing, need to have a great deal of say about where and how they spend their time.

For more on the significance of your child's developmental age for your parenting plans, see Chapter 8. This would be an excellent time to read *Children of Divorce* by Baris and Garrity or one of the books listed in the bibliography at the end of this guidebook that relate to your circumstances.

SIX-WEEK PARENTING PLAN AND CALENDAR

Directions: Using the material from the following page, fill in your parenting time for the next six weeks. This calendar ends the week with Saturday and Sunday together. Most published calendars divide the weekend by placing Sunday as the first day of the week and Saturday as the last—a picture which is generally confusing when working out parenting times.

Mon.	Tues.	Wed.	Thurs.	Fri.	Sat.	Sun.

USING YOUR SIX-WEEK CALENDAR

Fill in the following information on the calendar on the previous page. You may want to make several photocopies first for your rough draft(s). In addition, sometimes it is useful to use different colored pens for each parent or member of the family.

1. The dates for the six-week period you are planning and any holidays or other special days, such as a child's birthday.

2. Parents' fixed schedules, including work hours, fixed meetings, and appointments.

3. Children's fixed schedules, such as school hours, and planned regular activities, such as soccer practice, piano lessons, and Cub Scouts. Discuss whether a change in the children's day care schedule is desirable. On the one hand, it may be just the time to make a needed change. On the other hand, if both of you are moving, keeping the day care schedule the same may help a young child feel more secure at this difficult time.

4. Already scheduled appointments (doctor, dentist) and special events already committed to (recital, track meet, reunion).

5. Looking at the six weeks as a whole, begin to discuss and even pencil-in some possible parenting times, possibly including school nights with one parent; weekend or vacation nights with the other; alternating weeks with each parent; dividing each week four-three, five-two, or six-one; dividing each two-week period in half with a four-three-three-four schedule; or dovetailing with one or both parents' variable work schedule.

6. Be sure you take into account your children's ages and stages of development. The plan for an infant will be very different from the plan for a teenager.

7. Indicate on the calendar who will provide the transportation each time, that is, who will pick up and drop off. The further apart you live, the more important the transportation issue will become. Whenever you bring your children to their other parent, you demonstrate your support and willingness for your children to leave you and to relate to the other parent.

8. Be specific about any items which must move back and forth with the children, such as clothing, boots, homework, and musical instruments.

HOW TO TELL THE CHILDREN

How do you tell your children about your separation? If possible, both of you should be present to tell the children not only of your decision to separate but also about your plans. Help them understand that you are not separating from or "divorcing" them. Tell them that you will always take care of them no matter what. Tell them how important it is to both of you that they continue to have both of you. Be concrete with them about your plans.

When appropriate, share your six-week calendar with your children and ask for their input. Listen to their concerns about the mechanics: "Where will my bicycle live?" "How will my ice skates get from one house to the other?" "I only have one computer—how will I do my homework?"

If you can, discuss with the children in advance the physical plans for your separation. Involve them by taking them with you to see possible new apartments or homes so they can participate in the creation of their second home. They will have their own ideas about which toys and books should be at which place and how they want their spaces to look. You may have to override some of their choices; but allow them to participate and express themselves—even to carry out some of their wishes in their own way—if you and your spouse agree.

The Budget Crunch

Two together still live more cheaply than two separately. Early negotiating about the reality of the high cost of two households is a major key to keeping peace throughout the separation and divorce process. As you separate, it is important that you and your spouse have a complete understanding of which income will pay for what expenses.

The purpose of this section is to help you keep track of your incomes and budget your expenses as your family moves from one household to two.

TRACKING YOUR INCOMES

The word "income" can mean very different things to different people. To the worker it probably means spendable earnings. To the IRS it means what is taxed. Under the law, it can mean potential earnings that are not actually coming in and even imputed income nobody actually receives. Using the "Income Tracker," write down the income you each expect to receive during the interim period

---

Agreement for Telling Our Children

We agree to tell our children about our separation on _____ (date) at _____ (time) at _____ (place).

Income Tracker

Husband *expects* to receive the following regular income (averaged per month) for the next _____ months:

$_____ gross; $_____ net.

Husband *may* receive the following additional income (averaged per month) over the next _____ months:

$_____ gross; $_____ net.

Wife *expects* to receive the following regular income (averaged per month) for the next _____ months:

$_____ gross; $_____ net.

Wife *may* receive the following additional income (averaged per month over the next _____ months:

$_____ gross; $_____ net.

Look at a Week Instead of a Month?

Cheryl managed the household but was never responsible for paying the bills. When she and Vernon separated, she was starting at the beginning when it came to thinking about a monthly budget. In fact, a month was too much for her to start with. So they began with a weekly budget. After a few weeks of experience, Cheryl was ready to begin looking at the monthly picture.

for which you are planning. List the incomes you are certain of receiving and those you might receive. Definite income includes your base pay before commission, salary, draw, guaranteed hours, required overtime, and regular bonuses. Possible income may include commissions, bonuses, one-time sales or liquidation, irregular overtime, irregular bonuses, income from assets and investments, pensions, and Social Security.

Write down both your gross and net incomes. The gross is the larger amount and the net is the amount you bring home after all the withholdings and deductions have been taken from your paycheck. This number may change as you make agreements about tax planning and saving for your futures, but use the present actual numbers for now.

If you are self-employed, your gross income is your business net, i.e., your total business receipts less your total necessary business expenses.

EXPENSES

The purpose of this section is to budget your expenses as your family changes from one household to two. You will have the ongoing expenses of both households, plus payments on any debt you may have.

You can divide the ongoing expenses for two households into three categories:

1. Bare bones: necessary expenses during this period of time ("survival");

2. Discretionary: expenses which either of you could live without, albeit with difficulty ("lifestyle"); and

3. Children: expenses that are directly for the children.

   You will find a three-page budget in Chapter 7. It lists your expenses in the three categories described above. Make several photocopies of the budget, and complete one for each household.

   Be sure that between your two budgets you include all your expenses and debts for both households but that you do not duplicate any of them. Do these budgets separately even if you are physically separating within the same residence. You will still have to decide how to share the expenses of the home.

BUDGETING YOUR SEPARATION

Now you are ready to compare your expected incomes with your expected expenses for this interim period.

Directions: Have in front of you the following:

1. Your DIN (Duplicate Items Needed) List, page 69-70.

2. Your Income Tracker, page 82.

3. Both of your budgets from Chapter 7. Use them to complete the following chart. You may want to make several photocopies of this chart for rough drafts.

Budget Analysis Chart

HUSBAND:

Basic Income (Inc. Tracker) $ _____	Extra Income (Inc. Tracker) $ _____	Total Income $ _____
Bare Bones Expenses (Budget) $ _____	Discretionary Expenses (Budget) $ _____	
Children's Expenses (Budget) $ _____	DIN List Expenses (Budget) $ _____	Total Expenses $ _____

WIFE:

Basic Income (Inc. Tracker) $ _____	Extra Income (Inc. Tracker) $ _____	Total Income $ _____
Bare Bones Expenses (Budget) $ _____	Discretionary Expenses (Budget) $ _____	
Children's Expenses (Budget) $ _____	DIN List Expenses (Budget) $ _____	Total Expenses $ _____

Budget Analysis

Step 1. A Look at Our Combined Picture

Your combined total incomes: $ _____

Your combined total expenses: $ _____

Difference: +/–$ _____

If your result is a positive number, this means that you have enough take-home money at the present time to meet the total short-term expenses for both households. Make a clear agreement about what you will do with the surplus so that the whole family can benefit from it during this time. You are not unusual if you have a negative number here. Most people do not have enough income to meet the total "wish lists" of two households.

Step 2. One Household Shortfall

If you have a combined negative number, go to Step 3. If you have a combined positive number, you must now check if you individually have a positive number. Subtract your individual total expenses from your individual total income as follows:

Husband's Total Income $ _____		Wife's Total Income $ _____	
Husband's Total Expenses $_____		Wife's Total Expenses $ _____	
Difference: +/–$ _____		Difference: +/–$_____	

If one of you has a positive difference and the other a negative, some money must change hands between you to enable both households to meet all expenses. It may be possible to increase the net income to your whole family by decreasing income taxes in this situation. In principle, this type of planning lowers the tax burden of the higher-income spouse by allocating some of his or her income to the lower-income spouse, who is in a lower tax bracket. This may generate significant savings from which you can both benefit. See the next section of this chapter and Chapter 11 (Alimony) and Chapter 12 (Taxes) for more about this.

Step 3. Mutual Belt-Tightening

If the result in your Budget Analysis is a negative number, there is not enough combined income to meet your total combined expenses. Look at both of your budgets and your DIN List. What can you agree together to cut back on? The discretionary column on your budget is the most likely place where you can cut. If, by doing this, you can at least break even in your combined numbers, then go back to Step 2.

Step 4. Rethinking Your Budgets

If, after Step 3, you still have not broken even or achieved a positive number, then you will probably need to take a hard look at the assumptions underlying your two-household budgets:

- Can either of you increase your income by decreasing your withholding, working additional hours, or taking interest or dividend incomes which you would normally not do?

- Is this the time for either of you to go from part-time to full-time employment or to find employment?

- Is this the time to sell the house? Should you consider refinancing the mortgage or taking out a second mortgage?

- Is this really the time to buy the second home? Can one or both of you rent or lease-with-option-to-buy for a time?

- Is this the time to sell an asset or use a savings account?

- Is this the time to borrow against an asset: i.e., take a second mortgage on the house or borrow against your life insurance?

- Do you have friends or relatives who will help you through this interim period?

- If your short-fall is primarily due to large debts or bill payments, is this the time to call Consumer Credit Counseling or to consider a Chapter 13 bankruptcy?

This is a difficult time for everyone who faces these circumstances. This may be the time when you are most tempted to give up working together and let someone else take over. Don't panic. This may be a good time to put the numbers aside and review your purpose agreement in Chapter 3. Be careful not to lose yourself in fear about money. Keep your eyes focused on the big picture.

If you can agree on a solution using one or more of the above suggestions, thereby bringing your combined totals to break-even, then go back to Step 2.

Step 5. If there is nothing you yourselves can do to make your two-household budgets happen, then ask:

- Must you separate at this time? Can you put off the separation until one of you finishes school or is no longer laid off? Is this the time to reconsider sharing the house "upstairs/downstairs?"

- Is this the time to do a Chapter 7 or 13 bankruptcy?

- Is there a source of community, church, or family assistance, such as Food stamps, unemployment compensation, workers' compensation, Social Security, or Supplemental Security Income?

Temporary Support Between Spouses: Alimony and Tax Considerations

Chapter 11 (Alimony) and Chapter 12 (Taxes) discuss the benefits of good tax and financial planning for even the most straightforward divorce or separation. Reading these now may help you plan for temporary support.

DIFFERENT WAYS TO MEET YOUR SHORTFALL

If the result of your budget analysis on the previous pages is that some money needs to change hands between you so that you both may meet your ongoing living expenses, you may need to agree upon temporary support. Following are two basic ways that you can take care of this shortfall and the tax considerations of each. Just as your arrangements about your children can benefit from a "dry run" during this temporary period, so can your financial arrangements.

1. *All married couples have ways that they deal with their financial issues on a day-by-day basis.* One way of looking at this is that, when married, there is a "marital economy." For most couples, all of the income and assets are merged into joint accounts and used for joint expenses. Other couples keep their finances very separate. When the decision is made to divorce, one option is to continue the marital economy until the final decisions are made to construct the separate economies. In some cases, the marital economy only needs slight adjustments to accommodate changes to the family as a result of the decision to divorce.

 When married taxpayers file separate returns, both must either itemize or use the standard deductions. If one spouse itemizes and the other does not, the second spouse's standard deduction will be reduced to zero.

2. *One spouse pays some or all of the other spouse's expenses directly.* Many couples set up their temporary agreement so that the higher-income spouse directly pays certain items for the lower-income spouse: mortgage; health, life, and car insurances; credit card bills; and, perhaps, utilities and telephone. Doing this permits the paying spouse to take the tax deduction for the home mortgage interest *if and only if* the mortgage is still in the paying spouse's name, that spouse does not yet have another primary residence, and the couple is planning to file separate tax returns for the year of the payments (including married/separate). If the couple is planning to file a joint tax return for this last year, they will share the tax deduction for the home mortgage as usual, even if only one of spouses lived in the home.

The higher-income paying spouse can also pay some of the children's expenses directly, such as day care, babysitting, and medical and dental bills. The child care credit which is available to single working parents may then be taken by the paying spouse IF AND ONLY IF he or she: 1) files separately, 2) has been separated for more than six months before the end of the calendar year, and 3) has sufficient custodial time to qualify as head of household.

3. The *higher-income spouse gives the lower-income spouse the money to pay directly some or all of the lower-income spouse's bills or marital bills.* This method helps the lower-income spouse establish credit, work out a realistic budget, and test how much money will need to change hands on a permanent basis.

Any money which meets the IRS definition of alimony is deductible by the paying spouse and taxable to the receiving spouse (*see* Chapter 11). If you expect to file separate tax returns this year, this will save the paying spouse substantial taxes. If the paying spouse increases the payments by the amount of the lower-income spouse's taxes on that money, the lower-income spouse feels no effect of the increased taxes, and the higher-income spouse may still save money. The effect of this planning is that the higher-income spouse is now paying tax on all these dollars at the receiving spouse's lower tax rate.

If you structure your temporary agreement so that the bills the lower-income spouse is paying are themselves tax deductible or lead to a credit, then the receiving spouse offsets these against the taxable payments from the paying spouse and everyone saves more money. Examples of payments which reduce taxes in this way are the mortgage interest and property tax deductions on a personal residence and work-related child care for the child care credit. If the lower-income spouse is the custodial parent who is remaining in the family home, then this way of doing things may be tailor-made for you.

Temporary alimony may maximize payments between the spouses in pre-tax dollars. Child support, by contrast, is entirely post-tax dollars (after the paying spouse has already paid taxes on it). Child support is not taxable to the receiving spouse and not a tax deduction for the payor. Alimony shifts taxable income from the higher tax bracket spouse to the lower.

If the return date on your complaint is after September, you cannot have permanent alimony this year because your divorce will not be final before the end of the year. You may file either mar-

Temporary Alimony: Payments made by one spouse to the other, prior to the final judgment, that for tax purposes may be deductible from income for the paying spouse and included in income for the receiving spouse provided the spouses do not file a joint tax return.

Section 71 Payments: Same as alimony or maintenance (refers to a section in the Internal Revenue Code).

To be tax deductible as temporary alimony, the payment must be part of a court order or a written separation agreement specifically providing for temporary alimony between the parties that ends on the death of the recipient.

Checklist of Temporary Alimony and First Year Filing Status

☐ **We plan to obtain our final judgment of dissolution of marriage (legal separation) this calendar year.**

We will file our taxes this year as:

Wife: ☐ Single   ☐ Head of Household

Husband: ☐ Single ☐ Head of Household

_____ (paying spouse)
will pay $ _____
per month as temporary alimony to

_____ (receiving spouse)
starting _____ (date), until the
decree. _____ (paying spouse)
will pay $ _____ per month as
alimony between the final judgment and
the end of the calendar year, for a total
of $ _____.

We ☐ will ☐ will not make our alimony
agreement into a temporary court order,
so that the total paid before the judgment
☐ will ☐ will not be counted in the first
separation year alimony total for testing
under the recapture rule (*see* Chapter 12).

☐ **We don't plan to obtain our final judgment this calendar year.**

We will file our taxes this year as follows:

☐ Married filing jointly

☐ Married filing separately
  ☐ Wife ☐ Husband

☐ Head of Household
  ☐ Wife ☐ Husband

_____ (paying spouse) will pay
to _____ (receiving spouse)
$ _____ per month for temporary
alimony ☐ by ☐ not by court order for
a total of $ _____ which
☐ will ☐ will not be our first separation
year for alimony recapture test calculations (*see* Chapter 12).

ried filing jointly (no alimony deduction can be utilized) or married filing separately (providing for temporary alimony if you choose). This decision is likely to hinge on how comfortable you are with each other's accounting. It also depends on whether you wish to provide for temporary alimony in a written temporary separation agreement. If you wish to deduct temporary alimony during this period, you may not file a joint return. You will need to decide how you will allocate the deductions each of you will take. These include the home mortgage interest and property taxes, other taxes paid, and the dependency exemptions for the children.

If you have been separated for more than six months before the end of the year (i.e., you physically separated before July 1 of this year) there is an additional option for one or both of you. Any separated (but still legally married) person who has provided the primary home for his or her dependent child for more than six months of the year may file as head of household even if still married. If you have more than one child and are sharing physical custody, you might each have this option. Each parent who can file as head of household also gets the child care credit for that child and is likely to save money over filing jointly. If only one parent qualifies and elects head of household status, the other must file married/separate (since you are not yet single).

If the return date on your complaint is before October, then you may have the option of completing your final judgment of divorce in this tax year. You may agree to alimony both before and after the final judgment. The tax consequences and rules vary for temporary or permanent alimony (regardless of whether you are involved in a dissolution or legal separation), as discussed below and in Chapter 12.

Permanent alimony, after the judgment of divorce, requires that you be physically separated at or within thirty days of the first payment. There is no such separation requirement for temporary alimony (such as in an upstairs/downstairs agreement as discussed earlier in this chapter) during the temporary period.

Permanent alimony may be subject to recapture rules if it decreases by an amount specified in the tax laws over the first three years. Alimony treatment may be disallowed if the payments decrease on a date related to a child's age or an event related to a child. Review these rules in Chapter 12 if you are planning permanent alimony or alimony to pay expenses for the custodial parent's household that may include some children's expenses that decline or terminate at certain times during the period of the alimony.

Temporary alimony can help you avoid the recapture problem, if you have one. If you can reach an agreement quickly about high-end temporary alimony and ask the court to approve your written agreement as an order of court, then any amounts paid as temporary alimony covered by the agreement will not count in the recapture rules.

If you have a written agreement about temporary alimony and do not make it into a court order, any amounts paid that you want to term alimony will count in the recapture rules. If you do not complete your final judgment of divorce this year and your temporary alimony is not by court order, it will constitute your first post-separation year for purposes of measuring alimony against the recapture rules. The recapture rules can sneak up on you in this manner, so carefully review the amounts you want to label alimony. (See Chapter 12, Taxes.)

Remember that tax issues are complicated. You should consult a CPA, attorney, or financial planner while planning your temporary or permanent agreement to make sure it accomplishes what you intend.

TEMPORARY CHILD SUPPORT

If you choose to file your temporary agreement with the court, the law requires that you use the Connecticut Child Support Guidelines if your combined net income is no more than $2,500 per week. You must include a Child Support Guidelines worksheet and financial affidavits for both of you. See Chapters 7 and 9 for instructions about preparing and using these forms.

If you are bargaining between yourselves about how to get the bills paid, including those of your children, you do not necessarily have to follow the Connecticut Child Support Guidelines in calculating support. If you have the temporary agreement made into a court order, the court may permit you to deviate (change) from the amount guidelines if you can give the judge a good reason and explain how you will pay the children's expenses. (See Chapter 9, Child Support.)

TEMPORARY TEETH

If you worry that you or your spouse may not keep the agreement, consider writing in some "teeth." In an alimony agreement, for example, consider providing that if your spouse is substantially late in making a payment, the money, when paid, will not qualify as alimony. The paying spouse loses the tax deduction, and the receiving spouse does not pay tax on it. (The IRS allows you to

Temporary alimony payments are subject to income tax, both federal and state, for the receiving spouse but are not subject to F.I.C.A. (Social Security) taxes.

"The IRS doesn't care if the court approves our temporary agreement about alimony."

This is incorrect. Temporary alimony with a court order *IS NOT* subject to the recapture rules while temporary alimony without a court order *IS*. See Chapter 12 for this important distinction, especially if you are negotiating toward alimony of more than $15,000 per year.

"Once we separate, if one of us qualifies to file as 'head of household,' the other can file as 'single.'"

This is incorrect. As long as you remain legally married, if one of you qualifies to file as head of household, the other must still file as married filing separately—unless he or she also qualifies as head of household.

"Once we separate, we can make our own alimony agreement."

This is true but incomplete. Once a couple is separated they may have a private contractual agreement—without a court order for payments—for alimony. But the IRS requires for tax purposes that such an agreement be in writing and signed by both spouses.

File the Complaint First

To make your temporary agreement a temporary court order, you must file your Divorce Complaint so that you have a docket number and an action in court. See Chapter 6. You may file your Divorce Complaint and your temporary agreement at the same time.

"My object all sublime I shall achieve in time—To make the punishment fit the crime."

Sir William Schwenk Gilbert, *The Mikado*

say whether something that looks like alimony to the IRS will still not receive the deductible/taxable treatment.) In this case, make the tax consequences strictly contingent on prompt payments.

The paying spouse might stipulate that if the money is not used as promised by the receiving spouse (for example, to pay the house mortgage), the affected asset will be put up for sale. It may or may not be appropriate for you to put such strict punishments in your own agreement. That's your decision. But, if you begin right away treating your agreement as a very serious bargain between you, there will be less chance that you will be tempted to take it lightly later on.

You may also give your temporary agreement legal teeth by making it an order of the court. If you do this, your agreement is then enforceable directly by the court. When you make your agreement an order of the court, the obligations in the contract become court orders and therefore enforceable through judgments, restraining orders, and even contempt.

HOW FORMAL DOES OUR TEMPORARY
AGREEMENT NEED TO BE?

Some couples do not need to write down their temporary arrangements because their communications are clear and there is complete trust and reliability. Others want something more formal or official. If the temporary agreement is made into an order of court, you increase enforceability through court measures.

If you want to make your arrangements very firm, write down your temporary agreements. You may have your signatures notarized to show the strength of your intent. Once your agreement is written and signed, you should be responsible for following through.

To have the judge approve your temporary agreement and make it a court order, you must file a *Motion for Order* with the court. See Chapter 6, page 125 for an explanation of how to prepare this form and the procedure you will follow. Chapter 6 also explains the procedure for filing a request with the court for temporary orders if you and your spouse have not yet reached an agreement and need the judge to enter these orders. Remember that you should obtain legal advice before signing any temporary agreement or filing it with the court.

CHAPTER 6

GETTING DIVORCED: PROCEDURES AND PAPERWORK

Who May File in Connecticut

To obtain a Connecticut divorce or a legal separation, one of you must fulfill the following requirements:

1) Either spouse has been a resident of Connecticut for at least twelve months before filing the Divorce Complaint.

Most divorces filed in Connecticut satisfy this requirement. After twelve months of residency, you can file any time. You can then move out of Connecticut after you file the Divorce Complaint and still have your case completed here.

2) Either spouse has been a resident of Connecticut for at least twelve months before the entry of the final divorce judgment.

Many states have "waiting periods" for people who have moved into the state and want to file for divorce. Connecticut is different in that you may file for divorce as soon as you move here. However, your divorce may take longer because you must wait until you have lived in Connecticut for twelve continuous months before it can be finalized.

Domicile: To live; to make a place one's permanent home.

3) Either spouse was domiciled in Connecticut at the time of the marriage and has returned to Connecticut with the intention of permanently remaining before filing the Divorce Complaint for divorce.

You would use this provision if you were to file after you moved to Connecticut and wanted to cut short the twelve-month waiting period to complete your divorce. However, you must be "domiciled" in Connecticut when you file and at the time of the marriage.

4) The cause of the dissolution of the marriage arose after either party moved into the state.

Broken Down Irretrievably: Most common reason for divorce, also known as "no fault divorce."

Since you do not have to allege fault to get a divorce in Connecticut, this provision is rarely used. Most people establish jurisdiction to get a divorce in Connecticut under one of the other provisions.

Where Do We File?

Divorces take place in the Connecticut Superior Court, as distinguished from federal courts. State courts in Connecticut are organized into separate judicial districts. Each judicial district contains at least one superior court.

Which judicial district should you file in? In legal terms, this is a question of "venue." You should file civil cases (divorce is a civil rather than a criminal matter) in the judicial district where either of you lives. If your spouse lives out of state, the correct judicial district is where you live. You find the judicial district where you and/or your spouse live by looking at Appendix A at the end of this book. Appendix A lists each town in Connecticut, the judicial district in which it is located, and the address of the court or courts where you can file divorce actions. If your judicial district has more than one courthouse (or if your town qualifies you to file in more than one judicial district), you can choose the one you want to file in.

If there is a choice, you and your spouse should agree on which judicial district and courthouse you will use before you file. You may pick the court that is more convenient for both of you. If your divorce remains friendly and cooperative, you will not have to spend much time in court anyway.

What Forms Do We Need?

You will need some, but not necessarily all, of the forms on the following list. Read the entire list, and check off the ones you think you will need. Your attorneys can prepare all of these papers for you if you hire them for this purpose. This is true if they negotiate all the terms of the agreement for you or if you negotiate by yourselves or with a mediator and tell your attorneys of your agreements. You can prepare all or some of these papers by yourself if you are representing yourself. Some mediators may also be willing to prepare some of these documents as part of the mediation process.

There are sample copies of these forms printed in this chapter, unless otherwise indicated, with line-by-line instructions for completing the forms yourself. Court staff may answer basic procedural questions. However, court staff cannot act as your attorney or give you legal advice.

Venue: The location where a case will be heard; may refer to a choice of courts.

The Connecticut Judicial Branch publishes *The Do It Yourself Divorce Guide* to help you handle your own divorce or better understand the process. The booklet is available at the clerk's office in all judicial district courthouses or online at **www.jud.state.ct.us/publications**.

☐ **Summons:** The paper that notifies your spouse of the starting of the divorce case. Everyone needs this to start a case.

☐ **Divorce Complaint:** The legal paper that starts the case. Everyone needs this to start a case.

☐ **Notice of Automatic Orders:** Court orders that go into effect when the case starts. These orders are attached to every complaint.

☐ **Affidavit Concerning Children:** You must file this if you have minor children.

☐ **Motion and Order for Notice by Publication or Mail in Family Cases:** You will need these if you are serving your spouse out of state, by certified or registered mail, or by publication.

☐ **Appearance:** The defendant may use this.

☐ **Cross Complaint:** The defendant may use this; it is the same form as the **Divorce Complaint** (or use a different form called an **Answer**).

☐ **Application for Waiver of Fees:** You may use this form if you cannot afford to pay the filing fee, marshal's costs, and some other required costs. If the judge grants this request, you will also need the **Invoice-Voucher**.

☐ **Motions for Orders Before Judgment (Temporary Orders):** You may use these forms if you haven't reached temporary agreements and you want the court to decide for you.

☐ **Divorce Agreement:** This is signed by both spouses and contains all of the final agreements concerning property, debts, alimony, child support, and custody.

☐ **Case Management Agreement:** Everyone needs this form to track and schedule the final divorce judgment hearing.

☐ **Dissolution of Marriage Report:** Both spouses need this.

☐ **Advisement of Rights:** You need this form if there is an order for child support and/or alimony whether or not there is a withholding order for support.

☐ **Affidavit Concerning Military Service:** You need this form if you are the plaintiff and the defendant does not file an **Appearance** or appear in court for your final divorce judgment hearing.

☐ **Parenting Education Program—Order, Certificate, and Results:** You need this form if you have children and the court does not excuse you from the mandatory parenting education requirement.

☐ **Financial Affidavit:** Sworn statement of income, expenses, assets, and debts. Both spouses need to complete one of these forms unless one spouse, the defendant, does not appear (participate) in the case. The Financial Affidavit is in Chapter 7.

☐ **Child Support Worksheet:** You need this form in all cases if you have children. It reflects the guideline child support amount if the combined net income of you and your spouse is $2,500 per week or less. See Chapter 9.

☐ **Withholding Order for Support:** You need this form if there is an order for child support and/or alimony to be paid by means of wage withholding. See Chapter 9.

☐ **Qualified Domestic Relations Order:** This document is signed by the judge and then given to the plan administrator of your workplace to divide most pension and profit sharing plans. See Chapter 10.

☐ **Judgment File:** The permanent court record of the final divorce.

Preparing Your Papers for the Court

It is customary to file original forms with the court and keep photocopies for your records. Court forms are available at all Judicial District Court clerk's office's. Procedures may vary slightly in some judicial districts and sometimes change over time, but the basic process and forms are the same throughout the state.

On any paper you file with the court, write only what you know or believe to be true. If the form asks for something that is not part of your case write "not applicable" or "N/A" next to that question. Deliberately not telling the truth to a court, especially if you sign under oath, is a crime.

After you file your complaint with the court you will receive a notice by mail with the docket number. You can also look up your docket number and other information about your case by doing a search by name of the participants in the case at www.jud.state.ct.us. Be sure to make note of your docket number because you must write it at the top of any correspondence and all forms and papers you file with the court about your case. This is the only way to be sure that your document will find its way into your file and not get lost.

Pro se Divorce: Spouses represent themselves in court, signing all of the court papers instead of having attorneys do it for them.

You can download and print all court forms at the Connecticut Judicial Branch Web site. You can use the forms from this site by either downloading them and then typing them (or writing them if you must) or filling them out on the Web and then printing them in completed form. Go to **www.jud.state.ct.us**.

"My ninety-day waiting period before I can be divorced started when I filed the complaint."

The waiting period actually begins on the return date.

www.jud.state.ct.us/forms/fm003/htm

SUMMONS
FAMILY ACTIONS
JD-FM-3   Rev. 7-99
C.G.S. § 52-45a, Pr. Bk § 8-1

STATE OF CONNECTICUT
SUPERIOR COURT

CASE TYPE MINOR CODES
00 Dissolution of Marriage
10 Legal Separation
20 Annulment
90 All Other

INSTRUCTIONS

1. Type or print legibly; sign original summons and conform all copies of the summons.
2. Attach the original summons to the original complaint, and Notice of Automatic Court Orders (JD-FM-158) and attach a copy of the summons and a copy of the Notice of Automatic Court Orders to each copy of the complaint.
3. After service has been made by proper officer, file original papers and officer's return with the clerk of the court at least six days before the return date.
4. Do not use this form for actions in which an attachment or garnishment is being sought or for petitions for paternity or for support orders, or for actions in which an application for relief from abuse is being sought.

TO: Any proper officer
BY AUTHORITY OF THE STATE OF CONNECTICUT, you are hereby commanded to make due and legal service of this Summons and attached Complaint and Notice of Automatic Orders.

JUDICIAL DISTRICT OF **(1)**	AT *(Town)* **(2)**	RETURN DATE *(Month, day, year)* **(3)**	
ADDRESS OF COURT *(No., street, city)* **(4)**	CASE MANAGEMENT DATE* **(5)**	CASE TYPE *(From code list above)* Major **F (6)** Minor ___	PTY NO.
PLAINTIFF'S NAME *(Last, first, middle initial)* **(7)**	PLAINTIFF'S ADDRESS *(No., street, town, zip code)*		01
DEFENDANT'S NAME *(Last, first, middle initial)* **(8)**	DEFENDANT'S ADDRESS *(If known) (No., street, town, zip code)*		50

* See Form JD-FM-165A - C

NOTICE TO THE ABOVE-NAMED DEFENDANT

1. You are being sued.
2. This paper is a Summons in a lawsuit.
3. The Complaint attached to these papers states the claims that the Plaintiff is making against you in this lawsuit.
4. To respond to this Summons, or to be informed of further proceedings, you or your attorney must file a form called an "Appearance" with the Clerk of the above-named Court at the above Court address on or before the second day after the above Return Date.

5. If you or your attorney do not file a written "Appearance" form on time, the Court may enter judgment against you for the relief requested in the Complaint, which may result in temporary or permanent orders without further notice.
6. The "Appearance" form may be obtained at the above Court address.
7. If you have questions about the Summons, Complaint, or Notice of Automatic Court Orders (JD-FM-158), you should consult an attorney promptly. The Clerk of Court is not permitted to give advice on legal questions.

DATE	SIGNED *(Sign and "X" proper box)* **(9)**	☐ Comm. of Superior Court	TYPE IN NAME OF PERSON SIGNING AT LEFT
		☐ Assistant Clerk	

FOR THE PLAINTIFF Please enter the appearance of:	NAME OF ATTORNEY OR LAW FIRM *(If pro se, name of plaintiff)* **(10)**	JURIS NO. *(If attorney or law firm)*
MAILING ADDRESS *(No., street, town, zip code)*		TELEPHONE NO. *(Area code first)*

SIGNED *(Plaintiff, if pro se or attorney for plaintiff)* **(11)**

IF THIS SUMMONS IS SIGNED BY A CLERK:

a. The signing has been done so that the Plaintiff will not be denied access to the courts.
b. It is the responsibility of the Plaintiff to see that service is made in the manner provided by law.
c. The clerk is not permitted to give any legal advice in connection with any lawsuit.
d. The clerk signing this summons at the request of the Plaintiff is not responsible in any way for any errors or omissions in the Summons, any allegations contained in the Complaint, or the service thereof.

FOR COURT USE
FILE DATE
(12)

I hereby certify I have read and understand the above.	SIGNED *(Plaintiff, if pro se)* **(13)**	DATE SIGNED

The Judicial Branch complies with the Americans with Disabilities Act (ADA). If you need a reasonable accommodation in accordance with the ADA, contact the clerk's office indicated above.

DOCKET NO.

SUMMONS, Family Actions

The Summons and Divorce Complaint

The Summons and Divorce Complaint are the first documents that you must submit to the court and serve on your spouse. These combine to become your official request for a dissolution of marriage or a legal separation. In legal terms, you become the "plaintiff" and your spouse becomes the "defendant;" however, this does not necessarily imply that your spouse is contesting or disagreeing with your request for a divorce. Before you can begin to prepare the Summons and Divorce Complaint forms, you need to select the return date.

The return date is the Tuesday you select and put on your Summons and Divorce Complaint. This date starts the ninety-day waiting period between the beginning of the case and when you can finish it. No one has to go to court on the return date. The return date establishes two important time periods:

1) You must serve the Summons and Divorce Complaint on the defendant at least twelve days before the return date. You must return and file the Divorce Complaint with the court at least six days before the return date.

2) There is a waiting period between when you start your case and when it can become final, sometimes called the "cooling off" period. This ninety-day waiting period starts with the return date. You cannot have your final divorce hearing before the end of the ninety days even if you have an agreement and you are ready to proceed earlier.

To make sure you have enough time to serve the defendant with the Summons and Divorce Complaint and file the case, you should pick a Tuesday that is at least four weeks away from when you plan to fill out the Divorce Complaint and send it to the marshal for service.

INSTRUCTIONS FOR FILLING OUT THE SUMMONS

1. Name of the judicial district where you are filing your case.
2. Name of the town for the courthouse where you are filing your case.
3. Return date.
4. Court's address.
5. Case management date set by the return date on Form JD-FM-165 A, B, or C (depending on judicial district).
6. "OO" if you are filing for divorce and "10" if your are filing for legal separation.
7. Plaintiff's name and address.
8. Defendant's name and address.
9. These spaces are for the signature of the clerk of the court or your attorney, if any. Obtain the signature of one or the other. Do not date or sign here.
10. Your name, address, and telephone number.
11. Sign your name and write the date.
12. Leave this area blank. The clerk will fill in the file date and docket number.
13. Sign and date here, but not until you take your papers to the clerk's office so that a clerk can witness your signature.

www.jud.state.ct.us/forms/fm159/htm

DIVORCE COMPLAINT
(DISSOLUTION OF MARRIAGE)

JD-FM-159 Rev. 6-03
C.G.S. § 46b-40, et seq., P.B. § 25-2, et seq.

STATE OF CONNECTICUT
SUPERIOR COURT
www.jud.state.ct.us

CROSS COMPLAINT CODE ONLY
CRSCMP

(1) ☐ ***Complaint:*** *Complete this form. Attach a completed Summons (JD-FM-3) and Notice of Automatic Court Orders (JD-FM-158).*
☐ ***Amended Complaint.***
☐ ***Cross Complaint:*** *Complete this form and attach to the Answer (JD-FM-160) unless it is already filed.*

JUDICIAL DISTRICT OF **(2)**	AT *(Town)* **(3)**	RETURN DATE *(Month, day, year)* **(4)**	DOCKET NO.
PLAINTIFF'S NAME *(Last, First, Middle Initial)* **(5)**		DEFENDANT'S NAME *(Last, First, Middle Initial)* **(6)**	
1. WIFE'S BIRTH NAME *(First, Middle Initial, Last)* **(7)**			
2. DATE OF MARRIAGE **(8)**	3. TOWN AND STATE, OR COUNTRY WHERE MARRIAGE TOOK PLACE		

(9) 4. *(Check all that apply)*
☐ The husband or the wife has lived in Connecticut for at least twelve months before the filing of this divorce complaint or before the divorce will become final.
☐ The husband or the wife lived in Connecticut at the time of the marriage, moved away, and then returned to Connecticut, planning to live here permanently.
☐ The marriage broke down after the wife or the husband moved to Connecticut.

(10) 5. A divorce is being sought because: *(Check all that apply)*
☐ This marriage has broken down irretrievably and there is no possibility of getting back together. **(No fault divorce)**
☐ Other *(must be reason(s) listed in Connecticut General Statute § 46b-40(c)):*

_____

_____

Check and complete all that apply for items 6-13. Attach additional sheets if needed.

(11) 6. ☐ No children were born to the wife after the date of this marriage.
(12) 7. ☐ There are no minor children of this marriage.
(13) 8. ☐ The following children have been born to the wife or have been adopted before, on or after the date of this marriage and the husband is the father/adoptive father. *(List only children who have not yet reached the age of 23.)*

NAME OF CHILD *(First, Middle Initial, Last)*	DATE OF BIRTH *(Month, day, year)*

(14) 9. ☐ The following children were born to the wife **after** the date of the marriage and the husband **is not the father.** *(List only children who have not yet reached the age of 23.)*

NAME OF CHILD *(First, Middle Initial, Last)*	DATE OF BIRTH *(Month, day, year)*

(Continued...)

15 10. ☐ The wife is pregnant with a child due to be born on *(date)* _____

The father of this unborn child is *(check one)* ☐ the husband ☐ not the husband ☐ unknown.

16 11. If there is a court order about any child listed above, name the child(ren) below and the person or agency awarded custody or providing support:

CHILD'S NAME	NAME OF PERSON OR AGENCY
CHILD'S NAME	NAME OF PERSON OR AGENCY
CHILD'S NAME	NAME OF PERSON OR AGENCY

12. The husband, the wife, or any of the child(ren) listed above has received financial support from the State of Connecticut. *(Check one)* ☐ Yes ☐ No ☐ Do not know
If yes, send a copy of the Summons, Complaint, Notice of Automatic Court Orders and any other documents filed with this Complaint to the Assistant Attorney General, 55 Elm Street, Hartford, CT 06106, and file the Certification of Notice *(JD-FM-175)* with the court clerk.

17 13. The husband, the wife, or any of the child(ren) listed above has received financial support from a city or town in Connecticut. *(Check one)* ☐ Yes *(State city or town: _____*) ☐ No ☐ Do not know
If yes, send a copy of the Summons, Complaint, Notice of Automatic Court Orders and any other documents filed with this Complaint to the City Clerk of the town providing assistance and file the Certification of Notice *(JD-FM-175)* with the court clerk.

18 **The Court is asked to order:** *(Check all that apply)*

☐ A divorce (dissolution of marriage).   ☐ Visitation.

☐ A fair division of property and debts.   ☐ Name change to:
                                                  _____

☐ Alimony.
                                                  ☐ Sole custody.
☐ Child Support.
                                                  ☐ Joint legal custody, Primary residence with:
☐ An order for the post-majority educational support
of the child(ren) pursuant to C.G.S. § 46b-56c. _____

And anything else the Court thinks is fair.

19 SIGNATURE	PRINT NAME OF PERSON SIGNING	DATE SIGNED
ADDRESS	JURIS NO. *(If applicable)*	TELEPHONE *(Area code first)*

20
- *If this is a Complaint, attach a copy of the Automatic Court Orders before serving a copy on the Defendant.*
- *If this is an Amended Complaint or a Cross Complaint, you must mail or deliver a copy to anyone who has filed an appearance and you must complete the certification below.*

I certify that a copy of the above was mailed/delivered to all counsel and pro se parties of record on:

.DATE MAILED OR DELIVERED	SIGNED *(Attorney or pro se party)*
NAME OF EACH PERSON SERVED*	ADDRESS WHERE SERVICE WAS MADE *(No., street, town, zip code)**

*If necessary, attach additional sheet with name of each party served and the address at which service was made.

INSTRUCTIONS FOR PREPARING THE DIVORCE COMPLAINT

1. Check the first box, "*Complaint.*"

2. Name of the judicial district where you are filing your case.

3. Name of the town for the courthouse where you are filing is located.

4. Return date.

5. Your full name. You are now the "plaintiff" (the person asking for a dissolution or separation).

6. Full name of your spouse. He or she is now the "defendant."

7. Wife's birth name.

8. Indicate the date of the marriage ceremony and the city and state (or country, if you were married outside the U.S.A.) where your ceremony was performed.

9. Check the box that applies to you. See "Who May File in Connecticut" on page 92.

10. Technically, you can allege fault in this portion of the Divorce Complaint. Most couples check the no-fault grounds: "broken down irretrievably."

11. Check box 6 if the wife had no children born after the date of the marriage.

12. Check box 7 if you have children by this marriage but they are no longer minors.

13. List the names and birth dates of all children under age eighteen, or eighteen and still in high school but no older than nineteen, born or adopted to the wife since the date of the marriage, if the husband is the father.

14. List the names and birth dates of all children under age eighteen born or adopted to the wife after the date of the marriage, if the husband is not the father.

15. Check this box if the wife is pregnant and fill in the due date. Also, check the appropriate box for the designation of the father.

16. Enter the name of each child and the person or agency, if any, who has custody of, and/or is providing support for, the child by a court order.

If the Wife Is Pregnant

A child conceived during the marriage is presumed by law to be the child of that marriage. If the child the wife is expecting is not the husband's child, you must tell the court. You may then have to deal with issues of paternity which are beyond the scope of this book and will, in all probability, require that you seek legal advice.

---

17. Check the appropriate box in 12 and/or 13 if the state of Connecticut or any city or town is currently providing or has provided state aid or support (such as welfare) to either party and/or the children.

18. Read this list carefully, and check the boxes that apply to you.

> "A divorce (dissolution of marriage)." Always check this box unless you are asking for a legal separation, in which case you should cross out "divorce" and insert "legal separation."

> "A fair division of property and debts." Always check this box if you and/or your spouse own any assets or have any debts.

> "Alimony." Check this box if your spouse agrees to pay you alimony. Also check it if you have not yet agreed about alimony, but you want to keep this issue open during your discussions.

> "Child Support." Always check this box if you have minor children.

> "An order for the post-majority educational support of the child(ren) pursuant to C.G.S. § 46b-56c." Check this box if you have a child under the age of twenty-three and you are requesting a court order for contribution to post-secondary education.

> "Visitation." Always check this box if you have minor children.

> "Name change to:" Include this provision if you want to return to your birth or former name. Type or write the complete restored name. The final divorce judgment will reflect the restored name and, when signed by the judge, becomes the official document that the spouse may use to change his or her Social Security card, driver's license, bank accounts, etc. Either spouse may use the divorce proceeding to restore his or her birth or former name but not to change to an entirely new name. To do that, an individual must file a separate court action for a change of name.

> "Sole custody." Check this box if you are requesting sole custody.

> "Joint legal custody, primary residence with:" Always check this box if you have minor children, unless you are requesting sole custody. Specify your intentions for the children's residence. (See Chapter 8.)

19. Sign and date the Divorce Complaint, and type or write your full name, address, and telephone number.

20. Attach a copy of the Notice of Automatic Orders, an additional form that you obtain from the clerk of the superior court.

When you finish preparing the Summons and Divorce Complaint, take them to the office of the clerk of the superior court in the town in the judicial district where you are filing for divorce. The addresses and telephone numbers of the clerk's offices are in Appendix A. The clerk will review the documents and, if they are acceptable, sign the Summons, assign a case management date, and insert the case management date in the Notice of Automatic Orders (if you have not already done so). The clerk will return the Summons and Divorce Complaint to you for service of process. Before filing, you must:

1. Make two copies of the Divorce Complaint and attach a copy of the Summons to each. One set of copies is for your spouse and will be served by the marshal. The other set of copies is for you.

2. Attach the original Summons (the copy you filled out) to the original Divorce Complaint. These originals, and the set of copies for your spouse, will go to the marshal for service.

The Automatic Orders of the Complaint

When the plaintiff begins the divorce, certain automatic court orders go into effect and last until the divorce is final. The plaintiff is bound by the automatic orders upon signing the Divorce Complaint, and the defendant is bound by the automatic orders when served with the Divorce Complaint. You should not ignore these orders because the court has the power to punish you by a contempt action initiated by the other party if you disobey them.

You and your spouse can enter into written temporary agreements varying the terms of the automatic orders. If you do so, you should submit your written agreements to the court following the procedures at page 125 to file a *Motion for Order*. If you want to terminate, modify, or amend any automatic order and your spouse will not sign a written agreement, you must file a Motion for Relief from Automatic Orders with the court. You should also consult with an attorney concerning the automatic orders.

The automatic orders are attached to the Divorce Complaint. In summary, they provide the following:

1. Neither party shall "sell, transfer, encumber, conceal, assign, remove, or in any way dispose of" any property either spouse owns separately or together. You are permitted to transfer or dispose of the property in one of the prohibited ways if it is in the ordinary course of business, for customary and usual household expenses, or for reasonable attorneys' fees in connection with the divorce.

2. Neither party shall incur unreasonable debts. The definition of the term "unreasonable" depends on the case and the written agreement of the parties. Generally, however, borrowing against any credit line secured by the family residence or further encumbering assets or unreasonably using credit cards or cash advances against credit cards is prohibited.

3. Within thirty days of the return date, both spouses must complete and exchange sworn financial affidavits. See Chapter 7 for instructions for completing the Financial Affidavit.

4. The case management date is designated according to the return date on Form JD-FM-165 A, B, or C depending on your court location. You may or may not have to appear at court on that date for a case management conference.

When you begin a divorce case, you can file and serve a Notice of *Lis Pendens* against the title to real estate owned by either or both of the spouses. If you file a Notice of *Lis Pendens*, any creditors of the other spouse, or other people to whom that spouse may attempt to convey the property, are on notice of the pending court action and the spouse's claim of an interest in the property. Anyone with a concern about protecting title to real estate pending completion of the case should contact an attorney to prepare, file, and serve a Notice of *Lis Pendens*. Consult with an attorney to help you with this procedure.

5. Neither party shall permanently remove the minor child or children from Connecticut.

6. If you have children, both parties must participate in parenting education classes within sixty days of the return date. See page 180 for information about parenting education classes.

7. Neither party shall remove the children and/or the other party from medical, hospital, and/or dental coverage. If the coverage is in existence, the parties are ordered to maintain it in full force and effect for the benefit of the children and/or the other party.

8. Neither party shall change the beneficiaries of any existing life insurance policy. Any life, automobile, homeowner's, and/or renter's insurance all must be continued in full force and effect.

9. If the parties are living together on the date the Summons and Divorce Complaint are served, neither party can deny the other party use of the primary residence without a court order.

10. If you have children and one party is moving out of the family residence, the party moving out must notify the other party, or his or her attorney, in writing within forty-eight hours of the move with an address where he or she can be located.

11. If you have children and are living apart, you shall assist your children in having contact with the other party. This contact can be in person, by telephone, and/or in writing, "consistent with the habits of the family."

www.jud.state.ct.us/forms/fm158/htm

NOTICE OF AUTOMATIC COURT ORDERS

JD-FM-158 Rev. 4-2000
P.B. § 25-5

Attach to Divorce (Dissolution of Marriage) Complaint/Cross Complaint (JD-FM-159), Custody/Visitation Application (JD-FM-161), and any Annulment or Legal Separation Complaint

www.jud.state.ct.us

The following automatic orders shall apply to both parties, with service of the automatic orders to be made with service of process of a complaint for dissolution of marriage, legal separation, or annulment or of an application for custody or visitation. An automatic order shall not apply if there is a prior, contradictory court order. The automatic orders shall be effective with regard to the plaintiff or applicant upon the signing of the complaint or application and with regard to the defendant or respondent upon service and shall remain in place during the pendency of the action, unless terminated, modified, or amended by further order of the court upon motion of either of the parties:

1. Neither party shall sell, transfer, encumber (except for the filing of a lis pendens), conceal, assign, remove, or in any way dispose of, without the consent of the other party in writing, or an order of the court, any property, individually or jointly held by the parties, except in the usual course of business or for customary and usual household expenses or for reasonable attorney fees in connection with this action. (This section only applies to divorce, annulment, and legal separation cases.)

2. Neither party shall incur unreasonable debts hereafter, including but not limited to, further borrowing against any credit line secured by the family residence, further encumbrancing any assets, or unreasonably using credit cards or cash advances against credit cards. (This section only applies to divorce, annulment, and legal separation cases.)

3. The parties shall each complete and exchange sworn financial statements substantially in accordance with a form prescribed by the chief court administrator within thirty days of the return day. The parties may thereafter enter and submit to the court a stipulated interim order allocating income and expenses, in accordance with the uniform child support guidelines. (This section only applies to divorce, annulment, and legal separation cases.)

4. The case management date for this case is _____ · The parties shall comply with Sec. 25-51 to determine if their actual presence at the court is required on that date. (See JD-FM-165A - C or court clerk for local Case Management Dates.)

5. Neither party shall permanently remove the minor child or children from the state of Connecticut, without written consent of the other or order of the court.

6. The parties, if they share a minor child or children, shall participate in the parenting education program within sixty days of the return day or within sixty days from the filing of the application.

7. Neither party shall cause the other party or the children of the marriage to be removed from any medical, hospital, and dental insurance coverage, and each party shall maintain the existing medical, hospital, and dental insurance coverage in full force and effect.

8. Neither party shall change the beneficiaries of any existing life insurance policies, and each party shall maintain the existing life insurance, automobile insurance, homeowner's or renter's insurance policies in full force and effect.

9. If the parties are living together on the date of service of these orders, neither party may deny the other party use of the current primary residence of the parties, whether it be owned or rented property, without court order. This provision shall not apply if there is a prior, contradictory court order.

10. If the parties share a child or children, a party vacating the family residence shall notify the other party or the other party's attorney, in writing, within forty-eight hours of such move, of an address where the relocated party can receive communication. This provision shall not apply if there is a prior, contradictory court order.

11. If the parents of minor children live apart during this dissolution proceeding, they shall assist their children in having contact with both parties, which is consistent with the habits of the family, personally, by telephone, and in writing unless there is a prior court order.

BY ORDER OF THE COURT

FAILURE TO OBEY THESE ORDERS MAY BE PUNISHABLE BY CONTEMPT OF COURT. IF YOU OBJECT TO OR SEEK MODIFICATION OF THESE ORDERS DURING THE PENDENCY OF THE ACTION, YOU HAVE THE RIGHT TO A HEARING BEFORE A JUDGE WITHIN A REASONABLE TIME.

(Continued on back/page 2)

SUMMARY OF AUTOMATIC COURT ORDERS

The court orders on the reverse side/page 1 apply to both parties in this case, unless there is already a court order which contradicts one of these orders. The automatic court orders apply to the plaintiff or the applicant when the attached Complaint or Application is signed. They apply to the defendant or respondent when a copy of the Complaint or the Application and the Notice of Automatic Court Orders are served (delivered to the defendant/respondent by an authorized person). The automatic court orders are summarized below, but you are subject to the full text of the orders on the reverse side/page 1. If you do not understand the full text of the automatic court orders, you may want to talk to an attorney.

Neither party shall:

• Sell, mortgage, or give away any property without written agreement or a court order. (Only applies to divorce, annulment, and legal separation cases.)

• Go into unreasonable debt by borrowing money or using credit cards or cash advances. (Only applies to divorce, annulment, and legal separation cases.)

• Permanently take your children from Connecticut without written agreement or a court order.

• Take each other or your children off any existing medical, hospital, doctor, or dental insurance policy or let any such insurance coverage expire.

• Change the terms or named beneficiaries of any existing insurance policy or let any existing insurance coverage expire, including life, automobile, homeowner's or renter's insurance.

• Deny use of the family home to the other person without a court order, if you are living together on the date the court papers are served.

Both parties shall:

• Complete and exchange sworn financial affidavits within thirty days of the return date. (Only applies to divorce, annulment, and legal separation cases.)

• Participate in a parenting education program within sixty days of the return date or, for a custody or visitation case, within sixty days from the filing of the Application (if you share children under 18 years old).

• Attend a case management conference on the date specified on the reverse/page 1, unless you both agree on all issues and file a Case Management Agreement form with the court clerk on or before that date.

• Tell the other person in writing within forty-eight hours about your new address or a place where you can receive mail if you move out of the family home (if you share children under 18 years old).

• Help any children you share continue their usual contact with both parents in person, by telephone and in writing.

IF YOU DO NOT OBEY THESE ORDERS WHILE YOUR CASE IS PENDING, YOU MAY BE PUNISHED BY BEING HELD IN CONTEMPT OF COURT. IF YOU OBJECT TO THESE ORDERS OR WANT THEM CHANGED, YOU HAVE A RIGHT TO A HEARING BEFORE A JUDGE WITHIN A REASONABLE TIME, BY FILING A MOTION TO MODIFY THESE ORDERS WITH THE COURT CLERK

Affidavit Concerning Children

If you have minor children, the Uniform Child Custody Jurisdiction Act as adopted in Connecticut requires that each party file the Affidavit Concerning Children. In it, you name any people, including the parents, with whom your children have resided and/or who had legal custody of them in the last five years, anyone who has been involved in court custody actions concerning your children, and/or anyone who currently wants custody of or visitation rights with your children. The purpose of this requirement is to prevent multiple custody actions concerning the same children in different courts or different states.

You must sign this affidavit before a notary, attorney, or clerk of the superior court. Both federal and state laws require this information. You will be signing this affidavit under oath and therefore swearing to the truth of this information. Be sure that it is accurate and complete to the best of your knowledge and belief.

The Connecticut General Statutes technically require the filing of this affidavit before any orders enter about child custody, visitation, and/or support. This way the court knows from the beginning if there are any jurisdictional problems that involve the children, and it can address these problems before the case proceeds too far. In practice, however, most people in Connecticut have historically waited until the end of the case to file this affidavit. It is good practice to file the affidavit at the beginning of the case.

If you completed this form at the beginning of the case and are the plaintiff, have the affidavit served with the Divorce Complaint. The marshal will list the affidavit on his or her affidavit of service so it is not necessary to complete the certification. If you are the defendant, mail a copy of the affidavit to the other spouse along with your Cross Complaint and/or Appearance and/or Answer—note on your copy the date you mail it and the address you use. You can change the form so that you both sign one affidavit, keeping copies for your files. If you serve and file the Affidavit Concerning Children at the beginning of the case and any children are born after the date of the filing of the Divorce Complaint, you must file an amended affidavit to reflect the information about new children.

www.jud.state.ct.us/forms/fm164.htm

AFFIDAVIT CONCERNING CHILDREN

JD-FM-164 Rev. 4-03
C.G.S. § 46b-115s
P.B. § 25-57

STATE OF CONNECTICUT
SUPERIOR COURT
www.jud.state.ct.us

INSTRUCTIONS

Complete form. You must swear that your statement is true and sign it in front of a court clerk, a notary public, or an attorney who will also sign and date the affidavit.

COURT USE ONLY
AFFACUS

1

JUDICIAL DISTRICT OF	AT *(Town)*	DOCKET NO.
PLAINTIFF'S NAME *(Last, first, middle initial)*	DEFENDANT'S NAME *(Last, first, middle initial)*	

Information about the past five years for each child affected by this case is required. Provide information below. If more space is needed, use form JD-FM-164A.

2

CHILD'S NAME *(First, middle, last)*			DATE OF BIRTH *(Month, day, year)*
DATE(S) OF RESIDENCE	LOCATION *(Town or city, and state, unless confidential by court order)*	NAME(S) AND PRESENT ADDRESS(ES) OF PERSON(S) CHILD LIVED WITH *(unless confidential)*	RELATIONSHIP TO CHILD

3

TO THE PRESENT			
TO			
TO			
TO			
TO			

4

CHILD'S NAME *(First, middle, last)*	DATE OF BIRTH *(Mo., day, yr.)*	☐ RESIDENCE INFORMATION IS SAME AS FOR CHILD ABOVE. *(If not same, provide information)*	
DATE(S) OF RESIDENCE	LOCATION *(Town or city, and state, unless confidential by court order)*	NAME(S) AND PRESENT ADDRESS(ES) OF PERSON(S) CHILD LIVED WITH *(unless confidential)*	RELATIONSHIP TO CHILD
TO THE PRESENT			
TO			
TO			
TO			
TO			

5

☐ Check here if additional children are listed on JD-FM-164A.

(Continued...)

1. *(Check one)* ☐ I have ☐ I have not been a party or a witness or participated in any other capacity in cases in Connecticut or any other state concerning custody of or visitation with any child listed in this affidavit. If yes, identify the name of the court, the court case number and date of determination:

(Check item 2 or 3 below)

2. ☐ I do not know of other civil or criminal proceedings in Connecticut or any other state, now or in the past, that could affect the current proceeding, including enforcement proceedings and proceedings relating to family violence, protective orders, termination of parental rights and adoption.

3. ☐ I know of the following civil or criminal proceedings, in Connecticut or any other state, now or in the past, that could affect the current proceeding, including enforcement proceedings and proceedings relating to family violence, protective orders, termination of parental rights and adoption.

CASE NAME	DOCKET NO.	COURT LOCATION *(Including state)*
NATURE OF PROCEEDING		

CASE NAME	DOCKET NO.	COURT LOCATION *(Including state)*
NATURE OF PROCEEDING		

4. *(Check one)* ☐ No one except the plaintiff/applicant and defendant/respondent has physical custody or claims to have custody or visitation rights regarding any child listed here.

☐ The following person(s) has physical custody or claims to have custody or visitation rights regarding any child listed here:

NAME: _____

ADDRESS: _____
(unless confidential)

5. The mother of the child(ren) named in the Complaint or Application is pregnant.

☐ Yes   ☐ No   ☐ Do not know

6. A child has been born to the mother named in the Complaint or Application after the filing of the Complaint or Application.

☐ Yes   ☐ No   ☐ Do not know   If yes, complete the following:

CHILD'S NAME	DATE OF BIRTH *(Month, day, year)*

SIGNATURE	PRINT NAME OF PERSON SIGNING
SWORN TO BEFORE ME *(Asst. Clerk/Comm. of Superior Court/Notary Public)*	DATE SIGNED

JD-FM-164 *(Back)* Rev. 4-03

You have an ongoing duty to tell the court about any case that could affect the current proceeding, in Connecticut or any other state, if you learn about it during this case.

INSTRUCTIONS FOR FILLING OUT THE AFFIDAVIT CONCERNING CHILDREN

Obtain an Affidavit Concerning Children from the office of the clerk of the superior court.

1. Fill in the information at the top the same as you did on the Divorce Complaint. If you are filling out this form after the return date, leave that space blank and insert the docket number assigned by the court.

2. Type or write the name and birth date of one of your children, even if he or she is not living with you or your spouse (for example, if the child lives with a grandparent).

3. List the dates and locations by address where your child has lived, except for vacations or visits, for the last five years. Include your name and address and that of your spouse if the child has lived with either or both of you during the five-year period, and write in your relationship ("mother" or "father").

    List the dates, names, present addresses, and relationships of individuals, other than you or your spouse, with whom your child has lived during the last five years. This may include, for example, grandparents, other relatives, or foster parents. You do not list camps, day care centers, babysitters, or other child care providers.

4. For your second child, insert his or her name and birth date. If the information for your second child is identical to that of the first child you listed, check the box provided. Otherwise, fill in all the information for the second child.

5. Check this box if you have more than two children. Fill in and attach Form JD-FM-164A.

6. Check the appropriate box and if necessary, fill in the information about any custody case involving your children in which you participated or that you know about but were not involved in.

7. Check item 2 or 3 (providing requested information if applicable to 3).

8. Check the appropriate box for items 4, 5, and 6. Fill in any applicable information.

9. You must sign and print your name before a clerk of the superior court, commissioner of the superior court (a licensed Connecticut lawyer), or a notary public.

Jurisdiction: Jurisdiction is the legal word for the power of the court to take action about something.

If your spouse is in the military service, he or she is protected by the Soldiers and Sailors Civil Relief Act. This law provides that military personnel cannot have orders or judgments entered against them if they cannot attend the hearing because they are in the military. It does not prevent the serviceperson and his or her spouse from entering into a separation agreement to settle all issues and having the judge enter the divorce based on that agreement. The serviceperson, his or her spouse, or any dependent can receive counseling and legal advice from the Judge Advocate General's (JAG) office where he or she is stationed. This includes advice to the serviceperson about the jurisdictional effect of waiving his or her rights under the law. If your spouse is on active duty away from home and will not waive the protection of the act, your divorce case may be very difficult at the present time and you should consult with an attorney for advice on this issue. (See page 142 for the Affidavit Concerning Military Service.)

Jurisdiction

The court has jurisdiction to grant your divorce when you serve your spouse personally in the state of Connecticut. The court also has jurisdiction to grant your divorce if you serve your spouse out of state personally or by certified or registered mail as long as you can prove that he or she received the papers. If you do not know the address for personal service or mailing, you can give notice by publication and the court has jurisdiction to grant your divorce.

If you serve your spouse while he or she is physically in the state of Connecticut, the court has jurisdiction not only to grant your divorce but also to determine child custody and visitation and order either of you to transfer property, make payments on debts, or pay alimony and/or child support. If you are unable to serve your spouse in Connecticut, the question of the power of the court to enter custody and financial orders becomes much more complicated. If you want the court to do more than just give you a divorce, you may at this point be well advised to consult with an attorney.

For the most part, the court can enter custody and visitation orders as long as it has jurisdiction to grant your divorce in one of the three ways discussed here. However, this power to enter custody and visitation orders only exists if Connecticut is the "home state" of the children (with certain technical exceptions). Generally, Connecticut is considered the children's home state if they have resided here for the last six months immediately before you start the divorce. "Home state" is a technical legal issue which, in doubtful cases, needs to be discussed with an attorney.

The court's power to award child support or alimony or to divide property or debts may be in doubt if the defendant has not been served within the state of Connecticut. While there are means by which the court can properly enter these financial orders even with out-of-state service, if this is your situation, you should be sure to consult with an attorney.

A defendant who files an Appearance and/or Cross Complaint and/or Answer with the court is treated as consenting to the court's full jurisdiction, no matter where or how service was made.

If you cannot personally serve your spouse and you subsequently find out that your ex-spouse is now in Connecticut, immediately consult with an attorney. You may be able to obtain full jurisdiction over him or her and get additional financial orders.

Notifying Your Spouse/Service of Process

In the American civil legal system, the court generally cannot enter orders against anyone unless the court is certain that person has notice of what is going on. If you decide to file for a divorce, you are responsible for proving to the court that you have properly notified your spouse about the filing and what you are asking for. The papers that notify your spouse of your filing are the Summons and Divorce Complaint. Proving to the court that your spouse got a copy of both is called *service* and *return of process*.

Jurisdiction and Service of Process Checklist

Directions: Check the statement which fits your situation. Then see the instructions in this chapter for that procedure.

☐ **Personal service**—The marshal personally serves your spouse with the Summons and Divorce Complaint in Connecticut and then submits documents to the court to prove how service was completed.

☐ **Service by certified or registered mail**—If your spouse lives out of state, you can serve him or her by certified or registered mail. You must obtain the prior permission of the court to make service by mail. See page 114.

☐ **Publication**—If you do not know the whereabouts of your spouse, you can serve your spouse by publication. You must obtain the prior permission of the court to serve by publication. See page 115.

☐ **Appearance**—To guarantee full personal jurisdiction (even if you weren't properly served) and/or to insure that you receive all court notifications, the defendant files an appearance.

☐ **Cross Complaint**—If your spouse filed the Complaint but you do not agree, see page 121 for issues that you may respond to. Filing a Cross Complaint gives the court personal jurisdiction over the defendant even if the manner of service of process did not, unless the response is specifically limited to the jurisdictional issue. If you are the defendant and do not believe the court has jurisdiction, you should consult with an attorney before filing a Cross Complaint or Appearance to discuss the procedure to contest the court's jurisdiction.

PERSONAL SERVICE

If you know where to find your spouse in Connecticut, have him or her personally served with the Summons and Divorce Complaint. You have a choice of how to serve your spouse. Generally, the best approach is to have the service occur at a prearranged mediation or collaborative session. If you are doing an uncontested divorce on your own, you and your spouse can make an appointment with the marshal to have the papers served. If your spouse is in Connecticut, you must use a marshal to serve the papers. Ask the clerk of the superior court for a list of local marshals. You can also find the list at www.jud.state.ct.us/faq/marshals.htm. From this list, call a marshal to let him or her know you want the papers served and to obtain the marshal's rate for civil service of process (usually between $35–$50). Then send the ORIGINAL AND A COPY of the Divorce Complaint, and the ORIGINAL AND A COPY of the Summons, marking the originals (with pencil or with a sticky note) "to be served." Enclose a stamped envelope addressed to yourself and a check for the amount for service (unless the marshal tells you he or she is willing to bill you after service). If your spouse is not cooperating in the divorce process, you may write a cover letter to the marshal like the following sample. Include the Spouse's Whereabouts Information Sheet from page 113 that will give the marshal valuable information.

Sample Cover Letter to Marshal

Your Name
Your Address

Date of your letter

Dear Marshal:

Please serve the enclosed copies of a Divorce Complaint (Dissolution of Marriage) (or Legal Separation), Automatic Orders, and a Summons on_____
(name of your spouse). The originals are also enclosed.

Information for locating _____ (name of your spouse) is on the attached Spouse's Whereabouts Information Sheet.

I have enclosed a photograph to help you identify him/her.

After you have completed the Return of Service on the back, please return the original Summons, Divorce Complaint, and Automatic Orders to me in the enclosed stamped legal-size envelope.

My check to you for $_____ is enclosed.

Sincerely,

Enclosures: original Summons
               photocopy of Summons
               original Divorce Complaint
               photocopy of Divorce Complaint with Automatic Orders
               Spouse's Whereabouts Information Sheet
               your check to the marshal
               stamped legal-size envelope addressed to you

FILING YOUR SUMMONS AND COMPLAINT

After serving your spouse with his or her copies of the Divorce Complaint and Summons, the marshal will return the originals to you along with another sheet of paper called a *Return of Service*. The Return of Service sets forth the necessary factual information about the service and is the proof for the court that your spouse was properly served. Keep a copy of the Return of Service for your records since you need to file the original with the court.

When you receive the papers from the marshal, you should immediately file them by mail or in person with the clerk of the superior court where you are filing your case. If you do not file the papers at least six days before the return date, you may have to prepare new papers and serve your spouse again. Along with the original Summons, Divorce Complaint and Automatic Orders, the filing fee is $225 (as of the publication of this guidebook). Most courts will accept cash or a money order or a personal check payable to "Clerk, Superior Court." However, if you feel you cannot afford to pay all or part of the court costs (filing fee, marshal's fee, and/or cost of the parenting education class), complete the Application for a Waiver of Fees Form JD-FM-75 or complete it online at www.jud.state.ct.us/forms/fm075.htm.

SPOUSE'S WHEREABOUTS INFORMATION SHEET

To serve your spouse, you will find it useful to complete this form. It will help you to gather and clarify necessary information. Copy this form, complete the information, and give it to the marshal.

Spouse's full name: _____

Other names used by spouse: _____

Last known address:

     Street, Apt. #: _____

     PO Box: _____

     City, State, Zip: _____

When there: _____

Work information:

     Company name: _____

     Company office address: _____

     _____

     Position/title: _____

     Hours: _____

     Supervisor: _____

Physical Description: _____

_____

Family members and others who might know where spouse is:

Name: _____ Relationship: _____

Address: _____

Phone: (work)_____ (home) _____

Name: _____ Relationship: _____

Address: _____

Phone: (work)_____ (home) _____

Name: _____ Relationship: _____

Address: _____

Phone: (work)_____ (home) _____

Serving the Absent Spouse By Certified or Registered Mail

There is a way to get jurisdiction for the court to dissolve your marriage even if you cannot serve your spouse personally. If you have a current address for your spouse, you will need to get permission from the court to serve him or her by certified or registered mail in or out of state. To do this, prepare the Motion for First Order of Notice and Order of Notice.

When you go to court to have the clerk sign the Summons, take the original and two copies of the Motion for Notice By Publication or Mail in Family Cases with you. The clerk will review the order and approve it. Then, send the marshal the original Order of Notice attached to the original Summons and Divorce Complaint as well as a copy of the Order of Notice with the copy of the Summons and Divorce Complaint for your spouse. Keep a copy of the motion and order yourself.

The marshal does the actual mailing of the papers and will bill you for it. The marshal then completes a Return of Service, including an affidavit setting forth the facts of the mailing and attaching the post office receipt. When you receive the Return of Service, file it with the original Summons and Divorce Complaint as described earlier.

If your spouse signs the post office "green card," this is the proof that your spouse received the papers. The marshal will get the signed card from the post office and will send it to you. You must then make a copy of the signed certified mail receipt for your file and send the original on to the clerk's office asking that it be placed in your file. When you file the signed mailing card with the court be sure that you put the docket number on it. If you file it by mailing it to the court, be sure to put your docket number on your cover letter to the clerk of the superior court. It is also important for you to keep a copy of the signed certified or registered mail card as your proof of notice to the defendant should the original card not be in your file when you appear for the final hearing.

If someone else signs for your spouse or the card is never returned, the judge may find that your spouse did not have notice of the case and refuse to enter the divorce. You can insure that the divorce will go through if your spouse files an Appearance and/or Answer and/or Cross Complaint. These forms acknowledge that your spouse is aware of the case and give the court the power to enter the full range of divorce orders.

www.jud.state.ct.us/forms/fm167/htm.

MOTION FOR NOTICE BY PUBLICATION OR MAIL IN FAMILY CASES

JD-FM-167 Rev. 6-03
C.G.S. § 46b-46, P.B. §§ 11-4, 25-28

STATE OF CONNECTICUT SUPERIOR COURT
www.jud.state.ct.us

COURT USE ONLY
MFORNOT

1 JUDICIAL DISTRICT OF	AT *(Town)*	DOCKET NO. *(If any)* **2**

3 PLAINTIFF'S NAME *(Last, first, middle initial)*	DEFENDANT'S NAME *(Last, first, middle initial)*

4 PARTY TO BE NOTIFIED *(Check one)* ☐ Plaintiff ☐ Defendant	RETURN DATE, IF APPLICABLE *(Mo., day, yr.)* **5**

6 1. This court case asks for: *(Check all that apply)*

☐ Divorce (dissolution of marriage) based on _____
(Legal grounds)

☐ Legal separation   ☐ Visitation with children

☐ Custody of children   ☐ Other *(specify)* _____

☐ Annulment

7 2. *(Check one)*

☐ The party to be notified lives out of state at:

_____
(No., street, town, state, zip code)

Therefore, I ask the Court's permission to serve the party to be notified by registered or certified mail or by an authorized person in the state where the party to be notified lives.

> **If this motion accompanies a complaint for divorce (dissolution of marriage), legal separation or annulment, or an application for custody or visitation, the defendant or respondent, when served, will be subject to automatic court orders which are attached to the complaint or application.**

☐ The current address of the party to be notified is unknown and all reasonable efforts to find him/her have failed: I have made the following efforts *("X" all that apply)*:
   ☐ contacted directory assistance
   ☐ contacted relatives/friends of the party
   ☐ contacted current/previous employer(s) of the party
   ☐ other *(specify)*: _____

The last known address of the party to be notified was:

_____
(No., street, town, state, zip code)

Therefore, I ask the Court's permission to publish notice of this case in the local newspaper named:

_____ in *(town, state)* _____

(Local newspaper chosen must circulate in the town of the defendant's last known address.)

8 SIGNATURE *(Attorney or pro se party)*	PRINT NAME OF PERSON SIGNING	DATE SIGNED
ADDRESS *(No., street, town or city, state, zip code)*		TELEPHONE NO. *(Area code first)*

INSTRUCTIONS FOR FILLING OUT THE MOTION FOR NOTICE BY PUBLICATION
OR MAIL IN FAMILY CASES

1. Name of the judicial district and court location just like you did for the Summons and Divorce Complaint.

2. Leave this space blank. The clerk will fill in the docket number of your case.

3. Type or write your name and your spouse's name as they are on the Summons and Divorce Complaint.

4. Check the appropriate box.

5. Type or write th return date.

6. Type or write "irretrievable breakdown." If you alleged a different ground for your divorce (or are filing a custody action) in paragraph four of the Divorce Complaint, state it here.

7. Choose the box that applies to you and provide the requested information.

8. Sign, and print your name, and the date. You must also provide your address and phone number.

INSTRUCTIONS FOR FILLING OUT THE ORDER OF NOTICE BY PUBLICATION
OR MAIL IN FAMILY CASES

1. Fill out the section above the gray line with the same information as on the Motion for Notice By Publication or Mail in Family Cases

2. Leave the rest of the form blank for the clerk to complete. The clerk will sign here.

www.jud.state.ct.us/forms/fm168/htm

**ORDER OF NOTICE BY
PUBLICATION OR MAIL
IN FAMILY CASES**
JD-FM-168 Rev. 6-02
P.B. §§ 11-6, 11-7, 25-28

**STATE OF CONNECTICUT
SUPERIOR COURT**
www.jud.state.ct.us

COURT USE ONLY
ORONOT

INSTRUCTIONS: To be used with the Motion for Notice By Publication or Mail form (JD-FM-167).

JUDICIAL DISTRICT OF	AT *(Town)*	DOCKET NO. *(If any)*

PLAINTIFF'S NAME *(Last, first, middle initial)*	DEFENDANT'S NAME *(Last, first, middle initial)*

NOTICE TO ➡	PARTY TO BE NOTIFIED *(Last, first, middle initial)*	RETURN DATE, IF APPLICABLE *(Mo., day, yr.)*

The Court has reviewed the Motion for Notice By Publication or Mail and the Complaint/Application/Motion which asks for:

❶

☐ divorce (dissolution of marriage) based on _____
(Legal grounds)

☐ legal separation   ☐ visitation with children

☐ custody of children   ☐ other (specify): _____

☐ annulment

COURT ORDER

☐ The Court finds that the party to be notified lives out of state at:

_____
(No, street, town, state, zip code)

THE COURT ORDERS that the party filing the Motion for Notice by Publication or Mail give notice to the party to be notified by mailing a true and attested copy of the *(Check all that apply)*:

❷

☐ Summons and Complaint plus Notice of Automatic Orders
☐ Application for Custody or Visitation and Order to Attend Hearing plus Notice of Automatic Orders
☐ Other *(specify)*:_____

and this Order of Notice by registered or certified mail, personal return receipt requested, to the party to be notified on or before _____ , or by having some authorized person in the state where the party to be notified lives serve the said party and file proof of service with this Court.

OR

☐ The Court finds that the current address of the party to be notified is unknown and that all reasonable efforts to find him/her have failed. The Court also finds that the last known address of the party to be notified was:

_____
(No, street, town, state, zip code)

THE COURT ORDERS that notice be given to the party to be notified by placing a legal notice in:
_____ a newspaper circulating in _____
containing a true and attested copy of this Order of Notice, and, if accompanying a Complaint for divorce (dissolution of marriage), legal separation or annulment, or if accompanying an Application for custody or visitation, a statement that Automatic Court Orders have been issued in the case as required by Section 25-5 of the Connecticut Practice Book and are a part of the Complaint/Application on file with the Court. *(Check one of the following)*

☐ The notice should appear before *(date)* _____ and proof of service shall be filed with this Court.

☐ The notice shall appear once a week for two successive weeks commencing on or before *(date)* _____ and proof of service shall be filed with this Court.

CLERK/ASSISTANT CLERK	DATE SIGNED

Why Should I Bother With Service by Publication?

If you can serve your spouse only by publication, the court generally only has jurisdiction to enter the divorce and sometimes to divide instate property and enter custody and visitation orders. So, why bother? Why not stay married?

As long as you are legally married, you are potentially obligating each other on debts you incur and arguably sharing all property you acquire, regardless of the names on either. Any children born or conceived by the wife are presumed to be fathered by the husband, even if the real father is present at the delivery and wants the child to carry his name.

"It's okay to tell the court that you don't know where your spouse is even when you actually do know or could easily find out."

This is not only a bad idea, it's also a crime, which is why a Motion for Notice By Publication or Mail in Family Cases is necessary to get permission to serve your case by publication. Lying about this might get you a divorce without initial hassle, but your divorce is null and void (can be wiped out) if your spouse finds out about it and can prove to the court that you knew his or her whereabouts all along or could have discovered it.

Serving the Absent Spouse By Publication

There is another way to get jurisdiction for the court to dissolve your marriage even if you cannot serve your spouse personally in Connecticut or by mail. With the court's permission, you can publish your Notice of Divorce in a newspaper or other periodical so that the court can give you the final divorce.

The court may not order alimony, child support, or division of property located outside of Connecticut without actual notice to the defendant by personal service or by mail actually received. Therefore, you should only use this procedure as a last resort. However, the court can enter the full range of orders if the defendant files an Appearance and/or Answer and/or Cross Complaint, separation agreement, and/or appears in person at the final hearing even if service was made by publication. If the defendant does not file an appearance or physically appear in court, you may need to provide additional notice by publication.

Complete the Motion for Notice By Publication or Mail in Family Cases. If you know the address for your spouse for certified mail, you should keep the signed certified mail receipt to show the judge your spouse got notice. Give the original and a copy to the clerk of the superior court. Ask the clerk to sign the order along with the Summons.

The completed Order of Notice must be published once a week for two successive weeks in a newspaper or other periodical with substantial circulation. The newspaper may be either where the defendant is most likely to be living or at his or her last known address. As a rule, local papers are much less expensive than the larger dailies. Call and find out what they charge. You may choose the least expensive if you wish, but make sure that the circulation is substantial enough that the court will believe the defendant will have an opportunity to see it.

Send the newspaper a letter enclosing a copy of the signed Order of Notice, their fee for publication, and a stamped envelope addressed to you. Some marshals will provide this service for you for a minimal fee (in addition to the newspaper's fee). After the publication is completed, the newspaper will send you a "publisher's affidavit" in the envelope you provided. Attach the original publisher's affidavit to your Motion to Dispense with Further Notice and file them with the court after you receive the publisher's affidavit.

www.jud.state.ct.us/forms/cl012/htm

APPEARANCE
JD-CL-12 Rev. 2-03
Pr. Bk. §§ 3-1 thru 3-6, 3-8

NOTICE TO PRO SE PARTIES
A pro se party is a person who represents himself or herself. It is your
responsibility to inform the Clerk's Office if you have a change of address.

STATE OF CONNECTICUT
SUPERIOR COURT
www.jud.state.ct.us

INSTRUCTIONS

1. *Type or print legibly.*
2. **Judicial District Court Locations:** *In any action returnable to a Judicial District court location, file only the original with the clerk. In criminal actions see instruction #4.*
3. **Geographical Area Locations:** *In any action returnable to a Geographical Area court location, except criminal actions, file original and sufficient copies for each party to the action with the clerk. In criminal actions see instruction #4.*
4. **In Criminal and Motor Vehicle Actions** *(Pr. Bk. Secs. 3-4, 3-5): Mail or deliver a copy of the appearance to the prosecuting authority, complete the certification at bottom and file original with the clerk.*
5. **In Summary Process Actions:** *In addition to instruction #2 or #3 above, mail a copy to the attorney for the plaintiff, or if there is no such attorney, to the plaintiff and complete the certification below.*
6. **In Small Claims Matters:** *File the original with the Small Claims area or Housing Session location. Mail or deliver a copy to the attorney or pro se party and complete the certification below.*
7. **For "In-lieu-of" Appearances** *(Pr. Bk. Sec. 3-8): Complete the certification below.*
8. *Pursuant to Pr. Bk. Sec. 17-20, if a party who has been defaulted for failure to appear files an appearance prior to the entry of judgment after default, the default shall automatically be set aside by the clerk.*
9. **In Juvenile Matters:** *Do not use this form. Use form JD-JM-13 Appearance, Juvenile Matters.*

DOCKET NO. **1**	
RETURN DATE **2**	
SCHEDULED COURT DATE *(Criminal/Motor Vehicle Matters)*	

3 NAME OF CASE *(FIRST-NAMED PLAINTIFF VS. FIRST- NAMED DEFENDANT)*

4 ☐ Judicial District ☐ Housing Session ☐ G.A. No. _____   ADDRESS OF COURT *(No., street, town and zip code)*

▼ **PLEASE ENTER THE APPEARANCE OF** ▼

NAME OF PRO SE PARTY *(See "Notice to Pro Se Parties" at bottom)*, OR NAME OF OFFICIAL, FIRM, PROFESSIONAL CORPORATION, OR INDIVIDUAL ATTORNEY **5** | **JURIS NO. OF ATTY. OR FIRM**

MAILING ADDRESS *(No., street, P.O. Box)* | TELEPHONE NO. *(Area code first)*

CITY/TOWN	STATE	ZIP CODE	FAX NO. *(Area code first)*	E-MAIL ADDRESS

in the above-entitled case for: *("X" one of the following)*

6
☐ The Plaintiff.
☐ All Plaintiffs
☐ The following Plaintiff(s) only: _____
☐ The Defendant.
☐ The Defendant for the purpose of the bail hearing only *(in criminal and motor vehicle cases only).*
☐ All Defendants.
☐ The following Defendant(s) only: _____
☐ Other *(Specify)* _____

Note: If other counsel or a pro se party have already appeared for the party or parties indicated above, state whether this appearance is:

☐ In lieu of appearance of attorney or firm or pro se party *(Name)* _____
already on file (P.B. Sec. 3-8) **OR**   *(Name and Juris No.)*
☐ In addition to appearance already on file.

7 SIGNED *(Individual attorney or pro se party)* | NAME OF PERSON SIGNING AT LEFT *(Print or type)* | DATE SIGNED
X

CERTIFICATION | *FOR COURT USE ONLY*

This certification must be completed in summary process cases (Pr. Bk. Sec. 3-5(a)); for "in lieu of" appearances (Pr. Bk. Sec. 3-8); in criminal cases (Pr. Bk. Sec. 3-5(d)); and in small claims matters.

I hereby certify that a copy of the above was mailed/delivered to:

☐ All counsel and pro se parties of record as listed below and on additional sheet. *(For summary process, criminal actions and small claims matters)*

☐ Counsel or the party whose appearance is to be replaced as listed below and on additional sheet. *(For "in lieu of" appearances)*

SIGNED *(Individual attorney or pro se party)* | DATE COPY(IES) MAILED OR DELIVERED
X

NAME OF EACH PARTY SERVED * | ADDRESS AT WHICH SERVICE WAS MADE

* If necessary, attach additional sheet with names of each party served and the address at which service was made.   **APPEARANCE**

Defendant's Appearance

While not required, it is best if the defendant files an Appearance with the court. This document insures that the defendant will receive all mailings from the court about the case, including notification of any court hearings. If the defendant files an Appearance and the plaintiff files any motions or takes action in the court, the plaintiff must notify the defendant by sending copies of anything filed. If the court sends any notices, schedules any hearings, or communicates with the parties in any way, the defendant will only receive these communications if he or she filed an Appearance with the court. If the defendant does not file an Appearance, he or she will not receive notification from the court and the plaintiff need not send copies of documents filed with the court.

The plaintiff does not have to file an Appearance. By signing and filing the Summons, the plaintiff enters his or her Appearance.

INSTRUCTIONS FOR FILLING OUT THE APPEARANCE

1. The court's docket number. If you do not know it, you can get it from the clerk of the superior court.

2. The return date that is on the Divorce Complaint.

3. Your spouse's name and your name as they appear on the Divorce Complaint.

4. Check the box for "Judicial District" and type the address of the superior court listed on the Divorce Complaint. See Appendix A for the addresses of the Connecticut judicial districts.

5. Your name, address, and telephone number. The Juris Number is for lawyers only, so you should leave it blank.

6. Check the box for "Defendant."

7. Sign your name, type or print your name, and enter the date.

You must mail or hand deliver the original to the court, mail a copy to the plaintiff, and keep a copy for yourself.

The Cross Complaint and/or Answer

If you are the defendant, you need not file a Cross Complaint or an Answer.

If you are concerned about whether or not you should file a Cross Complaint and/or Answer, consult with an attorney.

For the Cross Complaint, use the same form as for the Complaint. You may use the Cross Complaint to establish that:

- You want to get a divorce even if the plaintiff permits the complaint to be dismissed.

- The factual data on the Divorce Complaint is incorrect.

- You want general categories of results different from those requested by the plaintiff in the Divorce Complaint.

- You want to allege other grounds for the breakdown of your marriage.

- You disagree that the marriage is irretrievably broken.

Follow the instructions for filling out the Divorce Complaint on page 100. Check the box at the top for Steps 1–8, and fill in the information as it appears on the Divorce Complaint. Follow Steps 9–20 to fill in your version of the information requested in the form, designating yourself as defendant. Do not attach a copy of the Notice of Automatic Orders to the Cross Complaint because these orders go into effect when the Divorce Complaint is served. You also do not need to obtain a case management date because that date was scheduled when the Divorce Complaint was issued and served.

File the original Cross Complaint or Answer with the clerk of the superior court. Mail a copy to the plaintiff and note the mail date on the copy you keep for your records. There is no court fee for filing a Cross Complaint and/or Answer.

You do not necessarily have to be receiving welfare to qualify for a waiver of the fees and costs of a divorce case (Connecticut docket fee and marshal's service fee.) If you feel that you cannot afford these fees, file the application for Waiver of Fees to see if the judge will grant your request.

 The form that lets the court know you have notified the attorney general of the divorce case if you have received or are receiving financial assistance from the state can be found at **www.jud.state. ct.us/forms/fm175.htm**.

 The form to use to request a waiver of certain fees can be found at **www.jud.state.ct.us/ forms/fm075.htm**.

A Special Note for People Who Receive Welfare

If you, your spouse, and/or your children are now receiving financial assistance (from the state of Connecticut or a town) or have received such assistance during the marriage, you must follow some additional procedures.

1. Change paragraph seven of the Divorce Complaint to read: (Name of spouse) is/has received welfare and/or financial assistance from (name town and/or state of Connecticut).

2. Ask for alimony in the "Wherefore" clause of your Divorce Complaint. If you have minor children, ask for custody and child support.

3. After service, mail copies of the Summons, Divorce Complaint, Notice of Automatic Orders, and Affidavit Concerning Children, and marshal's Return of Service (or marshal's affidavit of registered or certified mail or publisher's affidavit) to: The Office of the Attorney General, 55 Elm Street, Hartford, CT 06106. Complete Form JD-FM-175.

4. If you are receiving welfare now or believe that you cannot afford the court's filing fee, marshal's charges, and/or publication costs, you may file an Application for Waiver of Fees/Appointment of Counsel JD-FM-75.

   The court grants these applications only for indigent people. If the court grants the application, the clerk will instruct you how to obtain the services.

5. File the original Summons, Divorce Complaint, Affidavit Concerning Children, and Certification of Notice with the clerk of the superior court.

An assistant attorney general (AAG) will file his or her Appearance. The AAG is the lawyer who represents the state. This means that besides you and your spouse, there is another party to the action—the state of Connecticut.

You must include the AAG along with your spouse in all mailings of court forms and documents. When you receive the AAG's Appearance, it will contain the name and address of the person to whom mail must be directed and with whom you will negotiate to finalize your agreement. If you do not receive an Appearance from the AAG before your final hearing, you should send the office another set of pleadings and call the office in Hartford to confirm receipt.

You are not free to settle your case without the approval and/or participation of the AAG. The state may want to negotiate and/or get court orders for child support and alimony as reimbursement of sums spent in the past and/or that will be spent in the future for the support of a spouse and/or children.

You should seriously consider obtaining legal advice about the impact of receiving welfare on your divorce case. If you are currently receiving welfare, you should contact the legal aid office near you to obtain free legal advice if you qualify.

The legal services system in Connecticut includes the following five programs:

Information about the legal services network in Connecticut with links to each of the five programs can be found at **www.larcc.org/common/ network.htm**.

1. Statewide Legal Services

   Statewide Legal Services (SLS) is available by phone to clients throughout Connecticut. Generally, SLS is the entry point for accessing legal assistance. SLS may provide advice over the phone, mail information, or refer clients to a legal services office or private attorney at no cost to the client.

2. Connecticut Legal Services, Inc.

   Connecticut Legal Services (CLS) provides legal representation to low-income persons throughout the state, except those living in the greater Hartford or New Haven areas.

3. Greater Hartford Legal Assistance

   The Greater Hartford Legal Assistance program (GHLA) provides legal representation to low-income persons who live in the greater Hartford area.

4. New Haven Legal Assistance Association, Inc.

   New Haven Legal Assistance Association (LAA) provides legal services to low-income persons in the greater New Haven and lower Naugatuck Valley areas.

5. Legal Assistance Resource Center

   The Legal Assistance Resource Center of Connecticut (LARCC) coordinates publications, policy advocacy, and staff training for the legal services programs. In addition, LARCC sponsors The Connecticut Alliance for Basic Human Needs (CABHN), a statewide advocacy network. CABHN publishes a free monthly newsletter and conducts community outreach education.

Call Statewide Legal Services first to find out if you qualify for services at (800)453-3320 or (860)344-0380 between 9:00 a.m. and 3:00 p.m., Monday through Friday.

www.jud.state.ct.us/forms/fm176/htm.

MOTION FOR ORDERS BEFORE
JUDGMENT (Pendente Lite)
IN FAMILY CASES

JD-FM-176 Rev. 3-03
C.G.S. § 46b-56, P.B. § 25-24

STATE OF CONNECTICUT
SUPERIOR COURT
www.jud.state.ct.us

COURT USE ONLY
MFORPL

JUDICIAL DISTRICT OF	AT *(Town)*	RETURN DATE *(Mo., day, yr.)*	DOCKET NO.
PLAINTIFF'S NAME *(Last, first, middle initial)*		DEFENDANT'S NAME *(Last, first, middle initial)*	
PLAINTIFF'S ADDRESS *(No., street, town, state, zip code)*		DEFENDANT'S ADDRESS *(No., street, town, state, zip code)*	

The ☐ Plaintiff ☐ Defendant requests court orders concerning *(check all that apply):*

☐ child custody

☐ child support

☐ child visitation (parenting time)

☐ alimony

☐ exclusive use of the family home

☐ appointment of an attorney for my child(ren) under 18

☐ genetic testing for paternity of child _____

☐ medical insurance/expenses

☐ other (specify) _____

I certify that a copy of this motion was mailed/delivered to all counsel and pro se parties of record on:	DATE MAILED OR DELIVERED
SIGNED *(Attorney or pro se party)* **X**	PRINT NAME OF PERSON SIGNING	TELEPHONE NO.
ADDRESS *(No., street, town, state, zip code)*	

NAME OF EACH PARTY SERVED AND ADDRESS AT WHICH SERVICE WAS MADE*

7 ** If necessary, attach additional sheet with name of each party served and the address at which service was made.*

ORDER - TO BE COMPLETED BY THE COURT

The above motion having been heard, it is ordered that:

BY THE COURT	SIGNED *(Judge/Asst. Clerk)*	PRINT NAME	DATE SIGNED

Temporary (*Pendente Lite*) Orders

You should review Chapter 5, Moving from One Household to Two, and Chapter 7, Gathering Information and Preparing Financial Affidavits. These chapters explain the procedures and issues that may be of concern to you between the time you file your case and when the court enters the final divorce judgement.

When you want the court to approve a written temporary agreement and make it into a court order, you should:

1. Prepare the agreement and both sign it in front of a notary, attorney as commissioner of the superior court, or the clerk of the superior court.

2. Prepare and sign Form JD-FM 176, Motion for Orders Before Judgment (*pendente lite*). Check all applicable boxes and the "other" block where you type "approve attached temporary agreement under date of (date) attached as Exhibit 1. Make two photocopies.

3. Write "Exhibit 1" on the first page of your temporary agreement.

4. Attach the original of your agreement to the Motion for Orders Before Judgment, and take or mail it to the clerk of the superior court along with both completed, signed, and notarized Financial Affidavits (see Chapter 7) and an Appearance form for the defendant, if not previously filed.

5. Be sure that you each keep signed copies of your agreement and the Financial Affidavits.

6. You will receive a Short Calendar in the mail from the court. Read the instructions on the Short Calendar and follow them to make your case "ready" by calling the court and notifying your spouse.

7. On the date assigned for your case, you both appear in court. Bring two additional copies of your Motion and Order, along with the Worksheet of the Connecticut Child Support Guidelines (*see* Chapter 9) and the Affidavit Concerning Custody if it is not already filed and your agreement adresses child-related issues.

   NOTE: Each party must file a sworn Financial Affidavit with the court at least five days before the temporary orders hearing date. Since you may not receive the Short Calendar in time to comply with this requirement, it is strongly recommended that the moving party file his or her Financial Affidavit with the motions and send a copy of the affidavit to the responding party with the copies of the motions. Upon receipt of the motions, the responding party should attempt to file his or her Financial Affidavit with the court and send it to the other party as soon as possible.

8. If you cannot appear on the scheduled date, your motion will "go off." Go to the clerk's office at the superior court and fill in and file a Short Calendar List Claim/Reclaim Form JD-CL-6 so that your motion will be scheduled on another Short Calendar. You cannot reclaim any motion that has been filed for more than three months on which no order has been entered or specific hearing date has been assigned beyond the three-month period. If you want to have the court hear the issues in any motion older than three months, you will need to file new motions to replace the old ones.

9. The Short Calendar should tell you the number of the courtroom to go to on the day of your temporary hearing. Otherwise, the clerk should post a docket listing all of the cases for the day in the

hallway. If you can't find the list, go to the clerk's office. When the judge calls your case, stand up and say "Ready, Your Honor." When the judge is ready to hear your motion, he or she will tell you to come to the front of the courtroom to stand at the tables in front of him or her. Ask the judge to approve your agreement and to sign the original order. The judge may ask you some questions about the agreement to be sure that it is fair and equitable.

10. After the judge signs the order you can have the clerk conform (show that the judge signed the order) the two copies.

IF THERE IS NO TEMPORARY AGREEMENT

If you and your spouse cannot agree on your temporary issues, the plaintiff or the defendant can file temporary motions with the court. These motions can address temporary issues of child support; child custody and visitation; alimony; exclusive possession of the home, automobile or other property; payment of debts, attorneys' fees, and costs; and relief from the automatic orders of the complaint.

Filing any temporary motions will result in your case being added to the court's docket for a temporary hearing before the judge. In a case that involves current or past receipt of welfare, the assistant attorney general may also file temporary motions for alimony and/or child support.

If you are considering filing temporary motions, you should obtain legal advice about the procedure and strategy for dealing with these issues. There may be reasons to have the other spouse personally served with an Order to Show Cause related to temporary motions. This guidebook does not cover this procedure. Legal advice is highly recommended if you cannot settle your temporary issues with your spouse. This guidebook only covers basic temporary motion procedures.

The plaintiff can serve the defendant with temporary motions along with the Summons and Divorce Complaint at the beginning of the case. The defendant can mail the plaintiff temporary motions with his or her Appearance and/or Answer and/or Cross-Complaint. Either party may, anytime before the end of the case, mail the temporary motions to the other party. Whether you serve the temporary motions on the other party or mail them to him or her, you must file the original motions with the clerk of the superior court.

1. Complete Form JD-FM-176—Motions for Orders Before Judgment (*Pendente Lite*), which can be found at www.jud.state.ct.us/forms/fm176.htm.

2. If you are the plaintiff and the marshal serves the motions on the defendant with the Summons and Divorce Complaint, you do not need to complete the Certificate of Mailing. In all other instances, whether you are the plaintiff or the defendant, for the Certificate of Mailing, fill in the date you mail the motion, the name and address of the other party (include the Attorney General if that office has entered an appearance), and sign and date it.

3. Make two copies of the motion, one to mail to the other party (or to serve with Summons and Divorce Complaint) and one for your file. File the original with the court.

4. You will receive a Short Calendar in the mail from the court. Read the instructions on the Short Calendar and follow them to mark your case "ready" by calling the court and notifying your spouse.

5. On the date assigned for your case, you both appear in court. Bring two additional copies of your Motion and Order, along with the Worksheet of the Connecticut Child Support Guidelines (*see* Chapter 9) and Affidavit Concerning Custody if the judge will be deciding child-related issues.

    NOTE: Each party must file a sworn Financial Affidavit with the court at least five days before the temporary orders hearing date. Since you may not receive the Short Calendar in time to comply with this requirement, it is strongly recommended that the moving party file his or her Financial Affidavit with the motions and send a copy of the affidavit to the responding party with the copies of the motions. Upon receipt of the motions, the responding party should attempt to file his or her Financial Affidavit with the court and send it to the other party, as soon as possible.

6. If you cannot appear on the scheduled date, your motion will "go off." Go to the clerk's office for the superior court and fill in and file a Short Calendar List Claim/Reclaim Form JD-CL-6 so that your motion will be scheduled on another Short Calendar. You cannot reclaim any motion that has been filed for more than three months on which no order has been entered or specific hearing date has been assigned beyond the three-month period. If you want to have the court hear the issues in any motion older than three months, you will need to file new motions to replace the old ones.

7. The Short Calendar should tell you the number of the courtroom to go to on the day of your temporary hearing. Otherwise, the clerk should post a docket listing all of the cases for the day in the hallway. If you can't find the list, go to the clerk's office. When the judge calls your case, stand up and say "Ready, Your Honor." If you settle your temporary issues with your spouse after you file the motions and before the hearing, you must put those agreements in writing. When the judge is ready to hear your motion, he or she will tell you to come to the front of the courtroom to stand at the tables in front of him or her. Ask the judge to approve your agreement and to sign the original order. The judge may ask you some questions about the agreement to be sure that it is fair and equitable.

8. If you have not agreed by the time the judge calls your case, inform the judge of that fact. In most judicial districts, the judge will then tell you to report to the Family Relations Counselor to attempt mediation of your agreement. If mediation is successful, the Family Relations Counselor will help you put your agreement in writing. You can go back into the courtroom to report to the judge's clerk that you are ready to go on with step 7. If you are unable to resolve your differences, you will have a hearing immediately before the judge, or the clerk will schedule you for another day. It is strongly recommended that you obtain legal advice and/or representation before going forward with a contested temporary orders hearing. In all likelihood, both spouses will testify at the hearing and there are many procedural and substantive issues that can be difficult if you do not have legal representation or advice.

Judgment: Final order signed by the court granting your dissolution of marriage or legal separation. Also known as a decree. Contains all of the terms of your divorce including child custody, alimony and child support, and property division.

This chapter assumes that the defendant has filed an Appearance and that you have reached an agreement so that your divorce will be uncontested. If the defendant does not file an Appearance or appear at the final hearing, the judgment will be by default. You must go before the judge so that orders can enter to the extent of the court's jurisdiction over the defendant. At the conclusion of the hearing, you prepare a different judgment form, called Judgment-Default and enter the terms of the court's order. If the defendant files an Appearance but you have no agreement, the judge will enter orders after a contested trial. You must then type the court's orders in the form of a Judgment of Dissolution of Marriage.

Finishing Your Divorce

After completing the Summons and Divorce Complaint, serving the defendant, and filing your papers with the court, you still have to wait ninety days from the return date before you can finish your divorce. When you are ready to ask the court to sign your final judgment of dissolution or legal separation, you must provide some or all of the papers that follow in this chapter.

If you reach a final agreement with your spouse on all issues, your case is called "uncontested" and you will obtain a "judgment of dissolution of marriage." If your spouse does not file an Appearance and/or Answer and/or Cross Complaint, he or she is a "non-appearing defendant" and you can obtain a "judgment by default." This too gives you a divorce. This section covers all of the forms and procedures to obtain your divorce in these two situations.

You may find, however, that although the defendant has filed an Appearance and/or Answer and/or Cross Complaint, you have not agreed on parenting and/or financial issues with your spouse by the time the ninety days have expired to obtain your divorce. A case that you do not settle that needs a judge to decide the issues is a "contested" case. If only financial and property matters are in dispute, your case is called "limited contested." If child custody and visitation (and financial and property issues, where applicable) are in dispute, the case is called "contested." Most contested cases become uncontested (settled) with time. However, five to ten percent of couples cannot settle all the issues and the judge needs to make the decisions at a trial.

This section does not cover the many complicated issues related to discovering all of the facts, financial and child-related, to present to the judge at your final divorce hearing. It also does not cover how to conduct the actual trial. A limited contested or contested trial is a very serious proceeding with long-term consequences for your entire family. You should seriously consider obtaining legal advice and/or representation if you are unable to settle your case.

DIVORCE AGREEMENT

Before you can get a divorce, you must resolve and write out all the financial and parental issues remaining from your marriage. This written document is sometimes called a separation agreement, settlement agreement, or stipulation, but the term most often used is "divorce agreement."

Your divorce agreement should do the following:

1. Account for and divide all property. See Chapter 10, Property and Debts.

2. Acknowledge and pay, or assign responsibility for paying, all debts, including taxes. See Chapter 10, Property and Debts, and Chapter 12, Taxes.

3. Establish a parenting plan for your children—custody and parenting time—and make commitments about their support. See Chapter 8, Children; Chapter 9, Child Support; and Chapter 12, Taxes.

4. Decide the amount and duration of alimony, if either spouse is to assist in supporting the other. See Chapter 11, Alimony, and Chapter 12, Taxes.

5. Arrange to pay for any costs of the divorce itself: the court filing fee, mediators, lawyers, accountants, recording fees, etc. See Chapter 10, Property and Debts.

6. State when and under what circumstances any of your agreements will change or terminate.

Chapters 8 through 12 are written to help you understand issues related to the negotiation of your separation agreement. Lawyers and/or mediators will probably write up the agreements you reach working with them. If there are still some issues that you work out by yourselves, you need to write them up. While there is no rule or law preventing you from drafting your own divorce agreement, it is strongly recommended that you at least consult with a lawyer or retain a lawyer to write it for you.

The judge will read your divorce agreement in court at the uncontested hearing to be sure it contains certain minimal provisions (support, if there are children; division of property and debts; etc.) The judge will also make sure that your agreement is fair and equitable and does not violate the law. The judge will not help you negotiate your agreement.

The divorce agreement is the most important legal document in your divorce process. Once you sign it and it is approved by the judge and made a court order, it is in virtually all circumstances final. For that reason, no matter what approach you use to resolve issues with your spouse and reach your divorce agreements, the actual written divorce agreement must be carefully crafted. In a collaborative or traditional adversarial case, attorneys draft the divorce agreement. If you mediate your case, many mediators who are licensed lawyers prepare the initial draft of the agreement (*see* Chapter 2 for a discussion of how to work with attorneys to review the draft divorce agreement) and advise you in the development of a final document.

Some people do not mediate but rather represent themselves throughout the process (*see* Chapter 2 for a more complete discussion of this approach and the role of coaching attorneys). For pro se parties, once the agreement is reached, they must prepare a divorce agreement suitable to protect the interests of both spouses (and the children) and that will pass the review and approval of the judge at the uncontested hearing.

If you are pro se and have not mediated your case (or if your mediator does not prepare the final written agreement), you have two choices for the preparation of your divorce agreement:

1. Hire an attorney to prepare the agreement for you (*see* Chapter 2 about coaching counsel). By using this approach, you will obtain legal advice about the terms of your agreement and know that the written document you are giving the court actually represents the deal that you made. The attorney can also help you anticipate the judge's questions and ways to draft the agreement that will be more acceptable to the judge.

2. Use Form JD FM-172 to prepare your own divorce agreement. However, use of this form in no way decreases (in fact it may increase) the need to have legal advice. Use of this form has great potential to cause more problems for you in a number of ways: you could have no agreement on an issue you do not know about but would be important to you if you did know about it; the way you draw up the agreement may be vague and cause you trouble in the future because it is drafted unclearly; you may not prepare it to the satisfaction of the judge, creating delay and problems at your uncontested hearing.

www.jud.state.ct.us/forms/fm172/htm.

DIVORCE (DISSOLUTION OF MARRIAGE) AGREEMENT JD-FM-172 Rev. 9-2000 C.G.S. § 46b-51	STATE OF CONNECTICUT SUPERIOR COURT www.jud.state.ct.us	COURT USE ONLY AGREMNT

JUDICIAL DISTRICT OF	AT (Town)	DOCKET NO.

PLAINTIFF'S NAME (Last, first, middle initial)	DEFENDANT'S NAME (Last, first, middle initial)

1

The wife and husband agree that:

1. Our marriage has broken down irretrievably. (No-fault divorce.)
2. The custody of the child(ren) shall be as follows:
   Legal Custody:

2

   Primary Residence:

3. As to visitation with the child(ren):

3

   Who will pick up/drop off for visits:

   Holiday and school vacation visits:

The amounts / percentages indicated below for child support, health insurance and unreimbursed medical costs, and child care costs must agree with the Child Support and Arrearage Guidelines (available at Clerk's Office) unless you meet one of the deviation criteria listed in the Guidelines.

4. As to current and/or past due child support:

4

☐ Agrees with Child Support and Arrearage Guidelines   ☐ Does not agree (give reason for deviation)   ☐ Do not know

5. As to health insurance and unreimbursed medical costs:

5

☐ Agrees with Child Support and Arrearage Guidelines   ☐ Does not agree (give reason for deviation)   ☐ Do not know

6. As to child care costs:

6

☐ Agrees with Child Support and Arrearage Guidelines   ☐ Does not agree (give reason for deviation)   ☐ Do not know

(Continued...)

7. As to alimony:

7
_____
_____
_____
_____
_____
_____

8
8. As to income withholding:
We agree to a(n)   ☐ IMMEDIATE   ☐ CONTINGENT   income withholding.

9
9. As to division of property:
_____
_____
_____
_____
_____
_____
_____
_____
_____
_____
_____
_____
_____

10
10. As to division of debts:
_____
_____
_____
_____
_____
_____
_____
_____
_____
_____
_____
_____
_____
_____

11
11. As to change of wife's name:
_____
_____
_____

12
12. Other:
_____
_____
_____
_____

We certify that the above statements are our agreement. (Sign in the presence of a Notary/Clerk/Comm. of Superior Court)

13

PLAINTIFF (Print name)	PLAINTIFF'S SIGNATURE	
DEFENDANT (Print name)	DEFENDANT'S SIGNATURE	
SIGNED AND SWORN TO BEFORE ME (Asst. Clerk/Notary Public/Comm. of Superior Court)	AT (Town, state)	DATE SIGNED

INSTRUCTIONS FOR FILLING OUT THE DIVORCE AGREEMENT

1. Fill in this information from the Divorce Complaint.

2. Specify whether you will have joint or sole custody, and designate the primary residence.

3. Details of your parenting plan (if you attended parenting mediation, you could attach the parenting agreement drafted by your mediator).

4. Details of the child support arrangement. Check the applicable box about the Child Support Guidelines.

5. Details of the health insurance and medical insurance payments for the children. Check the applicable box about the Child Support Guidelines.

6. Details of child care costs. Check the applicable box about the Child Support Guidelines.

7. Details of the alimony agreement.

8. Check the box about the wage withholding for child support and/or alimony.

9. Details about the division of the property.

10. Details about the division of debt.

11. If the wife is changing her name, put that name here.

12. If you have any other agreement not covered by the other agreements, list them here.

13. Print both names, and sign before a notary or clerk of the court.

SCHEDULING YOUR UNCONTESTED DIVORCE HEARING

The Notice of Automatic Orders attached to the complaint establishes a case management date. In some courthouses, the case management date is the date when you appear in court with the required documentation and have your uncontested hearing. However, if you plan on being divorced on the case management date, you should call the clerk's office just to make sure that the judge will be hearing uncontested cases on the case management date. If not, ask the clerk what day and time uncontested divorce cases are scheduled, and complete a Case Management Agreement.

There are a number of circumstances where you would not have the uncontested divorce hearing on the case management date:

1. The court is not hearing uncontested cases on that date.

2. Your settlement process, through mediation, collaboration, or your own discussions, may not be done. Or, you may have settled all the terms of your divorce but the paperwork is not done. Either way, you do not need to go on the "trial track" but you are not quite ready by the case management date.

3. The scheduled case management date is not convenient for your schedule, your spouse's, and/or the attorney's.

4. For tax, emotional, or other reasons, the case is settled but you have agreed to delay the entry of the actual divorce judgment.

In any of these circumstances exist in your uncontested case, you do not have to appear in court on the case management date if you do not want to. Complete Form JD-FM-163 Case Management Agreement) and mail or deliver it to the court before the case management date. You may also personally appear in court on the case management date and tell the judge the date you want to schedule your hearing.

If you do not have an agreement about custody and visitation, your case is considered *contested* and you must appear in court on the case management date.

Although Forms JD-FM-166 A, B, and C specify the dates for scheduling uncontested hearings, sometimes the date you pick consistent with the form is not acceptable to the court. If that happens, you will receive a notice in the mail with the new date.

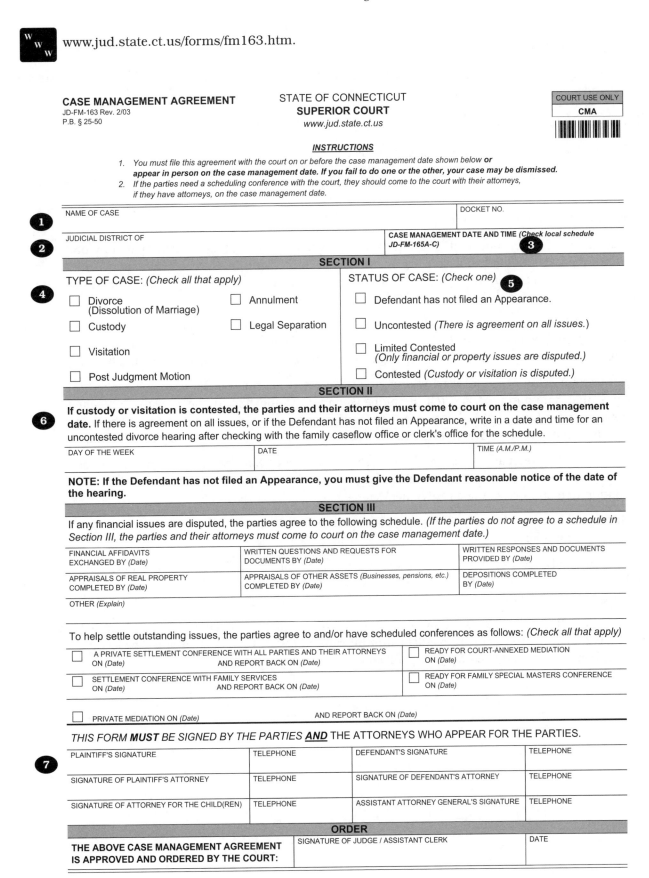

www.jud.state.ct.us/forms/fm163.htm.

CASE MANAGEMENT AGREEMENT
JD-FM-163 Rev. 2/03
P.B. § 25-50

STATE OF CONNECTICUT
SUPERIOR COURT
www.jud.state.ct.us

COURT USE ONLY
CMA

INSTRUCTIONS

1. *You must file this agreement with the court on or before the case management date shown below* **or** **appear in person on the case management date. If you fail to do one or the other, your case may be dismissed.**
2. *If the parties need a scheduling conference with the court, they should come to the court with their attorneys, if they have attorneys, on the case management date.*

1 NAME OF CASE | DOCKET NO.

2 JUDICIAL DISTRICT OF | CASE MANAGEMENT DATE AND TIME *(Check local schedule JD-FM-165A-C)* **3**

SECTION I

4 TYPE OF CASE: *(Check all that apply)*

☐ Divorce (Dissolution of Marriage)
☐ Annulment

☐ Custody
☐ Legal Separation

☐ Visitation

☐ Post Judgment Motion

STATUS OF CASE: *(Check one)* **5**

☐ Defendant has not filed an Appearance.

☐ Uncontested *(There is agreement on all issues.)*

☐ Limited Contested *(Only financial or property issues are disputed.)*

☐ Contested *(Custody or visitation is disputed.)*

SECTION II

6 **If custody or visitation is contested, the parties and their attorneys must come to court on the case management date.** If there is agreement on all issues, or if the Defendant has not filed an Appearance, write in a date and time for an uncontested divorce hearing after checking with the family caseflow office or clerk's office for the schedule.

DAY OF THE WEEK | DATE | TIME *(A.M./P.M.)*

NOTE: If the Defendant has not filed an Appearance, you must give the Defendant reasonable notice of the date of the hearing.

SECTION III

If any financial issues are disputed, the parties agree to the following schedule. *(If the parties do not agree to a schedule in Section III, the parties and their attorneys must come to court on the case management date.)*

FINANCIAL AFFIDAVITS EXCHANGED BY *(Date)* | WRITTEN QUESTIONS AND REQUESTS FOR DOCUMENTS BY *(Date)* | WRITTEN RESPONSES AND DOCUMENTS PROVIDED BY *(Date)*

APPRAISALS OF REAL PROPERTY COMPLETED BY *(Date)* | APPRAISALS OF OTHER ASSETS *(Businesses, pensions, etc.)* COMPLETED BY *(Date)* | DEPOSITIONS COMPLETED BY *(Date)*

OTHER *(Explain)*

To help settle outstanding issues, the parties agree to and/or have scheduled conferences as follows: *(Check all that apply)*

☐ A PRIVATE SETTLEMENT CONFERENCE WITH ALL PARTIES AND THEIR ATTORNEYS ON *(Date)* AND REPORT BACK ON *(Date)*

☐ READY FOR COURT-ANNEXED MEDIATION ON *(Date)*

☐ SETTLEMENT CONFERENCE WITH FAMILY SERVICES ON *(Date)* AND REPORT BACK ON *(Date)*

☐ READY FOR FAMILY SPECIAL MASTERS CONFERENCE ON *(Date)*

☐ PRIVATE MEDIATION ON *(Date)* | AND REPORT BACK ON *(Date)*

*THIS FORM **MUST** BE SIGNED BY THE PARTIES **AND** THE ATTORNEYS WHO APPEAR FOR THE PARTIES.*

7 PLAINTIFF'S SIGNATURE | TELEPHONE | DEFENDANT'S SIGNATURE | TELEPHONE

SIGNATURE OF PLAINTIFF'S ATTORNEY | TELEPHONE | SIGNATURE OF DEFENDANT'S ATTORNEY | TELEPHONE

SIGNATURE OF ATTORNEY FOR THE CHILD(REN) | TELEPHONE | ASSISTANT ATTORNEY GENERAL'S SIGNATURE | TELEPHONE

ORDER

THE ABOVE CASE MANAGEMENT AGREEMENT IS APPROVED AND ORDERED BY THE COURT: | SIGNATURE OF JUDGE / ASSISTANT CLERK | DATE

INSTRUCTIONS FOR COMPLETING THE CASE MANAGEMENT AGREEMENT
IN AN UNCONTESTED CASE

Obtain the Case Management Agreement from the clerk's office at the superior court. The form will be similar to the sample in this guidebook.

1. Fill in the name of the case and docket number.

2. Insert the judicial district where your case is filed.

3. Insert the date and time of the case management date from the Notice of Automatic Orders attached to the Divorce Complaint.

4. Check the "Dissolution of Marriage" box.

5. Check the box for "Uncontested" if you have a separation settlement agreement signed by both of you or if your case is settled and you are in the process of drafting your agreement. Check the box "Defendant has not filed an Appearance" if your spouse has not filed an Appearance and you do not have an agreement.

6. Forms JD-FM-166 A, B, and C list the dates and times uncontested divorce hearings are held at each court location. Depending on the reason you are scheduling the uncontested hearing after the case management date, you and your spouse need to agree to the date you will schedule the hearing.

    If you are not ready to go forward with your uncontested hearing on the date you picked, appear in court at that date and time and tell the judge when you would like the hearing to be rescheduled. In almost all cases the judge will accommodate your request, provided that you are planning to appear for the uncontested hearing at a date and time set aside for uncontested hearings at the court location.

    Section III of the form applies only to cases where the parties have not reached an agreement in their case. It requires these people to establish time limits for trial preparation and to elect a method of mediation to help in reaching an agreement.

7. Both parties (or only the plaintiff if the defendant has not filed an Appearance) sign here and include their phone numbers.

You must hand deliver the form to the clerk of the superior court or mail it if there is enough time for it to arrive before the case management date. Keep a copy of the completed agreement form with a notation of the date that you sent a copy to the defendant if he or she has not signed the form.

6. While Forms JD-FM-166 A, B, and C list the dates and times uncontested hearings are held at each court location, you may want to confirm this information with the court because procedures change and the form may be outdated for your judicial district.

What to Bring to the Final Uncontested Hearing

The copies referred to in this list are for the use of the court. Remember that each spouse should keep a signed copy of each document filed with the court. You should bring:

1. The original and two copies of your completed original divorce agreement signed by both of you and notarized. (See Chapters 8 through 12 for how to negotiate the terms of your agreement.) If your spouse cannot be found or refused to cooperate, then you will not have a separation agreement. You will tell the judge what orders you want, and to the extent that the court has jurisdiction, the judge's orders will be entered and you will write them on the judgment form.

2. A Financial Affidavit for each of you, signed and notarized. You will file a single Financial Affidavit for yourself if your spouse cannot be found or refused to cooperate. See Chapter 7.

3. The Child Support Worksheet. See Chapter 9.

4. The Dissolution of Marriage Report. See page 138.

5. The Advisement of Rights, if there is not going to be an immediate income withholding. Or, the Notice of Income Withholding an immediate income withholding. See page 140.

6. The Parenting Education Order for each of you if you attended parenting education classes. See page 144.

7. The Affidavit Concerning Children (if not filed previously). See page 106.

8. The Military Affidavit (if your spouse does not file an Appearance and does not appear at the hearing).

9. The Original and one copy of each Qualified Domestic Relations Order. The original is for the court, and you will ask the clerk to conform the copy (or provide a certified copy if required by the plan administrator) so that you can send it to the plan administrator for dividing the retirement account and/or pension. See page 268.

www.jud.state.ct.us/forms/fm181/htm

DISSOLUTION OF MARRIAGE
REPORT
JD-FM-181 Rev. 7/2001
P.B. § 25-58

STATE OF CONNECTICUT
SUPERIOR COURT
www.jud.state.ct.us

INSTRUCTIONS
1. To be completed by the Attorney for the Plaintiff or, if Pro Se, by the Plaintiff.
2. Clerk to complete section 2.

PART 1 *(To be completed by Attorney for the Plaintiff)*

HUSBAND

1

NAME OF HUSBAND *(First, middle, last)*

USUAL RESIDENCE *(Number and street)* | CITY OR TOWN

COUNTY | STATE | BIRTHPLACE *(State or Foreign Country)* | DATE OF BIRTH *(Mo., Day, Year)*

WIFE

2

NAME OF WIFE *(First, middle, last)* | MAIDEN NAME *(Last name only)*

USUAL RESIDENCE *(Number and street)* | CITY OR TOWN

COUNTY | STATE | BIRTHPLACE *(State or Foreign Country)* | DATE OF BIRTH *(Mo., Day, Year)*

MARITAL HISTORY

3

PLACE OF THIS MARRIAGE *(City)* | COUNTY | STATE

DATE OF MARRIAGE *(Mo., Day, Year)* | APPROXIMATE DATE COUPLE SEPARATED *(Month, Year)*

4

NUMBER OF CHILDREN BORN ALIVE OF THIS MARRIAGE | NUMBER OF CHILDREN STILL LIVING | NUMBER OF CHILDREN UNDER 18 YEARS OF AGE

5

PLAINTIFF
☐ HUSBAND   ☐ WIFE | CSSD FAMILY SERVICES EVALUATION
☐ YES   ☐ NO | CSSD FAMILY SERVICES MEDIATION
☐ YES   ☐ NO

PUBLIC ASSISTANCE RECIPIENT
☐ YES   ☐ NO | AMOUNT OF ASSISTANCE MONTHLY

6

ATTORNEY FOR MINOR CHILD(REN)
☐ YES   ☐ NO | GUARDIAN AD LITEM FOR MINOR CHILD(REN)
☐ YES   ☐ NO

ATTORNEY FOR PLAINTIFF (IF APPLICABLE) *(Name)* | ATTORNEY'S ADDRESS (IF APPLICABLE) *(No., street, city, state, zip code)*

INFORMATION FOR STATISTICAL PURPOSES ONLY: (To be completed by Attorney for the Plaintiff or, if Pro Se, by the Plaintiff)

7

	RACE *(White, Black, Native American, etc., specify)*	NO. OF THIS MARRIAGE *(First, Second, etc. specify)*	IF PREVIOUSLY MARRIED, HOW MANY ENDED BY		EDUCATION - SPECIFY HIGHEST GRADE COMPLETED		
			DEATH	DIVORCE OR ANNULMENT	ELEMENTARY *(0,1,2,3, thru 8)*	HIGH SCHOOL *(1,2,3, or 4)*	COLLEGE *(1,2,3, 4 or 5+)*
HUSBAND		FOR HUSBAND	FOR HUSBAND	FOR HUSBAND	HUSBAND	HUSBAND	HUSBAND
WIFE		FOR WIFE	FOR WIFE	FOR WIFE	WIFE	WIFE	WIFE

PART 2 *(To be completed by the Clerk of Superior Court)*

DECREE

DATE OF DECREE *(Mo., Day, Year)* | TYPE OF DECREE
☐ ABSOLUTE DIVORCE   ☐ ANNULMENT | DATE WRIT RETURNABLE *(Month, Year)*

COUNTY OF DECREE | DOCKET NO.
FA | LEGAL GROUNDS FOR DISSOLUTION *(Specify)*

CASE CONTESTED
☐ YES   ☐ NO | CUSTODY OF MINOR CHILDREN TO
☐ HUSBAND   ☐ WIFE   ☐ JOINT   ☐ NOT APPLICABLE

DECREE GRANTED TO
☐ HUSBAND   ☐ WIFE | TITLE OF OFFICIAL | SIGNED *(Clerk or Assistant Clerk)*

INSTRUCTIONS FOR FILLING OUT THE DISSOLUTION OF MARRIAGE REPORT

1. Husband's full name, address, birthplace, and date of birth.

2. Wife's full name, address, birthplace, and date of birth.

3. Place and date of marriage, along with the approximate date of your separation.

4. Total number of children, the number currently living, and the number under eighteen years old.

5. Check the box designating which spouse is the plaintiff.

6. Check the applicable boxes.

7. Fill in statistical information for husband and wife.

Leave the rest of the form blank.

www.jud.state.ct.us/forms/fm071/htm

ADVISEMENT OF RIGHTS

Re: Income Withholding

I. You have the right to present any evidence to the court as to why an order for withholding effective immediately should not be ordered.

II. EXEMPTIONS: If your income is subject to a withholding order, a portion of your income will not be withheld. Only disposable income is subject to a withholding order. Disposable income means that part of the income of an individual remaining after deduction from that income of amounts required to be withheld for the payment of federal, state and local income taxes, employment taxes, normal retirement contributions, union dues and initiation fees and group life and health insurance premiums. The amount withheld may not exceed the maximum amount permitted under section 1673 of title 15 of the United States Code: If you are supporting a spouse or dependent child other than the spouse or child with respect to whose support the order is issued, the maximum amount of your disposable income that may be withheld is 50% of such income, unless you are twelve weeks or more in arrears in which case the maximum is 55% of such income. If you are not supporting a spouse or dependent child other than the spouse or child with respect to whose support the order is issued, the maximum amount of your disposable income that may be withheld is 60% of such income unless you are twelve weeks or more in arrears in which case the maximum is 65%. In no event, however, under state law may you be left with less than 85% of the first $145 of disposable income per week.

III. You have the right to claim the exemptions listed above or any other applicable state or federal exemptions with respect to income withholding orders.

IV. The computation of the amount withheld will be done by the payer of the income based on information supplied by the court. If you believe that an incorrect amount of your income is being withheld due to incorrect information being supplied to the payer of the income and you would like the amount withheld modified, you must request a court hearing.

V. You have a right to seek a modification of, or raise a defense to, the support order by filing a proper motion with the court.

This is to certify that this document was read to me or read by me in a language that I understand. A copy of this statement has been given to me.

1
_____   _____
Signature   Date

This is to attest that the above document was signed in my presence.

2
_____   _____
Signature/Title   Date

3 *Check the box below if the parties have completed the "Waiver" on the back/page 2 of this form.*

☐ "Waiver of Right to Immediate Income Withholding Order" completed on back/page 2.

JD-FM-71 Rev. 6-03
C.G.S. § 52-362

Advisement of Rights

This form is required in all cases with child support or alimony. Even if you are not activating immediate income withholding, the obligor must complete the Advisement of Rights form.

INSTRUCTIONS FOR FILLING OUT THE ADVISEMENT OF RIGHTS FORM

1. The obligor (spouse who owes the child support and/or alimony) signs on the line that says "signature" and fills in the date signed.

2. Any person (including the other spouse) may witness the obligor's signature. The witness signs on the signature/title line and repeats the date.

3. Check this box if there is not going to be an immediate wage withholding.

Waiver of Right to Immediate Income Withholding Order

If you and your spouse agree to make the Income Withholding Order "contingent" (meaning it will go into effect only if the obligor defaults on his support obligation), you both sign the Waiver of Right to Immediate Income Withholding Order.

If the support is going to be withheld from income, you would bring the Income Withholding Order to the final hearing. If you waive the immediate income withholding and if your spouse fails to pay child support and/or alimony in the future, you can request activation of the contingent wage assignment. See Chapter 13.

The waiver is on the reverse side of the Advisement of Rights Form. Check the box at the bottom of the advisement, and complete the following on the reverse side:

WAIVER OF RIGHT TO IMMEDIATE INCOME WITHHOLDING ORDER

NAME OF CASE			DOCKET NO.	
The undersigned parties agree that a contingent and not an immediate income withholding order shall issue in this case.				
OBLIGOR	DATE SIGNED	OBLIGEE		DATE SIGNED
OTHER	DATE SIGNED	OTHER		DATE SIGNED
WITNESS	DATE SIGNED	WITNESS		DATE SIGNED

INSTRUCTIONS FOR FILLING OUT THE WAIVER OF RIGHT TO IMMEDIATE INCOME WITHHOLDING ORDER

1. Fill in this information from the Divorce Complaint.

2. The obligor signs here and fills in the date signed.

3. The obligee (recipient spouse) signs here and fills in the date signed.

4. A witness signs and repeats the date on this line. Any person may witness the obligor and/or the obligee's signature.

www.jud.state.ct.us/forms/fm178/htm

AFFIDAVIT CONCERNING MILITARY SERVICE

JD-FM-178 Rev. 7-99
P.B. § 17-21

STATE OF CONNECTICUT SUPERIOR COURT

COURT USE ONLY
AE

INSTRUCTIONS

Anyone who knows the military status of the defendant may complete the form below. You must swear that your statement is true and sign it in front of a court clerk, a notary public, or an attorney who will also sign and date the affidavit. Make one copy for yourself and give the original to the court clerk.

EXPLANATION: A military service affidavit is required in every case where the defendant has not filed an Appearance form with the court clerk's office by the time of the court hearing. The purpose is to protect men and women serving in the U.S. military from getting a court judgment against them without first receiving notice of the lawsuit and a chance to defend the case. The affidavit gives the court the necessary facts to find that the defendant is not in the U.S military.

①

JUDICIAL DISTRICT OF	AT *(Town)*	RETURN DATE *(Mo., day, year)*	DOCKET NO.
PLAINTIFF'S NAME *(Last, first, middle initial)*		DEFENDANT'S NAME *(Last, first, middle initial)*	

I certify that the following is true *(check all that apply and complete)*:

②

☐ 1. The defendant is in the U.S. Military.

☐ 2. The defendant is not in the U.S. Military. I know this because:

③

☐ the defendant is working at _____

☐ the defendant currently lives at _____

☐ the defendant is _____ years old.

☐ other *(state reasons)*: _____

_____

_____

☐ 3. I do not know whether the defendant is in the U.S. military service.

SIGNATURE		PRINT NAME	
SIGNED AND SWORN TO BEFORE ME *(Asst. Clerk/Notary Public/Comm. of Sup. Court)*		AT *(Town, State)*	DATE SIGNED

Affidavit Concerning Military Service

You only need this form to prove that the defendant is not in the United States Military Service if the defendant does not file an Appearance or does not appear at the hearing. If you absolutely do not know the whereabouts of your spouse, you must get military certificates to confirm that he or she is not presently in the military. You should mail your letter to each military branch no sooner than sixty days after the return date, preferably at the same time you file your Case Management Agreement Form.

Send a cover letter to each branch and ask for a Soldier and Sailor's Relief Act Certificate of Military Service for your spouse. You must include the following information:

1. Spouse's full name (including all names used by him or her), birth date, and Social Security number

2. Date of marriage

Enclose in each letter a certified check or money order for the fee indicated. If you file an Application for Waiver of Fees (*see* page 122) you may qualify for a waiver of this fee by putting "military certificates" in the "other" box and mailing a copy of the order with your cover letter stating that the court has found you to be indigent and you are therefore not required to send the fee.

When you receive all of the military certificates, you can prepare the military affidavit and attach your certificates to it.

INSTRUCTIONS FOR FILLING OUT THE AFFIDAVIT CONCERNING MILITARY SERVICE

1. Fill out this information as you did on the Divorce Complaint.

2. Check this box if the defendant is in the military.

3. If the defendant is not in the military, check the appropriate box. If you do not know the whereabouts of your spouse, attach your military certificates to the affidavit and state after the last box "See Attached Certificates." If you have not obtained military certificates because you have other information about his or her whereabouts check "other" and list your information (such as seeing your spouse, speaking with him or her, etc.).

You must sign and swear to this form before a notary, attorney, or clerk of the superior court.

www.jud.state.ct.us/forms/fm149/htm

PARENTING EDUCATION
PROGRAM - ORDER,
CERTIFICATE AND RESULTS
JD-FM-149 Rev. 9-2000
C.G.S. §§ 46b-1, 46b-56, 46b-69b, 46b-231(m)(12)

STATE OF CONNECTICUT
SUPERIOR COURT
www.jud.state.ct.us

FOR COURT USE ONLY
☐ ORDPEP (Order for participation)
☐ FNOPEPF (Finding of inability to pay)
☐ CERTPEP (Certification of results)
COURT LOCATION

INSTRUCTIONS

TO PARTICIPANT: 1. Provide docket number if available in designated box. 2. Complete Section III if you are attending the Program to comply with the Automatic Orders or to comply with an order of the court or family support magistrate. 3. If you believe you are indigent or are unable to pay, complete and submit form JD-FM-75, Application for Waiver of Fees/Appointment of Counsel prior to attending the program. 4. YOU MUST bring this form and any approved Fee Waiver form to the service provider. 5. Select service provider from a list available at the clerk's office and contact that provider to arrange attendance and to inform it of any individual that you name in Section III. 6. Give original and ALL copies of the form to service provider.

TO CLERK: 1. If program participation is ordered by the court or family support magistrate, enter court location and docket number at right and complete section I or II as appropriate. 2. Keep gold copy and give original and remaining copies to participant.

TO SERVICE PROVIDER: 1. Complete section IV and return original and green copy to the appropriate Family Division Office. 2. Give/send pink copy to participant. 3. Keep yellow copy for your records.

TO FAMILY SERVICES: 1. Upon receipt of Completion Certificate from service provider, complete section V and forward original to the superior court listed. 2. Keep green copy for your records.

DOCKET NO.

1

SECTION I - COURT ORDER (To be completed by Clerk)

2

NAME OF PARTICIPANT

The above-named participant has been ordered to participate in a parenting education program established pursuant to C.G.S.§46b-69b. The court finds that this individual:

☐   IS ABLE to pay directly to the service provider the appropriate fee for participating in a parenting education program.

☐   IS INDIGENT OR UNABLE to pay to participate in a parenting education program and all costs for participation in such a program shall be covered by the service provider pursuant to the provisions of C.G.S. §46b-69b.

BY THE COURT (Print or type name of Judge)	SIGNED (Judge, Asst. Clerk)	DATE ORDERED

SECTION II - FAMILY SUPPORT MAGISTRATE DIVISION ORDER (To be completed by Clerk)

NAME OF PARTICIPANT

All parties being present before the Family Support Magistrate Division, it is ordered that the above-named participant participate in a parenting education program established pursuant to C.G.S. §46b-69b. It is found that such participation is necessary and that this individual:

☐   IS ABLE to pay directly to the service provider the appropriate fee for participating in a parenting education program.

☐   IS INDIGENT OR UNABLE to pay to participate in a parenting education program and all costs for participation in such a program shall be covered by the service provider pursuant to the provisions of C.G.S. §46b-69b.

BY THE FAMILY SUPPORT MAGISTRATE DIVISION (Print or type name of FSM)	SIGNED (FSM, Asst. Clerk)	DATE ORDERED

SECTION III - PARTICIPANT INFORMATION (To be completed by Participant - print or type)

NAME AND ADDRESS OF PARTICIPANT (No., street, town and zip code)

3

"X" IF APPLICABLE   SPECIFY NAME OF INDIVIDUAL

☐   Participant requests not to be assigned by the service provider to same group as:

☐   "X" this box if you are attending the parenting education program to comply with the Automatic Orders (Practice Book § 25-5).

SECTION IV - COMPLETION CERTIFICATE (To be completed by Service Provider)

NAME OF SERVICE PROVIDER

DATE(S) OF PARTICIPATION	LOCATION AT WHICH PROGRAM WAS PROVIDED

TO: The Court Support Services Division, Family Services Unit of the Superior Court

The above-named participant was scheduled to participate in our Parenting Education Program. It is certified that the participant:

☐   satisfactorily completed the program.

☐   did not satisfactorily complete the program for the following reason(s):   ☐ lack of attendance.   ☐ other (specify below):

SIGNED (Authorized Person)	PRINT OR TYPE NAME OF PERSON SIGNING AT LEFT	DATE SIGNED

SECTION V - PARTICIPATION RESULTS (To be completed by Family Services)

TO: The Superior Court

The Court Support Services Division, Family Services Unit of the Superior Court certifies the results of participation as indicated above.

SIGNED (Authorized Family Division Person)	PRINT OR TYPE NAME OF PERSON SIGNING AT LEFT	DATE SIGNED

Parenting Education Program—Order, Certificate, and Results

If you have minor children, you must attend parenting education classes within sixty days of the return date unless the judge waives this requirement (*see* page 181). Take the Parenting Education Program Form to your parenting education class for the provider to sign. Each parent must complete his or her own form. This form certifies to the court your compliance with the requirement, and each spouse must sign and file one.

INSTRUCTIONS FOR FILLING OUT THE PARENTING EDUCATION PROGRAM—ORDER, CERTIFICATE, AND RESULTS

1. Docket number.

2. Your name.

3. If you do not want to attend classes in the same group as your spouse, check this box and fill in his or her name and place an "x" in this box.

Leave the other sections blank.

Uncontested Hearing: Appearance by one or both spouses before a judge to present their final separation agreement and request that a final judgement of divorce be entered by the court.

Directions to all Judicial District Courthouses can be found at **www.jud.state.ct.us/ directory/directory/ctinfo1.htm# directions**.

At the Hearing

Plan to be at the hearing on time, even fifteen minutes early, to allow for any delays you have getting to the court and parking.

If you are divorcing on a date after the case management date, you will have notified the court by filing a Case Management Agreement or by appearing in court on the case management date. You should receive written notification from the court of the date and time for your uncontested hearing. There may be a reason you are unable to attend the hearing on the scheduled date. If so, call the clerk of the superior court and ask to speak to the appropriate person. If the clerk is willing to reschedule the hearing over the phone, he or she will tell you the new date and time and mail out another notice. If you cannot reschedule it by phone, in most instances, your case will come up again on another uncontested calendar within a few weeks. After a certain number of times (usually about three), the case will be dismissed if you do not appear in court at any of the designated times.

If you do not receive notification of the date and time of your uncontested hearing in the mail or subsequent notices don't arrive after thirty to forty-five days, call or go to the office of the clerk of the superior court and ask about the status of your case. Your form may be lost and you may need to file another one.

The notification you get in the mail from the court may tell you the number of the courtroom at the courthouse where you will have your uncontested hearing. If the calendar does not give this information, the family docket may be on a list displayed on the wall when you first enter the building. Ask the marshal as you go through security if there is a posted list. If all else fails, go to the clerk's office and find out where your hearing will be.

Report to the clerk in the courtroom to let him or her know you are there to get divorced. Then, wait in the courtroom until the judge opens court. Whenever the judge is in the courtroom you must listen very carefully to what is going on. The judge may read a list of cases and you must listen for your name. In some cases, instead of calling the case by name the judge may ask if anyone is "ready." Either way, stand up and say to the judge "Ready, Your Honor." By doing this, you are letting the judge know that you are there and ready to have your hearing. The judge may ask you to come forward to start your hearing. However, it is more likely that you will wait until the judge calls your name a second time for the hearing to start. There will be other cases scheduled for your day so you may need to wait through other hearings. This is an opportunity to see how your judge handles uncontested hearings. Also, the judge could tell you to go to another court-room for your hearing. If so, go to that courtroom and wait for the judge to call your case there.

Your manner of dress should show respect for yourself and for the legal process. Avoid jeans, shorts, undershirts, tank tops, or halter tops.

When the judge calls your case, stand up and say "Ready your Honor," then come up to the tables before the judge. If you have not already done so, hand all your final papers to the clerk as you are directed. The judge or clerk will ask you to take the witness stand and swear you in. Remain standing until the judge or clerk administers the oath. Then, state your name, spelling your last name. Sit down and wait for the judge to ask you questions. Everything you say will be taken down either by a legal stenogra-pher or by tape recording.

When the plaintiff is done with the primary testimony, the judge may ask the defendant some questions. Whenever the judge is questioning or addressing you, listen very carefully and answer truthfully since you are sworn under oath to tell the truth in your testimony. You can look at your notes and the copies of your doc-uments in your file during the hearing. The judge has the right to ask you what you are reading from and even to ask to see it.

Sample Testimony for Final Uncontested Hearing

1. My name is _____ I am the plaintiff/defendant.

2. I (or _____) have been a resident in the state of Connecticut for more than one year. (See page 92 for other grounds if this does not apply to you). Neither I, my children, nor my spouse has received assistance from the state of Connecticut or any town (if applicable).

3. The defendant/plaintiff is _____. His/Her address is _____. He/She was served by _____ (personal service, mailing, publication). He/She is/is not present now.

4. We were married on _____ (date) in the town of _____ , county of _____ , state of _____ (or country of _____). The wife's maiden name at the time of the marriage was _____ (maiden name).

5. We have been separated since _____ (date) .

6. The following minor children were born or adopted as issue of this marriage: _____ (name), born on _____ (date).

(Repeat for all children.)

   OR

There were no children born or adopted during this marriage.

7. I am (or my wife is/is not) not/now pregnant. This child is/is not a child of this marriage.

8. My marriage to _____ is irretrievably broken. There is no reasonable prospect of a reconciliation.

9. Our minor child(ren) is (are) primarily residing with _____ and have been so since _____ (date). We have filed the required custody affidavit.

10. I request that the sole legal and physical custody, and control of our minor child(ren) be awarded to _____ . I believe that this is in the best interest of the children. I request visitation rights be granted to the plaintiff/defendant as written in our divorce agreement.

    OR

    I request that we be granted joint legal custody as written in our divorce agreement which includes a description of our agreement for parenting (visitation) time. I request that primary residential custody be awarded as detailed in our divorce agreement (if applicable).

11. We attended parenting education and have filed the certificate with the court.

12. I request child support in the amount of _____ be awarded to _____ and/or that other expenses for our children be shared as set forth in our divorce agreement. We have calculat-

ed the amount of child support by using the Connecticut Child Support Guidelines and Worksheet A, both of which we are filing with the court today. My total monthly income and expenses are shown on my Financial Affidavit. The defendant's income and expenses are shown on his/her Financial Affidavit. We have filed our Financial Affidavits with the court today.

OR

Our child support agreement deviates from the Child Support Guidelines and we ask that the court approve this deviation because _____ .

OR

Our joint net weekly income is more than $2,500 per week and the Child Support Guidelines Worksheet shows the presumptive amount. We request child support in the amount of $_____ , etc.

13. We have agreed to an immediate wage withholding or believe we should be excused from this requirement because _____ .

We have filed the Advisement of Rights and Waiver with the court today.

14. I request alimony in the amount of $_____ be awarded to _____ under the terms of our written divorce agreement.

OR

I do not desire that alimony be awarded to me and/or to _____ . I understand that if I/we do not ask for alimony now, we can never come back and ask for it.

 CAUTION You must include this waiver in your testimony and in your written agreement if you are waiving alimony.

15. I request the division of property that we have agreed to in our divorce agreement (and that this court sign the Qualified Domestic Relations Order provided, if applicable).

16. I request that the _____ and I be/ordered to be responsible for the marital debts as we agreed in the divorce agreement and that each of us be responsible for our own debts after that date.

17. All of the above requests are agreed to by the plaintiff and defendant as set forth in our divorce agreement. I request that the divorce agreement in its written entirety be approved by the court and adopted into the judgement as an order of court.

18. I request that the court enter a judgment dissolving my marriage to the defendant/plaintiff.

19. (Optional) I request that my former name of _____ be restored to me.

To see and print the record of your divorce, insert your name and the judicial district in which you were divorced at **www.jud2.state. ct.us/civil_inquiry/GetParty.asp**.

 Certified Copy: A copy of any order of court on which the clerk has signed under seal that it is a true copy of an actual order of court.

It's a Matter of Courtesy

You should generally stand whenever you are in court and are speaking to the judge, unless you are on the witness stand where you may sit in the chair provided. You should address the judge as "Your Honor" or as "Judge" depending on his or her last name.

HOW DO YOU KNOW THAT YOU ARE DIVORCED?

After the judge has read the documents and heard your testimony, he or she will verbally enter your divorce judgment and you will be divorced as of that moment.

However, some people like to have written evidence of the divorce.

When you are in court for the divorce, most courts will print from the computer a judgment form which is your written evidence of the divorce. To rollover IRAs, sometimes to remarry, and for insurance companies or other institutions you may need a certified (raised seal) copy of something officially showing you are divorced. Since this stays in the court file, you must ask the court clerk to provide certified copies. The fee for a certified copy of your judgment is $25. You may also obtain a statement from the court of your divorce for $2. If you need an official copy, make sure you ask what will be sufficient.

What to Do If the Judge Does Not Approve Your Agreement

If the judge does not approve your divorce agreement and/or does not enter the divorce judgment, he or she will tell you why. It might be that you left out one of the necessary forms, did not wait the full ninety days, or did not sign one of the papers. It may be that the court did not think some provision(s) of your divorce agreement was fair or complete. You may:

- supply the missing form

- provide the missing signature

- wait the correct number of days

- amend or complete your separation agreement to conform to the court's concerns

If the judge is questioning your divorce agreement, you may be able, if both spouses are present, to agree to the changes right there and hand-write the changes into your divorce agreement. You can also ask for a continuance to a later date to give you both time to deal with the objection.

If the judge does not approve your agreement even after you have had a chance to explain, don't give up. This would be a good time to consult a lawyer or lawyer-mediator with expertise in family law to find out either how to change your agreement to make it acceptable to the court or how best to go about persuading the court to approve your agreement as is.

What If You Can't Settle Your Case?

If the defendant has filed an Appearance and you have not reached an agreement by the case management date, you must comply with the legal requirements regarding the case management conference date (on your Divorce Complaint form). The Case Management Agreement Form on page 135 must be completed before the case management conference date and be signed by both of you. If you are unable to agree on the terms of the Case Management Agreement or you cannot get your spouse to sign the form, you both must attend the case management conference and report the status of your case to the judge who will enter case management and scheduling orders. You must also personally appear on the case management date if you do not have an agreement about parenting (i.e., you are contesting custody and/or visitation).

The Case Management Agreement form requires that you establish two types of deadlines. First, you must establish certain dates by which information will be exchanged and formal discovery conducted. Second, you must decide on procedures to address settlement (such as a Family Services conference or private mediation) and establish a deadline for these settlement procedures.

Because the procedures for contested and limited contested cases can be complex, you should, at least, obtain legal advice before the case management date or have an attorney represent you during the process.

Once your Case Management Agreement is approved or you appear on the case management date or other court-scheduled status conference, the various judicial districts have different approaches to pre-trial procedures. You should seek the advice of or retain a lawyer to make sure that you comply with these requirements. Many judicial districts will schedule certain pre-trial dates to include such things as Family Services settlement conferences, a status conference with a judge, a pre-trial conference with a judge to help you settle the case, a Special Masters conference where experienced divorce lawyers and/or mental health professionals work with you to try to settle the case, or a referral to private mediation.

Contested: No agreement to some or all issues, requiring a judge to decide after a hearing or trial.

Ultimately, if you cannot settle your case, the court will assign you a trial date. If you arrive at court for your limited contested or contested trial and have an agreement that day, you can proceed with an uncontested hearing that day, even if you literally reach an agreement "on the courthouse steps."

Trial discovery, strategy, and techniques are part of the special expertise of attorneys. Before participating in a limited contested or contested hearing, you should, at the very minimum, obtain legal advice. Retaining a lawyer to represent you in this process could save you a substantial amount of money. Too often parties represent themselves and only after the trial realize the dire financial consequences of failing to obtain legal advice and/or representation. Correcting these mistakes is frequently very difficult and expensive and often, impossible. The legal fees to correct mistakes may be more than it would have cost to do the case right the first time.

Remember that your goal should be to reach a reasonable settlement to which you can both agree. While it may look like you are too far apart to agree, an attorney may help you to settle the case before any contested trial. Mediation is a viable alternative at any stage of the case. Make sure that you are balancing your financial concerns about hiring attorneys, mediators, and other professionals with the value of that intervention to resolve your case and save financial and emotional costs in the end.

CHAPTER 7

GATHERING INFORMATION AND PREPARING FINANCIAL AFFIDAVITS

GATHERING INFORMATION AND PREPARING FINANCIAL AFFIDAVITS

This chapter lists all the financial information you will need to gather to negotiate your divorce. Your agreement should not be based on guesswork. You should have clear and accurate paperwork to back up every number you use in your final settlement and in the sworn Financial Affidavit each spouse must file with the court. The court will not approve your agreement and enter a divorce judgment without completed Financial Affidavits signed under oath.

Most people keep records by throwing receipts, canceled checks, and statements of all kinds, uncataloged, into a shoe box or file folder, sometimes marked "House," "Car," "Bills," "Taxes," or "Kids." Some couples manage all of their financial information on the computer. However you manage your records, gather as much of your financial information as possible before you begin any discussions—whether around the kitchen table or in your mediator's or lawyer's office.

Checklist of Things to Gather

Use the following checklist to help you gather the information about property, insurance, debts, and income that you will need to complete the budget and financial affidavit at the end of this chapter.

Directions: Initial each item which applies to you. This means that you are responsible for obtaining this information, statement, data, or item. Write the date you receive the information and put it in your joint file or the date you put it in your own file and make a photocopy for your spouse.

Assemble all documents you have showing the current fair market value of your major assets and any balances. If you still own assets you entered the marriage with, you may want to document their value at the time of your marriage. Gathering this data, if you have it, will help you focus on your specific situation.

REAL ESTATE

1. Home

Initials/Date   Initials/Date   a. Deed

Initials/Date   Initials/Date   b. Purchaser's closing statement

Initials/Date   Initials/Date   c. The cost of any capital improvements

Initials/Date   Initials/Date   d. Current balance, interest rate, and number of payments on remaining mortgage(s)

Initials/Date   Initials/Date   e. Market analysis or appraisal showing current market value

f.   Tax assessment valuation

g.   IRS Form 2119 for all previous primary homes sold by either of you showing any capital gain rolled over into this home. If you don't find any 2119s, gather your purchaser's closing statements and your seller's closing statements for the purchase and sale of any previous homes and your records of any capital improvements and cost of sale on those homes.

2.   Other real estate

a.   Deed

b.   Purchaser's closing statement

c.   Any depreciation taken by you if you have been renting the property or using it for business

d.   The cost of any capital improvements

e.   Current balance, interest rate, and number of payments on remaining mortgage(s)

f.   Market analysis or bank appraisal showing current market value

g.   Tax assessment valuation

PERSONAL PROPERTY

1.   Furniture, appliances, and household goods. List every item of significant value—you decide what *significant value* means to you. Remember, value isn't necessarily monetary. Something may be valuable to you because of its utility or because it reminds you of a person or the place where you got it. It is often useful to make your list with columns: "I want," "You want," "Both want," "Nobody wants." You can make a fifth column for value or comments if you wish. You can make columns for whether something was yours before the marriage or was a gift or inheritance or, for some other reason, feels more like "mine" than "ours." An interesting way to gather this information is for each of you to make a list and compare them. Be sure you leave time to walk through the house individually (or together if you wish) to prepare the list.

Many people do not detail their division of these assets in their settlement. It is possible to keep this as a private agreement after you physically divide the items between you. Therefore, this is an early agreement you can be working on while you gather data necessary to complete your larger settlement.

If you use a monetary value for these items in your settlement, consider using what you think you would get for an item if you sold it yourself.

2.   Art, antiques, jewelry. Start making a detailed list of these items with a description and market value.

3.   Necessary purchases of duplicate items needed for two households. As the two of you move from one household to two, inevitably you will need to acquire some

new furniture and household goods. If you anticipate some of these necessary purchases, complete the Duplicate Items Needed (DIN) List in Chapter 5.

MOTOR VEHICLES, BOATS, ETC.

Initials/Date   Initials/Date

NADA Blue Book retail and wholesale values for cars; ads for similar vehicles, boats, etc. from the newspaper classifieds; loan balance; and title. Unless your lender is holding it, provide the title(s).

CASH ON HAND

Initials/Date   Initials/Date

If you keep on hand more than small amounts of pocket money, list it here, whether it's in a safe, mattress, or buried in the backyard.

STOCKS AND BONDS

If all your securities are in a brokerage account, provide a current statement. For each security that you own, whether in a brokerage account or as a separate certificate, provide the following, including restricted stock, stock options, and similar interests:

Initials/Date   Initials/Date

a. Name of company and type and number of shares or bonds

Initials/Date   Initials/Date

b. How titled

Initials/Date   Initials/Date

c. Value/cost at acquisition and value now

HEALTH AND LIFE INSURANCE

Most of the information you need to answer the questions in this section may be in a benefits booklet from your employer. If you do not have a benefits booklet, ask your employer to provide the information to you in writing.

1. Answer the following with regard to your health insurance coverage:

Initials/Date   Initials/Date

a. Who is covered?

Initials/Date   Initials/Date

b. What is the premium for each person or category of person?

Initials/Date   Initials/Date

c. What is the coverage for each kind of medical expense? Dental? Eye glasses? Chiropractic? Preventive care? Office visits? Prescriptions?

Initials/Date   Initials/Date

d. Obtain the details on the COBRA option which permits a former spouse to purchase separate coverage as though he or she was an employee for up to three years after the divorce. (See Chapter 10 for more on this.)

2. For each life insurance policy you have, answer the following (and provide a copy of the most recent statement for each policy):

Initials/Date   Initials/Date

a. Is it whole life, term, decreasing term, hybrid (mixture of several kinds), or universal life?

b. Whose life do the policies cover? Spouse? Children? Initials/Date Initials/Date

c. Who is the owner of the policy? Initials/Date Initials/Date

d. Who are the beneficiaries of the policy? Initials/Date Initials/Date

e. What is the cash surrender value, if any? Initials/Date Initials/Date

f. What is the loan balance, if any? Initials/Date Initials/Date

g. What are the current and future premium payments? Initials/Date Initials/Date

h. How much is the death benefit? Initials/Date Initials/Date

PENSION, PROFIT SHARING, AND RETIREMENT FUNDS, INCLUDING 401KS AND IRAS

1. Your current and previous employers, plan administrators, or trustees have been giving you, or should have been giving you, the following documents regarding your pension, profit sharing, retirement, 401K, thrift savings, and IRAs. Provide the most current:

    a. Benefits statement telling what kind of retirement, pension, or tax-deferred benefit you have Initials/Date Initials/Date

    b. A current statement of the amount which is vested for you or in your name Initials/Date Initials/Date

    c. If there is a formula to determine the amount of your monthly benefit at retirement, obtain a copy of the formula and the current projected monthly amount. Initials/Date Initials/Date

    d. Is your plan subject to a Qualified Domestic Relations Order (QDRO)? If so, is there written information and/or "in-house" forms available from your employer or plan administrator? If so, provide them. Initials/Date Initials/Date

    e. The balance due of any loan taken against the plan Initials/Date Initials/Date

2. Check the accuracy of the factual data in the plan (since small discrepancies can create huge problems, including with the Social Security Administration). Not all this data will appear in every plan, but check your plan for the accuracy of the following data:

    a. Your name, address, Social Security number, birth date, and the exact date you began participating in the plan Initials/Date Initials/Date

    b. The exact name of the surviving spouse or alternate payee and his or her address Initials/Date Initials/Date

    c. The date of your marriage Initials/Date Initials/Date

3. For each plan or account, answer the following questions. If you don't know the answers to these questions, you can get help from the benefits office at your workplace.

    a. Does the plan continue, or pay, at the death of the participant? Initials/Date Initials/Date

Initials/Date Initials/Date	b. Does the plan have a separate death benefit? If so, state the exact name and address of the named beneficiary.
Initials/Date Initials/Date	c. How is the plan funded? Does the participant contribute? Does the employer contribute? If so, how much and when?
Initials/Date Initials/Date	d. How and when does the plan vest?
Initials/Date Initials/Date	e. When and under what circumstances does the plan pay out?
Initials/Date Initials/Date	f. Is the plan subject to divestment? Total? Partial? If so, when and how?
Initials/Date Initials/Date	g. Does the plan have a surviving spouse provision? If so, what are its terms?
Initials/Date Initials/Date	h. Does the plan have a separate death benefit? If so, what are its terms?
Initials/Date Initials/Date	i. What portion of the funds held in this plan are tax-deferred?
Initials/Date Initials/Date	j. What portion of the funds held in this plan have already been taxed?
Initials/Date Initials/Date	k. Can the participant receive a lump sum payout? If so, when and under what circumstances?
Initials/Date Initials/Date	l. Is any benefit or amount available to the participant now? Is there a "hardship" clause which permits a partial payout for:
Initials/Date Initials/Date	1) purchase of a primary residence
Initials/Date Initials/Date	2) college or higher education (self, spouse, or children)
Initials/Date Initials/Date	3) medical emergency
Initials/Date Initials/Date	4) divorce
Initials/Date Initials/Date	5) other
Initials/Date Initials/Date	m. May the participant borrow from the plan? If so, under what circumstances?
Initials/Date Initials/Date	1) purchase of a primary residence
Initials/Date Initials/Date	2) college or higher education expenses (self, spouse, or children)
Initials/Date Initials/Date	3) medical emergency
Initials/Date Initials/Date	4) divorce
Initials/Date Initials/Date	5) other
Initials/Date Initials/Date	n. What is the participant's expected date of retirement?
Initials/Date Initials/Date	o. What is the participant's earliest possible date of retirement?
Initials/Date Initials/Date	p. What change in benefits, if any, results from early retirement?
Initials/Date Initials/Date	q. Is any portion of this plan in lieu of Social Security (i.e., participant does not pay FICA and does not have FICA paid on his or her behalf)?
Initials/Date Initials/Date	r. If the answer to the previous question is yes, what is the value of the portion of the plan which is in lieu of Social Security?

s.   Are the benefits described above in questions h, i, and p affected by participant's Social Security benefits, estimated or received? If so, how? In what amount?

Initials/Date   Initials/Date

t.   Is the participant presently eligible for Social Security benefits? If so, what is the present anticipated monthly benefit? If not, how many more quarters are needed?

Initials/Date   Initials/Date

4.   If you have worked for forty full-time quarters, you will probably be eligible to receive Social Security—unless you work for a public entity which has a plan in lieu of Social Security. Call the local Social Security office and arrange to get a statement of your present earned credits and probable benefit, or visit www.ssa.gov/my statement.

Initials/Date   Initials/Date

BUSINESS INTERESTS

If either spouse owns a business you should consult with a lawyer, CPA, and/or business appraiser regarding the value of these assets. See Chapter 10.

Initials/Date   Initials/Date

MISCELLANEOUS ASSETS

The rest of your assets may include tools, pedigreed animals, craft supplies, rights to season tickets, frequent flyer and credit card miles and points, and sporting and exercise equipment. Start gathering titles, descriptions, and costs to acquire or maintain these assets. The paperwork should be ready to give to whomever will keep that asset after the divorce. Now is the time to start assembling everything so you avoid lost documents and nerve-wrenching last minute scrambles.

Initials/Date   Initials/Date

RECENT TRANSACTIONS

The period of the break-up of a marriage, and especially the physical separation, can be a time of high stress when people are likely to be less careful than usual—especially about finances. This section helps to remind you to keep track of all your recent transactions.

Initials/Date   Initials/Date

Provide documentation of any withdrawal (other than reasonable, day-to-day expenses) from or sale of an account or asset you made during the last year, especially since or around the time of your separation. If you can show the money went into a current asset (for example: home, car, furniture), then also provide that documentation (for example: bank statement, sales receipt, closing statement). If the money went into your own account, try to show what you used it for through your check register or other written records.

LOANS, GIFTS, AND INHERITANCES

If anyone gave you a substantial gift or loan of money, especially since or around the time of your separation, then obtain a written statement from that person showing

Initials/Date   Initials/Date

their understanding of the amount, whether they expect it to be paid back, and any interest rate.

Initials/Date   Initials/Date

If you inherited or received by gift any money or property during the marriage, provide written documentation of the date you received it, the value when received, and the value now.

PROPERTY OWNED BEFORE THE MARRIAGE

Initials/Date   Initials/Date

If you owned property of substantial value before the marriage, provide documentation of the property, the value at the time of the marriage, and the value now.

CREDIT REPORT

Initials/Date   Initials/Date

Obtain your individual (not joint) credit reports. Look under "Credit Reporting Agencies" in the Yellow Pages and call at least one or visit www.equifax.com. A recorded message will tell you how to obtain a copy of your credit report(s). See "Your Credit and Your Divorce" in Chapter 5 for why this is important.

DEBTS AND CREDIT CARDS

Initials/Date   Initials/Date

1. Assemble all the current debt, credit card, and loan statements you have, especially those since your separation. Note if any debt is secured by property, such as a mortgage on your house or a loan on your car.

Initials/Date   Initials/Date

2. Write out, in a manner you can refer to quickly, the present balance, minimum payment, and number of months left to pay on every debt you are legally responsible for, whether or not you are—or want to be—the one paying it.

Initials/Date   Initials/Date

3. Write out, in a similarly clear manner, all the payments and charges you have made since your separation.

Initials/Date   Initials/Date

4. Include any debt necessary to acquire items identified in the DIN Checklist in Chapter 5.

Information About Income

The word "income" can mean different things to different people. To the worker it probably means spendable earnings. To the IRS it means what is taxed. For calculating support, income may include earnings based on earning capacity but not current earnings. The list of items to be gathered and the income chart which follow are designed to help you assemble and organize your various kinds of income.

1. If you have a salary or regular pay (whether or not you receive additional income from commissions, tips, or performance bonuses), provide the following:

Initials/Date   Initials/Date

    a. All pay stubs or other evidence of income for the current year and your most recent basic paycheck stub

b. Employment contract or letter, if you have one, which states what your salary or hourly pay is and what you must do to earn it

<u>Initials/Date</u>   <u>Initials/Date</u>

2. If you are self-employed, put together, summarize, and average your monthly:

a. Gross business receipts

<u>Initials/Date</u>   <u>Initials/Date</u>

b. Necessary expenses to earn this income (For some ideas about categories, see IRS Schedule C from your federal tax return. Do not factor in depreciation on business assets, but consider allocating something for replacing equipment and/or repairs.)

<u>Initials/Date</u>   <u>Initials/Date</u>

c. Estimated tax payments and tax rate you are using

<u>Initials/Date</u>   <u>Initials/Date</u>

d. Average take-home pay (For all the paperwork on which you base your averages, keep a copy for yourself and make a copy for your spouse.)

<u>Initials/Date</u>   <u>Initials/Date</u>

3. If your business is a corporation, provide the last year's corporate tax return. Your gross (before tax) income should appear under officer's pay while your benefits (insurance, retirement, etc.) should appear as corporate expenses. The corporate tax return will also show any income you received from the profits as an owner.

<u>Initials/Date</u>   <u>Initials/Date</u>

4. If your business is a partnership, provide the IRS Schedule K-1 Form, Partner's Share of Income Credits, Deductions from your tax return to show income you actually received and/or paid tax on.

<u>Initials/Date</u>   <u>Initials/Date</u>

5. If you have income from investments, assemble at least a year of monthly or quarterly reports. Summarize the earnings, even if you left them in the account, and any expenses, and average them monthly. Do the same for any interest on bank accounts.

<u>Initials/Date</u>   <u>Initials/Date</u>

6. If your income for this last year included a one-time windfall such as profits from the sale of a home or stock, lottery winnings, or an inheritance, assemble all the information about this income, including any taxes paid at the time or which you expect to pay.

<u>Initials/Date</u>   <u>Initials/Date</u>

 There was a change in tax rules in 1993 regarding withdrawals from an IRA or other tax-sheltered or tax-deferred source. If you closed or took money from such an account, be sure to get current tax information. See Chapter 12.

7. Put together documentation of any additional income for the last year other than that listed previously.

<u>Initials/Date</u>   <u>Initials/Date</u>

8. Provide the last three years' federal and state income tax returns, including all attached schedules and W-2, 1099, and K-1 forms.

<u>Initials/Date</u>   <u>Initials/Date</u>

Weekly Income Chart

See directions for completing this chart on the next page.

1. Weekly gross base pay from principal employment $ _____

2. Extra income from principal employment (averaged over _____ weeks) $ _____

    a. Overtime $_____/week. Describe:

    b. Bonus: $_____/ week. Describe:

    c. Commissions $_____/ week. Describe:

    d. Tips $_____/ week.

3. Add the amounts on lines 1 and 2. $ _____

4. Rate of withholding: Married/Single claiming _____ exemptions.

5. Deductions from employment income:

    a. Federal withholding $_____

    b. State withholding $_____

    c. FICA (Social Security, Medicare) $_____

    d. Medical insurance $_____

    e. Life insurance $_____

    f. Credit union—savings $_____

    g. Credit union—loan $_____

    h. Pension/Retirement/401K $_____

    i. Union dues or fees $_____

    j. Other: _____ $_____

        Other: _____ $_____

        Other: _____ $_____

        Total deductions $ _____

6. Subtract the amount on line 5 from the amount on line 3. $ _____

7. List any additional interest or earnings:

        Interest $_____

        Dividends $_____

        Cash flow from rentals $_____

        Second (and third) job $_____

        Other $_____

        Total additional income $ _____

8. Estimate tax on additional interest or earnings. $ _____

9. Subtract the amount on line 8 from the amount on line 7. $ _____

10. Add the amounts on lines 6 and 9 for total weekly net income. $ _____

Directions for Completing Income Chart

Make copies of the income chart in this guidebook—at least one for each of you. Use it to show your respective incomes from all sources. Read each numbered paragraph before completing the corresponding section of the chart.

1. Write your gross weekly income from your principal employment, base pay, or salary only. If you are paid twice per month, multiply that amount by 2. If you are paid every two weeks (biweekly), multiply the gross income by 24 and then divide by 52. If you are paid monthly, divide the gross pay check by 4.3. If you own your own business or are self-employed, calculate the gross receipts and subtract your actual out-of-pocket expenses of doing business. This amount is not necessarily the same as the bottom line on Schedule C of your tax return.

2. List any bonuses, overtime, or commissions, and describe how often you receive them and how certain they are. For example, "I am guaranteed at least _____ hours of overtime per month," or "My bonus depends on company performance, it is not certain."

3. Write your total gross income from your principal employment. This should be the amount on line 1 plus the amount on line 2, especially if line 2 is regular income. (If line 2 is not so certain, you may wish to hold it for step 7.) This information will go in Section 1(A) of Page 1 of your Financial Affidavit.

4. Write your withholding classification. For example, "M-3" means filing "Married" claiming three exemptions. See your paycheck stub or the most recent W-4 that you filed with your employer.

If your paycheck stub does not show your withholding classification, obtain your W-4 form from your payroll office. If you changed your W-4 when you separated, or in anticipation of separation, then obtain one basic or typical paycheck under each designation. Ask your payroll office to calculate for you what your paycheck would be at your present rate if you filed "Single," claiming one exemption. This will give you a worst case scenario baseline for your tax planning (*see* Chapter 12).

 This information is important. Your status and the number of exemptions will change with your divorce. Understanding the effect of this change is vital to your budgeting. See Chapter 11.

5. What is being taken out of your weekly pay? You will need the following for both your basic pay and your extra income. If you are paid every two weeks (bi-weekly), divide the deductions by 2. If you are paid twice per month, multiply the deductions by 24 and then divide by 52. If you are paid monthly, divide the deductions by 4.3.

    *   Federal, state, and FICA (Social Security and Medicare) taxes being withheld. If all of your Social Security taxes are taken out before the end of the year, be sure you provide at least one typical paycheck each with and without this amount withheld.

    *   Spouse or family health and/or life insurance premium. Be *certain* you distinguish the amount you pay for your children's portion, if this is available, or see Chapter 9 if a separate premium cost is not quoted for your children.

    *   Car loans and/or credit union loans

    *   Required minimum retirement contribution

    *   Optional retirement, pension, and/or savings

    *   "Cafeteria Plan" pretax amounts for day care, family medical, etc.

    *   Mandatory union dues or fees, including initiation

6. Enter the deduction amounts from line 5 in Section 1(A) of your financial affidavit. Subtract line 5 from line 3. This will be the net weekly income in Section 1(B) of your Financial Affidavit.

7. List any additional income you receive, such as a second or third job, interest on interest, dividends, annuities, cash flow from rentals after reasonable and necessary expenses, Social Security, pensions, workers' compensation, alimony, or in-kind compensation (such as food, shelter, or transportation from your employer in lieu of salary). You may only receive this income annually or sporadically (or not at all with some unearned income). Convert the annual amount to a weekly amount. This information goes in Section 1(B) of your Financial Affidavit.

8. Write your deductions and/or estimated tax on income listed on line 7. Most people do not have taxes withheld from their secondary incomes. If you do not, you should estimate the probable tax on this income and pay it to the IRS quarterly, or put it into a savings account. For most people, tax on this additional income is 28 percent for federal tax, and 4.5 percent for Connecticut state tax. Include in this number your Social Security or Self-Employment Tax (if any) on this income. Unearned income, such as interest and dividends, is not usually subject to Social Security tax. This information goes in section 1(B) of your Financial Affidavit.

9. Subtract the amount on line 8 from the amount on line 7. This information is the total for section 1(B) of your Financial Affidavit.

10. List your total weekly net income from all sources—the amount on line 6 plus the amount on line 9. Report this amount in the shaded area, "A. Total Net Weekly Income," on your Financial Affidavit.

Budgeting Expenses

The purpose of this section is to budget your expenses as your family changes from one household to two. You will have the ongoing expenses of both households, plus any debt service payments.

There are three possible categories of ongoing expenses for two households:

1. Bare bones: necessary expenses during this period of time ("survival")

2. Discretionary: expenses that either of you could live without, albeit with difficulty ("lifestyle") (and for which there may not be adequate cash flow from income)

3. Children: expenses that are directly for the children, sometimes helpful in planning for how to share these expenses

The budget chart begins on page 166. The budget lists your expenses in the three categories described above. Be sure that between your two budgets you include all your expenses and debts for both households but that you do not duplicate any of them. Do these budgets separately, even if you are physically separating within the same residence. You will still have to decide how to share the expenses of the home.

Directions for Completing the Budget

Make several photocopies of each page of the budget. You will probably do several rough drafts to look at different possible plans. Use pencil so you can make changes as you go along. The budget will help you organize your information not only so it will be helpful to you in your negotiations but also so it will be in a form that is easy to transfer to section two of your Financial Affidavit.

You may want to prepare these separately and then share them with each other. As you do so, try not to let this process become an opportunity to tell each other how to spend. Write down the information which is true for you or is the best you can project that your expenses will be for each of you in your new households.

If you have not yet separated or have recently separated, much of your information will be based on your expenses when you were together. The information you write in this budget will be based on your individual experiences during separation if you have been separated for a period of time.

1. Using your check register(s) (or Quicken reports), list all the expenses you had in each of the categories on the budget over a period of time (six weeks to two years), then divide the total by the number of weeks. Write the number in the appropriate place on the budget, allocating it, if necessary, among bare bones, discretionary, and children. For example, the base rate for your telephone is bare bones; long distance and other services are probably discretionary; a second telephone line may be for the children.

    The Financial Affidavit you file with the court requires that you list your expenses by using a weekly amount. Divide monthly expenses by 4.3 and annual expenses by 12. If it is easier for you in your budgeting process, you can use monthly figures in the budget form and convert them to weekly figures when you complete your Financial Affidavit for the court.

2. If you have no experience with an expense on this budget, do some investigation:

    a. To determine rent or a mortgage, drive around the area you want to live in and call about homes for rent or sale. Be sure you ask about the average cost of utilities.

    b. Buy a simple budget book at your local office supply or discount store. Each day, write down every penny you spend. If you have a computer, use Quicken or some other financial management software.

    c. People rarely limit supermarket spending to groceries. Decide whether to keep the cleaning supplies, panty hose, and toiletries grouped with the groceries in your budget or list them in their own category. Be sure you know where you have allocated them in your budget.

    d. Obtain information regarding the balance not covered by insurance that you can expect to pay for any ongoing medical treatment for any members of your family, such as the deductible, dental care, mental health, physical therapy, and the like.

    e. Find out about one-time children's expenses such as prom, yearbook, school pictures, school trips, and summer camp.

3. Don't forget to include and average expenses which might not be paid weekly, such as car insurance, life insurance, or property taxes, if they are not part of the mortgage payment. Also be sure you average expenses that vary with the time of year: heat, water, birthday expenses, holiday gifts, summer activities, school clothes in the fall.

4. If you included your entire expense allowance as received from your employer in your income chart, include your actual expenses on this budget (or if you have excluded your expense reimbursements in the income section, exclude them here). Similarly, if you participate in a "cafeteria plan" pre-tax medical or day-care expense program, then either put the entire weekly amount on this budget with a notation that this is "prepaid" and do not add into the total expenses, or list the amount from the cafeteria plan in your income chart and put the amounts you actually spend for these services (averaged weekly, for example including summer day care) here and add them into your expenses.

5. Be sure that between your two budgets you list all your debts and debt payments, including the cost of paying for items from the DIN List. Debts are those bills which are not paid in full within the week, such as most credit cards and signature loans.

Weekly Budget

	BARE BONES	DISCRETIONARY	CHILDREN
HOUSING Mortgage/Rent			
Second Mortgage			
Real Estate Taxes (if not included in the mortgage)			
Condo Fee			
Other			
UTILITIES Fuel/Oil			
Electric			
Gas			
Water/Sewer			
Phone—Basic Service			
Long Distance			
Cellular			
Trash Removal			
Yard Care/Snow			
Alarm Fees			
Cable TV			
Other			
FOOD Groceries			
Eating Out			
School Lunches			
Wine and Spirits			
CLOTHING/SHOES			
TRANSPORTATION Gas/Oil			
Repairs			
Auto Loan			
Public Transportation			
License and Registration Taxes			

	BARE BONES	DISCRETIONARY	CHILDREN
Parking			
Replacement Reserve			
Car Wash			
Other			
INSURANCE Medical/Dental			
Automobile			
Homeowner's (if not included in mortgage)			
Renter's			
Life			
Disability			
Personal Umbrella			
MEDICAL/DENTAL (Unreimbursed) Doctor			
Dentist			
Therapist/Counseling			
Eye Care			
Prescriptions and Medications			
CHILD SUPPORT Court-Ordered			
Not Court-Ordered			
ALIMONY Court-Ordered			
Not Court-Ordered			
DAY CARE Work-Related			
Not Work-Related			
EDUCATION Tuition			
Books and Fees			
Room and Board			

	BARE BONES	DISCRETIONARY	CHILDREN
Extracurricular Expenses			
Tutoring/Lessons			
Other			
LAUNDRY/CLEANING			
RECREATION Travel/Vacation			
Video Rental			
Toys			
Books			
Children's Sports			
Children's Lessons			
Subscriptions			
Hobbies			
Summer Camp			
Health Club/Exercise			
Records/Tapes/CDs			
MISCELLANEOUS House Repairs			
Cleaning Service			
Domestic Help			
Allowances			
Toiletries/Cosmetics			
Gifts			
Pet Expenses			
Hairdresser/Barber			
Charities/ Contributions			
Worship			
Postage			

	BARE BONES	DISCRETIONARY	CHILDREN
Bank & Credit Card Fees			
Safe Deposit Box Rental			
Savings			
Retirement Contributions			
Child Visitation Expenses			
Other			
DIVORCE EXPENSES (Mediators, lawyers, etc.)			
TOTAL EXPENSES			
DEBTS (list individually; do not repeat those listed above—car payment or mortgage)	Creditor Original Amount Bal. Date Incurred Pmt.	Creditor Original Amount Bal. Date Incurred Pmt.	Creditor Original Amount Bal. Date Incurred Pmt.
	Creditor Original Amount Bal. Date Incurred Pmt.	Creditor Original Amount Bal. Date Incurred Pmt.	Creditor Original Amount Bal. Date Incurred Pmt.
	Creditor Original Amount Bal. Date Incurred Pmt.	Creditor Original Amount Bal. Date Incurred Pmt.	Creditor Original Amount Bal. Date Incurred Pmt.
TOTAL DEBTS			
TOTAL DEBT PAYMENTS			
TOTAL EXPENSES & DEBT PAYMENTS			
GRAND TOTAL: ALL EXPENSES PLUS ALL DEBT PAYMENTS			

Assets

The purpose of this section is to summarize your asset information. By completing the checklist, you have assembled information about all of the assets owned by each of you. This chart will help you to organize and summarize your asset information in a form you can use to negotiate your property settlement agreement and to prepare your Financial Affidavit for the court. Copy this chart if you need more space to list your assets.

Real Estate

Address	Title	Value	1st Mort.	2nd Mort.	Equity

Motor Vehicles

Year	Title	Make & Model	Value	Loan Bal.	Equity

Personal Property

Item	Title or Ownership	Value

Bank Accounts

Bank	Type of Account	Ownership	Value

Stocks, Bonds, and Mutual Funds

Name of Company	Title	No. of Shares	Value

Life Insurance

Insured	Company	Face Amount	Cash Value	Amt. of Loan	Equity

Employee Benefits and IRAs

Account or Plan Name	Title	Value

All Other Assets

Item	Title or Possession	Value

www.jud.state.et.us/forms/fm006/htm

FINANCIAL AFFIDAVIT
JD-FM-6 Rev. 1-03
P.B. 25-30

STATE OF CONNECTICUT
SUPERIOR COURT
www.jud.state.ct.us

COURT USE ONLY
FINAFF

DOCKET NO.

FOR THE JUDICIAL DISTRICT OF	AT *(Address of court)*	NAME OF AFFIANT *(Person submitting this form)*
NAME OF CASE		☐ **PLAINTIFF** ☐ **DEFENDANT**
OCCUPATION	NAME OF EMPLOYER	
ADDRESS OF EMPLOYER		

A. WEEKLY INCOME FROM PRINCIPAL EMPLOYMENT *(Use weekly average not less than 13 weeks)*

	DEDUCTIONS *(Taxes, FICA, etc.)*	AMOUNT/WEEK	DEDUCTIONS *(Cont.)*	AMOUNT/WEEK		
1. WEEKLY INCOME	1.	$	4.	$	GROSS WKLY WAGE FROM PRINCIPAL EMPLOYMENT →	$
	2.	$	5.	$	TOTAL DEDUCTIONS →	$
	3.	$	6.	$	NET WEEKLY WAGE →	$

B. ALL OTHER INCOME *(Include in-kind compensation, gratuities, rents, interest, dividends, pension, etc.)*

SOURCE OF INCOME	GROSS AMT/WK	SOURCE OF INCOME	GROSS AMT/WK		
1.	$	2.	$	GROSS WEEKLY INCOME FROM OTHER SOURCES →	$
DEDUCTIONS	AMOUNT/WEEK	DEDUCTIONS	AMOUNT/WEEK		
	$		$	TOTAL DEDUCTIONS →	$
	$		$	NET WEEKLY INCOME FROM OTHER SOURCES →	$
	$		$		
	$		$	*ADD "NET WEEKLY WAGE" FROM SECTION A, AND "NET WEEKLY INCOME" FROM SECTION B, AND ENTER TOTAL BELOW:*	
	$		$		
	$		$	**A. TOTAL NET WEEKLY INCOME** →	$

2. WEEKLY EXPENSES								
	1. RENT OR MORTGAGE	$			Gas/Oil	$	11. DAY CARE	$
	2. REAL ESTATE TAXES	$		6. TRANSPOR-TATION	Repairs	$	12. OTHER *(specify below)*	
	3. UTILITIES	Fuel	$		Auto Loan	$		$
		Electricity	$		Public Trans.	$		$
		Gas	$	7. INSURANCE PREMIUMS	Medical/Dental	$		$
		Water	$		Automobile	$		$
		Telephone	$		Homeowners	$		$
		Trash Collection	$		Life	$		$
		Cable T.V.	$	8. MEDICAL/DENTAL		$		$
	4. FOOD	$	9. CHILD SUPPORT *(order of court)*		$		$
	5. CLOTHING	$	10. ALIMONY *(order of court)*		$	**B. TOTAL WEEKLY EXPENSES** →	$

3. LIABILITIES (DEBTS)	CREDITOR *(Do not include mortgages or loan balances that will be listed under assets.)*	AMOUNT OF DEBT	BALANCE DUE	DATE DEBT INCURRED	WEEKLY PAYMENT
		$	$		$
		$	$		$
		$	$		$
		$	$		$
		$	$		$
		$	$		$
	C. TOTAL LIABILITIES *(Total Balance Due on Debts)* →	$		**D. TOTAL WEEKLY LIABILITY EXPENSE** →	$

(continued)

4. ASSETS	**A. Real Estate**	Home	ADDRESS			VALUE *(Est.)* $	MORTGAGE $	EQUITY $	
		Other:	ADDRESS			VALUE *(Est.)* $	MORTGAGE $	EQUITY $	
		Other:	ADDRESS			VALUE *(Est.)* $	MORTGAGE $	EQUITY $	
	B. Motor Vehicles	Car 1:	YEAR	MAKE	MODEL	VALUE $	LOAN BALANCE $	EQUITY $	
		Car 2:	YEAR	MAKE	MODEL	VALUE $	LOAN BALANCE $	EQUITY $	
	C. Other Personal Property	DESCRIBE AND STATE VALUE OF EACH ITEM						**TOTAL VALUE**	
								$	
	D. Bank Accounts	BANK NAME, TYPE OF ACCOUNT, AND AMOUNT						**TOTAL BANK ACCOUNTS**	
								$	
	E. Stocks, Bonds Mutual Funds	NAME OF COMPANY, NUMBER OF SHARES, AND VALUE						**TOTAL VALUE**	
								$	
	F. Insurance (exclude children)	NAME OF INSURED	COMPANY	FACE AMOUNT $	CASH VALUE $	AMT. OF LOAN $		**TOTAL VALUE**	
				$	$	$			
				$	$	$		$	
	G. Deferred Compensation Plans	NAME OF PLAN *(Individual I.R.A., 401K, Keogh, etc.)* AND APPROX. VALUE						**TOTAL VALUE (less loans)**	
								$	
	H. All Other Assets							**TOTAL VALUE**	
								$	
	I. Total				E. TOTAL CASH VALUE OF ALL ASSETS →			$	

5. HEALTH INSURANCE	NAME AND ADDRESS OF HEALTH OR DENTAL INSURANCE CARRIER
	INSURANCE POLICY NO. NAME(S) OF PERSON(S) COVERED BY THE POLICY

SUMMARY
(Use the amounts shown in boxes A thru E of sections 1-4.)

TOTAL NET WEEKLY INCOME (A)	$	TOTAL CASH VALUE OF ASSETS (E)	$
TOTAL WEEKLY EXPENSES AND LIABILITIES (B + D)	$	TOTAL LIABILITIES (TOTAL BALANCE DUE ON DEBTS) (C)	$

CERTIFICATION
I certify that the foregoing statement is true and accurate to the best of my knowledge and belief.

SIGNED *(Affiant)*	Subscribed and sworn to before me on	DATE	SIGNED *(Notary, Comm. of Superior Court, Assistant Clerk)*

JD-FM-6 Rev. 1-03 (Back)

Financial Affidavit

All of the financial information you gather must be put into a court form: Form JD-FM-6 (Financial Affidavit). The Financial Affidavit is a sworn statement that tells the court enough about your individual financial situations to allow the judge to determine if your written agreement is fair and to make full disclosure of all financial information to your spouse. The court will read the three documents (two Financial Affidavits, one Separation Agreement) side by side to see if you can each pay the debts you say you will be responsible for and the support and alimony you agree to pay, in addition to determining whether you each can live on the income you show yourself receiving, including any alimony or support you have agreed to. The judge will also determine whether your property and debt provisions are equitable. If you do not settle your temporary or permanent issues, each party will submit a Financial Affidavit to the judge who will use it as a part of the hearing to enter financial orders.

Each spouse must complete this form. If you do not have completed Financial Affidavits, the court will not consider your agreement or enter your judgment of divorce. The first page describes your weekly income, expenses, and debts. The second page lists all your assets. If something does not apply to you write "0" or "none" in the blank space.

INSTRUCTIONS FOR COMPLETING THE FINANCIAL AFFIDAVIT

The Financial Affidavit form requires weekly figures for income, deductions, expenses, and debt payments. To convert monthly numbers, divide by 4.3. To convert every-other-week numbers, multiply by 26 and divide by 12. If you are paid twice per month, divide by 2. For annual numbers, divide by 12.

Top portion:
- Fill out these lines the same way you did on your Divorce Complaint and all previous forms. Be sure to include the docket number.

- Place a mark in the box that applies to you as plaintiff or defendant.

- Your job title and name and address of your employer.

 Section A refers to your primary employment. This section calls for the income you receive regularly that is subject to tax withholding. If you regularly earn a bonus, overtime, or commissions, then you can include these amounts as additional income beginning at B(1). Income in kind, such as expense advances, reimbursements, or a car allowance, should also be reserved for the additional income in section B. "Cafeteria plan" (or "flex" dollars) are pre-paid expenses you may include. Any related expenses you actually pay from this income you can include in the expense section.

Part 1:
- The amount of your weekly paycheck before any taxes or other deductions.

- You can find out your weekly payroll deductions by looking at your paycheck stub. To calculate the amount of your taxes, see Chapter 12. You can use your pay stub if you believe that it accurately reflects your actual tax. You can use your last year's tax return but remember that your divorce may change your tax filing status and tax rate. The number of exemptions comes from the W-4 form you filed with your payroll office or the number you will claim on your income tax return.

- Your net weekly wage is the amount remaining after subtracting all the listed deductions from your gross income. Do not list expenses here that are not deducted from your paycheck—list them in the liabilities section later on page one of the affidavit.

- List gross income from all other sources averaged weekly. This includes dividends and interest, profits from rental property, alimony, child support, expense advances, car allowances, and second jobs. Add these up and write the total on the line provided.

- List any deductions from the income from other sources averaged weekly. Most people don't have actual deductions from additional income but instead pay estimated tax ,or tax at the end of the year, on their tax return. Be sure to list your estimated federal and state tax on all this income. To find out the amount of your taxes, see Chapter 12. You can use your last year's tax return but remember that your divorce may change your tax filing status and tax rate.

- This is your weekly net income from sources other than your primary employment (step 7 minus step 8).

- Add step 6 to step 9. This is your weekly net income from all sources combined.

Part 2:

- Type your weekly expenses for these items. If you do not know the exact amounts, estimate them. If you are separated from your spouse, list your current expenses. A good way to calculate these expenses is to take the total you have paid for each item over the last six months or year (or the length of time you have been separated) and divide by the number of weeks. For expenses not preprinted on the form, you can fill in the blanks after line 12. If there is still not enough room, type "see attached expense schedule" and on a separate piece of paper, list the additional expenses, total them, and carry the total forward to line 12. Don't forget to budget for monthly and annual expenses reduced to a weekly amount. See the budget for a complete discussion of this.

- Total all weekly expenses.

- List the debts for which you are currently personally liable. If you include joint debts your spouse is paying, do not include the weekly payment. Do not include mortgages or loan balances that will be listed in the assets section (i.e. car loan balances).

- Add step 6 to step 9. This is your weekly net income from all sources combined.

- Total all weekly expenses.

PAGE TWO OF THE FINANCIAL AFFIDAVIT

For a complete discussion of property, see Chapter 10, especially the property checklists.

If there is not enough room to list all of your assets in a particular category, type "see attached asset schedule" and then type the list of individual assets on a separate piece of paper. Carry the total forward to the "total value lines" of each section or class of assets.

- List the value of your assets using net fair market value (FMV minus any balance owing on that property). See Chapter 10 for how to value different kinds of assets. If you own the asset with anyone else (including your spouse) show the equity for your percentage of ownership. Example: $50,000 (fifty percent equity).

If you have reached agreement about the division of an asset or class of assets and cannot easily set specific values, then describe what you agreed to in words. For example, "household goods equitably divided by agreement."

- Type the total value of all your assets.

- If applicable, fill in this information about your health and/or dental insurance.

- Copy the totals from the sections of the financial affidavit as designated.

- Sign and date your financial affidavit in the presence of a notary, attorney or clerk of the superior court. Make sure that the person who witnesses your signatures completes the section immediately after the space for your signature.

CHAPTER 8

CHILDREN

CHILDREN

Who Is a Child?

For purposes of your divorce, a child is any person under the age of eighteen born to, conceived by, or adopted by both of you during your marriage. A child born to parents who later marry is also presumed to be a child of the marriage.

Until a child reaches eighteen, the parents may be liable for the child's financial needs, emotional welfare, and sometimes for his or her actions.

At age eighteen, children can do many things without their parents' consent. For example, they can go into the armed services or marry. At age eighteen anyone can sign a contract—to buy a car, for example—and be bound by his or her signature (they can also be sued on the debt). They can make a will and inherit outright.

Under Connecticut law, the duty of child support ends when the child reaches age eighteen, unless he or she dies, marries, or emancipates before that date. However, if at age eighteen the child is still a full-time high school student and resides with a parent, child support will continue until age nineteen or graduation from high school, whichever occurs first. There may also be a legal duty to contribute to higher education costs (up to the cost of the University of Connecticut), and parents can voluntarily agree to payment of higher education costs beyond this cap (*see* Chapter 9).

How to Be a Good Parent Through the Divorce Process

The time when parents begin living apart is one of the most stressful for children. Their worst fear is of losing a parent. They need both of you at this time. Each of you has a clear and distinct role to play. Children can adjust best to the separations and transitions in two-household parenting when the parents work together to support each other's relationship with the children. This chapter will help you.

Children feel more secure when they are confident that their parents can take care of themselves. If they feel you are not doing that, they will try to take care of you—reversing the parent-child relationship. Therefore, taking care of yourself at this difficult time is not only good for you but it is in the best interests of your children.

"Divorce always hurts children." "You just can't possibly be a responsible parent and get a divorce."

The truth, shown by extensive research, is that divorce does not necessarily hurt children. What does hurt them is ongoing hostilities between their parents whether or not there is a divorce. Research shows that children of divorcing parents who stopped fighting are as well-adjusted as those raised in successful marriages. The same research also shows that children of parents who stay together but continue to fight, have as much trouble adjusting as children of the continually hostile divorce. So it's not the divorce that hurts the children, it's the ongoing anger and hostility that are harmful.

Emancipation: When, as a matter of law, your child is no longer your legal or financial responsibility.

Attendance of both parents at the parenting education program is mandatory under the law. If you have both not attended the class and if you have not obtained a waiver from the judge, you run the chance that the judge will not allow you to get divorced until you comply with this requirement.

The list of parenting education providers in Appendix B was last updated in June of 2002. To see if there is any updated contact information you might want to check **http://www.jud.state.ct.us/forms/fm151P.pdf**.

Insulating children from any hostilities between the parents is critical to good parenting throughout the divorce process. This means managing your own conflict well. Work toward strengthening your children's sense of security while they navigate their own choppy waters as you separate and divorce. It's a time to be very careful about what you say and to whom you say it. Think your conduct through carefully.

PARENTING EDUCATION PROGRAM

Connecticut law requires that parties involved in divorce and other legal actions involving custody and/or visitation who share a minor child or children participate in a parenting education program within sixty days of the return date. The purpose of these classes is to educate parents about the impact divorce and custody cases have on children. The classes cover issues such as the developmental stages of children, adjustment of children to parental separation, dispute resolution, conflict resolution and management, guidelines for visitation, stress reduction in children, and cooperative parenting.

Classes are six hours, and each session is scheduled for a different time and length. The maximum cost is $100 per person, and the court can waive the fee if you can prove that you are unable to pay it. Court-ordered classes require that each parent have a Parenting Education Order Form signed by the provider (*see* page 144).

Parents are encouraged to attend the programs together, but this is not a requirement. If you want to attend a different program from your spouse, you may pick a different class location. If you want to attend classes at the same location, tell the provider when you call to register that you do not want to be in a class with your spouse.

A list of approved providers of parenting education programs can be found in Appendix B. You can attend any program in the state. You can also attend a comparable "unauthorized" program or participate in family therapy sessions instead of attending the parenting education class. However, the court must approve your participation in any unauthorized program. To get approval, you must file a motion with the court requesting permission.

You must arrange for the classes by calling the program directly. You will be provided with specific information concerning dates, times, and location of the classes along with the registration procedures and fee arrangements. You should take the parenting education form with you to the first class (*see* page 145 for instructions on preparing this form).

The law does provide that the court can enter an order exempting you from the requirement to take parenting education classes. (See Chapter 6 for an explanation about requesting relief from this and other automatic orders.) If the parties agree not to participate in the program and the court agrees, or if the court finds on its own that participation is not necessary, then you may be exempt. Some judges will exempt you from an authorized program if you have negotiated a solid parenting plan and you can demonstrate at your final hearing that you have participated in education and/or counseling to help you and your children with the divorce.

It is advisable that you take the parenting education classes even if the court does not require you to. Every judge is different, and if you count on not having to take the class, the judge may delay your divorce by requiring you to take it. In addition, these classes are extremely valuable for learning ways to help your children through the divorce process and to be a better divorced parent.

SAMPLE GROUND RULES FOR PARENTS

Here are some research-based ground rules for parents designed specifically for insulating the children from parental hostilities. They are abstracted from a section in Robert E. Adler's fine work, *Sharing the Children*, and are printed here by permission.

Directions: Discuss the statements below and initial those that you both agree to honor. Modify them as needed to fit your intentions. You may wish to circle or write down on a separate piece of paper any of the agreements you both initial. You can refer to them if you momentarily lose your way in your negotiations about your children.

Initial

_____ _____   1. We agree that we value our children's relationships and the time they spend with us.

_____ _____   2. We agree that we value our children's relationships and the time they spend with the other parent.

_____ _____   3. We agree to make numbers 1 and 2 clear to our children.

_____ _____   4. We agree to work out a fair and practical time-sharing schedule with each other, either temporary or long term, as soon as possible, and explain it to our children. If they are teenagers, we agree to get their input.

_____ _____   5. We agree to make every effort to live up to the agreement that comes out of number 4.

_____ _____   6. We agree to tell the other parent in advance of any necessary changes in plan.

_____ _____   7. We agree to be reasonably flexible in trading off time-sharing to accommodate the other parent's needs.

_____ _____   8. We agree to prepare our children, in a positive way, for each upcoming transfer to, and time with, the other parent.

_____ _____   9. We agree to work out our problems with the other parent in private and not to conduct adult business in the presence of our children, including at the time we transfer them between us.

_____ _____   10. We agree not to use our children as confidants, messengers, bill collectors, or spies.

_____ _____   11. We agree to overcome the temptation to enlist our children on our side of any issue.

_____ _____   12. We agree to listen caringly but to encourage our children to work out problems with the other parent directly.

Who Will Make the Major Decisions Regarding the Children?

LEGAL CUSTODY—SOLE OR JOINT?

Whoever has legal custody makes the major decisions regarding the children—for example, about their education, health, medical care, and religious training. Either both parents make decisions together—which is joint legal custody—or one parent makes those decisions alone—which is sole legal custody. Physical/residential custody—where the children live—is a separate matter discussed later in this chapter.

Each parent generally makes day-to-day decisions if the children are physically with him or her at the time of the decision. An example of such a decision is whether "our" child should go to Billy's birthday party during "my" time. Consistency of day-to-day rules is helpful to children if you can reach agreements on some of these issues.

If you and your spouse agree that you will have joint legal custody, you are agreeing that the major decisions regarding your children must be made by you together. You must discuss any such decisions with each other until you reach agreement. Neither of you has the power to make these decisions alone. Examples of major decisions might be: whether your child will attend private, public, or parochial school or whether to treat your child's bed-wetting problem medically, psychologically, or some other way.

If you agree that one of you will have sole legal custody, then you are agreeing that the major decisions will be made by the parent with whom the child primarily resides. There is no duty to consult with the other parent, although some sole custodians do, and there is no obligation to reach agreement. Input from the non-custodial parent need not, but may, be taken into account by the decision maker.

The decision of whether to have joint or sole decision making should be taken seriously and made with planning and commitment. The most difficult joint custody cases for children result from parents who use their joint decision making responsibilities as the arena for carrying on their hostilities from the marriage. On the other hand, the most difficult sole custody arrangements for children occur when one parent becomes distant or disappears and the other becomes overwhelmed, bearing a huge responsibility alone. Consider getting some counseling if a desire to defeat or exclude the other parent seems to be the basis of wanting sole custody.

 Legal Custody: The parent or other person who has the legal right to make the major decisions concerning a child.

 Sole Legal Custody: The one parent or other person who has the legal power to make *all* the major decisions concerning a child.

 Joint Legal Custody: Both parents have equal legal power to make the major decisions concerning their child.

 Primary Physical Custody: If the parents agree to joint legal custody, one parent may be designated as the parent with whom the child primarily lives.

 "Don't ever agree to joint custody. That means nobody really has custody, and if one of you disappears with the kids nobody will help you get them back."

This is not accurate. For the most part, a court will protect the rights of joint legal custodians just as much as full or sole custodians. However, if geographical relocation of a child is even a remote concern for either of you, then be sure your agreement contains very clear provisions about what will result if this occurs.

HOW DO WE DECIDE?

In order to carefully consider whether to have joint or sole legal custody, think about the likely decisions that you will be making about your children—for example, schools and medical care, activities and lessons, driver's license, car insurance, birth control. List below six anticipated important decisions regarding your children:

a.

b.

c.

d.

e.

f.

In the following table, using different colored pens, answer "yes" or "no" for each question in the left column relating to the anticipated decisions you have listed.

PARENTAL DECISION-MAKING QUESTIONNAIRE

Decisions:	a	b	c	d	e	f
1. Can I bear to be left out of this decision?						
2. Must I have veto power over this decision (if I don't agree, it does not happen)?						
3. Is consultation about my opinion sufficient?						
4. Is being informed of the decision before the fact sufficient?						
5. Do I have to be part of the fact-gathering (interviewing day care providers and pediatricians, checking out ballet school or karate class, visiting colleges, etc.)?						
6. If I'm not part of the decision, am I willing to pay my fair share of the cost?						

Interpreting the Parental Decision-Making Questionnaire

- If both of you answer "no" to 1 and "yes" to 5 for most or all of your decisions, then joint legal custody would probably work for you.

- "Yes" by either of you to 3, 4, and 6 for most of the decisions indicates that parent may be content with not being part of the decision making and therefore comfortable with sole legal custody for the other parent.

- If either of you answers "yes" to 2 for most of the decisions, it might indicate that power and control over the other parent is important to that person. This can be a problem in joint decision making.

- If either of you answers "yes" to 1 and 2 about some but not all of your six decisions, this may indicate that those decisions are very important to that parent. In such a case, you might want to make that parent the final decision maker in those areas.

CAN WE HAVE JOINT LEGAL CUSTODY?

Can parents who could not get along during their marriage really be good joint decision makers? The answer to this question depends on whether or not the joint custody arrangement becomes a vehicle for continuing the marital hostilities. In fact, making joint decisions does not require that you get along, or even that you like each other. It requires mutual respect and maturity—the ability to trust and to cooperate. Ask yourselves whether you can discuss and negotiate fairly with each other, keeping your children's interests as your primary goal.

Research shows that there are some qualities that enable parents to overcome their hostilities and to work together as joint custodians. Many of these qualities are important to parenting in general and apply to a sole custody situation as well.

"Joint custody means a 50-50 split right down the middle." Joint custody does not mean the children live half the time with each parent. The schedule for children varies regardless of legal custodial title and is based on the best interests of each child.

Should We—Can We?

For most parents, the issue is not whether to share major decisions about their children after divorce; the issue is whether they can.

186   CHAPTER 8

Who Is Not (Quite) Ready for Joint Custody?

Parents who have great difficulty making joint custody work have many of these characteristics:

- They maintain intense, continuing conflict and hostility that they are unable to divert from the children.

- They exhibit overwhelming anger and the continuing need to punish the former spouse.

- There is a history of physical abuse.

- There is a history of substance abuse.

- One or both maintain a fixed belief that the other is a bad parent.

- One or both is unable to separate his or her own feelings and needs from those of the children.

If any of these apply to you or your spouse, joint legal custody may still be a possibility for you if your determination is great enough, but you will probably require some professional help. There are therapists who specialize in teaching parenting skills and mediators who can help you work out a parenting plan.

Parenting Qualities Chart

Directions: Rate yourselves and each other individually and as a team, on a scale of one to ten, ten being excellent, on the following chart using different colored pens.

Mom	Dad	Team	Qualities of Good Joint Legal Custodians
			1. Makes clear to our children that he/she values relationship and time with self and with other parent, despite all his/her anger and disappointment from the ending of our marriage.
			2. Maintains some objectivity throughout our divorce process and insulates our children from our conflicts.
			3. Empathizes with our children's point of view and with that of other parent.
			4. Successfully shifts his/her emotional expectations of the other from the role of mate to that of co-parent and recognizes the boundaries of the new roles.
			5. Maintains high self-esteem, shows flexibility, and is open to both giving and receiving help from outside sources and especially from the other parent.

Interpreting the Parenting Qualities Chart

- If your evaluations of yourselves and each other coincide and the estimate of your joint functioning is a 5 or better, you are probably candidates for successful joint legal custody.

- If your evaluation of yourselves and each other directly contradict and the estimate of your joint functioning is a 4 or less, then joint legal custody might be difficult for you.

- If your answers are not consistent and you still want to try joint legal custody, you should be aware that to make this decision work for your children will be hard work for both you and your spouse.

HOW TO MAKE JOINT LEGAL CUSTODY WORK

If you agree to be joint legal custodians, it is crucial that you define the decisions that you will make jointly and decide the process you will use if you do not initially agree.

Use the following shopping list to write your Must-Share Decisions List together.

Shopping List of Must-Share Decisions

1. Any major expense (whether one-time or ongoing) that we expect the other parent to share in. We define a major expense as anything over $_____. For example: your child's teacher says you should enroll him or her in piano lessons and buy or rent a piano in each home.

2. Any activity that may take place on the other parent's time. For example: soccer league where the games are every Saturday and you plan on alternate weekends with each parent.

3. Any major change in our basic plan for time we each spend with the children and/or the basic support plan.

4. Choice of school, including whether it should be private, public, or parochial.

5. Orthodontia or other medical and dental treatment.

6. Mental health counseling.

7. When our children will drive, whose car, and who pays for the extra insurance.

8. The birth control teaching and decisions of our children.

9. In-school electives and activities, whether or not they cost more money.

10. Parent-teacher conferences.

11. Results of medical/dental exams and recommended treatment.

12. Elective medical or dental treatment. Be sure you say that either parent is able to sign for emergency medical care when the other parent cannot be reached immediately. State that any follow-up care is a joint decision.

Must-Share Decisions List

Our list of decisions that we both agree are to be made jointly:

1.

2.

3.

4.

5.

6.

7.

8.

The parent who has the children at the time will make any decisions not on this list.

AVOIDING DEADLOCK THROUGH GOOD COMMUNICATION

One key to making your joint legal custody agreement work is to write out your communication process in detail. This may sound too silly to work but it usually does. Some couples find this very helpful at the beginning of their separation. It is up to you. It is also up to you whether you wish to include any of your agreements about communication processes in your final separation agreement.

Communications Process Checklist

Directions: Discuss each of the following carefully, and decide which, if any, will work for you. Alter them as needed. Initial those statements below that you both agree will work for you.

Initial

———— ————   1. We agree to meet at the same time and place for at least fifteen minutes a week (every other week, month) whether we have anything earthshaking to report or not. (This will get you in the habit of talking face to face and listening carefully before you have to do it when a problem comes up.)

———— ————   2. We agree to share (or exchange) a written agenda in advance of our meetings. (Big surprises are nearly always unpleasant and difficult.)

———— ————   3. Each of us agrees to present issues without our own "pet" solution already in place. Instead, each of us will keep an open mind by suggesting a number of possible options.

———— ————   4. If we really get stuck on something, we will each produce two alternate plans, solutions, or suggestions that each of us can live with in the event one's favorite solution does not meet with the other's favor.

———— ————   5. We agree to rank the three best solutions, any one of which are acceptable to both of us, and let the children select.

———— ————   6. If we agree, we may invite the child in question to the discussion.

———— ————   7. We agree that unless there is real-time urgency, we won't shake hands on the deal on the spot. We will write it up and exchange drafts the next day, then meet again.

———— ————   8. We agree to suspend discussions until both of us have had time to cool off, if necessary, to gather more data, to get other input, or to ask the children. In other words, we agree to force ourselves to look past our initial reaction and develop other alternatives.

———— ————   9. We agree to seek together the opinion of someone with special knowledge about the problem, such as a teacher, counselor, pediatrician, or pastor.

———— ————   10. We agree to initiate a short-term trial to gain more information and to check out our assumptions. For example: we agree to reevaluate the school at the end of the semester or reevaluate after three sessions with the counselor.

LONG-DISTANCE JOINT LEGAL CUSTODY

Can "long-distance parents," parents too far apart geographically to meet face to face on a regular basis, be effective joint decision making parents? Yes, with great commitment by both parents. Just as time heals much, distance may lend clarity and decrease pressure.

The following is some suggested language that you may wish to include in your agreement if you are considering becoming long-distance joint custodians.

1. We will work together to make our list of must-share decisions as clear and well-defined as possible.

2. We agree to develop, at the outset, a communication process or sequence that will work for us and to stick with it until and unless we both agree to change it. For example: "We will talk by phone until we disagree, then we will exchange our thinking in writing." OR, "We will never call each other on the phone (except in emergency). We will only communicate face to face three times a year."

3. Each of us agrees to present to the other, as early as possible, any question or future decision to be made—even if it might not occur.

4. Each of us agrees that if we get stuck on a particular joint decision we will find a mediator who will work with us via conference call.

5. Each of us will develop a plan for exchanging news and information, i.e., use mail, fax, e-mail, and audio and video tapes, as well as the telephone.

RESOLVING DEADLOCK

Even with the best communication processes it is possible to get stuck. If you agree to joint legal custody, you should include a paragraph in your agreement about what you will do if after concerted effort you really get stuck on one of your major decisions. The court needs to be sure you are not agreeing to joint legal custody because you do not have the stomach to choose between yourselves and that you will not come back to court every time you cannot agree on a joint decision. The more confident your agreement sounds about how you are going to go about sharing your joint decisions, the more likely the court is to approve it without

---

Communications with the Other Parent

Poor: "Jennifer got a scholarship to Europe, so she won't be coming to see you."

Better: "Jennifer has a chance at a choir trip to Europe for June and July. Unfortunately, it is during your time with her. What do you think?"

Best: "Jennifer is getting so serious at her music, I wonder if we should explore, with her options for camp, clinics, performance experience. For instance ...."

What We Will Do If We Get Stuck:

Directions: Write here what you agree to do if and when you get stuck.

1.

2.

3.

4.

5.

More Communications with the Other Parent

Poor: "Jennifer is going to Europe in June and July. I put down the first payment last night. It's not refundable."

Better: "Jennifer said she would like to consider the Europe trip for this summer, but she doesn't want to miss seeing you or hurting your feelings. Can you give her a call and discuss some alternatives with her?"

Best: "Here is Jennifer's vacation calendar with the dates of the possible Europe trip penciled in. I will see that she has no other activities scheduled for the summer. She also has nothing scheduled for spring break this year. (Spring break for her is _____ to _____.) By the way, parents are allowed to go on the Europe trip. Would you be able to go for all or some of it? I know Jennifer would be thrilled."

Our Information Exchange List

We agree to share with each other information about the following:

1.

2.

3.

4.

5.

6.

7.

8.

question. If you find yourselves stuck, there are some very effective ways to get unstuck. The following are some sample ideas.

- Assign a "sphere of influence" to each of you as separate decision makers for times you cannot reach a decision jointly after trying all your agreed-upon deadlock-breaking techniques. For example, mother makes the medical decisions, father makes the educational decisions.

- Seek input from a person with special knowledge in the area of the decision you are stuck on. For example, ask the school counselor about whether your child should repeat kindergarten.

- Take the particular issue to mediation. A neutral third-party may help you find your solution.

- Choose a third party to make the decision for you. For example, let your priest or pastor decide a question about religion, or let your child's teacher make the decision about school.

- Take the particular issue to formal arbitration. You will each have the opportunity to argue for your position, then the arbitrator will decide.

INFORMATION EXCHANGE—FOR ANY KIND OF CUSTODY

In most custody plans, regardless of whether they are for sole or joint legal custody, there are matters both parents must stay informed about. Some parents think that something is a must-share decision when the real issue is that they do not want to be left out. An Information Exchange List is very useful not only for joint legal custody plans but also for keeping peace within sole custody plans. The following are some suggestions for your consideration.

- If you have trouble arranging for the school, pediatrician, or dentist to send a copy of everything concerning your children to both of you, then make arrangements for doing this yourselves. Be very specific about who will copy and send what to whom.

- The parent who first learns of child's upcoming activity must agree to notify the other parent (by making and sending a photocopy, by leaving a message on the other parent's answering machine, or by putting a note in an agreed upon pocket in the children's backpacks).

- Come to a clear understanding about notifying the other parent about any minor injury or illness that occurs on your time with the children. This can be hard because you worry that it will reflect badly on your parenting. Sometimes having a promise in your parenting plan will make these difficult phone calls easier.

- Inform the other parent of any change in the normal behavior, sleep, or eating pattern of a child. These are also often hard calls to make for fear the other parent will take the opportunity to criticize or worse.

- Let the other parent know about any special award or accomplishment of a child. Sometimes having the child make this call or write this note is a very positive way of reinforcing your commitment to the importance of the other parent to your children.

- If any child repeatedly complains about something in the other home and/or tells of something you consider dangerous or probably untrue you will then immediately call the other parent to verify (with the child in earshot only if appropriate).

Use e-mail and the Internet for maximum communication.

SOLE LEGAL CUSTODY

The parent who has sole legal custody makes decisions without having to consult with the other parent. Sole legal custody is appropriate when parents cannot or will not work together. Sometimes sole custody is a continuation of the way things were during the marriage in that one parent has historically been the decision maker. Things may change, however, after you get beyond your initial fear, hurt, and anger. Be open to the possibility of wanting to share decisions about your children at a later date.

As a sole legal custodian you may never get a break. You will never be able to say, "Go ask your father/mother." Some people say single parenting is burdensome and lonely—the hardest job on earth. Even joint custodians have feelings of loneliness and being burdened when they realize their former means of communication and decision making have to change so radically. The sole legal custodian may have to do without any communication at all with the other parent.

Some parents evolve a kind of hybrid: sole legal custody with some designated must-share decisions. For example, when Johnny drives and whose car or what college and who pays. Designating certain shared decisions need not change the legal custody from sole to joint. Having some shared decisions can be both an act of self-preservation for the sole legal custodian and an

 An excellent family calendaring system is located at **www.our-familywizard.com** or **www.myevents.com**.

Single Parent Overload?

Family counselors, therapists, churches, and single-parent groups can provide counsel and assistance for single parents. Many of them sponsor support groups for single parents to provide insight and mutual support, and even family activities. These resources can be helpful to the sole legal custodian who needs psychological and moral support, as well as to the joint legal custodian who finds the going rough.

Sole Custody with Shared Decisions

In practice, although most courts approve sole custody agreements which require the sole custodian to consult with the other parent, some courts may be resistant to enforcing them. If your agreement requires either of these, be very clear and specific, especially about what you will do if this part of your agreement breaks down.

Primary Physical Custody: Legal designation of where a child lives—sometimes called "primary residential custody."

Primary or Residential Custody: The child lives primarily with one parent or other person.

opportunity for involvement of the other parent in shaping the child's life.

Beware the link between decisions and dollars. If you have sole legal custody and have no provision about discussing extraordinary expenses for your children, you may create an uncomfortable situation for everyone. The custodial parent might enroll the child in music lessons, sports, even private school, and simply send a bill to the non-custodial parent for his or her share. If the sole custodian makes all the decisions without input from the other parent, this can happen. How likely is payment of this bill? How does this unplanned process make everyone feel? This may be a blueprint for conflict.

No matter what label you put on your legal custody arrangement, you will inevitably need or want to talk together at some point about your children. Your agreement should leave room for that. Even if you do not wish to require joint decision making, you have to be ready to talk with each other.

Where Will the Children Live?

The question of where your children live is the legal issue of physical/residential custody. The specific legal label or name hinges on where the children primarily live. Since most parenting happens while the children are awake, you should probably begin with your day-to-day schedules as they are now. Let your parenting plan—as you work it out—define the label rather than naming your plan and then forcing it to fit the label.

The amount of time the children spend with each parent is what Connecticut calls "physical custody." This in turn creates a presumption about the amount of basic child support as well as who gets the children as tax exemptions. There are two kinds of physical custody: primary physical or shared.

Primary or residential physical custody means that the children have one primary home (home base). The time with the other parent, is called visitation, but is now sometimes referred to as parenting time, custodial time or on access schedule. The sole legal custodial parent usually has primary physical custody, subject to visitation rights to the non custodial parent. If legal custody is joint, there may not be a designation of primary physical custody.

Shared physical custody means that the children have two homes. They have substantial clothing, toys, and possessions at both homes. The designation "shared physical custody" does not arise just because the overnights reach a certain magical number. It occurs because the parents commit to having two homes for the children, with a schedule for sharing time.

Shared Physical Custody: Both parents agree, and the court approves, that each parent will have the children living with them, usually with a designation of a primary residential parent.

Whether legal custody is sole or joint, *split physical custody* means that the primary home of at least one child is with one parent and the primary home of at least one other child is with the other parent. For example, if one child is a teenager and is having difficulty fitting in or sharing with other siblings, then some intense, one-on-one attention from one parent may be just right. However, if one child has special needs, having two primary parents in different homes may be too confusing.

Split Physical Custody: Each parent has sole or primary physical custody of a different child.

Physical custody can feel like the most important part of your agreement, and counting overnights can stall or foreclose your agreement. If you find yourselves getting stuck and angry about this issue, then consider the following information:

- Children change as they grow. The agreement you agonize over today may not work a year from now. One of the most important things which changes is how long a child can be away from the primary parent, or from either parent if you have both been active. Small children have an extremely short separation tolerance—less than a day for infants.

- Frequent transfers between parents can be stressful once a child is no longer so much in need of frequent contact.

Visitation: The scheduled time for one parent, usually the non-custodial parent, to spend time with the child. Less emotionally charged terms that mean the same thing are "parenting time" or "custodial time."

PARENTING TIME AND THE DEVELOPMENTAL STAGES OF YOUR CHILD

Children have different needs at different stages in their growth and development, meaning that they should learn certain things at certain expected ages. It's vitally important in putting together your parenting plan to meet the developmental needs of your children.

Bear in mind that there is no single right way to do physical or residential custody. What's right is what works best for all of you. Every family succeeding in parenting from two households works out a unique schedule that makes sense for both the children and the parents. Generally, from infancy to age six, one primary home is advisable with the other parent spending time with the child that reflects the pre-separation care-taking history. After age six, parents need to decide if they will stay with a "home base" approach or move to a more equitable time-sharing arrangement.

The following is a summary of children's stages taken largely from *Sharing the Children* by Robert E. Adler, PhD. See also *Children of Divorce* by Mitchell Baris, PhD, and Carla Garrity, PhD.

Infancy—Birth to Eighteen Months:

The developmental tasks from birth to six months are physiological stabilization and bonding to one or more parental figures. Babies need consistent care and nurturing, which includes feeding, diapering, talking to, playing with, holding, and cuddling.

From six to eighteen months, the developmental tasks are the deepening of loving attachments to caretakers, development of basic trust and security, and exploring the environment from a secure base. Babies continue to have the same needs as the previous stage, with emphasis on the addition of predictability, familiarity, and a safe environment to explore.

Care must be consistent and continuous, with responsive caretakers. The number of caretakers should be small, the settings stable, and routines smooth and predictable.

Visits with the non-custodial (or "non-primary") parent should be frequent and fairly short (rather than longer contacts farther apart). Overnight visits are probably not in babies' best interests, and separation from either parent should not be longer than a few days. Both parents may have the ability to provide for and nurture the child. However, the separation and individuation process, which is very important at this stage, is best if it proceeds at a normal pace.

Our Infant

Our child _____ (name) is in the birth to six months age range. He or she fits the description given here in the following ways:

He or she does not fit the description given here in the following ways:

"Children, especially very young ones, must be with their mothers. Besides, a woman who doesn't keep custody of her children must not be a real woman!"

The facts do not bear out this stereotyping. Children need to be wanted. Research shows that single parents of both sexes struggle with the same problems.

Try to match schedules to the child's temperament. An easy child can handle longer times away from each parent and a more flexible schedule. A slow-to-warm-up child may need to stay with frequent, short contacts until older. A difficult child may require even shorter visits on a very predictable schedule. Overnight stays are still likely to be stressful to the child. An easy and adaptable child with motivated and cooperative parents may handle them well, but other infants in less ideal circumstances will probably do better if overnights do not start this early.

Some possible parenting plans for this age:

- The other parent spends two or three hours, for a *minimum* of two or three times per week with the child, preferably in the home of the primary parent.

- Starting at about eight months, three-hour visits away from the primary home gradually increasing to six hours.

Toddlers—Eighteen Months to Three Years

The developmental tasks at this age are becoming an individual, developing autonomy, and experiencing safe separation from parents.

Children need firm support, meaning that the parents, secure and patient, need to set firm limits while allowing the freedom to explore. During the "terrible twos," parents need to allow children to resist on unimportant issues but must stand firm when it comes to safety, self-control, and interacting with others. The parents must be attentive monitors at this time. They must have the patience to provide verbal explanations and reassurance, repeated over and over.

Children need close, consistent, frequent contact with both parents. Secure, well-adjusted children toward the end of this age range can handle longer stays, entire days, or overnights, spaced up to three or even four days apart. Entire weekends away from home base may still be too much for children this age.

Less adaptable children, or those still not familiar with a parent, may still need shorter, more frequent contacts without overnight stays.

Some possible parenting plans for this age:

- One primary home. The other parent has the child during the day up to three times per week on a predictable schedule, in or out of the primary home.

Our Eighteen-Month to Three-Year-Old Child

Our child _____ (name) is in the eighteen months to three years age range. He or she fits the description given here in the following ways:

He or she does not fit the description given here in the following ways:

Our Three- to Five-Year-Old Child

Our child _____ (name) is in the three to five years age range. He or she fits the description given here in the following ways:

He or she does not fit the description given here in the following ways:

- One primary home. The other parent has the child as above, but with one overnight per week at the end of this age range.

- One primary home plus good day care. Schedule as in either of the two previous examples.

Preschoolers—Three Through Five Years

The developmental tasks at this age are development of initiative, impulse management, sex role identification, and peer relationships.

At this age children need clear parental roles, values, and cooperation. Children of this age react strongly to parental conflict. They need frequent and continuing contact with the same-sex parent. Do not encourage children this age to feel that they have driven away the same-sex parent and that they now have a unique relationship with the opposite sex parent.

Children need frequent and predictable contacts with plenty of reassurance, love, and support. Predictability of schedules is at least as important as frequency or duration. Children this age need to know that the divorce is not their fault and that they don't have the power to undo it.

Pre-school children need access to nursery school or other settings for stimulation and socialization, and both parents need to maintain the children's schedule.

Even during holiday periods, children this age should not go longer than one week without contact with a parent. Supplement longer separations with phone calls. For vacations, schedule one week, once or twice a year, with the nonprimary parent.

Some possible parenting plans for this age:

- One overnight per week starting at about age two and a half to three, increasing gradually to a maximum of a split week at the end of the age range.

- Two or three nights at one home, spaced throughout the week, with the remaining time at the other home.

- Same as above but supplemented by good day care.

- Three consecutive days and nights with one parent, four with the other.

- Every other weekend with the non-primary parent, with or without time during the week.

A full week should not pass without the child spending an evening, half-day or overnight with the other parent.

School-age Children—Six Through Twelve Years

The developmental tasks at this age are to free energy from family concerns in order to focus on friends, school, learning, self-discipline, and cooperative play; to gain a sense of personal competence and self-esteem; to develop logical thought applied to concrete objects; and to develop a sense of fairness.

School-age children need enough stability and security at home to allow full involvement outside the home, a reasonably well-structured schedule with some flexibility, exclusion from parents' conflicts, and insulation from their negative views of each other.

These children, especially the older ones, suffer when they feel they have to choose between their parents. They may respond with intense anger or by rejecting one parent completely. They need lots of explanation, discussion, and listening. They need geographical proximity to and continuity of school and friends. Both parents continuing to live in the same area is an ideal arrangement for these children.

Children this age also need flexibility. This becomes important as these children develop strong friendships and activities outside the home. Parental insistence on a planned contact at the expense of a much desired activity can generate resentment.

Contacts with parents can be spontaneous. A parent dropping in on these children, or the children initiating a contact with a parent, can be valuable as long as such contacts do not stir up parental conflict. Particularly for younger school-age children, two weeks without contact with a parent is too long. Supplement longer separations by brief contacts, spontaneous visits, and phone calls.

If parental conflict is low, school-age children can do well with many different parenting plans as long as the plans provide for relatively frequent and adequate contact with both parents. Generally, children in this age group do better with blocks of time, spending the majority of the school week with one parent. One test to use in assessing the appropriateness of a proposed schedule is for the parent to ask the question: "Will the children move homes more frequently than the parent would find tolerable if the parent were doing the moving?"

Some possible parenting plans for this age:

The Case of the Reappearing Parent

An absent parent, physically or otherwise, may reappear. A parent without interest in babies may be much better at and more interested in parenting an older child. A parent who is excellent with toddlers may be at a total loss with teenagers. Things change. The best parenting plans give the children access to the best of each parent at any given time.

Our Six- Through Twelve-Year-Old Child

Our child _____ (name) is in the six to twelve years age range. He or she fits the description given here in the following ways:

He or she does not fit the description given here in the following ways:

"When children reach a certain age, they have the legal right to choose which parent they want to live with."

There is no age at which the law in Connecticut shifts this decision to the child, although judges will consider, but not necessarily implement, the child's wishes.

Our Teenager

Our child _____ (name) is in the thirteen to eighteen years age range. He or she fits the description given here in the following ways:

He or she does not fit the description given here in the following ways:

- Friday after school through Sunday evening or Monday morning, every other week, plus one or two nights during the two-week stay with the other parent.

- Three days with one parent, four days with the other.

- Alternating weeks with each parent, with midweek after school time.

- Alternate weekends with each parent, two or three days at each home during the week.

- Three and a half days with each parent—weekends are also split.

- One or two weeks with each parent, with one or two midweek overnights with the other starting around age eight.

- Older children may be able to handle even longer stays if they are supplemented by phone calls and some contacts with the other parent.

- Some parents find it manageable to have the child spend the school year at one home and the bulk of vacation time at the other. Supplement contact with frequent and regular calls and visits.

Teenagers—Thirteen to Eighteen Years

The developmental tasks of teenagers include separation, peer involvement, development of own identity, sexual identity, and independence.

Teenagers need emotional stability and maturity on the part of both parents. They need adequate but flexible and age-appropriate parental controls and continuing, meaningful contact with both parents.

Schedules must be flexible enough to respect teenagers' needs for involvement with peers and independent activities. The level of parent-parent conflict about scheduling should be low.

Parents should be sensitive to teenagers' needs to be consulted, informed, and listened to without giving up the adult/child relationship. Treat teenagers as individuals. Teenagers do not need the same extended time with either parent that they once did.

Some possible parenting plans for this age:

- Home base with one parent, and a mixture of scheduled and spontaneous overnights, shorter visits, and outings with the other parent.

- Children spend school year as above. During summer vacation and other long holidays, reverse the arrangement.

- For some teenagers, the more structured plans discussed for younger age groups may continue to work, particularly if the parents are geographically close.

- Some families work out year-by-year arrangements with older children. These plans need to respect teenagers' needs for continuity in friendships and school placement, and telephone and other contacts should supplement contact as frequently as possible.

MORE THAN ONE CHILD

Although it usually makes sense for all the children to share the same schedule, be open to the needs of each of your children, even if that means making different arrangements for each child. Infants have special needs for feeding and holding, teenagers for peer involvement and controlling their own lives.

Having an older brother or sister along can be important support for a younger child. Nevertheless, the children don't always have to be together for their time with parents. One-on-one time with a parent is important for all children. Sometimes it's best for one child to live primarily with the mother and the other to live primarily with the father. If the children are split, then the schedule should also allow for times for the children to be together with each parent.

TIME SHARING

Some parents want equal time sharing when it may or may not be in the children's best interests. For example, infants and very young children may not be developmentally ready for two homes on a fifty-fifty basis. You may better serve small children by gradually expanding the overnights with the other parent, with a goal of reaching fifty-fifty or by establishing roughly equal time sharing by an older age. However, a younger child may do quite well in equal time sharing if his or her connections have been strong with both parents and/or if there is an older sibling making the same transitions on the same schedule. Teenagers, who can do well with equal time sharing, need to have input about where and how they spend their time.

"Kids can't make it if they go back and forth between very different parents."

Some experts say that for two households to work well together, they shouldn't be too terribly far apart in value systems. For example, if one parent lives a "laid-back" hippie lifestyle and the other household uses linen napkins, the child may begin to wonder whether to be like mom and her household, or dad and his. Studies show that children can make these transitions with support and preparation from both parents.

Four-three-three-four and Alternating Weeks

Florence and Fred separated within the same neighborhood when their two children were in first and third grade. They began with a four-three-three-four schedule, splitting the children's time equally between them over a two-week period. After three months of this type of schedule, the children asked if they could alternate weeks, rather than splitting each week. The parents made the change.

Developing Your Parenting Schedule

Don't expect to know right away what arrangements are going to be best for your children in the long term. Your first plan may well not be your final agreement. If you are just starting to work out your parenting plan, you may want to review Chapter 3 to begin planning your separation.

BASIC SCHEDULE

Most parents begin a discussion of basic schedules by talking about whether it is in their children's best interests at the present time to have one primary home or two equal homes. To some parents this means dividing the children's time between mom's house and dad's house nearly equally and having close to a complete set of clothes, toys, and equipment at each home. To others it means locating the child's bedroom set, bicycle, and computer with one parent, and the child carries a backpack with clothes and other items to the other parent's home and sleeps on a day bed or in a sleeping bag. For most parents, the distinction between having one home or two for the children is not so cut and dried. To decide this for yourselves, consider your children's developmental ages, the geographic distance you will be from each other, and your respective parenting styles. Remember that things change. What works today for your family will, in all probability, not work at some later time, perhaps sooner than you expect.

Sometimes, at divorce, one parent has clearly been the major caregiver for the children and the other has been less involved. Sometimes divorce brings the more distant parent "out of the woodwork" to become a more interested and active parent. Sometimes the less involved parent just wants to fade away. Sometimes the historical major caregiver resents that the other parent wants now, at the end of the marriage, to become a more active parent. If a parent has been distant from the children, it may be in the children's best interests to phase in the changes gradually. Parenting plans do not need to blindly perpetuate the status quo. Divorce is a time of great change for everyone. Getting away from a difficult or destructive marriage often enables people to become better parents.

Realistically, equal or substantial time-sharing usually requires that the parents live near each other, optimally within the same school district. In that situation, the children really can enjoy having two homes. This is feasible, usually, if the parents live close together—a few minutes driving or within bicycling or walking distance.

You can create a calendar with everyone's schedule to use online. Graphics and printouts may help to involve children in knowing about their schedule. Visit **www.myevents.com** for more information.

Parents who live a significant distance apart, but still within driving distance, usually look for a weekend arrangement (every weekend, alternate weekends, one or two a month) during the school year, complemented by some other arrangement during the summer. If you don't live in the same area you will need to look at an arrangement that is more appropriate for this longer distance area. These ideas reflect what appears to work for most people, not hard and fast rules. You must develop what will work for you, your spouse, and your children.

The two-home concept requires a plan for those times when you will transfer the children between you. The following are some of the questions you will need to consider and discuss. Remember, you may have different responses for each of your children. You may want to photocopy these questions so that each of you can make notes.

- Is it important for your children to be in the same house on all school nights?

- How important is it that your children settle in on Sunday night before school?

- Is it important for your children to go to the same church with the same parent every week?

- Can either parent take your children to recurring activities (soccer practice, Scouts, doctor's appointment)?

One Home or Two?

We believe our children would (would not) benefit from having two homes at the present time because:

☐ All our children look to both of us for day-to-day parenting.

☐ We will live too far apart to make frequent transportation between two households possible.

☐ One or more of our children is/are at a stage which makes frequent shifts from one home to another troublesome for them.

☐ Two homes are not possible now, because:

but we anticipate that it will be appropriate for _____ (name) by _____ (date/age/stage/circumstance).

Our Basic Schedule

Our initial basic time-sharing plan for our children will be:

☐   Every other weekend

☐   Other weekend arrangement

☐   Alternating weeks

☐   Alternating two-week periods

☐   Alternating months

☐   Alternating semesters

☐   4-3-3-4 every two-week period

☐   5-2-4-3 every two-week period

☐   6-1 each week

☐   5-2 each week

☐   4-3 each week

☐   One of us works a variable shift. We will arrange the children's schedule around this work schedule as follows:

☐   One of us works twenty-four hours on, forty-eight hours off. That parent will have all days-off with the children, or:

☐   School sessions with one parent, school breaks with the other.

☐   Other:

- Can your children go to the same school from either home, and return home from school to either home?

- Is there a maximum amount of time that any of your children can tolerate being away from either of you?

- How frequently do any of your children need to see each of you?

- Do you live so far apart geographically that your children will probably stay with one parent during school sessions and with the other during non-school time?

- Is this the time to change the day care schedule or provider for one or more of the children?

- Is it important to keep your children's day care schedule the same for the time being, in the face of other changes in their lives right now?

SIX-WEEK CALENDAR

Fill in your basic schedule for six weeks. This may be any six weeks, or the next six weeks, whichever is more useful to you. On the following page are suggestions.

This calendar ends the week with Saturday and Sunday together, unlike most published calendars that divide the weekend, generally a confusing picture for divorcing parents.

Mon.	Tues.	Wed.	Thurs.	Fri.	Sat.	Sun.

Directions for Six-week Calendar

Fill in the following information on the calendar on the previous page. Make several photocopies first for your rough drafts. Sometimes it is useful to use different colored pens for each parent or each member of the family.

1. Parents' fixed schedules, for example: work hours, fixed meetings, and appointments.

2. Children's fixed schedules, such as school hours, day care, and planned regular activities such as soccer practice, piano lessons, Scouts, and doctor's appointments.

3. If you are planning a specific six weeks, fill in the dates you are planning for and any holidays or other special days that fall during that time, such as a child's birthday.

4. Sketch in your agreement from "Our Basic Schedule." For example, school nights with one parent, vacation nights with the other, alternating weeks with each parent, etc., coordinating with the information in 1–3 above.

5. Indicate on the calendar who will provide the transportation each time. The farther apart you live, the more important the transportation issue will become. If you each agree to bring the children to the other parent, you demonstrate your support and willingness for your children to leave you and relate to the other parent.

7. Make a note about any items which must move back and forth with the children, such as clothing, boots, homework, and musical instruments.

HOLIDAYS AND OTHER SPECIAL DAYS

Many parents begin by listing all the holidays recognized by their school, church, or wall calendar. They then alternate each of these by odd- or even-numbered years or some other mathematical formula. When it comes to writing down your shared holidays, it may be easier to say that Mom will have the children for such-and-such holidays in even-numbered years while Dad has them in odd-numbered years.

Typically, arrangements for holidays and special days preempt the regular schedule. Your parenting plan must include agreement about how and when this happens. You may alternate the days themselves as discussed above or consider one of the following.

Consider merging federal, state, or school holidays, including teacher in-service days, that fall on a Monday or Friday with the weekend next to it. If you are doing an alternating weekend physical custody plan, these three-day weekends will even out between you over a period of two or three years. If you can tolerate unequal sharing of holiday time within a single year, this can work out well in the long run.

Be sure to include on your list those days that are special to your children. For example, children typically care much more about Halloween than they do about New Year's Day. Not all children or families feel the same way about the same holidays. These may change as the make-up of your new families changes. If you have any hesitation about where holidays fit on your children's list, ask them. Be prepared for some surprises. It is possible they will list Mother's Day and Father's Day or your birthdays, but don't be disappointed if they don't.

Most parents alternate the days that are special to their children from year to year or let them fall into place in the course of the usual schedule. Others agree that one parent has the children on the day itself, and the other parent celebrates the occasion on their next regular time with the children. If your children are small and/or your relationship is amicable, you might consider spending these important days together with your children. For example, give a joint birthday party. If sharing the event is not possible and your children are old enough, you might try alternating portions of these days, for example Christmas morning at Mom's, Christmas afternoon at Dad's. For all but the most stable of children, however, this usually results in emotional overload and an exhausted child trying to be cheerful.

Our Important Days

Directions: Circle any of the following which are important to you, using different colored pens for each parent and each child. Be sure to add to this list any other days or events which are important to you to share with the children such as, Russian Easter, St. Lucy's Day, Ramadan, or County Fair.

New Year's Eve	Father's Day
New Year's Day	Fourth of July
Martin Luther King, Jr. Day	Labor Day
Super Bowl	Columbus Day
Valentine's Day	Rosh Hashanah
President's Day	Yom Kippur
St. Patrick's Day	World Series
Passover	Halloween
Good Friday	Thanksgiving
Easter	Hanukkah
Mother's Day	Christmas Eve
Cinco de Mayo	Christmas Day
Memorial Day	Kwanzaa
	Other

Mother's Birthday

Father's Birthday

Children's Birthdays

Does the "Year" Start in January or September?

Your list of days might begin with Labor Day and the start of school rather than New Year's Day and the start of the calendar year. Experience has shown that most parents and children plan in terms of the school year rather than the calendar year.

Three-day Weekends

The holidays which we agree to add to or include in the previous or following weekend, including teacher in-service days, are:

Special Handling

We will handle the following holidays in the following special way:

Winter and/or Spring Break

Our plans for winter and/or spring break are:

Spring Break

Our plans for spring break are:

Thanksgiving Break

Our plans for Thanksgiving break are:

Summer Vacation

Our plans for summer vacation are:

Make a parenting plan for the long school breaks, usually summer, winter, and spring, and sometimes Thanksgiving. Many parents try to equalize the time in these school breaks over a calendar year. If you have a long-distance parenting arrangement in which the children spend the school year primarily with one parent, these breaks will constitute the other parent's time.

Where the children will spend the winter break and holiday is of great importance in most families, partly because it contains important holidays and partly because it is a two-to-six-week period in which the children are out of school. Here are some ideas:

- For short-distance parenting time, some parents remain with their regular weekly schedule. You may divide the entire break into two parts: one parent for the first half, the other for the second, to be reversed for the next year. The two-week break will usually divide December 26 or 27.

- If the winter break contains an important holiday to you (Christmas, Hanukkah, Kwanzaa), then your planning will probably focus on that holiday. You may specify that the holiday will be spent with Mother in even-numbered years and with Father in odd-numbered years. You may wish to divide the holiday between the parents. For example, Christmas Eve with Mother, Christmas Day with Father; first half of Hanukkah/Kwanzaa with Father, second half with Mother. You can then alternate each year if you wish, but you will have to decide at what time the children travel from one home to the other and who will provide the transportation.

- Thanksgiving break is usually four or five days, Wednesday or Thursday through Sunday. Spring break is usually nine days, starting and ending with a weekend. Many parents just continue their usual schedule, focusing on the holiday itself (sometimes spring break includes Easter). Some parents take part of their vacation during the school break and travel with the children. This is especially true if that parent works in a field in which summer or Christmas is the busiest time of year. For long-distance parents, these can be additional times for travel to the home of the other parent. If you are long-distance parents and the children spend the school session with one of you and school breaks with the other, you may wish to discuss reserving either Thanksgiving, winter or spring break, or both for the school-year parent.

- Summer vacation in most of Connecticut starts in June and ends around the last week in August. Most parents agree that the children need to be at the primary home for a few days to two weeks before school starts. Some parents reverse primary physical custody for the summer. In some long-distance situations, the children simply travel to the other home and spend the entire summer there. Others continue their regular pattern (alternating weeks, alternating weekends). Some continue their regular pattern, but agree that either parent has the right to take the children on a vacation for a designated number of weeks, with a certain amount of notice to the other parent. Some parents agree to meet every April or so to make their summer plans.

TRANSPORTATION

If you are a short distance apart, consider the responsibility for driving as a shared problem. It's usually difficult for one parent to have to provide it all the time, and it can, in itself, put an unfair burden on that parent's relationship with the child. Find a way to divide the picking-up and the dropping-off that creates the maximum convenience—or minimum inconvenience—for each of you. Sharing the transportation is a good way to demonstrate that you support the children's relationships with the other parent. Use transportation time to help the children in their transition to the other home.

If you live far apart, then your parenting plan will have to take into account longer travel time for both you and your children. Look at how much time (how many days) make a long-distance visit worthwhile.

Children five and younger must have someone travel with them by air. Children aged six through eight can fly unaccompanied on direct flights, while connecting flights require an adult. Airlines consider "adults" for this purpose to be anyone age twelve or older. Children aged nine through eleven may fly as unaccompanied minors on all flights. Many airlines provide escorts for children for a fee (usually about $50). This service is helpful in reducing the cost of providing adult supervision for minor children when traveling. If this service is not available or you decide not to use it, you may decide that the parent will do the traveling rather than very young children. Another option is to have a parent accompany the child on the trip.

Your parenting plan should be clear about who pays for the transportation of the children between you. Travel tickets are more expensive if you purchase them at the last minute. Be sure to discuss who will pay the cost of a missed flight or if plans change after purchasing tickets.

Transporting Our Children

Our agreement about transporting our children between us is:

 There are some countries that will not admit children traveling with only one parent without the signed permission of both parents. Likewise, there are some foreign-based airlines that will not allow such children to board their aircraft. If you have joint legal custody, a notarized statement signed by both parents authorizing any trip is probably a very good idea.

How to Tell the Children

How do you tell your children about your separation? If possible, both of you should be present to tell the children not only of your decision to separate but also about your plans. Help them understand that you are not separating from or divorcing them. Tell them that you will always take care of them no matter what. Tell them how important it is to both of you that they continue to have both of you. Be concrete with them about your plans.

When appropriate, share your six-week calendar with your children and ask for their input. Listen to their concerns about the mechanics: "Where will my bicycle live?" "How will my ice skates get from one house to the other?" "I only have one computer—how will I do my homework?"

If you can, discuss with the children in advance the physical plans for your separation. Involve them by taking them with you to see possible new apartments or homes so they can participate in the creation of their second home. They will have their own ideas about which toys and books should be at which place and how they want their spaces to look. You may have to override some of their choices; but allow them to participate and express themselves—even to carry out some of their wishes in their own way—if you and your spouse agree. The older your children, the more likely they are to have their own ideas about what they want out of your divorce, and the more willing they are to let you know about it. Working toward agreement between the two of you without any input from the children sends them the clear message that you do not care what they think. On the other hand, having them as part of the negotiations from the beginning is to give them far too much power over the outcome. They, after all, are the children and you are the adults—a fact which is not always evident when the adults are dealing with the stress of a divorce.

So, how do you give your children the chance to tell you what they think will work without deferring decisions to them which you must make as parents? The following are some rules of thumb that may help:

- Do a rough cut of the parenting and support plans by yourselves. Discuss what you each think would be acceptable to the children, but do not ask them yet.

- Invite the children to sit with you and read through the rough cut and react to it. Do this with both of you present. You can do it with the children individually if you think they will speak more freely when the other children are not there, but it is

Our Agreement About Telling Our Children

Our agreement about telling our children is:

usually the reverse. Many mediators are willing to have you do the sharing of your rough cut in a regular mediation session or in a shorter session just for that purpose.

- Be certain when you share your ideas with the children that you promise to listen carefully to what they have to say but that you do not promise to do exactly what they ask.

- If any child objects continuously to an aspect of your proposed plan, then you may want to consider having that child meet with a therapist. It is possible to listen to the children but not hear what they are saying due to your own need to have them endorse your options. It is possible for the children not to feel free to speak because they feel any request they might make would sound disloyal to one or both of you.

- If the children have chosen their own confidant who is not one of you (such as a grandparent or babysitter) then you may wish to get the children's permission to have their confidant come to a discussion or mediation session instead of them.

- If there is a person with a special relationship to the children in addition to yourselves, you may want that person to attend the session when you present the agreement to the children or to sit in on your early sessions about parenting so that you can begin being mindful of the children's wishes.

Involve the Children

Sometimes children have trouble understanding the parenting schedule you have agreed to. This depends on the age of the child and the complexity of scheduling school, activities, and time with each parent. It is fun and helpful for them to see their schedule written down in a way they can understand. After all it is their schedule! You can buy a Keep Track Calendar kit. This calendar includes colorful stickers that say "Mom" and "Dad," stickers that show transition days, holiday and activity stickers, and blank stickers for children to write down their own important events. The stickers are bright and cheerful, and children will enjoy seeing their weeks, months, and years displayed in an understandable and upbeat way! Call Free Spirit Publishing at (800)735-7323 or visit www.freespirit.com for information about ordering this package.

Signing for Emergency Medical Care for Your Children

There are still a few emergency care facilities that will require both parents' signatures in joint custody situations in order to admit children for care and treatment—unless there is a written court-ordered stipulation that says either parent may sign. Not only should you have a clear agreement about this but you should carry a copy of this agreement with you and give one to your child's pediatrician, day care provider, and school.

Glad We Asked

Matt and Claire were successful in equally sharing their time with their daughter, Bonnie, for two years after their divorce. When Bonnie was in second grade, however, Claire remarried and moved about an hour away. The distance made the equal sharing unfeasible. They were at a stalemate until they asked their mediator to find out what Bonnie thought. Bonnie wanted most not to have to spend the summer in day care. That meant spending summers with her mom, who was not employed outside the home, and the school year with her dad who was.

Odds and Ends

As you get close to a working draft of your parenting plan, try to have discussions about the following, even if those discussions never find their way into your written agreement:

- Describe what each of you will do to keep and strengthen your children's connection with the departing parent in his or her new home and to minimize any sense of loss or abandonment they may feel.

- What is the role of grandparents and extended family? Should they have fixed times with the children? Will you count it as part of either parent's time?

- What is the role of your own adult friends, especially a live-in relationship, "significant other," or stepparent. The concern here is to what extent this person may participate in parenting. May this person discipline your children? May this person transport your children between you? May this person attend parent-teacher conferences, be a Scout leader, coach the soccer team, or be a teacher's aide?

- Do you want to make special commitments about religious upbringing?

- Do you want to put in restrictions about not taking the children out of the state or country without written agreement?

- What happens if the children are too sick to change houses? Go to school? Go to day care?

- How do you handle make-up days? What is the procedure for making a one-time change in the time schedule with the children?

- How do you want the other parent to handle it if the children start complaining about something that is going on at your house?

- What do you do if any child shows signs of stress or exhibits changes in behavior?

Teeth

Most people worry, from time to time, that they might not completely fulfill their end of the bargain they are negotiating. If your ex has a new lover, will you be less likely to deliver the children on time or to tell your ex about the teacher's conference? If you re-marry, will conflict between your loyalties to your new spouse and your former spouse interfere with your parental communications with your ex so that cooperation would begin to break down? In a money crunch, would you try to increase the children's time with you in order to increase child support? Most people would answer "yes" to at least one of these or at least admit that temptation may exist.

If you have any doubts about yourself, or some secret doubts about your soon-to-be-ex, then try putting in some creative incentives to follow through with all your agreements about your children. Some examples are:

- The parent who delays deciding about travel dates for the summer pays the additional cost for late plane tickets.

- The parent who delivers the children late to the other parent becomes responsible for all transportation for the children for the next week, two weeks, or month.

You can design baby teeth for minor misses, molars for larger defaults, and even fangs if you need them—but use these last carefully. Giving notice about problems and maintaining flexibility in dealing with them are frequently the best solutions.

These incentives to correct behavior are limited only by your imagination. Try having the person against whom the penalty would act set the penalty. What your former partner fears may surprise you!

Anticipating Changes

Change happens. Unexpected and last minute events require flexibility and cooperation. Your children's needs, as well as your own, will change before your children emancipate. Write down the changes you anticipate in the foreseeable future and commit to them now. Here are several samples, along with two extra spaces to write in your own:

- "We expect our basic time schedule to change for each child when he or she begins first grade/middle school/high school/ or reaches puberty."

Our Agreement About Anticipated Changes and When We Expect Them to Occur

Write here your agreement about when and under what circumstances you expect to discuss changing your parenting plan.

Parenting Plan Checklist

Directions: Use this outline to check off each element of your parenting plan as you complete it.

I. Legal Custody

☐   A. State whether you will have sole or joint legal custody.

☐   B. Spell out areas for joint decision making, if any.

☐   C. Spell out areas for consultation before separate or sole decision making.

☐   D. Spell out areas for information exchange.

☐   E. Dispute Resolution

1. Spell out your agreements for communication and process.

2. Spell out your agreements about what to do to avoid and resolve deadlock and what you will do when you find yourselves stuck.

3. State your more formal dispute resolution mechanism (if any) that you wish to have in place as a condition before either of you may take a matter to court.

II. Physical Custody

☐   A. State the pattern of parenting times you will start with and whether it is primary, split, or shared custody.

☐   B. State your exceptions to A, if any, for holidays and vacations.

☐   C. State who will provide and pay for the transportation of the children between parents.

III. Odds and Ends
☐

IV. Teeth
☐

V. Anticipated Changes
State what, if anything, you will look at to determine whether that pattern needs to change in the future.
☐

• "We expect to discuss changing physical custody if one of us moves so far away that regular transportation is no longer possible."

• "We expect to discuss changing legal custody if one of us moves back into close proximity to the other and wants to be included in the important parenting decisions."

You are finished with your first rough look at your parenting plan. It will probably not be your final version. Go on to the next chapters. The agreements you reach as a result of each of those chapters may necessitate changes in your parenting plan.

Take heart. Understanding the issues and settling your divorce case is hard work. Don't expect to get it all done in one sitting. Don't even expect to complete your agreement about the children in one sitting. Give yourself and each other the time you deserve to make the best decisions for both of you and your children.

CHAPTER 9

CHILD SUPPORT

CHILD SUPPORT

The Connecticut Child Support Guidelines

The Connecticut Child Support Guidelines are the cornerstone for calculating child support for parents whose combined net income is not more than $2,500 per week. The guidelines presume that divorcing parents will share the support of their children in the proportion of their individual net (after tax) incomes to the total family net income. The guidelines establish a certain minimum dollar amount that the parents are presumed to spend on the basic needs of their children. This minimum amount appears in a schedule that is part of the guidelines. These presumptions are rebuttable—that is, you can overcome them by showing the court that the guidelines should not apply to your family.

HOW TO MAKE THE CHILD SUPPORT GUIDELINES
WORK FOR YOU

If you agree to the child support award that results from the worksheet, it becomes an order of court. You may deviate (have an amount different from that calculated by the guidelines) provided the judge approves your explanation and agreement. You may pay child support directly to your spouse, have it withheld from your paycheck by an immediate wage withholding order, or make arrangements to have it paid by an automatic bank transfer to your spouse's account.

IF YOUR NET INCOME EXCEEDS THE GUIDELINES
($2,500 PER WEEK NET)

If your combined monthly net income is greater than $2,500 per week, the guidelines establish the minimum presumptive child support amount. In this case, work through this chapter and complete the checklists to assist you in defining the actual costs of your children, as well as your incomes and budgets, as a foundation for coming to an agreement about child support. You must, however, complete a worksheet and submit it to the judge with your child support agreement. If your agreed child support award is less than the minimum presumptive child support award calculated on the worksheet, you must have an explanation that is acceptable to the judge.

"Child support is cut and dried. You have to pay whatever the chart says."
Connecticut does have a formula-based child support statute that states how much parents must pay to cover certain expenses for their children. However, for most couples, latitude exists regarding how to apply their facts and circumstances to the guidelines.

**State of Connecticut
Child Support Services**

The state of Connecticut provides services to locate absent parents, to determine who is the legal father of a child (paternity), and to get a child support order. There is a modest fee for certain services if you do not receive AFDC. To get more information about the procedures and cost, you can obtain the booklet, *Child Support: A Guide to Services in Connecticut,* by calling the Department of Social Services *Voices* hotline 7 days per week from 6:00 a.m. to midnight at (800)647-8872.

Child Support Money: Money paid by one parent to the other to help financially support the needs of the child(ren).

"The Child Support Guidelines will tell us how much we have to spend on our kids."

Not quite. The schedule estimates your children's basic minimal monthly expenses: housing, ordinary clothing, ordinary food, and ordinary medical. As you know, your children may cost more than this. You may want to decide which expenses will not be paid from the basic amount on the schedule and how you will share them.

To establish the amount of child support where the combined net income is more than $2,500 per week, Connecticut's statutes (C.G.S. § 46b-84(c)) require that the court consider the following factors:

1. With respect to the parents:

    a. Age

    b. Health

    c. Station

    d. Occupation

    e. Earning capacity

    f. Amount and sources of income

    g. Estate

    h. Vocational skills

    i. Employability

2. With respect to the child(ren):

    a. Age

    b. Health

    c. Station

    d. Occupation

    e. Educational status and expectations

    f. Amount and sources of income

    g. Vocational skills

    h. Employability

    i. Estate

    j. Needs

Using the Guidelines and Schedule of Basic Child Support Obligations

The centerpiece of the Connecticut Child Support Guidelines is the Schedule of Basic Child Support Obligations printed at the end of this chapter. The schedule contains the percentage of combined net incomes that the guidelines expect the parents to pay for their children's basic needs.

The amounts of this schedule vary from about 10 to 24 percent for one child and from about 10 to 35 percent for two children on a curve. Actual national studies of child-rearing costs adjusted for Connecticut economic circumstances are the basis for these percentages. The studies found that lower income families spend a higher percentage of their family income on the basic expenses of their children than higher income families.

The basic support amount on the schedule increases with the number of children but not in strict arithmetical increments. The schedule recognizes that the second child does not cost as much as the first and that there are some basic expenses incurred with one child that are not incurred again with additional children. Therefore, although the amount on the schedule increases with each additional child, it does not double for the second or triple for the third, etc. This is an important concept to remember as you decide how to change support as each child goes to college or emancipates.

The guidelines expect parents to be responsible for the amount on the schedule in proportion to their net incomes. For example, if the father's income is 60 percent of the family's total income and the mother's is 40 percent, then the father pays child support to contribute to 60 percent of the children's basic costs and the mother is presumed to contribute 40 percent.

To calculate child support, the law (C.G.S. § 46b-215a-1) provides that gross income is made up of earned and unearned income, including the following:

1. Salary

2. Hourly wages for regular, overtime, and additional employment up to a maximum of fifty-two total paid hours per week

3. Commissions, bonuses, and tips

4. Profit sharing, deferred compensation, and severance pay

"We'll just plug our incomes into the guidelines, and they will tell us what we should do for our children."

You can do it this way if you wish, but the result may not be affordable or sufficient for your children's needs. In addition, you are far more likely to carry out a support agreement that you have thought out yourselves rather than simply obeying a number from a schedule.

While you can agree to an amount different than the amount the Child Support Guidelines require, you must obtain court approval. You must carefully articulate the reason for deviation on your child support worksheet and separation agreement. You must provide the court with an accurate Child Support Guidelines calculation.

Our Children's Basic Expenses

Directions: Complete the following sentence using the name of each expense, not the amount.

We agree that the basic expenses for our children are housing, basic food, basic clothing, and:

Our Children's Regular Additional Expenses

We do not consider the following expenses for our children to be included in the basic amount on the schedule, and we do not believe these expenses can be foreseen or quantified monthly:

- [ ] School expenses $_____
- [ ] Unreimbursed medical expenses $_____
- [ ] Day care $_____
- [ ] Babysitting $_____
- [ ] Private school tuition $_____
- [ ] Religious training $_____
- [ ] Transportation between parents (especially long distance) $_____
- [ ] Other visitation expenses $_____
- [ ] Gifts to and from the children $_____
- [ ] Sports: including fees, special clothing, equipment $_____
- [ ] Music and art: including lessons and equipment $_____
- [ ] Clubs $_____
- [ ] Scouts $_____
- [ ] Travel $_____
- [ ] Tutoring $_____
- [ ] Special education $_____
- [ ] Automobile: payments, insurance, fuel and maintenance $_____
- [ ] Camping $_____
- [ ] Family activities $_____
- [ ] Summer camp, activities and programs $_____
- [ ] Regular babysitting, other than work-related (parent at school, meetings, etc.) $_____
- [ ] Chronic medical, dental, mental health (insulin, medication, braces, counseling) $_____
- [ ] Infant expenses (shots, well-baby checkup, equipment) $_____
- [ ] Other $_____

5. Employment prerequisites and in-kind compensation (any basic maintenance or special need, such as food, shelter, or transportation, provided on a recurrent basis in lieu of or in addition to salary or wages)

6. Military personnel fringe benefit payments

7. Benefits received in place of earned income, including but not limited to workers' compensation benefits, unemployment insurance benefits, strike pay, and disability insurance benefits

8. Veterans' benefits

9. Social Security benefits (excluding Supplemental Security income, or SSI), including dependency benefits on the earnings records of an insured parent that are paid on behalf of a child whose support is being determined

10. Net proceeds from contractual agreements

11. Pension and retirement income

12. Rental income after deduction of reasonable and necessary expenses

13. Estate or trust income

14. Royalties

15. Interest, dividends, and annuities

16. Self-employment earnings after deduction of all reasonable and necessary business expenses

17. Alimony being paid by an individual who is not a party to the support determination

18. Regularly recurring gifts, prizes, and lottery and gambling winnings, except the income and regularly recurring contributions or gifts of a spouse or domestic partner.

19. Education grants (including fellowships or subsidies that are available for personal living expenses)

The following are not considered gross income:

1. Support received on behalf of a child who is living in the

home but not subject to this child support calculation

2. Federal, state, and local public assistance grants

3. Earned income tax credit

4. Income and regularly recurring contributions or gifts of a spouse or domestic partner

From the total gross income, you must decide how you are going to compute the net (after tax) income for each parent to calculate the basic child support amount under the Connecticut Child Support Guidelines. Chapter 12 explains many issues that go into your net income calculation, including these options:

- *Use pay stub figures.* If you are not under- or over-withholding, this may be an accurate reflection of your net income. You should be careful, however, because your withholding may not accurately reflect your year-end tax obligation. Many people do not take all tax factors into consideration in claiming their payroll deductions and may not have considered the tax consequences of the divorce. Also, the pay stub does not reflect gross income and taxes from other income sources.

- *Last year's tax return.* You may choose to use the annual numbers from your last tax return to calculate net income for the next year. Some couples even agree to review their child support annually, using the prior year's tax return as the measure of net income. However, if your filing status (married, single, head of household) and other tax factors will be different this year, last year's tax return may not give you an accurate net income amount.

- *Calculate your own taxable income for this year.* Be sure to include all sources of income, deductions, and credits.

- *Consult with a CPA, financial planner, lawyer, and/or mediator.* Trained professionals can help you accurately calculate net income and future tax estimates and/or answer tax questions.

You may need to determine potential income if one or both of you is unemployed or underemployed. There are very few circumstances under which a parent would have no financial responsibility for his or her children, however, there is a special worksheet calculation for "low income obligors."

The guidelines require you to prepare and file with the court a Child Support Guidelines Worksheet if you have any minor children at the time of your divorce, at the time of temporary orders, or when changing any child support order.

Our Children's Irregular Expenses

We anticipate the following irregular expenses may occur for our children. (List average monthly amount at right.)

One-time major purchases (full-size bed, bicycle, skis, etc.):

Description $

Special events (birth, graduation)

Description $

Other

Description $

www.jud.state.ct.us/external/news/childsupport.htm (Part iv)

CCSG-1   NEW 8-99
C.G.S. §46b-215a
§46b-215a-5a, Regulations of
Connecticut State Agencies

STATE OF CONNECTICUT

COMMISSION FOR CHILD SUPPORT GUIDELINES

WORKSHEET for the *Connecticut Child Support and Arrearage Guidelines*

MOTHER		FATHER		CUSTODIAN ☐ MOTHER ☐ FATHER OTHER:	
COURT				D.N./CASE NO.	NUMBER OF CHILDREN

CHILD'S NAME	DATE OF BIRTH	CHILD'S NAME	DATE OF BIRTH

I. NET INCOME (Weekly amounts)

		MOTHER	FATHER
1.	Gross income (attach verification)	$	$
2.	Federal income tax (based on all allowable exemptions, deductions and credits)	$	$
3.	State and local income tax (based on all allowable exemptions, deductions and credits)	$	$
4.	Social security tax or mandatory retirement	$	$
5.	Medicare tax	$	$
6.	Medical, hospital, dental, or health insurance premium payments (for other than child)	$	$
7.	Mandatory union dues or fees	$	$
8.	Non-arrearage payments on court-ordered alimony and child support awards (for other than child)	$	$
9.	Imputed support obligation for qualified child (Current support for all children/total number of children x number of qualified children)	$	$
10.	Sum of lines 2-9	$	$
11.	Net income (line 1 minus line 10)	$	$

II. CURRENT SUPPORT

12.	Combined net weekly income (rounded to nearest $10)	$	
13.	Basic child support obligation (from *Schedule of Basic Child Support Obligations*)	$	
14.	Check here if noncustodial parent is a low-income obligor and refer to instructions:		
15.	Child's health insurance premium	$	$
16.	Total current support obligation (line 13 minus noncustodial parent's line 15 amount if line 14 is checked; line 13 plus total of line 15 amounts for all other cases)	$	
17.	Each parent's decimal share of line 12 (If line 14 is checked, skip this line and line 19, and enter the line 16 amount in the noncustodial parent's column on line 18.)		
18.	Each parent's share of the total current support obligation (line 17 times line 16 for each parent)	$	$
19.	Health insurance premium adjustment (enter line 15 amount for each parent)	$	$
20.	Social security dependency benefits adjustment	$	$
21.	Sum of lines 19 and 20 (for each parent)	$	$
22.	Presumptive current support amounts (line 18 minus line 21)	$	$
23.	Recommended current support order (noncustodial parent only) (If different from line 22, state applicable deviation criterion on line 47.)	$	$

	III. UNREIMBURSED MEDICAL EXPENSE		MOTHER	FATHER
24.	Net disposable income (line 11 plus noncustodial parent's line 23 amount for custodial parent; line 11 minus noncustodial parent's line 23 amount for noncustodial parent)		$	$
25.	Each parent's decimal share (rounded to two places) of combined net disposable income (each parent's line 24 amount divided by the sum of the line 24 amounts)			

	IV. CHILD CARE CONTRIBUTION			
26.	Qualifying costs (enter contribution amount on line 43)		$	$

	V. ARREARAGE	(OBLIGOR ONLY)
27.	Delinquencies on current support orders	$
28.	Unpaid court-ordered arrearages	$
29.	Support due for periods prior to the support action (not court-ordered)	$
30.	Total arrearage (sum of lines 27 through 29)	$

	VI. ARREARAGE PAYMENT	
31.	Recommended current support order from line 23 (*OR* imputed support obligation if there is no current support order or the child is living with the obligor)	$
32.	20% of line 31 (but see instructions below)	$
	⇨ (If line 14 is checked, skip line 32 and go to line 37.)	
	⇨ (If the child for whom the arrearage is owed is deceased, emancipated, or over age 18, skip line 32 and go to line 39.)	
	⇨ (If the child is living with the obligor, skip lines 33-39 and: (1) if the obligor's gross income is not more than 250% of poverty level, enter $1 on line 40; *OR* (2) if the obligor's gross income is greater than 250% of poverty level, enter the line 32 amount on line 40.)	
33.	Obligor's line 11 amount	$
34.	55% of line 33	$
35.	Line 34 minus line 31	$
36.	Lesser of line 32 or line 35 (Enter here and on line 40, and skip lines 37-39.)	$
37.	10% of line 31	$
38.	Greater of line 37 or $1 (Enter here and on line 40, and skip line 39.)	$
39.	50% of line 31 (Enter here and on line 40.)	$
40.	Recommended arrearage payment (If different from line 45, explain on line 47.)	$

	VII. ORDER SUMMARY		
41.	Current support order	$	
42.	Unreimbursed medical expense order		
43.	Child care contribution		
44.	Total arrearage	to state	to family
45.	Arrearage payment order		
46.	Total child support award: $		

	VIII. DEVIATION CRITERIA	
47.	Reason(s) for deviation from presumptive support amounts: *(Attach additional sheet if necessary)*	

PREPARED BY	TITLE	DATE

WORKSHEET FOR THE CONNECTICUT CHILD SUPPORT GUIDELINES

To complete the worksheet form you must calculate your net weekly income. Remember to divide monthly figures by 4.3 and annual figures by 52 to arrive at the weekly amount. If you are paid every other week, divide by 2. If you are paid twice per month, you must multiply by 2 and divide by 52.

The date of the divorce determines your tax filing status and what your taxes will be. See Chapter 12, Taxes, for more information.

INSTRUCTIONS FOR FILLING OUT THE WORKSHEET

To begin, list the names of the mother and the father, and check the box for which parent will be the primary custodial parent of the child. The custodial parent is the parent who provides the primary residence and pays the basic expenses. If someone other than a parent is the custodian of the children, fill in that person's name. Enter the court judicial district location and the court/docket number from the court caption. This information will be on all your court papers. Fill in the number of children covered by the calculation, and list their names and birth dates.

1. Fill in the total gross weekly income (before deductions or taxes) for each parent in the appropriate columns. The income figure that you include is the total income from all sources identified in your income chart in Chapter 7. Attach verification of your total income in the form of pay stubs, tax returns, or other documents.

2. Calculate your annual federal income tax (*see* Chapter 12 to estimate your annual tax), divide by 52, and enter the amount.

3. Calculate your annual state and local income taxes (*see* Chapter 12 to estimate your annual tax), divide by 52, and enter the total.

4. Calculate your Social Security tax for W-2 employees (6.2 percent) or self employment tax (12.4 percent) on annual earning up to $87,000 per year (2003 rates). If you are not a Social Security taxpayer, enter your mandatory retirement plan deduction for an amount not to exceed the maximum amount permissible under Social Security.

5. Now calculate your Medicare tax: 1.45 percent for W-2 employees or 2.9 percent for self-employed taxpayers.

6. Enter any amounts a parent pays out of pocket for medical, hospital, dental, and/or health insurance premiums for the parent and other legal dependents not subject to the support order. If you do not know or are unable to verify the portion of the premium attributable just to the parent and not to the children you are calculating child support for, divide the total premium by the number of persons covered by the policy and multiply that number by the combined total of the parent and other legal dependents not subject to the support order. (See the formula following step 15 of these instructions.)

7. Enter any amount for mandatory union dues or fees.

8. Enter any amounts paid by the mother and/or father for court-ordered alimony and child support awards (for a child other than the one whose support is to be determined) to the extent of actual pay-

ment. Do not include arrearage payments for children not involved in this support determination. Disregard this deduction if the current court-ordered payments are not being made.

9. If either parent has another child or other children not subject to this child support calculation for whom the parent is legally responsible but for whom there is no current support order, that parent may qualify to deduct an "imputed support." However, the imputed support amount deduction is only permitted in an initial child support award calculation or if the parent is defending against a proposed increase to a current child support amount.

For a child to be a "qualified child" for the purposes of the imputed support deduction amount, he or she must meet all four of the following requirements:

    a. The child must currently reside with the parent if the parent is the child's legal guardian or if such parent is not the child's legal guardian, has lived in the same household with such parent for at least the six months preceding the support determination or six of the twelve months preceding the support determination.

    b. The child must be a dependant of the parent.

    c. The child must not be a subject of the child support calculation being made.

    d. The child has not been claimed on the child support worksheet.

To calculate the imputed support amount if it applies, complete a separate child support worksheet. Enter the income information for the parent claiming the qualified child for imputed support purposes in the "mother" or custodial column. Assume income of zero for the person who is the other parent of the qualified child. In calculating the basic child support obligation, count the total number of children (qualified imputed children plus the children for the main child support calculation). Then, after arriving at the basic child support amount, divide it by the total number of children used, then multiply by the number of imputed qualified children. This amount is the "imputed amount" for line 9.

10. Add lines 2 through 9, and enter the total amount on line 10.

11. Subtract line 10 from line 1 and enter the resulting amount on line 11. This is the net weekly income for each parent for purposes of applying the Child Support Guidelines.

12. Add both parties' net incomes from line 11 and enter the total of their net incomes on line 11 rounding to the nearest $10.

13. Turn to the Schedule of Basic Child Support Obligations at the end of this chapter and find the combined net income from line 12 in the left-hand column. Then read across the top columns for the number of children for whom you are calculating child support. The dollar amount in the block that intersects these two lines is the basic child support obligation. Enter this amount on line 13.

14. On the Schedule of Basic Child Support Obligations, find the block for the non-custodial parent's weekly net income and the number of children. If that block is in the darker shaded area of the schedule, he or she is a "low income obligor." Place a check on this line and follow the Instructions for Low Income Obligors on page 226.

15. Enter any amount a parent pays out of pocket for medical, hospital, dental, and/or health insurance premiums for the children whose support is being calculated. You may not know or be able to verify the portion of the parents' total premiums attributable to the children. If not, use the following formula to divide the total premium by the number of persons covered by the policy's out-of-pocket premium amount and multiply by the number of children covered by this support calculation. Attach proof of the children's enrollment in the insurance plan and the cost of the premium attributable to them.

$ _____	÷ _____	= _____	x _____	= _____
Total Premium	Number of Individuals Covered by the Policy	Per Person Cost	Number of Children Who Are the Subject of This Order	Children's Portion of Cost of Premium

The balance of the insurance premium is the parental portion subtracted from the gross income to determine net income on line 6.

16. Enter the total child support obligation here by adding the total insurance premium on line 15 to the basic support amount on line 13.

17. Divide each parent's net income from line 11 by the combined net weekly income on line 12 to figure out each parent's percentage share of the combined net weekly income. Enter the result (rounded to two decimal places) for each parent.

18. Multiply the amount on line 16 by the percentage amount on line 17 for each parent. Enter the result for each parent as each parent's dollar share of the total current support obligation.

19. Enter the same amount for each parent as on line 15.

20. In the non-custodial parent's column, enter the weekly amount of any Social Security dependency benefits the children are receiving on the earnings record of the non-custodial parent.

21. Enter the total of lines 19 and 20 for each parent.

22. Subtract the amount on line 21 from the amount on line 18 for each parent. The results are the presumed support amounts for each parent to enter on line 22.

23. The presumed child support amount for the noncustodial parent on line 22 is the recommended amount for line 23. This is so unless the parties agree to a different child support amount—in which case they must enter that amount on this line—or the court orders a different amount. (See page 228 for a discussion of the deviation criteria used to support a recommended amount higher or lower than the presumed amount.)

Note that if your combined net weekly income on line 12 is more that $2,500 per week, the presumed child support amount on line 22 is the minimum presumed amount of child support.

24. Add the custodial parent's line 11 net income to the noncustodial parent's line 23 recommended sup-

port amount. Enter this sum on line 24. Subtract the non-custodial parent's line 23 support amount from his or her line 11 net income. Enter the result on line 24.

25. Divide each parent's revised net income amount on line 24 by the combined net income amount on line 12 to figure out each parent's revised percentage share of the total net disposable income (rounded to two decimal places). Enter this amount on line 25.

26. Do not enter any figure on line 26 if you are calculating child support for the first court order or if you and your spouse do not agree to use this line (see step 43 for instructions about calculating payment for child care costs).

For child care costs to be included in the calculation on this line, they must meet all four of the following criteria:

    a. reasonable,

    b. necessary to allow the parent to maintain employment,

    c. not otherwise reimbursed, and

    d. do not exceed the level required to provide quality care from a licensed source.

27.–40. If there is an arrearage (court-ordered child support that has not been paid) follow the instructions on the worksheet to fill in these lines.

41. Enter the recommended support amount from line 23.

42. Write a statement that provides that any unreimbursed medical and/or dental expenses for the children in excess of $100 per child per year will be paid by each parent by using the line 25 percentages. (See page 232 "Health and Dental Expenses for Your Children.")

43. Write a statement that provides that qualified child care costs will be paid by each parent using the line 25 percentages. (See page 233 "Child Care Expenses for Your Children.") However, if there is a prior order for contribution to child care costs and if that order has not been complied with or if you decide that you want a set amount for child care costs to be added to the basic child support amount, multiply the noncustodial parent's decimal share from line 25 times the amount of qualifying costs on line 26 for the custodial parent. Enter the product on line 43 in the noncustodial parent's column.

44.–45. Follow the instructions on the worksheet for these lines if there is an arrearage (past due support) amount due as calculated on line 40.

46. Enter on line 46 the total of the recommended support amount and the arrearage payment, if calculated.

47. If the total child support award as calculated on the worksheet is not satisfactory for both of you, see "What if the Recommended Support is Too High or Too Low for You?" later in this chapter. If you want to ask the court to deviate from the amount of child support on line 23, state your reasons and the amount of deviation on line 47, page 2, of the worksheet.

48. Finally, sign and date the worksheet.

INSTRUCTIONS FOR LOW-INCOME OBLIGORS

You are considered to be a "low-income obligor" if you are the non-custodial parent and your net income from line 11, when located on the Schedule of Basic Child Support Obligatorions for the number of children for whom you are calculating support, shows a dollar amount in a block in the darker shaded area on page 1 of the schedule. If this applies to you, place a check on line 14 of the worksheet and follow these steps:

1. If the amount of the noncustodial parent's income from line 11 is in a darker shaded block and is not in white italics, the amount in the block is the noncustodial parent's basic child support obligation. As such:

    a. Enter the amount on Line 13.

    b. Follow the instruction for line 15 on page 224 and enter children's health insurance amount, if paid by the noncustodial parent.

    c. Subtract the amount on line 15 from the amount on line 13, and enter the result on line 16. This is the total child support obligation of the low-income obligor. Skip line 17 and fill in the amount from line 16 on line 18. (Skip line 19 because the medical insurance adjustment was made on line 15). If there is no Social Security adjustment, line 18 is the presumptive current child support obligation for the non-custodial parent to enter on line 22.

    d. If the child is receiving Social Security on the noncustodial parent's account, enter the amount on lines 21 and 26.

    e. Subtract line 20 from line 18. This is the presumptive current child support amount of the non-custodial parent for line 22.

2. If the amount in the darker shaded block is in white italics and the custodial parent has some income:

    a. Calculate the net income for the custodial parent by following the previous instructions through line 11, and enter the combined total of both parents' income on line 12.

    b. Find the block in the Schedule of Basic Child Support Obligations that corresponds to the net income for the noncustodial parent and the number of children for whom you are calculating support. Note the applicable percentage in that shaded block.

    c. Find the block in the Schedule of Basic Child Support Obligations that corresponds to the combined net income of both parents and the number of children for whom you are calculating support. Note the percentage in that shaded block.

    d. Compare the percentages found in steps b and c. If the percentage for the noncustodial parent's income alone is lower than the percentage in the combined net income block, the amount in the dark shaded block for the noncustodial parent is his or her basic support obligation. Enter this amount on line 13, place a check mark on line 14, and continue with the calculation starting with the first paragraph above.

    e. If the percentage for the noncustodial parent's income alone is higher than the percentage in the combined net income block, enter on line 13 the basic child support amount stated in the combined income block. Place a check mark on line 14 and continue with the calculation starting with the first paragraph in this instruction section.

3. If the amount in the darker shaded block is in white italics and the custodial parent has no income, follow the instructions for low income obligors beginning with the first paragraph on page 226.

4. Under all circumstances, low-income obligors do not make contributions to qualifying day care in addition to the basic child support amount.

"Shared physical/ residential custody makes your child support go down."

This is a widely-held misconception. The payments between the parents may go down, but each parent is still expected to contribute to the costs of rearing their children. The presumption shifts from expecting the custodial parent to be disbursing all the children's basic expenses to expecting the parents to be disbursing them in proportion to their parenting time and/or income.

Deviation: An amount of child support that is higher or lower than the amount specified by the Child Support Guidelines. To obtain court approval of the deviation amount, you must supply the judge with a completed Child Support Guidelines worksheet that includes a statement of the reasons you believe the deviation is in the best interest(s) of your child(ren).

SPLIT CUSTODY

You and your spouse may choose to split the physical custody of your children. This means that each parent is the primary custodial parent of at least one child. For split custody, complete two worksheets so that you can calculate the amount of support due to each parent for the number of children living principally with him or her. Then subtract the lower amount from the higher amount. The net difference is the presumptive amount that the higher amount parent pays to the lower amount parent.

Deviations: What If the Recommended Support Is Too High or Too Low for You?

The Child Support Guidelines create a rebuttable presumption, or something that will happen unless you can convince the court that it should not. This means that the court will require the payment of the amount on line 22 unless the court finds a legal reason to order an amount higher or lower ("deviation"). In practice, most courts will approve an agreed child support amount that is higher than the presumptive amount. This "deviated" amount is entered on line 23 as the "recommended" support order. Court approval for a deviation is sometimes more difficult to obtain when the amount you agree to is lower than your worksheet calculation.

You can always pay more money to each other voluntarily for your children, but you are only officially credited with child support paid by court order—side deals are not binding! The issue here is what amounts you want to make binding and enforceable by the court as regular monthly court-ordered child support.

The guidelines may allow you to deviate from the recommended support amount under a variety of circumstances. If you fit any of the circumstances in the statute, you may convince the judge that the recommended child support amount should not apply to you. You must give the judge your own recommended amount for support and your reasons for asking for a deviation. You also must provide the judge with your complete worksheet so he or she can compare the guidelines with your agreed recommended presumptive amount.

The law specifies the following criteria that the judge may consider in adjusting the child support amount. If you have other reasons to deviate, the judge may approve those as well if you provide an adequate explanation.

1. Other financial resources available to a parent

In some cases, a parent has financial resources that are not in the legal definition of "income" but could be considered income if they benefit the child or meet the needs of the parent. For example, a spouse might have substantial assets, including non-income producing property. You could also consider a parent's earning capacity. In some instances the parent may have a new spouse (or "domestic partner") who financially contributes to the parent so that he or she can reduce income and/or has an extraordinary reduction of living expenses.

2. Extraordinary expenses for the care and maintenance of the child

A parent may be paying extraordinary expenses essential for the proper care of the children. If these expenses are substantial and continuing, you may use them to adjust the child support depending on who is making the payments.

You can share payment of extraordinary expenses in any number of different ways. Some parents use the child support amount as a regular baseline amount and share the extraordinary expenses by the same worksheet line 25 percentage share of day care and medical expenses. For example, if one spouse has 70 percent of the income after child support and the other has 30 percent, they could agree to pay uncovered medical expenses, private tutoring, or other special needs on the same 70-30 basis. Alternatively, you can decide which parent will pay the expenses in a way that feels fair to you, considering the child support amount you agree to. Or, you may decide to increase the child support received by the parent who pays the extraordinary expense. You could also decrease the child support payment if it is the child support payor who is paying the extraordinary expense.

3. Extraordinary parental expenses

Sometimes a parent may incur extraordinary expenses for him- or herself that are not considered an allowable deduction from gross income by the guidelines. However, these expenses may be necessary for the parent to maintain a satisfactory parental relationship with the child, continue employment, or provide for the parent's own medical needs. These expenses, if they are substantial and paid regularly, may justify a deviation. These kinds of extraordinary expenses could include significant visitation expenses, job-related unreimbursable employment expenses of a parent who is not self-employed, or unreimbursed medical and disability expenses for the parent.

4. Needs of a parent's other dependents

A parent may be legally responsible for the support of individuals other than the children for whom you are deciding support. The formula in the worksheet at line 9 for "imputed support" attempts to deal with this situation.

However, in some cases it still may be appropriate to deviate from the guidelines particularly if the child not subject to the child support calculations has other financial resources or the imputed adjustment is insufficient when reviewed in the context of the budget for the entire family.

5. Coordination of total family support

Sometimes, the judge may approve a deviation after considering the amount of the child support along with the total family support (including alimony), property settlement, and tax planning considerations.

6. Special circumstances

There may be other situations where you believe the Child Support Guidelines do not adequately address your family's circumstances. One special circumstance may be a shared custody arrangement. The Child Support Guidelines assume that the children reside primarily in one home and that the parent in the primary home pays all of their basic expenses. In practice, however, the children may spend substantial time in each home and with each parent assuming a substantial share of the costs of the children normally covered by the child support amount. In these situations, the parent may arrange to meet the children's financial needs by reducing the amount of support paid by one spouse to the other. (See the section that follows entitled "Dealing with Children's Expenses.")

7. Any other equitable factor or situation that results in serving the best interest(s) of the child(ren)

Dealing with Children's Expenses—The "Budgeting" Approach to Deviation

There are two categories of expenses for rearing children: basic expenses and extraordinary ones. Basic expenses include housing, food, clothing, regular transportation, school lunches, medical and dental expenses, allowances, and other customary and regular child expenses. The Connecticut Child Support Guidelines are designed to cover these expenses. If you can agree, designate your children's expenses that you believe the basic support payment amount includes and whether the basic child support amount is right for your family.

Extraordinary expenses are any other expenses. Work-related day care, medical insurance costs, and uncovered medical and dental expenses are shared proportionately if you use the guidelines' approach. You can decide whether the guidelines' treatment of these extraordinary expenses is right for your family.

Extraordinary expenses vary with each family. Some other expenses beyond basic needs not specifically addressed in the guidelines are:

- For infants: special clothing, diapers and perhaps diaper service, and special foods

- For school-age children: private school tuition, school supplies, school trips and activities, school clothes, lessons, activity fees, special clothing and equipment, and organization fees

- For teenagers: car and car insurance, birth control, advanced lessons and clinics, activity fees, special clothes including shoes and equipment, and graduation expenses.

- For all children: babysitting expenses (not work related) and travel/vacation costs

- Gifted and talented children may have additional costs. Special needs children (handicapped, developmentally or educationally delayed, ill, injured, or emotionally troubled) have additional extraordinary expenses unique to their conditions.

Extraordinary expenses for your children (in addition to the costs of the children's medical insurance, uncovered medical and dental expenses, and work-related day care):

- can be assumed to be covered by the presumed child support amount or some other child support amount agreement

- can be shared in any proportion you choose, including the percentage determined by the worksheet

- can be shared between you when the expense comes up instead of estimating ahead of time, allowing you to adjust for the unexpected and the irregular (such as a broken leg or summer camp)

- can be estimated and averaged monthly in advance and paid in addition to the basic child support amount

- will not be enforceable if you don't include them in your agreement

- require communication on an ongoing basis since the decision about whether to incur an extraordinary expense may be what you termed a "major" decision earlier on

Sometimes you don't know about an extra expense at the time of divorce and the calculation of child support. It is therefore a good idea to make some agreement about these future unknown expenses. Most people provide that they must agree ahead of time to any extraordinary expenses for their children (except emergencies) and share them in a certain percentage. Sometimes parents agree to pay a certain category of expenses in one percentage and another category in another percentage. For example, you could agree to pay medical expenses in proportion to the parent's income but split special activities 50-50.

HEALTH AND DENTAL EXPENSES FOR YOUR CHILDREN

If either of you maintains health insurance for your children, the guidelines' calculation includes the premium cost attributable to the children. Health insurance premiums include medical, hospital, and dental insurance. The amount you each pay in premiums for the children's insurance is added to the basic child-support obligation. The parent who pays child support subtracts the cost of the child's insurance premium if he or she is providing the insurance. The parent receiving the child support who also pays the children's medical insurance receives the child support amount plus a contribution to cover the cost of the medical insurance premium. You can deviate from this arrangement if you can agree.

The Child Support Guidelines further provide for the proportionate sharing of uninsured medical and dental expenses for the children. Under the guidelines, the custodial parent pays the first $100 of unreimbursed medical and dental expenses per calendar year, per child. Thereafter, the unreimbursed medical and dental expenses are paid by the parents in proportion to the percentage calculated on line 25 of the worksheet. Examples of these expenses could be orthodontic treatments, asthma treatments, physical therapy, and any other chronic health problem not covered by insurance. They may also include professional mental health counseling or therapy. Your agreement should specify which unreimbursed expenses you will share.

You may want to define for yourself the meaning of extraordinary medical expenses to include some or all of the following:

- Your insurance deductible—the amount you pay out each fiscal year per person or per family before the insurance starts paying

- Co-payment—the amount you pay up front in HMO (health maintenance organization) plans and/or the amount you pay after the insurance has paid for medical expenses. This is 80-20 on many plans and is usually 50-50 on mental health and dental expenses, if covered.

- Payment for injuries or illnesses not covered by the insurance or over the limit for that particular kind of illness or injury

- Well-child care, inoculations, preventive care—unless you included this in your definition of basic expenses

- Alternative treatments such as chiropractic, acupuncture, massage, or holistic healing

- Dental expenses including cleaning—unless you included this in your definition of basic expenses

- Orthodontia

- Eye exams and glasses

- Counseling/therapy

After identifying these current and/or future medical expenses, you can agree who will pay them or how you will share them, should you decide to share.

CHILD CARE EXPENSES FOR YOUR CHILDREN

If you follow the Child Support Guidelines in the calculation of your child support, they provide a mechanism for determining the contribution of the noncustodial parent to the qualified day care costs incurred by the custodial parent. To qualify for this contribution, the day care costs must meet all four of the following criteria:

1. reasonable,

2. expended to allow the custodial parent to maintain employment,

3. not otherwise reimbursed, and

4. not in excess of the level required to provide quality care from a licensed source.

Under the guidelines, the way in which the contribution is paid depends on the time that the child support obligation is established. If the calculation is for the first court order for child support, then the noncustodial parent pays his or her percentage share from line 25 of the worksheet of qualifying day care costs as incurred by the custodial parent. In practical terms, this works on an "invoice" basis. The custodial parent should keep records of the qualifying costs that he or she pays and give copies to the noncustodial parent with an informal written invoice requesting reimbursement. However, if there has been a prior child support order including contribution to day care costs and if the noncustodial parent has not complied with that order (hasn't made the payments when invoiced by the custodial parent), then you should enter the annual amount of qualifying day care costs divided by 52 for a weekly amount on line 26 of the worksheet. Multiply line 26 by the noncustodial parent's percentage on line 25 and enter the product on line 43. Add lines 41 and 43 (and other lines, if applicable) for a total child support amount (that includes day care) on line 46.

Both of you may agree to an arrangement for payment of day care costs that differs from the child support guidelines. Examples of those deviations include:

- Decide when you initially set up the child support arrangement to estimate the child care costs and add a regular payment to the base child support amount instead of invoicing expenses as they occur

- Include day care expenses that are not considered qualified by the guidelines

- Use a different percentage for the sharing of the day care expenses

Organizing Parents' Income and Children's Expenses

Dividing your income and children's expenses into the categories on the following Child Support Plan Questionnaire will help you decide which income to use to pay certain expenses. Being clear about this will help you remember expenses you are apt to forget and not count on income you may never see.

The Connecticut Child Support Guidelines only apply if your combined net income is $2,500 per week or less and may not adequately address all of the children's expenses. The Child Support Plan Questionnaire is particularly helpful if your combined net income exceeds this amount because by using it, you can negotiate a child support arrangement that will work for both of you as well as the children.

Child Support Plan Questionnaire

Directions: Discuss the numbers/amounts on your income charts and budgets from Chapter 7 and the lists of your children's basic and extraordinary expenses from this chapter. Then write down the answers to the following questions:

1. For each of you, what income do you want to use in determining the amount of basic child support? All your income from every source (total income on income chart)? Only income each receives regularly (#1 on income chart)? Additional income (#2 on income chart)? Occasional income (#7 on income chart)? You may also want to read the definition of income from page 160. Describe the sources of income for each of you and your estimated amounts.

Although the guidelines do not technically permit the payment or receipt of alimony as a factor in gross income, do you want to include the impact of alimony in your calculation?

2. Do you want to estimate all the foreseeable additional expenses for your children, average them weekly, and then apply your relative income percentages so that they are pre-paid monthly between you? Do you want to use some other formula or assignment for these expenses? Which expenses would you include? List those expenses, averaged monthly, that you agree to pay or prepay between you and the estimated amount:

3. Are there any expenses for your children that you cannot estimate weekly or that you do not want to pre-pay between you weekly? If so, what are these expenses? List them and the estimated amounts.

You may share any expense that you identify and agree to as it arises—in any proportion or assignment you feel is fair. While not part of the guidelines support amount, you can include this responsibility in your court order. How are you going to handle these types of occasional expenses (example: proportional to income, 50-50, 60-40, or one of you pays all)?

4. Have you set aside some occasional or irregular income sources from which to pay these occasional expenses, such as annual performance bonus or sale of stock? If you have an agreement about this, write that agreement here.

Post-secondary Education Checklist

Directions: Complete the following statements:

1. We agree that we want _____
_____ (child's name) to
attend _____
(college or other postsecondary
institution).
(Repeat for each child.)

2. We agree to be responsible for paying
all of the following expenses for post-
secondary education for _____
_____ (name of child):

   We agree that the upper limit on these
   expenses is:

   We agree that we will pay these
   expenses in the following proportion:

3. We agree that we will share the following expenses with the child:

   We agree that we will share these
   expenses with the child in the
   following proportion:

4. We agree that we will establish
(have established) a bank account at
_____ (bank)
by_____ (date) to pay the
following postsecondary education
expenses for _____
_____ (name of child).

   We agree to contribute to this amount
   in the following amounts or
   proportions:

5. We agree that _____
(name of child) shall be responsible for
paying the following postsecondary
education expenses himself/herself:

Post-secondary Education

For any divorces finalized after October 1, 2002, the judge has the authority to enter orders for payment of certain post-secondary education expenses if the parents do not otherwise agree. For cases where the initial support order was entered prior to this date, the court does not have the authority to force a parent to contribute to these expenses. However, if a court order entered before October 1, 2002, incorporated the parents' voluntary provisions for the payment of college expenses, the court has the authority to enforce those agreements.

The law permits the judge (absent an agreement by the parents) to enter an educational support order if he or she finds that it is more likely than not that the parents would have provided support for the child for these expenses had the family remained in tact. The judge decides how much each parent must contribute after considering a number of factors, including the relative financial situation of the parents, availability of financial aid, and the child's aptitude for and commitment to higher education. The expenses that the judge can require the parents to pay are limited to the amount charged by the University of Connecticut for a full-time in-state student and can also include the cost of books and medical insurance. The parental obligation under this law is limited to the equivalent of a four-year undergraduate degree, and the child must be under the age of twenty-three.

Under the law, you must make decisions about the college education expenses of your children at the time of your divorce even if the children are not yet old enough to attend college. Basically, you have the following choices:

1. Agree to waive your rights under the law. This means that the judge will never have the authority to force either one of you to pay college expenses. If there is going to be any parental contribution to these expenses, it would be by informal agreement and not enforceable by the court.

2. Agree to share the costs required by the law (essentially the UCONN cap, books, and medical insurance) through age twenty-three in a proportion that you agree on now. If either parent fails to pay the agreed amount, the order can be enforced by the court. Any expenses over this amount or those incurred after the child reaches the age of twenty-three would be subject to an informal, unenforceable agreement.

3. Have the judge reserve jurisdiction under the law. By doing this, you are not making a decision now as to how you will

share the expenses provided by the law but are acknowledging that you want to wait until your child is actually planning to attend college. If you can't reach an agreement at that time, you can go to court and the judge will decide how to apportion the UCONN cap, books, and medical insurance.

4. You can arrive at an agreement of your own for the funding of your child's college expenses and not restrict yourself to the limitations of the law. If you make this agreement a part of your final divorce agreement, it will become an order of the court and the judge has the power to enforce it, including the provisions in excess of the law. The rest of this section discusses some of the ways you can handle this option.

POST-SECONDARY EDUCATION EXPENSES MIGHT INCLUDE THE FOLLOWING:

- tuition, books, and lab and other fees

- room and board (on or off campus)

- transportation to, from, and on campus, including a car and car insurance

- medical insurance and medical expenses not covered by the insurance

- spending money, clothing, allowance, and other miscellaneous living expenses

Most colleges now apply their financial aid test to all admitted students, but divorced parents need creative cooperation to navigate through college financial issues. The college tells the parents what portion of the overall costs it expects them to carry. It then assesses the student a fair share to pay or earn on his or her own. The college then decides what part of the balance, if any, to cover through scholarships, grants, and guaranteed loans. The easiest kinds of college education expense agreements are those that focus on the amounts the parents must pay and the amount to be borrowed. You can decide whether you think it is fair for you to help your child repay any of the loans and if so, in what proportion. Some parents also agree in advance to help the child pay the amount the college assesses him or her.

Besides the direct costs for higher education, parents may agree about the payment of reasonable amounts for room and board when the student returns from school to live with a parent on vacation or is living at home while attending post-secondary school.

 To find resources for financial aid for post-secondary education go to **www.finaid.org**.

 Post-secondary Education: Attendance at an institution of higher education or a private occupational school for the purpose of attaining a bachelor's or other undergraduate degree or other appropriate vocational instruction.

You may agree to maintain health insurance for the child who is in college if it is available at a reasonable cost. Most policies allow you to keep a full-time student in good standing on your policy until about age twenty-four. Additionally, most colleges and private schools offer minimal life and health insurance coverage to full-time students at a very reasonable cost.

YOU CAN PROVIDE FOR THE PAYMENT OF COLLEGE COSTS IN YOUR AGREEMENT BY:

- Stating that you acknowledge that your child or children will probably attend an institution of higher education and that you will share this expense when the time comes

- Reserving the choice of school and setting of costs (what you will and will not pay for) as a shared decision

- Determining the percentage you will apply to carry these expenses or providing that it will depend upon your proportionate incomes at that time

- Setting a ceiling on the amount, either in dollars per year or for the whole cost, or by establishing a standard such as the in-state costs for UCONN that year

You could agree to begin a fund for your children to use for higher education or any other purpose now. You could base the goal for this account on your estimate of total future college costs, then set a monthly savings amount that you will share in proportion to income. For example, if you feel $20,000 is what you both want to pledge for a child's higher education and that child is now two years old, you would have that amount in savings if you shared an investment of $100 per month beginning now. If the ratio of your incomes were 60-40 now, you would put aside $60 and $40 respectively and adjust these amounts if the ratio of your income changed.

If you agree on college expenses, you may include the provisions in your final separation agreement that you submit to the court. However, you must remember that once the judge approves the agreement and makes it a part of the court judgment, you may be subject to court sanctions (including wage garnishment and contempt of court) if you fail to pay your share. However, if you don't include these issues in the separation agreement, you will have no legal remedy if the other spouse does not comply.

The Best Laid Plans

Suppose you save now for your five-year-old to attend your alma mater, but at nineteen he or she wants to travel or attend a vocational school. Would that be acceptable to you? Would your college savings fund this alternate plan? Which of you would have the right to decide? What if you did not agree?

Life Insurance and Other Security for Child Support

Both parents may want life insurance to secure the financial support of their children. Though only one parent may have a weekly child support payment to make, both parents contribute to the support of the children. Think about whether your children will have adequate support without life insurance if either one of you dies.

One way to roughly calculate the value of your future contribution is to take the annual amount of child support and multiply that number times the years you expect to support your children. Then add your best guess as to your likely share of unexpected extraordinary expenses not included on the worksheet and your expected share of post-secondary expenses. This will give you some guidelines for how much life insurance you need. To do a more accurate projection, consult with a divorce financial planning professional.

Try to agree on the total amount of life insurance you each will carry. You may want to name each other as trustee for the benefit of the children as long as the children are minors. You can use decreasing term insurance, i.e., the death benefit and the premium cost decrease each year over a certain term—usually the number of years until your last child emancipates or finishes college (age twenty-three is a good guess). Term insurance is usually the least expensive and most common insurance available as a benefit through your employer. Some parents prefer, however, to purchase an annuity which will pay out as life insurance in the event of death or be available as a lump sum in time to pay for higher education.

If you include life insurance or other security agreements in your separation agreement, they become enforceable court orders at the time the judge approves the agreement and enters your judgment of divorce.

Teeth for Your Child Support Agreement

If your ex has a new lover, will you be less likely to pay the child support or make the payments on time? If you lose your job or the bonus does not come through, will you look for a way out of your agreement? Most people would have to answer yes to at least one of these—or, at least admit that the possibility of temptation exists.

There are several kinds of internal enforcement to use in agreements about child support. These "teeth" are voluntary, private, and effective ways of penalizing yourselves with more or less costly consequences if you don't do what you say you will do. What does each of you need to put into your agreement to make sure you keep the promises you make to each other about supporting your children? Try having the person against whom the penalty would act set the penalty; what motivates each of you may be surprising.

Here are some examples of teeth in a child support agreement: You can say that the parent who has the tax exemption for the child loses it automatically to the other parent if his or her part of the child support agreement is not kept or is not current as of December 31 or some other date. You can state that if either parent does not pay his or her share of the extraordinary expenses, then that parent carries 100 percent of the extraordinary expenses for the next month.

Besides the internal teeth you negotiate, the law provides other available remedies. At the time of the support order, you can implement wage withholding to insure payment. A person who does not comply with child support orders may have his or her income garnished, assets levied, or tax refund intercepted. He or she may also face contempt charges. These enforcement mechanisms are available even without being specified in the actual separation agreement.

Conclusion

You are finished with your first rough look at your child support plan. It will probably not be your final version. Go on to the next chapters. The agreements you reach as a result of each of those chapters may necessitate changes in your child support arrangement.

Income Withholding Order: A court order to deduct child support and/or alimony automatically from wages. All support is paid this way unless the spouse receiving support waives his or her right to an immediate wage withholding order.

CONNECTICUT CHILD SUPPORT GUIDELINES
SCHEDULE OF BASIC CHILD SUPPORT OBLIGATIONS

NOTE: *Noncustodial parent income only for the darker shaded areas of the schedule on the first page; combined parental income for the remainder of the schedule. Use amounts in white italics only when the percentage in white italics is lower than the percentage for combined parental income.*

Combined Net Weekly Income	1 Child %	1 Child $	2 Children %	2 Children $	3 Children %	3 Children $	4 Children %	4 Children $	5 Children %	5 Children $	6 Children %	6 Children $
10	10.00%	1	10.13%	1	10.25%	1	10.38%	1	10.50%	1	10.63%	1
20	10.00%	2	10.24%	2	10.49%	2	10.73%	2	10.98%	2	11.22%	2
30	10.00%	3	10.36%	3	10.72%	3	11.09%	3	11.45%	3	11.81%	4
40	10.00%	4	10.48%	4	10.96%	4	11.44%	5	11.92%	5	12.40%	5
50	10.00%	5	10.60%	5	11.20%	6	11.79%	6	12.39%	6	12.99%	6
60	10.00%	6	10.72%	6	11.43%	7	12.15%	7	12.86%	8	13.58%	8
70	10.00%	7	10.83%	8	11.67%	8	12.50%	9	13.34%	9	14.17%	10
80	10.00%	8	10.95%	9	11.90%	10	12.86%	10	13.81%	11	14.76%	12
90	10.00%	9	11.07%	10	12.14%	11	13.21%	12	14.28%	13	15.35%	14
100	10.00%	10	11.19%	11	12.38%	12	13.56%	14	14.75%	15	15.94%	16
110	10.00%	11	11.31%	12	12.61%	14	13.92%	15	15.22%	17	16.53%	18
120	10.00%	12	11.42%	14	12.85%	15	14.27%	17	15.70%	19	17.12%	21
130	10.00%	13	11.64%	15	13.28%	17	14.93%	19	16.57%	22	18.21%	24
140	10.00%	14	11.66%	16	13.32%	19	14.98%	21	16.64%	23	18.30%	26
150	12.37%	19	14.99%	22	16.90%	25	18.68%	28	20.40%	31	22.08%	33
160	14.44%	23	17.89%	29	20.04%	32	21.92%	35	23.69%	38	25.39%	41
170	16.27%	28	20.46%	35	22.80%	39	24.78%	42	26.59%	45	28.31%	48
180	17.90%	32	22.74%	41	25.26%	45	27.32%	49	29.17%	53	30.90%	56
190	19.36%	37	24.79%	47	27.46%	52	29.59%	56	31.48%	60	33.22%	63
200	20.67%	41	26.62%	53	29.44%	59	31.64%	63	33.56%	67	35.31%	71
210	21.85%	46	28.29%	59	31.23%	66	33.49%	70	35.44%	74	37.20%	78
220	22.93%	50	29.80%	66	32.86%	72	35.17%	77	37.15%	82	38.92%	86
230	24.03%	55	31.18%	72	34.35%	79	36.71%	84	38.71%	89	40.49%	93
240	24.02%	58	32.44%	78	35.71%	86	38.11%	91	40.14%	96	41.93%	101
250	24.01%	60	33.61%	84	36.97%	92	39.41%	99	41.46%	104	43.25%	108
260	24.01%	62	34.68%	90	38.12%	99	40.60%	106	42.67%	111	44.47%	116
270	24.00%	65	35.58%	96	39.19%	106	41.71%	113	43.80%	118	45.60%	123
280	23.99%	67	35.57%	100	40.19%	113	42.74%	120	44.84%	126	46.65%	131
290	23.99%	70	35.56%	103	41.12%	119	43.70%	127	45.81%	133	47.63%	138
300	23.98%	72	35.56%	107	41.98%	126	44.59%	134	46.72%	140	48.54%	146
310	23.98%	74	35.55%	110	42.92%	133	45.43%	141	47.57%	147	49.39%	153
320	23.98%	77	35.54%	114	42.91%	137	46.21%	148	48.37%	155	50.19%	161
330	23.97%	79	35.53%	117	42.91%	142	46.95%	155	49.11%	162	50.95%	168
340	23.96%	81	35.52%	121	42.89%	146	47.59%	162	49.82%	169	51.65%	176
350	23.95%	84	35.49%	124	42.85%	150	47.55%	166	50.48%	177	52.32%	183
360	23.93%	86	35.46%	128	42.81%	154	47.51%	171	51.11%	184	52.95%	191
370	23.91%	88	35.44%	131	42.77%	158	47.47%	176	51.63%	191	53.55%	198
380	23.90%	91	35.41%	135	42.74%	162	47.44%	180	51.59%	196	54.11%	206
390	23.88%	93	35.39%	138	42.71%	167	47.40%	185	51.55%	201	54.65%	213
400	23.87%	95	35.37%	141	42.68%	171	47.37%	189	51.52%	206	55.26%	221
410	23.86%	98	35.34%	145	42.65%	175	47.34%	194	51.48%	211	55.23%	226
420	23.84%	100	35.32%	148	42.62%	179	47.31%	199	51.45%	216	55.19%	232
430	23.83%	102	35.30%	152	42.60%	183	47.28%	203	51.42%	221	55.16%	237
440	23.82%	105	35.28%	155	42.57%	187	47.25%	208	51.39%	226	55.13%	243
450	23.81%	107	35.26%	159	42.55%	191	47.22%	213	51.36%	231	55.10%	248
460	23.80%	109	35.24%	162	42.52%	196	47.20%	217	51.33%	236	55.07%	253
470	23.79%	112	35.23%	166	42.50%	200	47.17%	222	51.31%	241	55.04%	259
480	23.78%	114	35.21%	169	42.48%	204	47.15%	226	51.28%	246	55.01%	264
490	23.77%	116	35.19%	172	42.46%	208	47.13%	231	51.26%	251	54.98%	269

Combined Net Weekly Income	1 Child		2 Children		3 Children		4 Children		5 Children		6 Children	
	%	$	%	$	%	$	%	$	%	$	%	$
500	23.76%	119	35.17%	176	42.44%	212	47.11%	236	51.23%	256	54.96%	275
510	23.75%	121	35.16%	179	42.42%	216	47.09%	240	51.21%	261	54.93%	280
520	23.74%	123	35.14%	183	42.41%	221	47.07%	245	51.19%	266	54.91%	286
530	23.73%	126	35.13%	186	42.39%	225	47.05%	249	51.17%	271	54.89%	291
540	23.72%	128	35.11%	190	42.36%	229	47.02%	254	51.14%	276	54.85%	296
550	23.71%	130	35.09%	193	42.34%	233	46.99%	258	51.11%	281	54.82%	302
560	23.70%	133	35.07%	196	42.31%	237	46.97%	263	51.08%	286	54.79%	307
570	23.69%	135	35.05%	200	42.29%	241	46.94%	268	51.05%	291	54.76%	312
580	23.68%	137	35.04%	203	42.27%	245	46.92%	272	51.03%	296	54.73%	317
590	23.67%	140	35.02%	207	42.25%	249	46.89%	277	51.00%	301	54.71%	323
600	23.66%	142	35.01%	210	42.23%	253	46.87%	281	50.98%	306	54.68%	328
610	23.65%	144	34.99%	213	42.21%	257	46.85%	286	50.95%	311	54.66%	333
620	23.64%	147	34.98%	217	42.19%	262	46.83%	290	50.93%	316	54.63%	339
630	23.64%	149	34.96%	220	42.17%	266	46.81%	295	50.91%	321	54.61%	344
640	23.63%	151	34.95%	224	42.15%	270	46.79%	299	50.88%	326	54.58%	349
650	23.62%	154	34.93%	227	42.13%	274	46.77%	304	50.86%	331	54.56%	355
660	23.61%	156	34.92%	230	42.11%	278	46.74%	309	50.84%	336	54.54%	360
670	23.60%	158	34.90%	234	42.09%	282	46.72%	313	50.82%	340	54.51%	365
680	23.59%	160	34.89%	237	42.08%	286	46.70%	318	50.80%	345	54.49%	371
690	23.58%	163	34.88%	241	42.06%	290	46.69%	322	50.78%	350	54.47%	376
700	23.58%	165	34.87%	244	42.04%	294	46.67%	327	50.76%	355	54.45%	381
710	23.57%	167	34.85%	247	42.03%	298	46.65%	331	50.74%	360	54.43%	386
720	23.56%	170	34.84%	251	42.01%	302	46.63%	336	50.72%	365	54.41%	392
730	23.48%	171	34.72%	253	41.86%	306	46.46%	339	50.54%	369	54.22%	396
740	23.38%	173	34.58%	256	41.70%	309	46.28%	342	50.34%	373	54.01%	400
750	23.30%	175	34.44%	258	41.54%	312	46.11%	346	50.15%	376	53.80%	404
760	23.21%	176	34.31%	261	41.38%	314	45.93%	349	49.96%	380	53.60%	407
770	23.12%	178	34.19%	263	41.23%	317	45.77%	352	49.78%	383	53.41%	411
780	23.04%	180	34.06%	266	41.08%	320	45.60%	356	49.60%	387	53.22%	415
790	22.96%	181	33.94%	268	40.93%	323	45.44%	359	49.43%	390	53.03%	419
800	22.88%	183	33.82%	271	40.79%	326	45.29%	362	49.26%	394	52.85%	423
810	22.80%	185	33.71%	273	40.66%	329	45.14%	366	49.10%	398	52.67%	427
820	22.71%	186	33.57%	275	40.49%	332	44.96%	369	48.90%	401	52.46%	430
830	22.57%	187	33.37%	277	40.25%	334	44.69%	371	48.61%	403	52.15%	433
840	22.44%	188	33.17%	279	40.01%	336	44.42%	373	48.32%	406	51.85%	436
850	22.31%	190	32.98%	280	39.78%	338	44.17%	375	48.04%	408	51.55%	438
860	22.18%	191	32.79%	282	39.55%	340	43.92%	378	47.77%	411	51.26%	441
870	22.05%	192	32.60%	284	39.33%	342	43.67%	380	47.51%	413	50.97%	443
880	21.93%	193	32.42%	285	39.12%	344	43.43%	382	47.25%	416	50.69%	446
890	21.81%	194	32.25%	287	38.91%	346	43.20%	384	46.99%	418	50.42%	449
900	21.69%	195	32.07%	289	38.70%	348	42.97%	387	46.74%	421	50.16%	451
910	21.58%	196	31.91%	290	38.50%	350	42.74%	389	46.50%	423	49.90%	454
920	21.45%	197	31.71%	292	38.26%	352	42.49%	391	46.22%	425	49.60%	456
930	21.30%	198	31.50%	293	38.01%	354	42.21%	393	45.92%	427	49.28%	458
940	21.17%	199	31.30%	294	37.77%	355	41.94%	394	45.63%	429	48.97%	460
950	21.03%	200	31.10%	295	37.53%	357	41.68%	396	45.35%	431	48.66%	462
960	20.90%	201	30.90%	297	37.29%	358	41.42%	398	45.07%	433	48.36%	464
970	20.77%	201	30.71%	298	37.06%	360	41.16%	399	44.79%	434	48.07%	466
980	20.64%	202	30.52%	299	36.84%	361	40.92%	401	44.52%	436	47.78%	468
990	20.51%	203	30.34%	300	36.62%	363	40.67%	403	44.26%	438	47.50%	470

Combined Net Weekly Income	1 Child		2 Children		3 Children		4 Children		5 Children		6 Children	
	%	$	%	$	%	$	%	$	%	$	%	$
1,000	20.39%	204	30.16%	302	36.40%	364	40.43%	404	44.00%	440	47.22%	472
1,010	20.27%	205	29.98%	303	36.19%	366	40.20%	406	43.75%	442	46.95%	474
1,020	20.15%	206	29.81%	304	35.98%	367	39.97%	408	43.50%	444	46.68%	476
1,030	20.04%	206	29.64%	305	35.78%	369	39.75%	409	43.26%	446	46.42%	478
1,040	19.92%	207	29.47%	307	35.58%	370	39.53%	411	43.02%	447	46.17%	480
1,050	19.81%	208	29.31%	308	35.38%	372	39.31%	413	42.79%	449	45.92%	482
1,060	19.71%	209	29.15%	309	35.20%	373	39.10%	415	42.56%	451	45.68%	484
1,070	19.65%	210	29.07%	311	35.10%	376	39.00%	417	42.44%	454	45.55%	487
1,080	19.60%	212	28.99%	313	35.00%	378	38.89%	420	42.33%	457	45.43%	491
1,090	19.54%	213	28.91%	315	34.91%	380	38.78%	423	42.21%	460	45.31%	494
1,100	19.49%	214	28.83%	317	34.81%	383	38.68%	426	42.10%	463	45.19%	497
1,110	19.44%	216	28.76%	319	34.72%	385	38.58%	428	41.99%	466	45.07%	500
1,120	19.39%	217	28.68%	321	34.63%	388	38.48%	431	41.88%	469	44.96%	504
1,130	19.34%	219	28.61%	323	34.54%	390	38.38%	434	41.78%	472	44.84%	507
1,140	19.29%	220	28.54%	325	34.46%	393	38.29%	436	41.67%	475	44.73%	510
1,150	19.24%	221	28.46%	327	34.37%	395	38.19%	439	41.57%	478	44.62%	513
1,160	19.19%	223	28.39%	329	34.29%	398	38.10%	442	41.47%	481	44.52%	516
1,170	19.15%	224	28.33%	331	34.21%	400	38.01%	445	41.37%	484	44.41%	520
1,180	19.10%	225	28.26%	333	34.13%	403	37.92%	447	41.27%	487	44.31%	523
1,190	19.05%	227	28.19%	335	34.05%	405	37.83%	450	41.18%	490	44.20%	526
1,200	19.01%	228	28.13%	338	33.97%	408	37.75%	453	41.08%	493	44.10%	529
1,210	18.97%	229	28.06%	340	33.89%	410	37.66%	456	40.99%	496	44.01%	532
1,220	18.92%	231	28.00%	342	33.82%	413	37.58%	458	40.90%	499	43.91%	536
1,230	18.88%	232	27.94%	344	33.74%	415	37.50%	461	40.81%	502	43.81%	539
1,240	18.84%	234	27.88%	346	33.67%	417	37.42%	464	40.72%	505	43.72%	542
1,250	18.80%	235	27.82%	348	33.60%	420	37.34%	467	40.64%	508	43.63%	545
1,260	18.77%	236	27.77%	350	33.54%	423	37.27%	470	40.57%	511	43.55%	549
1,270	18.73%	238	27.72%	352	33.48%	425	37.21%	473	40.49%	514	43.47%	552
1,280	18.70%	239	27.67%	354	33.42%	428	37.14%	475	40.42%	517	43.40%	555
1,290	18.67%	241	27.62%	356	33.36%	430	37.07%	478	40.35%	521	43.32%	559
1,300	18.64%	242	27.57%	358	33.30%	433	37.01%	481	40.28%	524	43.25%	562
1,310	18.60%	244	27.52%	361	33.25%	436	36.95%	484	40.21%	527	43.17%	566
1,320	18.57%	245	27.48%	363	33.19%	438	36.89%	487	40.15%	530	43.10%	569
1,330	18.54%	247	27.43%	365	33.13%	441	36.83%	490	40.08%	533	43.03%	572
1,340	18.51%	248	27.39%	367	33.08%	443	36.77%	493	40.01%	536	42.96%	576
1,350	18.48%	250	27.34%	369	33.03%	446	36.71%	496	39.95%	539	42.89%	579
1,360	18.45%	251	27.30%	371	32.97%	448	36.65%	498	39.89%	542	42.82%	582
1,370	18.43%	252	27.25%	373	32.92%	451	36.59%	501	39.82%	546	42.75%	586
1,380	18.40%	254	27.21%	376	32.87%	454	36.53%	504	39.76%	549	42.69%	589
1,390	18.37%	255	27.17%	378	32.82%	456	36.48%	507	39.70%	552	42.62%	592
1,400	18.34%	257	27.13%	380	32.77%	459	36.42%	510	39.64%	555	42.56%	596
1,410	18.31%	258	27.09%	382	32.72%	461	36.37%	513	39.58%	558	42.50%	599
1,420	18.29%	260	27.05%	384	32.67%	464	36.32%	516	39.53%	561	42.43%	603
1,430	18.26%	261	27.01%	386	32.63%	467	36.26%	519	39.47%	564	42.37%	606
1,440	18.24%	263	26.97%	388	32.58%	469	36.21%	521	39.41%	568	42.31%	609
1,450	18.21%	264	26.93%	390	32.53%	472	36.16%	524	39.35%	571	42.25%	613
1,460	18.18%	265	26.89%	393	32.48%	474	36.10%	527	39.29%	574	42.19%	616
1,470	18.15%	267	26.84%	395	32.43%	477	36.05%	530	39.23%	577	42.12%	619
1,480	18.12%	268	26.80%	397	32.38%	479	35.99%	533	39.18%	580	42.06%	622
1,490	18.10%	270	26.76%	399	32.33%	482	35.94%	535	39.12%	583	42.00%	626

Combined Net Weekly Income	1 Child		2 Children		3 Children		4 Children		5 Children		6 Children	
	%	$	%	$	%	$	%	$	%	$	%	$
1,500	18.07%	271	26.72%	401	32.28%	484	35.88%	538	39.06%	586	41.94%	629
1,510	18.04%	272	26.68%	403	32.24%	487	35.83%	541	39.01%	589	41.87%	632
1,520	18.02%	274	26.64%	405	32.19%	489	35.78%	544	38.95%	592	41.81%	636
1,530	17.99%	275	26.61%	407	32.14%	492	35.73%	547	38.90%	595	41.76%	639
1,540	17.97%	277	26.57%	409	32.10%	494	35.68%	549	38.84%	598	41.70%	642
1,550	17.94%	278	26.53%	411	32.05%	497	35.63%	552	38.79%	601	41.64%	645
1,560	17.92%	280	26.49%	413	32.01%	499	35.58%	555	38.74%	604	41.58%	649
1,570	17.89%	281	26.46%	415	31.96%	502	35.53%	558	38.68%	607	41.53%	652
1,580	17.87%	282	26.42%	417	31.92%	504	35.48%	561	38.63%	610	41.47%	655
1,590	17.84%	284	26.39%	420	31.88%	507	35.44%	563	38.58%	613	41.42%	659
1,600	17.82%	285	26.35%	422	31.84%	509	35.39%	566	38.53%	617	41.36%	662
1,610	17.80%	287	26.32%	424	31.79%	512	35.34%	569	38.48%	620	41.31%	665
1,620	17.77%	288	26.28%	426	31.75%	514	35.30%	572	38.43%	623	41.26%	668
1,630	17.75%	289	26.25%	428	31.71%	517	35.25%	575	38.39%	626	41.21%	672
1,640	17.71%	290	26.19%	430	31.64%	519	35.18%	577	38.30%	628	41.12%	674
1,650	17.66%	291	26.11%	431	31.55%	521	35.08%	579	38.19%	630	41.00%	677
1,660	17.61%	292	26.04%	432	31.46%	522	34.98%	581	38.09%	632	40.89%	679
1,670	17.56%	293	25.97%	434	31.37%	524	34.88%	582	37.98%	634	40.77%	681
1,680	17.51%	294	25.89%	435	31.29%	526	34.78%	584	37.87%	636	40.66%	683
1,690	17.46%	295	25.82%	436	31.20%	527	34.69%	586	37.77%	638	40.55%	685
1,700	17.41%	296	25.75%	438	31.12%	529	34.59%	588	37.67%	640	40.44%	688
1,710	17.37%	297	25.68%	439	31.03%	531	34.50%	590	37.57%	642	40.34%	690
1,720	17.32%	298	25.61%	441	30.95%	532	34.41%	592	37.47%	644	40.23%	692
1,730	17.27%	299	25.54%	442	30.87%	534	34.32%	594	37.37%	646	40.13%	694
1,740	17.23%	300	25.47%	443	30.79%	536	34.23%	596	37.27%	649	40.02%	696
1,750	17.18%	301	25.41%	445	30.70%	537	34.14%	597	37.17%	651	39.92%	699
1,760	17.14%	302	25.34%	446	30.63%	539	34.05%	599	37.08%	653	39.82%	701
1,770	17.09%	303	25.28%	447	30.55%	541	33.96%	601	36.98%	655	39.72%	703
1,780	17.05%	303	25.21%	449	30.47%	542	33.88%	603	36.89%	657	39.62%	705
1,790	17.00%	304	25.15%	450	30.39%	544	33.79%	605	36.80%	659	39.52%	707
1,800	16.96%	305	25.08%	452	30.32%	546	33.71%	607	36.71%	661	39.42%	710
1,810	16.92%	306	25.02%	453	30.24%	547	33.63%	609	36.62%	663	39.33%	712
1,820	16.88%	307	24.96%	454	30.17%	549	33.54%	610	36.53%	665	39.23%	714
1,830	16.84%	308	24.91%	456	30.10%	551	33.47%	613	36.45%	667	39.15%	716
1,840	16.81%	309	24.86%	457	30.05%	553	33.41%	615	36.38%	669	39.08%	719
1,850	16.78%	310	24.81%	459	29.99%	555	33.35%	617	36.32%	672	39.01%	722
1,860	16.75%	312	24.77%	461	29.94%	557	33.29%	619	36.25%	674	38.94%	724
1,870	16.72%	313	24.72%	462	29.88%	559	33.23%	621	36.19%	677	38.87%	727
1,880	16.69%	314	24.68%	464	29.83%	561	33.17%	624	36.13%	679	38.80%	729
1,890	16.66%	315	24.64%	466	29.78%	563	33.11%	626	36.06%	682	38.73%	732
1,900	16.63%	316	24.59%	467	29.73%	565	33.06%	628	36.00%	684	38.67%	735
1,910	16.60%	317	24.55%	469	29.68%	567	33.00%	630	35.94%	686	38.60%	737
1,920	16.57%	318	24.51%	471	29.62%	569	32.94%	633	35.88%	689	38.54%	740
1,930	16.54%	319	24.47%	472	29.57%	571	32.89%	635	35.82%	691	38.47%	742
1,940	16.52%	320	24.42%	474	29.52%	573	32.83%	637	35.76%	694	38.41%	745
1,950	16.49%	322	24.38%	475	29.47%	575	32.78%	639	35.70%	696	38.34%	748
1,960	16.46%	323	24.34%	477	29.43%	577	32.73%	641	35.64%	699	38.28%	750
1,970	16.43%	324	24.30%	479	29.38%	579	32.67%	644	35.59%	701	38.22%	753
1,980	16.41%	325	24.26%	480	29.33%	581	32.62%	646	35.53%	703	38.16%	756
1,990	16.38%	326	24.22%	482	29.28%	583	32.57%	648	35.47%	706	38.10%	758

Combined Net Weekly Income	1 Child		2 Children		3 Children		4 Children		5 Children		6 Children	
	%	$	%	$	%	$	%	$	%	$	%	$
2,000	16.36%	327	24.18%	484	29.24%	585	32.52%	650	35.42%	708	38.04%	761
2,010	16.33%	328	24.14%	485	29.19%	587	32.46%	653	35.36%	711	37.98%	763
2,020	16.30%	329	24.11%	487	29.14%	589	32.41%	655	35.31%	713	37.92%	766
2,030	16.28%	330	24.07%	489	29.10%	591	32.36%	657	35.25%	716	37.86%	769
2,040	16.25%	332	24.03%	490	29.05%	593	32.31%	659	35.20%	718	37.80%	771
2,050	16.23%	333	23.99%	492	29.01%	595	32.26%	661	35.14%	720	37.75%	774
2,060	16.20%	334	23.96%	494	28.96%	597	32.22%	664	35.09%	723	37.69%	776
2,070	16.18%	335	23.92%	495	28.92%	599	32.17%	666	35.04%	725	37.63%	779
2,080	16.15%	336	23.88%	497	28.88%	601	32.12%	668	34.99%	728	37.58%	782
2,090	16.13%	337	23.85%	498	28.83%	603	32.07%	670	34.94%	730	37.52%	784
2,100	16.11%	338	23.81%	500	28.79%	605	32.03%	673	34.89%	733	37.47%	787
2,110	16.08%	339	23.78%	502	28.75%	607	31.98%	675	34.84%	735	37.42%	789
2,120	16.06%	340	23.74%	503	28.71%	609	31.93%	677	34.79%	737	37.36%	792
2,130	16.04%	342	23.71%	505	28.67%	611	31.89%	679	34.74%	740	37.31%	795
2,140	16.01%	343	23.68%	507	28.62%	613	31.84%	681	34.69%	742	37.26%	797
2,150	15.99%	344	23.64%	508	28.58%	615	31.80%	684	34.64%	745	37.20%	800
2,160	15.97%	345	23.61%	510	28.54%	617	31.75%	686	34.59%	747	37.15%	803
2,170	15.95%	346	23.57%	512	28.50%	619	31.71%	688	34.54%	750	37.10%	805
2,180	15.92%	347	23.54%	513	28.46%	621	31.67%	690	34.50%	752	37.05%	808
2,190	15.90%	348	23.51%	515	28.43%	623	31.62%	693	34.45%	754	37.00%	810
2,200	15.88%	349	23.48%	516	28.39%	625	31.58%	695	34.40%	757	36.95%	813
2,210	15.86%	350	23.44%	518	28.35%	627	31.54%	697	34.36%	759	36.90%	816
2,220	15.84%	352	23.41%	520	28.31%	628	31.50%	699	34.31%	762	36.85%	818
2,230	15.82%	353	23.38%	521	28.27%	630	31.45%	701	34.27%	764	36.81%	821
2,240	15.80%	354	23.35%	523	28.24%	632	31.41%	704	34.22%	767	36.76%	823
2,250	15.77%	355	23.32%	525	28.20%	634	31.37%	706	34.18%	769	36.71%	826
2,260	15.75%	356	23.29%	526	28.16%	636	31.33%	708	34.14%	771	36.66%	829
2,270	15.73%	357	23.26%	528	28.13%	638	31.29%	710	34.09%	774	36.62%	831
2,280	15.71%	358	23.23%	530	28.09%	640	31.25%	713	34.05%	776	36.57%	834
2,290	15.69%	359	23.20%	531	28.05%	642	31.21%	715	34.01%	779	36.53%	836
2,300	15.67%	360	23.17%	533	28.02%	644	31.17%	717	33.96%	781	36.48%	839
2,310	15.65%	362	23.14%	535	27.98%	646	31.14%	719	33.92%	784	36.43%	842
2,320	15.63%	363	23.11%	536	27.95%	648	31.10%	721	33.88%	786	36.39%	844
2,330	15.61%	364	23.08%	538	27.91%	650	31.06%	724	33.84%	788	36.35%	847
2,340	15.60%	365	23.05%	539	27.88%	652	31.02%	726	33.80%	791	36.30%	849
2,350	15.58%	366	23.03%	541	27.85%	654	30.98%	728	33.76%	793	36.26%	852
2,360	15.56%	367	23.00%	543	27.81%	656	30.95%	730	33.72%	796	36.22%	855
2,370	15.54%	368	22.97%	544	27.78%	658	30.91%	733	33.68%	798	36.17%	857
2,380	15.52%	369	22.94%	546	27.75%	660	30.87%	735	33.64%	801	36.13%	860
2,390	15.50%	371	22.92%	548	27.71%	662	30.84%	737	33.60%	803	36.09%	863
2,400	15.48%	372	22.89%	549	27.68%	664	30.80%	739	33.56%	805	36.05%	865
2,410	15.47%	373	22.86%	551	27.65%	666	30.77%	741	33.52%	808	36.01%	868
2,420	15.45%	374	22.83%	553	27.62%	668	30.73%	744	33.49%	810	35.96%	870
2,430	15.43%	375	22.81%	554	27.58%	670	30.70%	746	33.45%	813	35.92%	873
2,440	15.41%	376	22.78%	556	27.55%	672	30.66%	748	33.41%	815	35.88%	876
2,450	15.40%	377	22.76%	558	27.52%	674	30.63%	750	33.37%	818	35.84%	878
2,460	15.38%	378	22.73%	559	27.49%	676	30.59%	753	33.34%	820	35.80%	881
2,470	15.36%	379	22.70%	561	27.46%	678	30.56%	755	33.30%	822	35.76%	883
2,480	15.34%	381	22.68%	562	27.43%	680	30.52%	757	33.26%	825	35.73%	886
2,490	15.33%	382	22.65%	564	27.40%	682	30.49%	759	33.23%	827	35.69%	889
2,500	15.31%	383	22.63%	566	27.37%	684	30.46%	762	33.19%	830	35.65%	891

CHAPTER 10

PROPERTY AND DEBTS

PROPERTY AND DEBTS

Nearly anything of value is considered property. Property may include real estate; furniture; household goods; art, musical, and sporting equipment; any personal property; cars, trucks, and other motor vehicles; cash, bank accounts, stocks and bonds, and other investments; retirement and pension plans; profit-sharing; stock options; and business interests, including accounts receivable, furniture, fixtures, and good will. You must divide all your property and debt in your separation agreement.

In Connecticut, the law does not distinguish between "marital" and "separate" property. All property, titled in either spouse's name and whenever and however acquired, is subject to equitable division.

For purposes of agreeing to division, you may assign the property and debts each keeps as you wish. You could elect to identify property brought into the marriage and/or gifts and inheritances as separate property. You could consider property acquired during the marriage and/or the increase in value as separate property. If you are settling your case you can define and divide the property as you agree between you.

Valuing and Dividing Property and Debts

You may list your division of property and debts on the two-page Division of Marital Property and Debts Chart that follows. The value of an item of property, or the amount of a debt, will probably be an important part of this division. The next section of this chapter describes each kind of property that you may divide. Each discussion contains suggestions about how to find values for particular kinds of property. The following are some thoughts about value to keep in mind as you read this chapter.

What if the two of you are unable to agree on a value? This is not a reason to give up or to stop negotiating. Put down both values and agree that the value of that asset falls somewhere in between. It is possible to put together a property settlement in which several assets are assigned range-values only. Some assets are extremely difficult to value, such as small businesses. You can bring in a professional to tell you a value. You may list the value of such an asset for now as simply "unknown," and decide later if your negotiations necessitate honing in on a precise number or range.

You have the right to decide to allocate any or all of your assets between you without regard to monetary value at all. Value is not always monetary. The value an item has for you may be the mem-

"We have to divide our property equally. That's the law."

Nowhere is it written in Connecticut that you divide your assets equally. The word used in the statute is "equitable," which means fair.

Defining Our Sense of Fairness

A. We agree our marital property should be divided 50-50 because:

or

B. We agree that the first $ _____ in value of property should go to _____ because:

or

C. We agree _____ should get all the _____ because:

and _____ should get all the _____ because:

or

D.

Connecticut statute (C.G.S. § 46b-81) requires the court to consider the following factors in dividing property:

1. Length of the marriage

2. Cause of the dissolution of the marriage

3. For each of the parties

   a. Age

   b. Health

   c. Station

   d. Occupation

   e. Amount and sources of income

   f. Vocational skills

   g. Employability

   h. Estate

   i. Liabilities

   j. Needs

   k. Opportunity for future acquisition of capital assets and income

   l. Contribution to acquisition, preservation, or appreciation in value of their respective estates

Pre- and Post-marital Agreements

If you and your spouse have a signed agreement written before or after your marriage which defines "marital" and "separate" property and/or debts, it will probably control your definitions of these terms now. This is especially true if you were both represented by counsel. If you have any questions about the enforceability of such agreements you should consult an attorney.

ories it contains, its usefulness, or its beauty. Value to you may mean your need for an asset. For example, you might decide that certain items, such as the washer and dryer, may need to remain in the home with the children. You do not necessarily have to inventory and place values on such items unless you want to.

Many people try to divide each asset as they discuss it ("Your half of the house is $4,000, my half of the house is $4,000"). Since you will rarely divide the house like this, this may not be the most useful way to go about it. It may be more practical to begin by listing each asset under the name of the person who will keep it. For example, in the wife's column, list the equity in the house if she is thinking of continuing to live there. List the entire value of the husband's retirement in his column, if that is your initial inclination. An advantage to this method is that it allows you to see the balance, or lack of it, of your initial plan as you develop it.

If you want to know dollar values, you may need a third party, such as an appraiser, to help you determine them. To avoid expensive competing professional opinions, agree on whom you will hire as your appraiser and how you will pay him or her. Agree on what you will do if one of you strongly disagrees with the value offered by the appraiser.

The law considers such factors as the age, health, station, occupation, amount and sources of income, vocational skills, employability, estate, liabilities, needs of the parties, the opportunities of each party to acquire capital and assets in the future, and the contribution of each spouse to the acquisition, preservation, and appreciation in value of each other's property. The court may consider the cause of the breakdown of the marriage. There is no legal formula, so you should consult with an attorney if you have any questions about the law of property and debt division. If you can agree on a generic plan that meets each of your ideas of fairness, you will find you have an agreement that practically writes itself.

This is the time for a really frank discussion about the range of your sense of fairness. Is the only possibility for you a 50–50 division of things by value? By number? Do you have more interest in cash than in other assets? Will you take less than 50 percent if your share is all cash? Do you have more interest in future security than in present assets? If you are willing to wait for a buy-out of your share, such as house or retirement, are you looking for more than 50 percent to compensate you for waiting? Does a "lopsided" agreement (more to one than the other) to compensate for the larger earnings of one of you now interest you? Do you want to be "made whole"—end up where you were at the beginning of the relationship? Do you need compensation "off the top" for some contribution you made to the acquisition of property?

As you divide assets, write down on the Division of Property and Debts Chart, page 252, the costs to maintain each asset, the debt that comes with it, and the potential for growth or income. This will help you make a more balanced settlement.

As you allocate your other debts, agree who will pay off the balance of each. Remember that you may find it easier to handle the problem of unsecured debts as a budget issue rather than division of property. If you find yourselves getting stuck on the division of unsecured debts, including tax debt and divorce expenses, consider setting aside this issue for now. Look at these debts again in the context of alimony and tax planning after reading Chapters 11 and 12.

Think ahead to the long-term effect of the division of assets and debts you are considering. For example, suppose one spouse gets all assets that appreciate slowly (or not at all) and take money to maintain (home, car, furniture). As another example, one spouse may take assets with a lower (or higher) tax basis. Or suppose that one spouse takes all the assets that increase in value or produce income (stock, retirement, rental home). In such cases, even a few years after the divorce a "fair" or "equal" division may look quite different. The net worth of this spouse will far exceed the net worth of the other—and the gap will just continue to widen. Be sure to consider this information before you decide what is really fair or equal in your situation.

"If we can't agree on values, we can't agree on anything. We'll never be able to settle."

This is not true. You may elect to divide anything and everything without regard to monetary value. There are many kinds of value; dollars is only one of them. The only requirement is that you divide your property "equitably"—in a fair manner.

Division of Property Between Spouses Is Not a Taxable Event

Division of property in a divorce does not result in taxable income for anybody, even if one spouse pays off the other in cash. This is true as long as the transfers are directly between the two spouses, either before or after the divorce is final, as stated in the terms of a written separation agreement. The transaction is seen by the IRS as the division of something you already own, not as a taxable "sale."

DIRECTIONS FOR COMPLETING THE DIVISION OF PROPERTY AND DEBTS CHARTS

Make several photocopies of each chart. Do your first drafts and preliminary bargaining in pencil, as you may want to try different possibilities.

If you are treating any assets as separate in your division, use the Property and Debts Chart to list them in the appropriate column.

To divide the assets, use the following checklists found throughout this book to help you decide who gets what property and debt as well as the value or balance of each:

> Calculation of Your Value of Real Estate
>
> Personal Property Checklist
>
> Motor Vehicle Checklist
>
> Liquid Assets Checklist
>
> Stocks Checklist
>
> Bonds Checklist
>
> Life Insurance Checklist
>
> Retirements Checklist
>
> Business Interests Checklist
>
> Business Valuation Checklist
>
> Other Assets Checklist
>
> Debts Checklist
>
> Divorce Expenses Checklist

List under *husband* or *wife* every asset and debt each spouse will keep. If you are not placing a value on the asset, or if you are assigning a specific percentage or proportion of the asset between you, list that information also. Put debt balances in parentheses.

For each item of property or debt, you can choose to anticipate and calculate the expected earnings or cost and/or the increase or decrease in value in the cash flow/growth columns. Again, put decreases in parentheses. For example, if the wife will be retaining the family home, you can write all the costs of maintaining the home in the cash flow column of the chart, along with the probable rate of increase in value (est. x percent per year). You may want to include the increase in equity as the mortgage is paid as part of the growth of that asset. If the husband will retain his automobile, then the car payment, insurance, and costs of operating the car go in his cash flow column, as do the rate of decrease in value of this depreciating asset. List debt balances in either the *husband* or *wife* column as appropriate, and list the monthly payment in the cash flow column. Remember to list any debts secured by property along with the property.

After entering all your assets and debts, total the husband's assets minus the husband's debts and do the same for the wife. Then, for each spouse, total the cash flow column. These four totals will summarize your preliminary division of property. Refer now to your answers to Defining Our Sense of Fairness. Review your division with this in mind, and make changes as you need to.

DIVISION OF PROPERTY AND DEBTS CHART
WIFE

ASSET/DEBT	VALUE	CASH FLOW/GROWTH/ TAX BASIS
TOTALS		

DIVISION OF PROPERTY AND DEBTS CHART
HUSBAND

ASSET/DEBT	VALUE	CASH FLOW/GROWTH/ TAX BASIS
TOTALS		

Kinds of Property (Assets)

REAL ESTATE

Real estate includes your family home, condo, vacation home, time-share, commercial real estate, raw land, and real estate partnerships, as well as a contract for the purchase of real estate. Most people value real estate at current fair market value (the amount a willing buyer would pay a willing seller). There are three resources which may help you in determining fair market value: real estate appraisal, market analysis, and tax assessment value.

Getting the gross fair market value of your real estate is only the beginning. This is not the value to you in the divorce. You must take into account what is owed against the property: mortgages, liens, etc. The fair market value minus the amount owed is the equity. This is the most this property could be worth to the two of you.

You may want to adjust the equity value of your real estate for selling costs and capital gains taxes, if any. Unless you are going to sell the property immediately, the law does not specifically address whether these adjustments would occur in a contested trial. Therefore, whether these adjustments are made is up to you in the decisions and agreements you reach.

Selling Costs

Selling costs typically include brokerage commission, title insurance, and any fix-up and repairs to make the property saleable. If the property is to be sold immediately or in the near future (especially if the selling costs would wipe out the equity and the person keeping the property is not certain whether he or she can hold on to the property for very long), it makes sense to take out the costs of sale in arriving at what the value really is for you. Some selling costs to consider are:

- *Brokerage commissions.* To estimate this, multiply the probable sales price times approximately 6 percent or other rate (the commission on farm or commercial properties may be as high as 10 percent).

- *Cost of fix-up for sale.*

- *Conveyance tax.* The state of Connecticut charges a sales tax of approximately 2.05 percent. Towns also charge a conveyance tax, usually $1.10 for each $1,000 of the sales price. You should check with your town for the exact rate.

Difference Between Joint Tenancy and Tenancy in Common

Joint tenancy means that you each own an undivided 50 percent interest in the property, and the whole property goes to the survivor upon the death of the other joint tenant. Tenancy in common is a divisible interest, presumed to be 50-50, unless otherwise specified (60-40, 70-30) and each owner's share passes at death with his or her estate (does not go automatically to the other owner). Most couples own their family home in joint tenancy.

Real Estate Equity Calculation

(Complete for each property)

Fair Market Value
(FMV)   _____

Less: 1st
Mortgage Balance _____

Less: 2nd (& 3rd)
Mortgage(s)   _____

Equity   _____

Tax Carry-forwards

Some real estate, business, and other interests generate losses that are carried forward to be used as tax deductions for future years. Other business activities may generate profits that will have to be recognized in future years, requiring the payment of taxes on "income" that was actually received years before. Division of these carry-forwards as a part of the division of property is a complicated issue about which you should receive advice from an attorney or accountant.

The tax on capital gains is a "hidden" cost of real estate sales. Forgetting about this tax can be very costly.

- *Attorneys' fees.* Depending upon the complexities of the sale, attorneys' fees are usually $400 to $800.

If the spouse receiving the property is likely to keep it for a number of years—until the children are grown for example—then you may not want to subtract future selling costs now.

Whether you subtract the costs of sale to determine the equity is up to you. Making a clear agreement about selling costs is one of the ways in which you can fine tune your settlement.

Capital Gains Taxes

The capital gains tax is a real cost that stays with real estate and other assets and will have to be paid when the property is eventually sold. Whoever keeps the property will ultimately be responsible for this tax.

Capital gains is the difference between the adjusted selling price and your investment in the property. You may pay income tax on the gain as though it were additional income earned by you in the year of sale. The amount of your investment for tax purposes is called the basis.

If you bought your principal residence, your original basis is the purchase price. If you acquired the property by means other than a purchase (built it yourself, hired someone to build it for you, or received it as a gift or inheritance), see IRS Publications 523 and 551 for how to determine your original basis.

During ownership, the basis in the property may increase or decrease. You increase the basis by additions or capital improvements; you decrease the basis by rolling over a prior capital gain or taking depreciation. The lower your basis, the greater your gain and the greater your tax. See IRS Publication 551 for a detailed discussion of these and other adjustments to basis.

To determine your likely capital gain, subtract your adjusted basis from the fair market value. Then you may adjust for probable selling costs. Next, figure out your taxes.

Your gain is taxed at your federal and state tax rate. However, the IRS caps the federal tax at certain maximum rates. Generally, the maximum federal tax under the Taxpayer Relief Act of 1997 is 20 percent. The actual rate can be lower depending upon how long you hold the property and your tax bracket. To calculate the federal and state rate for capital gains tax on your home accurately, you should consult with a CPA.

The Taxpayer Relief Act of 1997 establishes a system for excluding all or part of your gain from taxation. The new law allows homeowners to avoid paying taxes on the first $500,000 of capital gains from the sale of their principal residence if they are married at the time they sell the home. After the divorce, each spouse as a single taxpayer may exempt $250,000 of capital gains from taxation. To qualify for this tax exemption, the house must be the taxpayer's principal residence for two out of the five years preceding the sale.

If you sold a previous personal residence, you may have rolled over the capital gain from that sale into your present home. Pull your tax return for the year in which you sold your previous residence, then check your tax return from the year you purchased your new home. These forms should help you to determine the basis in your present home as well as the capital gain and the rolled over basis in your new home.

If you can't determine this information from your tax return forms, then you will need to assemble the same information about your previous home that you are gathering about your present home, particularly the following: Purchaser's Closing Statement (at the time you bought it), Seller's Closing Statement (at the time of sale), and proof of the cost of capital improvements.

The new law eliminates the old provisions, permitting rollover of capital gain when selling your home. If you have owned several homes over the years and have built up rolled-over profits, all of the accumulated profits will be subject to tax (and the $500,000 or $250,000 exemption) on the sale of your current home.

Because under the old law you could roll capital gains over and were subject to a one-time $125,00 exemption at age fifty-five, most judges did not consider capital gains when valuing the marital home unless the divorce order included selling it. It remains to be seen whether judges will take the new approach to capital gains tax under consideration in valuing the marital home if it was not sold as part of the order. However, you may want to calculate and consider the capital gains tax as you decide what to do with the marital home. To evaluate the capital gains tax impact on the sale or retention of your home, you should consult with a CPA and/or divorce lawyer familiar with these issues.

Different Ways to Divide Real Estate

Before you take out the chain saw or sign the listing agreement, think about all the possible ways you might divide real estate:

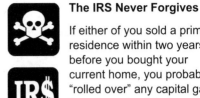

The IRS Never Forgives

If either of you sold a primary residence within two years before you bought your current home, you probably "rolled over" any capital gain from the sale of that residence into your present home. If so, it's still there. You must include this old gain in your calculation of the capital gain on the present home.

For more information on the tax consequences of selling your home see IRS Pub. 523, *Selling Your Home* at **www. irs.gov/pub/irs-pdf/p523.pdf**.

1. Sell it together now and divide the proceeds. You may:

   - Give more than half the proceeds to the spouse who needs more down payment to qualify for a new mortgage; and/or

   - Offset some or all of the proceeds with some other kind of property to the other spouse, business interests for example, or savings, stocks, or present value of retirement; and/or

   - Use the proceeds to pay off the marital debts.

2. One of you keeps the home, and the other gets:

   - Some other property as you negotiate; or

   - Cash or other assets; or

   - A promissory note (with or without interest) promising to pay at some later date (a balloon payment), due on sale or in payments over a period of time (months or years). You may secure this promise to pay by a mortgage lien that you record with the town clerk in the town where the property is located. Although the principal amount of these payments is not taxable, the interest on them is taxable to the recipient in the year received. An attorney should draft these papers for you.

3. You can retain shared title and ownership of the home. Either one of you can live in the home without transferring the title, and you can agree to keep the home for a time, even for many years, and then sell it and share the profits at a later time. Note that you would share responsibility for the tax on the capital gain in proportion to your ownership at the time of sale. In addition:

   - You should make your agreements clear about your respective responsibilities for payment of the following: mortgage, property taxes, insurance, homeowners' association dues, special assessments, day-to-day upkeep and repairs, major repairs, capital improvements, and selling costs.

   - Be sure you agree about how to share the profits in the full light of who has paid for what during the period of joint ownership.

- You can rent it to a third party and wait for a better market. Each can depreciate his or her share of the home.

- You should consider whether you want to retitle ownership as joint tenants or as tenants in common. Make certain if you change title ownership to record the new deed on the land records showing your respective interest.

Once you decide how you want to divide all or some of your real estate, write the appropriate information on the Division of Marital Property and Debts Chart. You may do this even if you are not certain this is your final agreement. Noting your interim thinking in pencil is a good idea. You will probably look at several different property divisions before you reach a final agreement.

PERSONAL PROPERTY

Your personal property includes furniture, appliances, stereo system and TV, linens, all your kitchen items, musical instruments, art, collections, sporting equipment, pets and animals, and all the stuff in the basement and the garage. This section addresses how to allocate these items.

Personal property usually does not include your personal clothing. Yours is yours, and your spouse's is your spouse's. Personal property to divide includes jewelry, furs, antiques, furniture, and the like. Personal property does not include personal business property, such as the computer, copier, or desk. Personal business property is discussed in "Business Interests" later in this chapter.

The division of personal property is often a discussion one spouse wants to avoid completely. "He/she can have it all! I just want out!" This is usually a great mistake. Both of you probably need some continuity with your tangible belongings even though the thought of having any of them may be painful at first.

Sometimes personal property becomes "larger than life." An item can become a metaphor for your time together or for your marriage or divorce. If you feel stuck on items of personal property, this is probably why. Take a little time to figure out what this hard fought–for item really represents for one or both of you.

Some people list all their personal property, place values on it, and then divide the value in some agreed upon proportion. Most people who do this use fair market value, which for most is the likely price at a garage sale. For more expensive items, such as

---

Personal Property Checklist

Directions: Check or complete those statements below which are true. Use a separate piece of paper for any itemized lists.

☐ We will divide our personal property by value.

☐ We will divide our personal property by need.

☐ We have set aside the separate personal property for each of us.

☐ We have agreed to walk through the house together on _____ (date).

☐ We will create THE LIST of items we both want by _____, 20___.

☐ We will divide the items on THE LIST by means of _____ _____, on _____(date).

These pieces of personal property have debts against them:

Item   Amount of Debt

George's Tools

Mary thinks George spends all his time in the garage tinkering with small motors that appear to propagate overnight. She proves, through a review of the check register, that they have spent more than $5,000 on his tools and equipment. She wants to value his things in the garage at the original cost. He says they "might be worth $500 on a good day," if he could find someone who wanted them.

Louise's Dining Room

Louise and Charles bought a Chinese Chippendale dining room set for $8,000, fifteen years ago because it was "just like" the one Louise grew up with—and her parents gave to her sister. Charles has no objection to Louise keeping it, but he wants to be allocated $8,000 to buy his own dining room set. Louise says that it might bring $800 at a garage sale.

We need to research the values for the following items of personal property:

Who will do it? When will it be done?

☐　We completed our DIN List (*see* Chapter 5), or will complete it by _____, 20___.

You can obtain information to estimate the value of your car at **www.kbb.com** or **www.nadaguides.com**.

musical instruments, art, antiques, and collections of any kind, you may want to pay for an appraisal. Other items you may consider are "separate" because you brought them into the marriage, inherited them, or bought them with "your" money. The importance you put on the value of items is up to you.

Another approach is to divide things by need. Walk through the house together and see if you can agree on who gets what with a view to setting up two households that are as complete as possible. Inevitably some new purchases will be necessary. See the "DIN" list in Chapter 5. Many people try to find an equitable way to bear that burden/benefit too. It's a burden because you have to spend money, and it can be a benefit or a burden because one of you gets the "new" item while the other gets the used one with all the memories. Remember, the replacement cost of an item is probably much higher than the fair market value of the existing one.

There may be items you don't agree on. You can always sell what neither of you wants, but what to do about items you both want? First of all, just list them and don't argue about them. You can begin to deal with this list after allocation of everything else. See if you can strike a bargain about any of those items. "You can have #4 if I can have #3." "I'll give you $40 if I can have #6." Agreements like these can shorten the list. Finally, you can flip a coin to decide who goes first to pick one item off the list. The other then takes the next two items from the list (in exchange for not being first). You then take turns until nothing remains.

If you have now agreed on a division of personal property, you may enter the appropriate information on the Division of Marital Property and Debts Chart. If you have agreed not to monetarily value your personal property, there is no need to enter the information.

CARS AND OTHER MOTOR VEHICLES

Motor vehicles may include cars, pick-ups, RVs, boats, motorcycles, trailers, snowmobiles, and aircraft. You may divide these by value, need, or any other measure you agree to.

To divide by financial value, you may start with the automobile values obtained from the NADA (National Automobile Dealers Association) Blue Book, available at any public library, car dealer, bank, or lending institution. This will give you the retail, wholesale, and loan values. "Retail" in the Blue Book is often slightly higher than fair market value to you since it is the price a dealer would get. Likewise, "wholesale" is probably too low, as it is the price a dealer would pay. The value of your automobile is probably between these. You can further refine these values by looking for used vehicles like yours in the weekend classified ads of major newspapers.

You can call and survey dealers and brokers, especially of used items like yours, and find out what they are asking. You can find these dealers and brokers through the Yellow Pages under the type of item you are valuing, such as "Aircraft" or "Boats." To get a professional appraisal, you can start your search by looking in the Yellow Pages under "Appraisers." See also "Asset Evaluators" in Chapter 2.

If you drive a leased vehicle, you do not own it and therefore it has no value for property division purposes. You should state in your agreement who will drive the car and be responsible for the remainder of the lease payments and the right to the buy-out option.

If you have an agreement about dividing your motor vehicles, you may enter the appropriate information on the Division of Marital Property and Debts Chart. If you have agreed not to monetarily value your motor vehicles, there is no need to enter the information.

LIQUID ASSETS: CASH AND BANK ACCOUNTS

Cash and bank accounts, the most liquid of assets, are easiest to value. Certificates of deposit, even if not mature, are also known as liquid assets. You may include money market accounts here too. Savings accounts, certificates of deposit, and some checking accounts earn interest, and money market accounts increase in value. See your most recent statements for their current values. You may want to adjust your valuation of these assets in your settlement if the person keeping them will have to cash them out soon—therefore realizing less than full face value.

If you have agreed on how you are going to divide your liquid assets, enter the appropriate information on the Division of Marital Property and Debts Chart.

LIFE INSURANCE

There are two basic kinds of life insurance policies: whole life and term. Various hybrids also exist. A whole life policy has cash surrender value, which is an asset. The cash surrender value is the amount of money you would receive if you cashed in the policy, but this may be reduced by outstanding loans. The policy

---

Motor Vehicle Checklist

Provide the following information for each of your motor vehicles:

Make and Model:

Blue Book Value:

Wholesale:

Retail:

Loan balance:

How titled:

Make and Model:

Blue Book Value:

Wholesale:

Retail:

Loan balance:

How titled:

Make and Model:

Blue Book Value:

Wholesale:

Retail:

Loan balance:

How titled:

Liquid Assets Checklist

Bank name:
Type of account:
Name(s) on the account:
Account number:
Balance:
Date of balance:

Bank name:
Type of account:
Name(s) on the account:
Account number:
Balance:
Date of balance:

Bank name:
Type of account:
Name(s) on the account:
Account number:
Balance:
Date of balance:

Life Insurance Checklist

Complete the following for each life insurance policy on either of your lives or owned by either of you on anybody's life:

Company:

Person insured:

Death benefit:

Accidental death benefit, if any:

Beneficiary(ies):

Type of policy:

Premium:

Cash value:

Loan balance:

Surrender value:

Ownership:

Stock Checklist

Repeat as necessary, for each stock held:

Company:
# of shares:
Value per share:
Basis per share
Date of value:
How titled:
Who holds certificate:

Bond Checklist

Repeat as necessary, for each bond held:

Name on bond:
Face value:
Current value:
Basis:
Date of maturity:
Estimated current value:
How titled:
Who holds the bond:

statement usually sets forth the value, or you can ask your insurance agent.

A term policy, including most group policies offered by employers, has no cash value and usually does not have value in the division of assets. A policy such as this is useful to secure, or underwrite, your agreements about child support and/or alimony. See Chapters 9 and 11.

Many so-called insurance policies are really annuities, similar to retirement plans. You may want to include these policies or portions of these policies here or in your discussion of retirement assets.

If you have agreed about dividing your insurance policies, you may enter the appropriate information on the Division of Marital Property and Debts Chart. If you are dividing some or all of your insurance policies according to some value other than monetary, you do not need to make an entry on the chart.

STOCKS, BONDS, AND OTHER SECURITIES

If your holdings are in an investment account at a brokerage, then the current fair market value is in your most recent statement. For individual stocks, bonds, and some limited partnerships, look up their values in the *Wall Street Journal* or similar periodicals.

If the value of stocks (or bonds) increases, the spouse who keeps them will face a capital gains tax on sale. For example: You bought 1,000 shares of ABC Corp. at $14 a share in 1979—a $14,000 investment. Now it is worth $60 a share—$60,000. The gain is therefore $46,000.

According to the Taxpayer Relief Act of 1997, the tax rates on profits from sales of stocks, bonds, and other assets depend on your income and how long you own an asset and are a maximum federal rate of 20 percent and a maximum Connecticut rate of 4.5 percent.

As a matter of law in a contested case, the judge will not consider capital gains taxes in valuing your assets. You must decide whether you want to consider this tax burden in your bargaining. Keep in mind one spouse's marginal tax rate may be lower than the other's. Therefore, the potential tax liability may not be the same for each of you. Consult a CPA or tax attorney for help calculating capital gains tax on investments.

Limited partnerships may be especially tricky to value. Some enable the owner to take depreciation year after year. This lowers the basis. The lower the basis, the greater the gain on sale—and the higher the tax on the sale. Some call this *phantom income*. You must investigate each limited partnership interest you own to discover its fair market value (what a willing buyer would pay for it currently) plus the potential tax burden that may accompany ownership or sale.

If you now have an agreement about dividing your stocks and bonds, enter the appropriate information on the Division of Marital Property and Debts Chart. If you are dividing some or all of your stocks and bonds according to some value other than monetary, you do not need to make an entry on the chart.

BUSINESS INTERESTS

This section deals with businesses in which you or your spouse have an ownership interest. They could be professional practices like dentistry, psychotherapy, massage, medicine, law, or accounting; majority shares in a closely held corporation or family business; or active partnerships or joint ventures. You might be an independent contractor or a sole proprietor or pay rent and other fees to a broker with the franchise name. You might be a cosmetologist or stylist in a beauty salon. You and your brother might be running an old and very successful clothing store that has been in your family for three generations and is owned by the two of you and your mother. One of you might sell Amway or Mary Kay products either as supplemental or primary income. You might have a cottage industry or a small manufacturing or repair business in your home or in a workshop, or you may be an artist, writer, or graphic designer.

Active businesses come in many forms:

- If your business is a *corporation*, your interest is a percentage of the stock. In this case, your actual asset is the stock and not the assets owned by the corporation itself, although the value of those assets underlies the value of the stock. If your shares make up a majority or controlling interest, then your actions directly control the conduct of business and this control impacts the value of your stock ownership. If you are a *minority shareholder*, your actions may not directly affect the business. In this case, lack of control may impact value.

- If your business is a *sole proprietorship*, you personally own all the assets and are personally responsible for all the debts of the business.

Business Interests Checklist

Directions: Complete the following information for each business interest either one of you has:

☐ Corporation (majority or controlling interest): _____ (spouse) owns _____ shares of common/preferred/ other stock in _____ corporation, at _____
_____
(address) constituting ____% majority or controlling interest. Shares are held by

_____
(broker or agent).

☐ Corporation (minority interest): We have listed these shares in our Stocks and Bonds Checklist.

☐ Sole Proprietorship: _____ (spouse) is the sole proprietor of _____ _____ business at
_____
_____ (address)

☐ Partnership: _____ (spouse) is a ____% partner in _____
business, at _____
_____ (address) .
Managing partner is _____
_____ at
_____
(address).

☐ Limited Partnership.
_____ (spouse) is a ____% limited partner in _____
_____
(business) which we have listed in our Stocks and Bonds Checklist.

☐ Joint Venture.
_____ (spouse) is in a joint venture: _____
_____ (name of business) at
_____
_____ (address) with _____ (other persons), whose names are:

Business Valuation Checklist

Directions: Complete the following information for each business interest either one of you has:

☐ We will hire _____
(name of appraiser) to value our business
_____
(name of business).

☐ We will try to value our business
_____
(name of business) and will therefore need to gather the following:

Who will gather	Date Done	
_____	_____	P & L statement for _____ (date/period of time) prepared by _____ (accountant, if any)
_____	_____	Balance sheets for _____ (dates) prepared by _____ (accountant)
_____	_____	K-1 tax return for _____ years.
_____	_____	Income tax Schedule C for _____ years.

As a result of the above information gathered, we believe the following is true about _____ (business):

Assets are
worth $ _____

Liabilities are
worth $ _____

Value of
business $ _____   (assets minus liabilities)

In addition, we agree this business has (does not have) a good will value of $_____, figured using the following formula:

If your business is a *partnership*, your interest is your agreed percentage of that business. For example, if there are two of you, you may have agreed to be 50–50 partners, 60–40 partners, or some other percentage. You then own that agreed percentage of the assets of the business and are responsible for that same agreed percentage of the partnership's debts and obligations.

If you are a *limited partner*, by definition you do not have any control over the operation of the business.

Valuing a Business

There are appraisers who value businesses as a specialty. (See information about divorce services and consultants in Chapter 2.) However, agree on a single appraiser who will be working for both of you. Be sure you tell him or her that this is a friendly divorce and that you will not be asking for legal testimony as an expert witness. You may want to put that in writing. The price of the appraisal or valuation may be less this way. If you want to try to find a value acceptable to both of you on your own, begin by gathering all the fiscal year-end accounting and balance sheets and tax reports, such as the corporate tax return, partnership K-1 tax forms, or Schedule C.

There are some simple concepts which may make it possible for you to come to agreement about the value of your business. All businesses can be valued, at least in part, by adding up the business assets and subtracting the business debts. Business assets include real estate, unsold inventory, accounts receivable (money others owe the business for services rendered or goods purchased) that you may want to discount if they are old or you know the person or company that owes the money is having financial troubles, business equipment (copier, fax, car), furniture (desks, chairs), and supplies (paper, stamps, etc.). It is customary to use the fair market value of assets such as furniture and equipment rather than what you paid for them or what it would cost to replace them.

Business debts (liabilities) include loan balances and bills not yet paid this month or quarter. The result when you subtract the liabilities from the assets will give you the net book value of the business.

The difficult part of valuing a business is that someone will buy some established businesses for more than the net book value. The buyer is then paying for something called "good will." Good will is what makes the business desirable because it already has loyal customers, a good reputation, a known name, or those other qualities which make the consumer come to this business rather than any other offering the same service or selling the same goods. If your business is very new or very small or very shaky, you may agree that it has no, or very little, good will and therefore you will value it at assets minus liabilities.

If you think your business has good will, refer to some of the excellent books on the subject of valuing (usually for purposes of sale) a small or family business. These books are available both at local bookstores and at libraries. These books describe a variety of formulas for valuing businesses based on personal income of the owner, how much more than the average business of this kind the particular enterprise earns, or the gross income stream of the business. There are many other formulas, and each industry lends itself to different ones. Trade magazines and journals will contain articles about buying and selling business in that particular field.

Dividing a Business

If you are dealing with a very small family business or a business which has been in one of your families for some time, you may feel like you are getting two divorces at once. If the business in question is also the primary support for the two of you, it can be deeply threatening both emotionally and financially. A helpful technique might be to think of the business as a child of your marriage to shield from your hostilities. A business, like a child, must survive the divorce of its parents and be given the opportunity to grow and flourish. Here are some suggestions for how to do this:

- Evaluate every possible way of allocating or dividing the business between you in light of which is most likely to enhance the business itself.

- Avoid any way of allocating or dividing the business that is likely to destroy it.

- Remember that you each have much more than money invested in this business.

The following are some options for you to consider for dividing your business:

1. *One of you keeps the business.*

Your Business Is Your Baby

If your business was created by both of you, it may feel as though it were your child. If you cut it in half, as Solomon threatened, it won't survive. Better to work out for one or the other of you to have it, and then compensate the other in some way. Or apply some of the ideas about joint custody so that you both continue to own it.

Don't kill the goose that lays the golden eggs.

"Divorced people can't possibly go on sharing a business."
This is not necessarily true if it is done carefully. The key is to differentiate between your relationship as spouses and your relationship as business partners.

Don't Pay More Tax Than You Need To

Ted and Betty, husband and wife, and their friend Arthur founded Friendly Corporation, Inc., "FCI." After a few years Arthur wanted out, so their corporate attorney arranged for the corporation to redeem (purchase) Arthur's stock, resulting in Ted and Betty each owning 50 percent of the outstanding stock. This corporate redemption is taxed as a capital gain to Arthur.

When Ted and Betty divorced, they agreed that Betty would keep the corporation and Ted would start up his own company with the funds he would receive for his half of FCI. To save attorney fees, they followed the same paperwork their attorney had prepared when Arthur left. Ted paid capital gains tax on the increase in value of the shares he sold back.

If they had, instead, arranged for Betty to purchase Ted's shares directly from Ted, it would have been a transaction between husband and wife, "incident to divorce," and not taxable at all. Betty would keep all the shares at their original basis.

- Buy the other out with cash, offset with other assets, or use a mix of cash and assets.

- Trade stock in the business for other stock or assets.

- Do a long-term buy-out. You may do a long-term buy-out as a straight property settlement, or structure it like alimony to provide some real tax advantages (*see* Chapter 11).

2. *Sell the business.*

- If you have a friendly buyer, you can often keep control or feel as though you have. This is an option for some people, but it is very important to be clear about your ongoing role in the business when you invite a buyer in. The friendly buyer, however, can enhance the likelihood of payment since the buyer cares about you. The friendly buyer may also ease the transition for the clients and customers of the business so that there is less danger of loss of business in the transfer.

- If the buyer is a stranger, the transaction and the transition may feel like a terrible loss to you. However, this is often the surest way to solve the issue of valuation.

- If you cannot agree on a value between yourselves despite your best efforts, you may need to sell to get on with your separate lives.

3. *Don't divide it.* Plan for both of you to be active in the business in either the short or long run, but do this cautiously! If you choose this, here are some things to remember:

- Protect the baby. Don't allow your personal animosities to overflow into your conduct of the business. If that keeps happening despite your best efforts, then this is probably not a viable option for you in the long run. Equal ownership between ex-spouses with no other partners can lead to real problems in decision making unless both are operating cooperatively and in good faith.

- Try a plan which allows you to re-evaluate at the end of six months or a year. This may be enough time for you both to go through the changes in yourselves which happen during separation. You can then look at your changed relationship with each other and evaluate whether it will support your being business partners for the long term.

- Separate your roles within the business as much as possible. Have separate offices or different hours. Share the necessary business travel so one of you is always there but there are times when each of you is alone with the business. Be responsible for different departments or different functions. Try to be independent in your authority and responsibility within the business.

- One of you takes an active role (managing partner, runs the store), and the other keeps only a passive role (limited partner). The difficulty with this model is the possibility that the passive partner may feel frustration or be critical of the active partner. Another consideration is compensation for the active partner in profits and/or salary or profit-based incentive or bonus as contrasted with payment to the less active partner.

RETIREMENT, PENSIONS, AND PROFIT SHARING

Retirement plans are of two general types: those defined by the benefit paid at retirement and those defined by the contributions made. Many plans combine both these elements.

A plan defined in terms of its benefits is usually called a *pension*. It tells you what it will pay you at retirement and is usually based on a percentage of your highest earnings at the time of retirement. Typically the employer contributes directly to this benefit, and nothing, as a rule, is withheld from your paycheck for this purpose. Some benefits vest over a period of years. Vesting means you own that portion and it cannot be taken away. If a plan vests gradually, you might own 20 percent of your plan after one year of employment, 40 percent after two years, etc. You may lose unvested benefits if you leave that workplace before vesting occurs.

Examples of defined benefit retirement plans are private pensions, Civil Service Retirement System, Federal Employee Retirement System, military retirement, most railroad retirements, and many state and town pension plans such as those held by teachers and police.

Retirements Checklist

Complete the following information for each retirement or pension plan either one of you has:

Name of Plan:

Kind of plan, if known:

Name of participant:

Vested?

Current vested value:

Date of vesting:

Future benefit?

At what age?

Monthly amount, lump sum or formula?

Reductions for early retirement?

Subject to divestment?

Divisible by QDRO?

Loans available?

Early payout option?

Survivor benefit?

Name of Plan:

Kind of plan, if known:

Name of participant:

Vested?

Current vested value:

Date of vesting:

Future benefit?

At what age?

Monthly amount, lump sum or formula?

Reductions for early retirement?

Subject to divestment?

Divisible by QDRO?

Loans available?

Early payout option?

Survivor benefit?

For additional retirements, repeat on a separate sheet of paper.

A plan defined in terms of its contribution sets the amount which you contribute from your gross pay and is often a combination of a required percentage of your pay plus an optional amount. Then the employer may "match" the amount you put in. Frequently the employer's contribution may vest over time. If you leave employment before vesting, sometimes you lose a portion or all of the employer's contribution but you do not lose your own contribution. The vested and unvested amount in your account is shown at least once a year in a statement from your employer or the trustee or institution which manages your account or plan.

Examples of defined contribution plans are 401K, profit sharing, ESOP, tax sheltered annuities, money purchase plans, Keogh, 401(3)(b), and TIAA-CREF.

The first step in negotiating about retirement plans is to find out exactly what you have. Most of us don't really know. Today's plans are often complex hybrids of the simple plans that existed only a few years ago. There are tax pitfalls to be wary of, some of very recent origin.

How Do We Value Our Retirement Plans?

There are two ways of looking at the value of retirement plans. For defined contribution plans the value is the actual amount of your contributions plus those of the employer that are vested to you (if any), as well as accrued interest to date. This is the most readily obtainable value because it is the balance on the periodic statement from the plan administrator, trustee, or agency holding your account.

For defined benefit plans, or pensions, you can look at the present value of a future flow of payments. For example, assume you will receive $680 per month starting at age sixty-five. You can translate this amount into a current cash value: the amount of money you would need now, invested at 7 percent (or some other interest rate), which would pay you your monthly pension amount, starting at age 65 through your life expectancy.

The plan administrator may or may not tell you the present value of your account. If he or she does, be sure you know the interest rate and other assumptions used to calculate it. (A low interest rate means a higher present value, and vice versa.) The plan administrator may make other assumptions that can substantially affect the value. If your plan administrator does not provide the present value, or if you want an independent and more accurate calculation of value, you may need to hire a CPA, actuary, or attorney who specializes in this kind of valuation. The values provided by any of these professionals may vary based on the evaluator's assumptions concerning interest and/or discount rates.

Dividing Pensions in Divorce

This section covers the mechanics of dividing your retirement accounts and pensions if you choose to do so. Dividing your pensions by present value is not the only way to handle them in your negotiations. You may choose, alternatively, not to divide them at all, but simply to allocate them—"You keep yours, and I'll keep mine." Some plans are divisible directly without a specific court order, some require a Qualified Domestic Relations Order (QDRO), and some are not divisible at all.

The most immediately divisible plans are Individual Retirement Accounts (IRAs), a form of defined contribution plan that is really a tax-deferred savings plans. You may directly transfer by rollover all or some of the balance to a similar account in the name of your spouse. Obtain the forms for the rollover from your banking institution.

Federal pensions require special court orders to divide them at divorce. These include military pensions, CSRS (Civil Service Retirement System) and FERS (Federal Employee Retirement System), and railroad retirement. For division of these types of pensions, write to the accounting office for the military service in question, FERS, CSRS, or your employer. Request information about the procedure and forms, if any, for division of your retirement at divorce. For these and all other pension divisions that require a special court order, you should consult with an attorney to be sure the order properly divides the pension as you intend.

The Retirement Equity Act, a federal statute, gives domestic relations courts the power to order the division of certain private pension and retirement plans. The divorce court signs a Qualified Domestic Relations Order (QDRO, pronounced "Q-dro" or "Quadro") that requires the plan administrator to divide the retirement account according to the proportion stated in the order, often by opening up a second account in the name of the non-employee spouse. The plan administrator manages the non-employee spouse's account just like that of the employee spouse, except that there are no further contributions to the account of the non-employee spouse other than interest earned.

Plans divisible by QDROs include defined benefit plan pensions and defined contribution plans such as 401Ks (thrift savings plans), some profit sharing and money purchase plans, Keogh

Death Benefit

There are two kinds of death benefits attached to retirement or pension plans. The first is the remainder of the retirement (if any) after the death of the participant, usually payable to the surviving spouse. The second is a separate amount, that, like a life insurance policy, is payable in a lump sum upon the participant's death to the designated beneficiary. Be certain your agreement is clear about what happens to any death benefit. Does it stay with the current spouse, or will it be available to a future spouse, if any?

Tax Status of the Money in the Plan

For the most part, your account carries contributions—whether yours or your employer's—in a tax-deferred status. This means that you have not paid income tax on this money but that you will pay tax on it when you receive it—typically at retirement. Since your tax bracket will usually be lower at retirement than now, you usually can save by deferring or putting off tax on this money until later. By contrast, some of your or your employer's contributions may have already been taxed, or be tax-free, and you should not be taxed again when those dollars are paid out to you. If you are considering an early payout, when you examine the present value of the plan be sure you understand which dollars are in which tax status because it will substantially change the value of each dollar you receive.

In some defined contribution plans, it is usually possible for an employee spouse to rollover retirement assets of a non-employee spouse into his or her own qualifying account without paying taxes or the 10 percent penalty if the distribution is made to the non-participant spouse under a divorce court order, and within 60 days of distribution by the plan administrator. Be sure to consult with a CPA or attorney who specializes in divorce tax matters to see if this can work in your situation.

A spouse can sometimes avoid the 10 percent penalty for withdrawl of defined contribution plan funds at the time of the divorce property division by QDRO. To explore this option, consult with a CPA or attorney who specializes in divorce issues.

Divestment

Whatever the nature of your retirement (defined contribution, defined benefit, or a hybrid) all or some of it may be subject to full or partial divestment (you may lose it) under certain circumstances if you have not worked the required number of years. If your retirement is subject to divestment, you may want to consider dividing it with an agreement that goes into effect only if it pays.

If your plan administrator provides a QDRO form for you, be sure to read it carefully and obtain an opinion from an attorney or CPA. You must check that it does what you want it to do (transfers exactly what you want transferred to the person you want it transferred to) and that it does not add something that you do not want to do.

plans, tax-sheltered annuities, and ESOPs (Employee Stock Ownership Plans).

A QDRO instructs the plan administrator to set aside now, in the name of the non-employee spouse, either a specific amount or a certain percentage of the present amount in the employee's name. Or the QDRO may instruct the plan administrator to pay the non-employee spouse a percentage of what is in the employee's account when the employee retires. You may give the plan administrator a formula for how you want this done. For example, create a fraction: the numerator is the number of years of the marriage while the denominator is the total number of years the employee spouse will have worked there at the time of retirement. Divide this amount in half (or multiply it by 50 percent), or determine whatever portion you think is fair for the non-employee spouse to receive.

The formula you negotiate after filling in all the numbers (except the number of years employed if the employee-spouse is still working there) is a part of your QDRO. Some plans may require exact numbers instead of formulas.

Some plans may have their own QDRO forms that you can request and use. Ask the plan administrator to review your draft QDRO before you send it to the court with the rest of your final papers (*see* Chapter 13). There is no legal requirement for the plan administrator to review your proposed QDRO and tell you if it is acceptable. However, some administrators will tell you what needs changing for approval. You must allow enough time for them to respond and for you to make amendments and resend it. You may run into difficulties if you just have the court sign the QRDO and you then submit it to the plan administrator to review and approve. If the plan administrator requires changes, you must resubmit the revised QDRO to the court.

QDROs and other court orders dividing retirement plans are complicated and important documents. Mistakes can have serious economic repercussions years down the road. You should have a CPA or attorney well versed in divorce issues draft the pension division order for you. While there is an immediate cost to this, the money is well worth it for the future protection it provides.

Early Payout Options

In addition to transferring all or part of the retirement to the other spouse, the employee spouse may have some options to access funds in defined contribution plans. Depending on the terms of the plan, the payout option may be lump sum, hardship, or loan.

1. *Lump sum.* Some plans offer a lump-sum payout at retirement or on the occurrence of certain events, such as leaving the job. The lump-sum options on defined contribution plans are usually available at retirement, leaving employment, or death. It is important in your bargaining and planning to know the options in your plan. Even if your periodic account statement gives your balance as a projected monthly payout or account balance, don't assume that these are the only options for you.

2. *Hardship.* Some plans offer a lump-sum payout of all or a portion of the balance on the occurrence of certain events. Most common are purchase of a primary residence, second mortgage for capital improvements, college or higher education expenses, a medical emergency, and sometimes divorce. The payouts, if available, are taxable as additional income in the year you receive them. Some hardship option clauses allow you to get money out, but you have to pay a penalty and/or tax. Be sure you know which kind of hardship clause you have, if any.

3. *Loan.* Some plans permit you to borrow against the balance, which is similar to borrowing against a whole-life insurance policy. Often you must prove need. The terms are strict; they usually require repayment within five years. This can be a valuable planning tool for you to meet short-term emergency needs at the time of your separation or divorce.

Social Security

To be eligible for Social Security benefits, a worker must accumulate forty working quarters in which the worker paid FICA or self-employment taxes. Once you become eligible, the amount of your benefit payable at retirement depends on your earnings during your working lifetime. To find out whether you or your spouse is eligible, contact your local Social Security office for the necessary request forms.

These payments represent a future income stream that may not be the same for each spouse. The law does not treat Social Security benefits as assets. They are often considered when discussing whether alimony or child support payments should still be payable after retirement of either the recipient or the payor.

CAUTION When your QDRO is complete, be sure to send it to the plan administrator before you ask the court to sign it. Ask the plan administrator if he or she will approve it as written. The plan administrator is not required by law to tell you specifically if there are any problems with it before the court signs it. But many will, and that allows you to correct any problems before giving it to the court for signature.

New IRS regulations require the withholding of 20 percent if you take money from an IRA or other tax-deferred plan even for the purpose of transferring it into another IRA for yourself or your spouse. The trustee must take out the 20 percent and send it to IRS. You must then replace the 20 percent out of your own pocket to transfer to the new IRA, or pay tax on that 20 percent as though you had received it as income that year. You therefore not only lose this money from the IRA but you also pay tax on it. If you do replace the 20 percent out of pocket, the IRS will then return the 20 percent, without interest, if you request it as a tax refund on your next income tax return. If you put it back into the IRA, you won't pay tax on it. The only way to avoid this 20 percent is to never let your hands touch the funds being transferred from the IRA. Have the trustee transfer it directly to the trustee of the new IRA for yourself or your spouse as part of your divorce agreement.

Do We Have to Put a Value on Our Pensions?

A QDRO that gives a formula for a percentage division of future defined benefit pension payments is a way to avoid a defined benefit determining the pension's present value.

Applying for Social Security

When applying for Social Security benefits, you should have the following records:

• Your Social Security card

• Your birth certificate

• Your marriage certificate

• Your divorce judgment or decree showing the date that your marital status terminated

You may contact the Social Security Administration either in writing or by phone to obtain information regarding your Social Security account and future benefits, or apply for Social Security benefits online at www.ssa.gov.

Department of Health and Human Services
Social Security Administration
Baltimore, MD 21235
(800)772-1213

All phone calls are confidential.

Social Security laws are constantly changing and may affect your future benefits. To be sure of your exact benefits and earliest eligibility to receive them, contact the Social Security Administration directly.

 For helpful information, including a benefits calculator visit **www.ssa.gov**.

Future Income Stream as Property

If you treat a future income stream as property, the employee pays the tax on it when he/she gets it at retirement, and the payment from the retiring spouse to the former spouse is tax-free (in after tax dollars). These payments would not necessarily cease at either remarriage or death of the recipient.

If you were married for at least ten years, as an ex-spouse you may collect Social Security disability and/or retirement benefits from your ex-spouse's account. You cannot "negotiate away" this entitlement in your agreement.

Plans in Lieu of Social Security

Some retirement plans take the place of Social Security. Common examples are Connecticut State Retirement, Connecticut Teachers Retirement, and some specific plans for other public employees. The difficulty in valuation of these plans is that there is usually no way to accurately determine the equivalent Social Security portion. If, in your bargaining, you choose to treat pension and other retirement benefits—but not Social Security—as property, you may consider setting aside from the property division some part of any plan as though it were Social Security. However, keep in mind that if you have been married at least ten years at the time of your divorce, the non-Social Security-covered spouse can elect benefits under his or her ex-spouse's Social Security account in addition to retirement amounts from his or her own employment.

Plans Not Divisible at All

Plans not divisible at all include those of small employers not covered by E.R.I.S.A. (Employee Retirement Income Security Act of 1974) and some public employee group funds. For these plans, the best you can do in your negotiations is to balance them with other property or income. If you can calculate a current value for the plan or a portion of it, then you can set this aside for the employee spouse and offset it with other property for the other spouse.

You could agree that when the benefit starts, the retiree spouse will pay to the former spouse a percentage of the amount the retiree receives. You might consider using the QDRO formula to determine what this percentage should be. However, since there would be no QDRO, you have to rely on your ex-spouse to make the payments.

If you are trying to divide an interest in these types of pensions, you should consult an attorney when drafting your separation agreement.

If you have an agreement for how you are going to divide your retirements, enter the appropriate information on the Division of Marital Property and Debts Chart. If division of some or all of your retirement accounts is according to some value other than monetary, you do not need to make an entry on the chart.

OTHER ASSETS

Other assets include intellectual property such as a patent or a copyright, sports and symphony tickets and ticket priorities, frequent flyer miles, hunting rights, club memberships, and debts that people owe you. You can divide all of these between you in your separation agreement even if you choose not to place a monetary value on them. You can also value these kinds of assets and pay the other spouse his or her share with cash or other property to affect an equitable division.

The rights to a spouse's creation of a song, book, software program, or picture have value. How can these rights be divided in a divorce? You can transfer ownership of patents and copyrights, and you can assign a certain portion of income from them—even a certain percentage of future income.

If you have rights to season tickets to sporting activities, the symphony, or hunting areas, you can alternate their use ("I'll take them this year, you take them next year."), divide the season or time they cover, or trade them between you ("I'll take the football tickets, you take the theater tickets.").

If you belong to a private membership club such as a country club, you may find these permit only one member of a divorced couple to continue the membership. You will have to reach agreement on this one. Trade for some other right or assets, or flip a coin if you have to.

Frequent flyer miles have value but often cannot be transferred. A clever way to divide them is to use them for the benefit of both of you—by using them for your children's travel, for instance—or to limit their use to the family business.

Suppose you loaned your best friend $1,000 when his car broke down. This is an informal but real loan, and his obligation to pay it back to you is an asset, as is a more formal loan with a signed promise to pay. You can assign your friend's obligation to pay to either one of you, divide the payments between you when received, or use them to pay one of your marital bills.

Future Income Stream as Alimony

On the other hand, if you treat future income stream as income rather than property, the employee spouse may be able to deduct the payments to the ex-spouse. They then become alimony payments, deductible by the employee spouse and taxable to the former spouse. Such alimony payments normally terminate on the former spouse's remarriage unless you state specifically that they are to continue beyond that event. In any event, such payments normally terminate at the receiving spouse's death.

Other Assets Checklist

Directions: Complete the following information for each additional asset either one of you has.

We have the following additional assets to divide in our agreement:

☐ Intellectual property:
  ☐ Patent #_____ for _____ in the name of _____ (spouse).
  ☐ Copyrighted (book, song, poem, art work, name, software, other) _____ _____ (describe) in the name of _____ (spouse).

☐ Priority rights:
  ☐ Season tickets: _____ _____ (describe).
  ☐ Fishing/hunting rights: _____ _____ (describe).
  ☐ Frequent flyer miles: _____
  (# of miles) in name of _____

  (# of miles) in name of _____

☐ Membership in _____ _____ (club, organization).
☐ Accounts receivable
  $_____ owed to _____ (spouse) by _____
  (name of debtor) under the following terms:
☐ Other: Describe:

Kinds of Debts

You can organize debts into four major categories:

1. Debts that go with the property—"secured" debts that are tied to an asset, like your mortgage to your house or your car loan to the car

2. Freestanding or "unsecured" debts—debts not tied to any asset, like most credit cards

3. Tax debt

4. Divorce expenses

SECURED DEBTS

The best examples of secured debts are the mortgage(s) on your home or other real estate and loans on cars and trucks. To secure a loan, you sign a document that says that if you default on your loan payments the lender can take possession of the property and sell it. If this happens, it's called *foreclosure* in the case of a house, it is called *repossession* if it's your car.

Usually in divorce the person who gets the asset also gets the responsibility for the loan. Be sure in your negotiations you bear in mind that the value you place on any asset should take into account any outstanding loan balance on it. Keep in mind also any negative cash flow that goes with these assets. One way of managing both debt repayment and negative cash flow is through alimony (see Chapter 11).

UNSECURED DEBTS

Unsecured debts are those obligations not tied to an asset; they are "freestanding." Examples are most credit cards, personal bank loans, some lines of credit, and most loans from parents and friends.

TAX DEBTS

Taxes rate their own category because Uncle Sam and the Connecticut Department of Revenue are the most difficult creditors of all. One of your largest joint obligations may be your joint tax returns. The IRS can do random audits for three years after the filing and can question your return for good cause for seven years or anytime for fraud. Therefore, your separation agreement should have some provision for what you will do about any additional taxes, penalties, or interest, as well as the cost of a possible audit.

Your separation agreement should also clearly state your plan for filing your taxes for the last full year of your marriage. Your separation agreement should state how you will deal with any audits or questions raised about tax returns which you filed together. See Chapter 12, Taxes.

DIVORCE EXPENSES

While focusing on the marital debts, you must not forget to negotiate the expenses of the divorce as well. Be certain that your separation agreement sets forth who will pay the direct and indirect costs of becoming divorced. The most obvious ones are usually the court filing fee and the costs of appraisals, mediation, and attorneys. Some not-so-obvious divorce expenses are joint or individual accounting, financial planning, and counseling. Treat these like any unsecured marital debt, no matter whose lawyer's bill it is or who asked for an appraisal.

Some of the divorce expenses may have been paid by one or both of you before you began bargaining together. You may want to remember these in your agreement by giving credit to the person who paid them (setting aside assets in that amount to the payor). Some of these expenses might be the court filing fee or professional fees for a mediator, attorney, accountant, or appraiser.

There may be divorce expenses after the divorce. Examples of these are attorney fees for doing QDROs and title transfers, tax preparation for the final joint return, mediation fees, and long-term divorce counseling for you or your children. You will need to be clear about these in your budgets and in your bargaining. You may want to write these arrangements into your separation agreement.

Dealing with Debt

Talk about debts early on since most must be paid regularly or you risk a credit problem. It's very easy in a separation to have your debts fall through the cracks by assuming that your spouse is paying them all.

GATHER THE DATA

To avoid lots of heartbreak, expense, and recriminations later, begin by gathering all the information either of you has about

Debts Checklist

Directions: Provide the following information for each secured, unsecured, or tax debt either or both of you owes:

Creditor	Amount	Payment Terms

Uneasiness About Tax Returns

You are both legally responsible for any tax return you sign. Physical separation, when emotions are running high and expenses running even higher, is a time when people are tempted to be unwise on their tax returns (by exaggerating deductible expenses, claiming doubtful deductions, or "forgetting" to list income). If either of you is likely to be less forthcoming than the other, consider filing married/separately so you are not legally bound by a tax return you are uncomfortable with. You may pay more tax this way, but the peace of mind may be worth it.

Divorce Expenses Checklist

Directions: Provide the following information for each divorce expense owed by either or both of you or expected to be incurred by either or both of you:

Divorce Expense	Amount	Payment Terms

"I'm not responsible for paying that VISA bill, my ex-husband/wife promised to pay it in our divorce agreement, and the judge approved it."

Any agreement you two make about who is going to pay this debt does not affect the creditor because the person or company you owe a debt to is not a "party" to your divorce negotiation or agreement. If one of you defaults, the lender will attempt to collect from the other and the default is on the credit report in each of your names.

Hold Each Other Harmless

Here is a typical hold harmless clause: Wife will be solely responsible for paying the loan at ABC Credit Union, indemnifying and holding Husband harmless therefrom.

"But screw your courage to the sticking place, and we'll not fail." *Macbeth I, vii, 59*

your current and recently-paid debts, as delineated in Chapter 5. You must know whether bills such as the car insurance are up to date. If you are having any trouble agreeing about whether a certain purchase or expense was for the family, gather all the statements and/or charge slips that relate to the expense. Collect all this data before you begin talking about that particular expense or debt.

Once you have all the data about the debts, agree which part of each debt you will share or consider in the property division. For example, you may want to say that the expenses or charges incurred since your separation are your own to assume fully without contribution from your spouse.

DEBT STRATEGIES

Try to pay off as many debts as possible before or at the time of the final judgment. Consider using liquid assets (bank accounts, stocks, bonds) or other saleable assets (the extra car, the time-share condo, non-essential furniture) to do this.

If it is not possible to pay off your debts right away, then you must be clear about who will pay which debt and within what period of time. Debts are a good place to consider putting "teeth" in your agreement. For example, if you fail to make a payment on a debt that is secured by an asset, you lose that asset to the other spouse. Or, if one of you fails to pay the loan on the washer and dryer, then the other spouse may have the washer and dryer and pay off the remaining debt.

To back up your agreement about who will pay your unsecured debts, include a hold harmless clause in your agreement. This will *indemnify* the non-paying spouse; that is, the paying spouse gives the non-paying spouse the right to collect from him or her all missed payments and possibly interest and attorneys' fees resulting from the failure to make the payment.

After dividing the responsibility for paying the debts, examine the effect on your respective budgets. Some tax planning through alimony may be very helpful here to generate some cash with which to pay bills (*see* Chapters 11 and 12).

Failure to allocate all your debts between you and to give teeth to this part of your agreement may come back to haunt you years later.

BANKRUPTCY AT THE TIME OF YOUR DIVORCE

In the frustration over money issues, the threat of one spouse declaring bankruptcy may come up. Try approaching the discussion of possible bankruptcy as the kind of thing that might happen in spite of both of your best efforts, like being laid off at work or becoming seriously ill.

There are two basic kinds of bankruptcy for individuals. Chapter 7 bankruptcy provides complete discharge of all (unsecured) debts and the forfeiture of all assets over certain minimum protected amounts. Chapter 13 bankruptcy is the "Individual's Debt Adjustment" plan that may preserve the assets. Chapter 13 bankruptcy allows the debtor to pay off all the secured and priority debts (usually mortgages, car loans, child support and alimony arrearages, and taxes) and some unsecured debts and discharge the rest of the unsecured debts. The impact of bankruptcy on a divorce is extremely complex. The advice of an attorney is absolutely necessary before you file a bankruptcy or if your spouse or former spouse files before, during, or after the divorce.

You should take several issues about bankruptcy into account in any settlement in divorce:

- If either spouse files for bankruptcy before, during, or after the divorce, the creditors will absolutely look to the other spouse to pay any of the originally joint debts, despite what the separation agreement says. If the possibility of bankruptcy is immediate, it may be better to do a joint bankruptcy filing before divorce rather than risk undoing your settlement.

- On the filing of a bankruptcy petition, all other legal actions are automatically stayed, or halted. First, this means creditors can't sue the person who filed for bankruptcy (remember, they can still sue the non-filing spouse). Second, it means that if there is no final judgment of divorce in a pending case, you may need to obtain written permission from the bankruptcy judge for the divorce court to proceed, especially if called upon to rule or act on any matters that are within the scope of the bankruptcy. Clearly, this can create chaos in your divorce negotiations.

- When you file a petition for bankruptcy, the law imposes an automatic stay on all the creditors listed in the petition, as discussed above. This means that they may not attempt in any way to collect the debt from the petitioner as long as the stay is in effect, usually around three months. The automatic stay in bankruptcy can be a good planning tool. You can use it to stop aggressive creditors and give yourselves time to reach agreement.

Filing the bankruptcy and the divorce at the same time can be very beneficial, especially if there is a possibility of using Chapter 13 to pay off your marital debts. It may take three lawyers to make this plan work smoothly—one for each of you in the divorce and one for both of you in the joint bankruptcy filing. Don't discard this option just because it is initially expensive or distasteful.

Declaring bankruptcy after your divorce may discharge (erase) unsecured property settlement payments but does not discharge alimony or child support payments either current or arrearages. You can anticipate a possible bankruptcy by saying in your separation agreement that if either spouse declares bankruptcy within a certain period of time, you will agree to renegotiate part or all of the separation agreement, particularly alimony.

Finalizing Your Division

Use the Final Division Calculation to test whether the division of property and debts on the Division of Property and Debts Chart on page 253 is what you want to agree to as a final settlement.

Suppose your definition of a fair division of property is 50–50. Add up the proposed property and debts for each of you in your separate columns, and compare these totals. If one of these totals is larger than the other, you will need to transfer one-half the difference to the spouse with the lower total. This can be done in a variety of ways. You can transfer a piece of property to affect this balancing or actually pay the amount in cash. If you do not have sufficient cash, this equalizing amount could be a promissory note—amortized over time or with a balloon payment when an asset such as the home sells.

Whether you decide that your fair division is 60–40, 70–30, or some other proportion, the method is the same, only the arithmetic changes. For example, if you have agreed to a 60–40 division, multiply the Net Estate from the Property and Debts Chart to determine how much property equals 60 percent. Then adjust the total for the spouse who is to receive 60 percent until you reach that number. You can make this adjustment (or whatever percentage you choose) by transferring property, cash, or future payments, as discussed above.

Final Division Calculation

Directions: Enter the appropriate numbers from the Marital Property and Debts Chart:

	Wife	Husband
Total Property	_____	_____
Less Total Debt	_____	_____
Total Net:	_____	_____
Difference (Subtract the lower from the higher)	_____	_____
1/2 the Difference (or whatever % you choose)		_____

Conclusion

Your first rough look at the division of property and debts is done. It will probably not be your final version. Go on to the next chapters. The agreements you reach as a result of each of those chapters may necessitate changes in the property division you have worked out so far.

Take heart. Settling your divorce case is hard work. Don't expect to get it all done in one sitting. Don't even expect to complete the work of dividing your property and debts in one sitting. Give yourself and each other the time you deserve to make the best decisions for both of you.

CHAPTER **11**

ALIMONY

Hot Words

There are certain incendiary words that can turn a healthy discussion of alimony into an inferno. Some of them are:

"I'm entitled…"

"You've got no right…"

"You owe me…"

"I owe you nothing…"

"It's my right…"

"You don't deserve…"

This guidebook avoids these hot words by taking a problem-solving, tax-saving approach to the question of alimony.

 Alimony: Money paid by one separated spouse to or on behalf of the other; also referred to as spousal support.

Connecticut statute (C.G.S. § 46b-82) requires the court to consider the following factors in making an alimony award:

1. Length of the marriage

2. Cause of the dissolution of the marriage

3. For each of the parties
   a. Age
   b. Health
   c. Station
   d. Occupation
   e. Amount and sources of income
   f. Vocational skills
   g. Employability
   h. Estate
   i. Needs

4. For the parent who has custody of minor children, the desirability of that parent securing employment

ALIMONY

Alimony is a series of payments (or a lump sum payment or payments) made by one spouse to the other or to some third party (such as a credit union for a car loan) on behalf of the receiving spouse. The IRS also refers to alimony as Section 71 payments, referring to the section covering alimony in the Internal Revenue Code.

Many who would or could pay alimony shy away from the idea because they don't want to be "on the hook," are angry at the thought of supporting ex-spouses, or don't want to feel tied to their ex-spouses. Other spouses who might receive alimony avoid the idea because they must pay taxes on it as income or because they don't want to be dependent on their ex-spouses through these kinds of payments, even for a short time. Some people worry about whether their ex-spouses will pay alimony. For many, if not most, alimony is an emotional subject.

Allowing your feelings to take over on this issue may prevent you from saving a great deal of money. Alimony may save money by providing an opportunity for smart tax planning at a time when you both need it. We recommend that you read the rest of this chapter so that you understand the potential value this tool has for you before deciding whether you wish to use it.

This chapter includes some general tax examples, but read Chapter 12 for more detailed information about taxes. Remember that for tax advice and opinions specific to your situation, you must consult an accountant or attorney familiar with divorce taxation.

None of the following statements is true:

"Alimony is always paid to the wife for life."

"Don't ever pay alimony—you're just opening up the door to more."

"Don't ever accept alimony—you have to pay taxes on it."

"Alimony has to be paid monthly."

"Once you open the door to alimony, you can't ever close it again."

"The trouble with alimony is it locks you into a certain payment for life."

None of the following statements is necessarily true:

"You can't use alimony to pay child support or property division."

"I don't have to pay alimony because she's just going to get remarried."

"He/she shouldn't get alimony—he/she doesn't need it."

"Nobody in this family needs alimony."

"I shouldn't have to pay for her/him to go to school when she/he can work and earn her/his own living."

"If I agree to alimony, I have to keep paying even if I lose my job."

SMART ALIMONY

Making alimony work for your unique circumstances is a smart way to save money for your family. This chapter first summarizes, then discusses in detail, some ways to do this. Alongside each discussion is a place for you to initial whether that particular use of alimony might work for you.

Open-ended alimony is of unlimited or undetermined duration. It may be used for a variety of purposes including:

- To balance income between spouses in two households

- To provide long-term, full, or supplemental income for a spouse based on need

- To meet ongoing expenses of the other spouse

Fixed-term alimony is for a designated period of time or until payment in full of a specific amount of money. It is generally for an identified purpose and is often called contractual or in gross. You may use it for a variety of purposes including:

- To pay specific marital debts

Tax Significance of Alimony
The tax significance of an alimony payment is that it is deductible from income by the person who pays it and taxable as income to the person who receives it.

"If we don't say anything about alimony in our agreement, then there won't ever be any."

This is not true. Unless both of you waive (give up your rights to) alimony in your agreement, the court can re-open the question in the future if either of you asks. If you do not want the court ever to have the power to consider alimony, then you both need to expressly waive it.

Maintenance: In some states this is the term used for alimony. Another term is "spousal support."

Open-ended Alimony: Alimony without either an explicit termination or total amount.

Fixed-term Alimony: The terms state the total amount of alimony. Also called contractual alimony and alimony in gross.

- To pay specific expenses for a spouse

- To pay for training, education, or therapy of a spouse

- To supplement while a spouse's income phases in or up

- To balance property division

OPEN-ENDED ALIMONY

Open-ended alimony is an alimony plan in which the total amount is unknown. Payments of this type of alimony are usually periodic and presumed to be modifiable if circumstances change substantially.

1. Alimony to Provide Long-term, Full, or Supplemental Income for a Spouse Based on Need

Long-term spousal support was the original concept of alimony. The divorcing wife in a long marriage, who dedicated her life to making a home and thus never worked outside the home, needed ongoing support for life or until remarriage. Now, depending upon the length of the marriage, marital standard of living, and other factors, spouses of either sex may request an award of alimony.

Central to planning for long-term alimony is the concept of need. Typically, plans of this type begin with the projected living expenses of the spouse who will receive the alimony. If your circumstances are like any of the following examples, long-term spousal support may be an appropriate solution for you.

- One of you has not worked outside the home, or not substantially so, and for reasons of age or mental and/or physical health, cannot look forward to adequate employment.

- One of you is taking care of a child or other dependent whose needs require that you be constantly available, making employment outside the home inappropriate. Perhaps you have an infant you both agree should not yet be in day care, a disabled or ill child, or an ailing parent. Your individual feelings about this situation may be very different, especially if the dependent is not a child of this marriage.

- One of you is in a line of work that pays significantly less than the other spouse's line of work, sometimes not enough to live

---

Alimony Checklist 1

We agree that _____ needs long-term, full, or supplemental alimony income because:

_____   _____
Initials   Initials

on. One of you may be an artist, musician, farmer, day care provider, piece worker, or a worker in other in-home or "cottage" industries. Even if you both endorsed this career choice while you were together, your feelings about it at this time may be very different. One of you may feel you will pay forever for the other's career choices. The other may feel vulnerable or angry with the difficulties that surround your career choice. It may feel like everyone is saying that one of you is less valuable or less worthy than the other. Be certain your negotiations around the question of alimony allow plenty of time to air these feelings.

If lifetime spousal support is payable until the death of the recipient, you can agree to adjust it upon the retirement of the paying spouse or when Social Security or other retirement benefits begin for either spouse so that both parties share in the usual reduction of income experienced at retirement.

If either of you is now struggling with feelings of righteousness, distrust, anger, helplessness, being trapped, dependence, guilt, or panic, you are not unusual. Most people feel some of these emotions at different times during this type of long-term arrangement. It may be that this is the time for both of you to seek professional help from a lawyer, therapist, financial counsel, mediator, medical evaluator, or employment evaluator rather than being weighed down by this emotional baggage long after the divorce is over. See Chapter 4 for some help with this, and see "Divorce and the Legal System," Chapter 2, for resources.

2.   Alimony to Balance Income Between Spouses in Two Households

If your goal after divorce is to equalize income between the two of you (or share it on some other percentage basis), then you may accomplish this with alimony paid by the higher-income spouse to the lower-income spouse. Sometimes separation will cause a drastic change in lifestyle for one spouse without the shifting of some income. When both spouses work full-time or have careers but there is a significant difference in incomes, income balancing can create a foundation for an equal or proportionate sharing of household expenses and debt payments after divorce.

Fred and Linda

Fred and Linda are the parents of two children, ages seven and twelve. Fred brings in 70 percent of the family income while Linda brings in 30 percent—percentages that are likely to continue into the foreseeable future. They have unsecured debts (debts

Alimony Checklist 2

We should consider alimony to balance our incomes:

_____   _____
Initials   Initials

If you are considering paying substantial alimony right from the beginning ($1250 per month or $15,000 per year or more) and if you are planning to have it decrease significantly within the first three years, read Chapter 12, Taxes.

"If we agree to monthly alimony, nobody can change it in the future, even the court."

Not true. If alimony is open ended, then it is presumed to be modifiable by the court on a "showing of a substantial change of circumstances," unless you specifically agree to make it nonmodifiable.

Alimony Checklist 3:

We should consider using alimony to pay the following expenses:

Expense:_____
Amount:_____

Expense:_____
Amount:_____

Expense:_____
Amount:_____

Expense:_____
Amount:_____

Expense:_____
Amount:_____

Expense:_____
Amount:_____

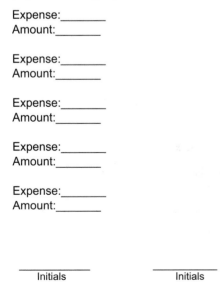

_____   _____
    Initials   Initials

not related to any piece of property) that will take three years to pay off if they make the minimum payments.

If Fred pays alimony to Linda of 20 percent of his gross income, Linda and Fred will then each have 50 percent of the family gross income. They would continue the income leveling for three years, and each then would contribute equally to the debt payments during that time.

If they have equal time with the children, they could agree to no child support and each pay 50 percent of the children's expenses. They can each file as head of household by agreeing to one more overnight per year of one child each. See Chapters 9 and 12 for how this works. They can share the dependency exemptions, thus equalizing the tax effects (see Chapter 12).

If either Linda or Fred has primary physical custody of both children, the other parent could then pay him or her 50 percent of the child support from the appropriate worksheet and half the unanticipated expenses. The custodial parent would file as head of household. The noncustodial parent could claim the dependency exemptions for the children. Linda and Fred could decrease the alimony to transfer less than 50 percent of the family income to the custodial parent to offset these unequal tax consequences. See Chapter 12, Taxes, for more about how to control the tax consequences of your divorce.

3.   Alimony to Meet Ongoing Expenses With Tax-deductible Dollars

You can use alimony to pay ongoing expenses such as a spouse's (or ex-spouse's) life insurance, medical insurance, or medical expenses or to pay all or a part of a mortgage. Some of these costs may be deductible as alimony by the person who pays them, provided the separation agreement specifies that these third-party payments will be made and the payments qualify under IRS regulations, including that they will terminate on the recipient's death. Such deductibility can make this alternative particularly attractive.

Or, you may consider paying alimony and having the recipient counterbalance the taxable income with a deduction for the expense. For example, medical insurance and medical expenses become deductible if they exceed 7.5 percent of your adjusted gross income. The interest portion of a home mortgage payment is deductible if the person paying it uses this property as a personal residence.

The following is an example of paying these expenses through alimony:

Charlie and Diane

Charlie and Diane pay $800 per month in mortgage payments on the family home where Diane will continue to live. $650 of the $800 is deductible interest and taxes. After the divorce, Diane's life insurance premium will be $25 per month and her health insurance premium will be $175 per month. The money Charlie could use to pay alimony would be taxed to him at 28 percent federal, 4.5 percent Connecticut. All of Diane's income will be taxed at 15 percent federal, 4.5 percent Connecticut, including the additional alimony income. See Taxes, Chapter 12.

Step 1: Add up the amount of the payments which you are considering paying as alimony. Charlie and Diane's total is $800 + $25 + $175 = $1,000

Step 2: Subtract Diane's tax deductions for these payments.

$1,000 – $650 = $350. (If Diane's medical insurance premium and medical expenses total more than 7.5 percent of her taxable income, she may be able to deduct some or all of the medical insurance premium. In our example, these are not large enough to be deductible.)

Step 3: Subtract Diane's combined tax rate from 100 percent (100% – 19.5% = 80.5%)

Step 4: Calculate Diane's likely income tax on the remaining alimony: $350 ÷ 80% = $435

$435 – $350 = $85

Step 5: Add together the payments and the remaining tax to figure the amount to be paid as alimony. $1,000 + $85 = $1,085.

Step 6: Charlie deducts the full amount as alimony. Charlie saves the following in taxes: $1,087.50 – 32.5% = $353

Step 7: Calculate their overall tax savings. $353 – $85 = $268. Charlie and Diane save $268 every month this alimony agreement is in effect. This total monthly tax savings is money they don't pay the IRS. The greater the spread between your tax rates, the more you can potentially save in taxes.

The more the amount of alimony paid exceeds the amount the recipient pays for taxes on the alimony, the more that spouse shares in the overall savings.

Step 8: Consider increasing the amount of alimony to share the tax savings each month.

Sometimes It's Alimony Whether You Like It or Not

The IRS may treat as alimony any payment made on behalf of a spouse which qualifies as alimony under their definition. If, for example, in your separation agreement you say that Husband will pay Wife's health and/or life insurance premium, or Wife's mortgage following the divorce, the IRS may treat this as alimony even if you did not call these payments alimony. This would give Husband an after-the-fact tax windfall and Wife unexpected taxes to pay. Be clear in your agreement whether a payment is or is not alimony, and what you intend in terms of tax treatment.

If Charlie and Diane continued to own the home together and Charlie paid the entire mortgage payment directly, the IRS might well assume that half the mortgage payment was on Diane's behalf—and therefore alimony—and unexpectedly deduct it from Charlie's taxable income and tax Diane on it. Charlie might not be able to deduct all or even half of the mortgage interest and property taxes because the home is no longer his primary residence.

Paying Spouse Pays FICA First

The spouse paying alimony does not save FICA (Social Security or Self Employment Tax) on the alimony amount, only the federal and state taxes. The recipient does not pay FICA on this money.

Alimony Checklist 4:

We are/should consider paying alimony through _____ business:

_____   _____
Initials   Initials

Alimony Checklist 1:

We should consider alimony to pay the following specific debts:

Creditor	Balance	Mo. Pmts.
_____	_____	_____
_____	_____	_____
_____	_____	_____
_____	_____	_____
_____	_____	_____

_____   _____
Initials   Initials

4. Alimony Paid from Business Income

You may define your alimony amount as a percentage of income from the paying spouse's business. This may feel exactly right if the receiving spouse has been part of the business and its development. It may be a way to get your share of the family business. This way of defining the amount has a unique tax advantage in that it may not be subject to the recapture rules (*see* Chapter 12, Taxes). Although this isn't a property settlement, it can feel like one and thereby help with accomplishing what feels like a fair division of your assets. You may, in these circumstances, want to consider alimony payments that survive the receiving spouse's remarriage.

FIXED-TERM ALIMONY

Fixed-term alimony is an alimony plan in which you calculate the total amount precisely. Payments of this type of alimony are often short term or lump sum, contractual (sometimes called "in gross"), or for a specific purpose, and their amount and term may be modifiable.

1. Alimony to Pay Specific Marital Debts

If there is a difference in your incomes—or a significant difference in the tax treatment at the same income level—then you can do some money-saving tax planning as you pay off your debts. Have the higher-taxed spouse pay to the lower-taxed spouse the amount of the debt payments for which the receiving spouse is exclusively obligated plus the receiving spouse's tax on the payments. Then the lower-taxed spouse makes the debt payments. You will save, outright, the difference between the paying spouse's federal income tax rate and the receiving spouse's federal income tax rate. The greater the difference in your tax rates, the larger the savings. However, if the debt is associated with an asset owned by the payor, the percentage of ownership limits his or her deduction.

• Alimony to pay off marital debts can stair-step down as the total of the debt payments goes down. See Chapter 12, Taxes.

• You can use alimony to pay off marital debts in a steady amount for a fixed period of time—paying less than the total minimum payments in the first years and more than the debt payment in the later years. A flat payment plan such as this has the advantage of looking more like traditional alimony to the IRS, as well as being predictable.

- You can also use alimony to pay marital debts in a lump sum or several lump sums. However, this could result in a recapture problem. Again, see Chapter 12.

- Some marital debts are single payment debts, such as joint taxes owed for the last year of the marriage or from an audit, a balloon payment on a mortgage, signature loans, and short-term loans from friends and family.

2. Alimony to Pay for a Spouse's Training or Education

You can use alimony to provide an opportunity to renew or rejuvenate a career, to obtain the education or training necessary to become self-supporting, or to supplement new income as it phases in and up. If you are considering alimony for any of these purposes, the spouse seeking alimony should gather the following data:

- What will your training or education cost be? What about direct costs, such as tuition, books, and parking?

- What are the indirect costs: babysitting, loss of income?

- What, if anything, will you earn during the training?

- How long will it take?

- When you complete your plan, what can you expect to earn?

Gathering this information can address some of the feelings that often accompany this situation: anger at paying for someone else's choices; anger at needing someone else to pay for your choices; guilt; fear of poverty, failure, the unknown; concern that your children lose something during this time; and worry about not being able to make ends meet.

In your agreement, tie the alimony directly to your purpose, being sure that it qualifies for deductibility under the IRS rules. For example, a clause could provide that alimony is payable only if the spouse is in school in good standing and working toward a degree or certificate. Sometimes it is easier on the family budget to pay some of this in a lump sum or several lump sums, such as from a year-end bonus or other occasional or irregular income of the paying spouse. Once the recipient spouse completes training, the alimony could reduce as the recipient's income increases.

If your alimony, including the lump sum options, will total more than $15,000 in the first post-separation tax year, you may be running into the recapture rules. A solution might be to pay the bulk of the alimony before your final judgment of divorce, since temporary alimony may be exempt from the recapture rules. See Chapter 12, Taxes.

Alimony Checklist 2: We should consider alimony to pay for _____'s training or education as follows:

Item:_____   Cost: $_____

Item:_____   Cost: $_____

Item:_____   Cost: $_____

Item:_____   Cost: $_____

Item:_____   Cost: $_____

_____   _____
   Initials   Initials

If your plan calls for a reduction in alimony within six months of any child reaching the age of eighteen, nineteen, or twenty-one, and/or you plan reductions in alimony during the time any two or more of your children are between eighteen and twenty-four, see Chapter 12, Taxes. The timing of these provisions may invalidate your attempt to establish deductible alimony.

Alimony Checklist 3:

We should consider alimony to supplement
_____'s income as follows:

_____   _____
Initials   Initials

Alimony Checklist 4:

There is an imbalance in our property
division of $_____ that we are con-
sidering using alimony to offset as follows:

_____   _____
Initials   Initials

**State Income Tax on
Alimony Too**

Remember in your planning to
add in the cost of Connecticut
income tax on alimony. The effective
percentage rate for Connecticut income
brackets up to 5 percent.

3. Alimony to Supplement a Spouse's Income as It Phases In or Up

If one spouse has recently re-entered the job market or changed careers, that spouse may be earning entry-level or probationary pay, which is probably less than that person's earning potential. It may take a while for the income to build.

Alimony that stair-steps down can complement a spouse's income that is stair-stepping up. Many people want to make the steps a dollar-for-dollar reduction: every time the receiving spouse earns $100 a month more, the alimony reduces by $100 the next month. Correlating the two this closely, however, can become a disincentive to the lower-income spouse (and also makes it open-ended alimony). Often, it is better to agree in advance to regular decreases in alimony over a fixed period of time based on your best estimates of the timing of the receiving spouse's future earnings. This way everyone knows what to expect and what not to expect.

4. Alimony to Balance a Property Division

Occasionally spouses will agree to a division of their property that makes sense to them but that places a larger amount of property with one spouse. If that property does not include readily transferable liquid assets, you may need to agree to a compensating amount to make the division feel fair.

Donald and Roxanne

In dividing their property, Donald and Roxanne have $20,000 more in value on Roxanne's side of the balance sheet due to a large retirement fund that she cannot touch now. Roxanne can pay $12,000 in alimony ($10,000 to equalize the property, plus $2,000 to pay Donald's tax on this amount). It can be a lump sum or periodic (quarterly, monthly), depending on how Roxanne receives income. If she gets quarterly income from stock or a twice-yearly company performance bonus, these can be a source of funding for this kind of alimony.

Be sure to disconnect this alimony provision from the section in your agreement about division of property since the IRS frowns on suspected payment for property with alimony. Say in the property division section of your agreement that your division is "equitable" although it is not 50-50. Then put your alimony agreement in another section. You may want to state that the receiving spouse needs alimony so that the alimony provision stands on its own. Also see Chapter 12, Taxes, for information about alimony recapture if the payments decrease by more than $15,000 in the first three years.

IRS ALIMONY RULES

To qualify as alimony which will be deductible by the payor and taxable to the payee, a payment must meet the following requirements:

1. It must be in cash or a cash equivalent, like a check, not property (i.e., not in-kind, like a car or horse).

2. It must be received by a spouse or former spouse of the payor or by a third party on behalf of a spouse or former spouse (where there is a written request or agreement to pay the third party rather than the spouse, and the agreement reflects that taxable alimony is intended).

3. The payments must be made according to a written agreement or court judgment of divorce.

4. You cannot be members of the same household at the time any payments are made after the final judgment of divorce (see Chapter 5 for temporary alimony payments).

5. The obligation to make the payment cannot continue after the receiving spouse's death.

6. The payment is not child support or considered child support by the IRS. See Chapter 12, Taxes.

7. The agreement (see 3, above) does not state that the payments are not to receive alimony tax treatment.

Before you finish your alimony agreement, be certain it meets all these criteria.

ORGANIZING YOUR INCOME AND EXPENSES

Because alimony is based on the ability of the paying spouse to pay as well as the needs of the receiving spouse you must be knowledgeable about your incomes and expenses to develop a sound alimony plan. Review the income charts and budgets you prepared for Chapter 7 and update them as needed. If you prepared budgets while designing a temporary agreement (Chapter 5), review and update them now.

The IRS provides an explanation of the tax impact of divorce, including alimony tax rules, in IRS Publication 504, *Divorced and Seperated Individuals.* Visit **www.irs.gov.pub/irs-pdf/p504.pdf**.

**Social Security Eligibility
in a Ten-Year Marriage**

Once you have been married for ten years or more, both spouses have the option of having their Social Security retirement benefit calculated on either their own earnings or on the earnings of their former spouse. If you choose the latter, the benefit is half of that of the former spouse. It is an independent entitlement and does not reduce the benefit of the former spouse.

Former Spouse's Medical Insurance—COBRA

Since 1986, every employer of more than twenty-five employees who is subject to the federal law called "E.R.I.S.A" (The Employee Retirement Income Security Act of 1974) must permit divorced spouses of their employees to continue coverage under the same health insurance policy by which they have been covered as the spouse of an employee. The non-employee spouse pays the premium, which may not be more than 105 percent of the full premium (including the amount the employer may have been paying on behalf of an employee as a benefit). Employers are now required to tell any employee what the cost of this COBRA (The Consolidated Omnibus Budget Reconciliation Act of 1985) option would be for their ex-spouse after a divorce. This option may be available for up to thirty-six months from the date of the final judgment. Since the ex-spouse does not have to qualify for this insurance, no pre-existing conditions will prevent him or her from being insured. However, to obtain COBRA coverage you should complete the paperwork with the employer within sixty days of divorce.

PUTTING YOUR ALIMONY PLAN TOGETHER

Putting together an alimony plan for your unique circumstances requires that you consider carefully each of the following:

- Purpose
- Amount needed
- Duration
- Reductions, if any
- Circumstances under which the amount and/or duration of alimony is modifiable, if any
- Tax consequences and amount to be paid
- Circumstances under which alimony terminates, if any
- Security, or "teeth"

Purpose, Amount, and Duration

Review any of the ways to use alimony at the beginning of this chapter in which either of you indicated interest. How many ways to use alimony are still of interest to you both? Review and discuss these. Write in detail each purpose for which you both agree to use alimony. For each purpose, calculate the amount needed based on your income charts and budgets.

- If one of your purposes for alimony is to level incomes or supplement the income of the lower-income spouse, then use the Budget Analysis Chart in Chapter 7. This chart will compare the incomes and budgets in your two homes.

- If your purpose for alimony is to supplement the income of the lower-income spouse for a specific purpose, you will base your analysis on that spouse's budget. For example, write down the amount for tuition, books, transportation, parking, and children's day care for a spouse entering college. Estimate the budget needs for the lower-income spouse for the immediate future.

- If another purpose for alimony is to pay specific expenses, be sure you look at both budgets. It is possible that a certain expense is now paid by the "wrong" spouse. Perhaps this expense might be better paid by the other spouse with money received as alimony.

For the duration of the alimony, you can either set forth a specific time period or specific event (not child related, see page 312). Long-term alimony may terminate or be reviewable at the retirement of the paying spouse, especially if the division of property included divisions of retirement or pension monies or if the receiving spouse has sufficient Social Security. See Chapter 10. You can also keep the alimony period "open ended." Some couples prefer to define their goals for alimony and set an amount for the first year only. They then meet toward the end of that year to adjust the amount according to their pre-defined criteria.

Reduction and Modification

The next step after determining the purpose, amount, and duration of your alimony is to decide if and under what circumstances the amount should change. You can agree ahead of time to change the amount on the occurrence of a certain event, after certain periods of time, when your incomes change in certain ways, or as a result of some other trigger.

When you decide on the purpose for alimony, you may want the amount to change when the purpose is satisfied either in whole or in part. You may set the modification amounts now. For example, you anticipate that the receiving spouse's income will increase in fairly predictable increments, so you plan for alimony to phase down at a certain amount per month each year whether either spouse actually earns according to the plan. Or, you can plan your future changes based on a formula. For example, alimony will decrease by a percentage of the amount of increase in the receiving spouse's income.

Lastly, you can agree now to review and adjust your alimony plan in the event circumstances arise later that you cannot foresee now. For example, the paying spouse loses his or her job, illness changes the earning capacity of either of you, or there is a change from one or several of the assumptions, such as a career choice that does not produce the anticipated income.

For more on the question of modifying alimony after the final judgment, see Chapter 13.

TAX CONSEQUENCES AND AMOUNT TO BE PAID

Now that you know how much the alimony should be, how long it should last, and under what circumstances the spouse will

Purpose, Amount Needed, and Duration of Our Alimony Plan

Directions: Fill in any of the following (1-3) uses of alimony to which you agree.

1. We will use lump sum alimony for these specific purposes:

    in this (these) needed amount(s):

    to be paid as follows (dates):

2. We will use monthly or periodic alimony for a specific period of time for the following purposes:

    In this (these) needed amount(s):

    To be paid monthly (or other frequency):

    For the following time frame:

3. We will use alimony with no built-in time limit (lifetime alimony for the following purpose:

    In the beginning needed amount of:

Future Changes

Directions: Complete the following statements as needed to reflect your unique circumstances:

We foresee predictable changes (for example, completion of degree, quitting school, payoff of a debt, child no longer needs day care, receiving spouse's income increases in a predictable amount, specific length of time from decree) in the amount of our alimony as follows:

We agree that the amount of our alimony may be re-examined and adjusted by us if the following (for example, unforeseen changes in either income or expenses) happens:

When you consider using alimony as a tax-planning tool and you have minor children, you must be extremely careful that you do not violate important IRS rules and regulations. Any reduction or termination of alimony related to a child contingency will result in the total disallowance of the planned tax treatment. Read Chapter 12 and consult a divorce attorney or CPA familiar with divorce taxation issues.

Our Plan for Terminating Alimony

Directions: Complete the following statement as needed to reflect your unique circumstances:

We agree that our alimony will end under the following circumstances:

 Alimony must not continue past the death of the receiving spouse. If it does, it is deemed to be a property payment not deductible from the taxable income of the payor. Similarly, alimony generally ends on the remarriage of the receiving spouse. You must specify in the separation agreement whether remarriage will terminate alimony.

receive it, you need to calculate how much to actually pay. To do that you must look at the projected tax status of each of you and the tax effect of your proposed alimony plan.

It is possible to agree that alimony is neither deductible to the payor nor taxable to the payee. In circumstances where the spouses are in the same tax brackets or you don't want to have the tax consequences apply to your situation, you might not want the presumed tax treatment to happen.

See Chapter 12 for an explanation of how to calculate your taxes and net income with alimony.

TERMINATION OF ALIMONY

Alimony usually ends on the death or remarriage of the recipient or the death of the payor. If your agreement to pay alimony arises from your division of property, you might want the payments to continue beyond the remarriage of the recipient. To be tax deductible, alimony must end on the death of the recipient.

Can alimony survive the death of the payor? There is no presumption about this, although it usually does not. Your agreement must specifically provide for termination of alimony on the death of the payor, if that is your intent.

If alimony will end on the death of the payor, consider using life insurance or other property as a way to compensate the recipient for the loss of expected cash flow. To calculate the amount of insurance, take the amount of the payments times the maximum number of months it could be paid. This is the maximum total amount for the initial amount of the death benefit. If the payor spouse died, the receiving spouse would presumably earn interest on the proceeds and this additional income would be available. You might choose to reduce, or discount, the initial amount in recognition of this factor. You could also have decreasing term insurance, i.e., the death benefit decreases each year over the term of the alimony.

COHABITATION

When divorcing couples are putting together an agreement about alimony that will last for some time after the final judgment, they are likely to end up in a discussion of cohabitation sooner or later. Connecticut law provides that the court may (it does not have to) terminate, suspend, or modify alimony if the recipient spouse is living with another person under circumstances that the court finds alter the financial needs of the recipient spouse.

As with many things divorcing couples argue about, the word *cohabitation* doesn't convey the real issue. The paying spouse wants the alimony to end when the receiving spouse marries or lives in a marriage-like arrangement. The thinking is that he or she should not pay for a former spouse if that spouse is living in an arrangement that implies someone else is taking care of or sharing expenses with the former spouse. From the receiving spouse's point of view, a cohabitation provision may feel like the former spouse is trying to tell him or her how to live— or at least trying to dictate the seriousness of his or her new sexual relationship.

TO MAINTAIN YOUR ALIMONY AGREEMENT

If your ex has a new lover, will you be less likely to pay the alimony? Will you be less likely to pay the debts you agreed to pay through alimony? If you lose your job or the bonus does not come through, will you look for a way out of your agreement to pay alimony? Would any of these be tempting for you?

There are several kinds of internal enforcement that you can use in alimony agreements. These "teeth" may be effective ways of penalizing yourselves with more or less costly consequences if you don't do what you say you will do. What do each of you need to put into your agreement to make sure you keep the promises you make to each other about alimony? Only your imagination limits these incentives. Try having the person against whom the penalty would act set the penalty. What motivates each of you may be surprising.

Agreements you might try: if the alimony payment is not made on time, the paying spouse loses the tax deduction and the recipient does not have to declare it as income. Or, if the recipient spouse does not use the alimony for the agreed-upon purpose (such as paying the house payment), the alimony will cease or reduce and the payor spouse has first option to assume the obligation and receive the property.

It may or may not be appropriate for you to put such strict "punishments" in your own agreement. That's your decision. But, if you begin right away treating your agreement as a very serious bargain between the two of you, there will be less chance that you will have the temptation to take it lightly later on.

Conclusion

Your first rough look at your alimony plan is now finished. It will probably not be your final version. Go on to the next chapter,

Taxes; the agreements you reach as a result of it may necessitate changes in your alimony plan.

Take heart. Understanding the issues and settling your divorce case is hard work. Don't expect to get it all done in one sitting. Don't even expect to complete your agreement about alimony in one sitting. Give yourself and each other the time you deserve to make the best decisions for your family.

TAXES

Reading this chapter is 90 percent likely to save you money; not reading it is 100 percent likely to cost you money.

"The art of taxation consists in so plucking the goose as to obtain the largest possible amount of feathers with the smallest possible amount of hissing."

Attributed to Jean Baptiste Colbert, (c. 1665)

"The wisdom of man never yet contrived a system of taxation that would operate with perfect equality."

Andrew Jackson, Proclamation to the People of South Carolina, Dec. 10, 1832

"Taxes, after all, are the dues that we pay for the privilege of membership in an organized society."

Franklin D. Roosevelt, Worcester, MA, Oct. 21, 1936

"The point to remember is that what the government gives it must first take away."

John S. Coleman, address to the Detroit Chamber of Commerce

TAXES

The purpose of this chapter, and the tax parts of other chapters, is to provide information about a variety of tax issues. Because taxes are a complex issue, this book provides a detailed overview and examples of the general application of tax laws and regulations.

To accurately calculate taxes you should seriously consider consulting a professional. Certified public accountants and tax lawyers are obvious choices for obtaining advice and accurate calculations. You might also consult with certified financial planners who incorporate tax issues in the analysis of financial planning. However, since not all CPAs, tax lawyers, and financial planners are familiar with divorce taxation, be sure the person you select is. Finally, some divorce lawyers and mediators are knowledgeable in the area of divorce taxation. They can be extremely helpful as you consider the tax implications of your divorce agreement.

Many professionals who work with divorce taxation use computer programs that help them analyze the tax aspects of your alternative settlement proposals. If you think that this technology would be helpful to you, be sure the professional you consult provides this service.

The Tax Effects of Divorce

Divorce affects taxes no matter how well you plan. There may be a profound change in your incomes, and there certainly will be a profound change in your taxes. Dollars that are exempt or deductible from taxable income will change as will your tax filing status and the tax credits for which you are eligible. This chapter supplements the discussion in Chapter 11 about alimony, a concept unique to divorce. Property transferred between spouses as part of a divorce is not taxed as if it was sold, but any built-in capital gain should be considered as you bargain about that property, as you saw in Chapter 10.

Your divorce impacts four aspects of your taxes:

1. Filing status

2. Exemptions

3. Deductions

4. Credits

Filing Status

The IRS taxes income in percentages: the federal tax rate for the first and lowest portion of your income is 10 percent; the second and higher portion, over a certain threshold, is 15 percent; and above that is 25 percent, then 28 percent, 33 percent, and 35 percent. Your filing status determines when your income requires that you move to the next highest bracket. Connecticut income taxes start at zero and graduate up to 5 percent for most taxpayers.

There are four statuses: married filing jointly, married filing separate, single, and head of household. Filing jointly with your spouse or married filing separately probably forms the basis of your current withholding rate at work. Therefore, it is important to begin your tax planning early in your negotiations because the divorce will change your tax status and your withholding for the year. This may turn out to be significantly more or less than your actual tax obligation.

The IRS publishes lots of pamphlets about all aspects of tax law and practice. One particularly useful publication for separating couples is *Divorced or Separated Individuals,* Publication 504. www.irs.gov.pub/irs-pdf/p504.pdf

2003 Federal Personal Income Tax Rates

Tax Rate	Single Filers	Married Filing Jointly	Married Filing Separately	Head of Household
10%	Up to $7,000	Up to $14,000	Up to $7,000	Up to $10,000
15%	$7,001–$28,400	$14,001–$56,800	$7,001–$28,400	$10,001–$38,050
25%	$28,401–$68,800	$56,801–$114,650	$28,401–$57,325	$38,051–$98,250
28%	$68,801–$143,500	$114,651–$174,700	$57,326–$87,350	$98,251–$159,100
33%	$143,501–$311,950	$174,701–$311,950	$87,351–$155,975	$159,101–$311,950
35%	$311,951 or more	$311,951 or more	$155,976 or more	$311,951 or more

This table illustrates taxable income according to your filing status for 2003 only. You can obtain current information for the year of filing from the IRS or your payroll department.

Initially, you determine your tax filing status by your marital status on December 31 of that tax year. If your final divorce is on or before December 31, you are single for that tax year and must file

Tax Filing Status: The category for figuring how much to tax your income, for example, married filing jointly.

This chapter deals with federal taxes. For information about Connecticut state taxes visit **www.drs.state.ct.us**.

If you, your spouse, or both of you file separate returns in any year when you are married, you can later file an amended joint return any time within three years from the due date (not including extensions) of the separate returns. However, if you file a joint return, you cannot change your mind later and file separate returns.

To get an overview of federal taxes see IRS Pub. 17 at **www.irs.gov/pub/irs-pdf/p17.pdf**.

"If we were married for most of the year, then we have to file our taxes as married."

No. You file your tax returns for the entire year according to your marital status on December 31. If your divorce was final that day you may not file as married. There may be some tax advantages to being divorced before year's end so that you can file separately. Or you may decide to stay married until early in the next year so that you can file jointly. This is a determination that you should make as part of your overall tax and divorce planning.

Judges do not necessarily consider anticipated tax consequences when they decide divorce cases. Working together, you have the advantage of being able to do tax planning.

as single or head of household. You no longer have a choice of filing married.

If you remain married through December 31, you may file married filing jointly or married filing separately. If you are still married on December 31 but you have been separated for more than six months, you may have the additional option of filing as head of household if you qualify.

Finalizing your divorce before or after December 31 may have significant financial consequences for the tax year. You can put off finalizing your divorce until after the first of the year if both of you will save money by filing married-joint or married-separate or by one filing married separate and the other as head of household. You might choose to finalize your divorce before the end of the year if at least one of you will save money by filing as single or head of household.

Head of household status is the most favorable way to file for divorced or separated persons because it results in the least amount of tax. The shift from 10 percent to 35 percent tax occurs at a higher income for head of household filers than for single filers, so more earnings are taxed at the lower rate.

A single taxpayer may file as head of household if he or she provides a primary residence for more than half the year for any legal dependent. A still-married person separated at least for the last six months of the tax year may file as head of household if he or she provides the main, or primary, home for a dependent child.

Uneasiness About Tax Returns

You are both legally responsible for any tax return you both sign. This is true even if you have an agreement as part of the divorce that one spouse will be responsible for all taxes, current and audited. Separation, when emotions are running high and expenses running even higher, is a time when temptation often causes people to make unwise decisions regarding their tax returns (by exaggerating deductible expenses, claiming doubtful deductions, or "forgetting" to list income). If either of you is likely to be less forthcoming than the other, consider filing married-separate so you are not legally bound by a tax return you are uncomfortable with. This might cost you some additional tax, but the peace of mind may be worth it.

Exemptions

A tax exemption is an opportunity to exempt, or take out, a certain amount from your taxable income. The exemption commonly discussed in divorce cases is the dependency exemption. This is a fixed amount per person: one for each parent, one for each dependent child. The exemption for one child cannot be split between you and your spouse in the tax year. If you have one child you may alternate years, but you should each adjust your wage withholding every year. If you have more than one child, you may allocate the exemptions between you. The amount of the personal or dependent exemption for yourself and your children depends on your filing status and varies annually ($3,050 in 2003).

The IRS will presume that the custodial parent gets the dependency exemption for that child. For tax purposes, the word *custodial* means either the sole custodian as designated by the court order or the parent with primary physical custody in a joint custody court order. If the court order does not establish custody this way, the person who has the child for the greater part of the year qualifies. However, you can bargain for the child-dependency exemption and allocate it to the other parent. Consider whether it will help the family budget or ease a significant tax burden for the non-custodial parent to have the exemption.

Remember, however, that the ability to use the dependency exemption phases out starting at $139,500 taxable income for single taxpayers and $174,400 for head of household.

The dependency exemption and the head of household filing status are not the same thing. They are two separate lines on your tax return. Compare line 4 with lines 6(c) and (d) of the 1040 form on page 303. To declare head of household status, you must list at least one qualifying person as your dependent, which means that your home was that person's principal place of residence for that tax year. The qualifying person is often a child.

If you want the dependency exemption to be claimed by the parent who does not name that child as the basis for his or her head of household filing status, the head of household parent for that child must sign IRS Form 8332. Both parents must file a copy with their tax return. See Form 8332 on next page.

D DEFINITION — **Tax Exemption:** Category of income on which you are not taxed, including the personal exemption for yourself and dependency exemption for members of your family.

"Filing head of household means that I get the tax exemptions for our children."

This is a frequent misunderstanding. Your filing status and dependency exemptions are different. Either parent may claim the dependency exemptions, if you agree. The IRS will presume they go to the "custodial" (head of household) parent unless you agree otherwise.

 Both parents declaring the same child as either a dependent or as the basis for head of household status will absolutely cause an audit by the IRS and may trigger a penalty. Be very clear about these arrangements in your agreement so that you do not duplicate claims with regard to the children.

 Begin with the assumption that the parent who has a child for more than half the overnights per year will file as head of household, claim the child care credit, and have the dependency exemption for that child. If you want to reverse the last of these—to balance the tax benefits of having children or as part of your overall bargaining—you may do so by using IRS Form 8332. See www.irs.gov/pub/irs-pdf/f8332.pdf.

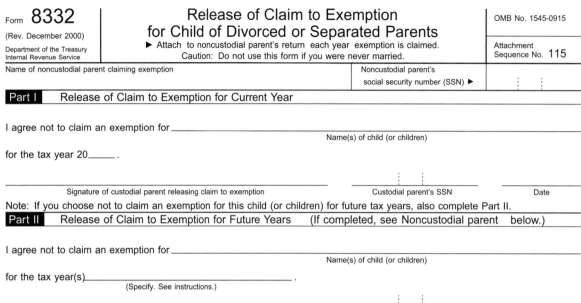

Form **8332**

(Rev. December 2000)

Department of the Treasury
Internal Revenue Service

Release of Claim to Exemption
for Child of Divorced or Separated Parents

▶ Attach to noncustodial parent's return each year exemption is claimed.
Caution: Do not use this form if you were never married.

OMB No. 1545-0915

Attachment
Sequence No. **115**

Name of noncustodial parent claiming exemption

Noncustodial parent's
social security number (SSN) ▶

Part I	Release of Claim to Exemption for Current Year

I agree not to claim an exemption for _____

Name(s) of child (or children)

for the tax year 20_____ .

Signature of custodial parent releasing claim to exemption   Custodial parent's SSN   Date

Note: If you choose not to claim an exemption for this child (or children) for future tax years, also complete Part II.

Part II	Release of Claim to Exemption for Future Years (If completed, see Noncustodial parent below.)

I agree not to claim an exemption for _____

Name(s) of child (or children)

for the tax year(s)_____ .

(Specify. See instructions.)

Signature of custodial parent releasing claim to exemption   Custodial parent's SSN   Date

General Instructions

Purpose of form. If you are a custodial parent and you were ever married to the child's noncustodial parent, you may use this form to release your claim to your child's exemption. To do so, complete this form (or a similar statement containing the same information required by this form) and give it to the noncustodial parent who will claim the child's exemption. The noncustodial parent must attach this form or similar statement to his or her tax return each year the exemption is claimed.

You are the custodial parent if you had custody of the child for most of the year. You are the noncustodial parent if you had custody for a shorter period of time or did not have custody at all. For the definition of custody, see Pub. 501, Exemptions, Standard Deduction, and Filing Information.

Support test for children of divorced or separated parents. Generally, the custodial parent is treated as having provided over half of the child's support if:

● The child received over half of his or her total support for the year from one or both of the parents and

● The child was in the custody of one or both of the parents for more than half of the year.

Note: Public assistance payments, such as Temporary Assistance for Needy Families (TANF), are not support provided by the parents.

For this support test to apply, the parents must be one of the following:

● Divorced or legally separated under a decree of divorce or separate maintenance,

● Separated under a written separation agreement, or

● Living apart at all times during the last 6 months of the year.

Caution: This support test does not apply to parents who never married each other.

If the support test applies, and the other four dependency tests in your tax return

instruction booklet are also met, the custodial parent can claim the child's exemption.

Exception. The custodial parent will not be treated as having provided over half of the child's support if any of the following apply.

● The custodial parent agrees not to claim the child's exemption by signing this form or similar statement.

● The child is treated as having received over half of his or her total support from a person under a multiple support agreement (Form 2120, Multiple Support Declaration).

● A pre-1985 divorce decree or written separation agreement states that the noncustodial parent can claim the child as a dependent. But the noncustodial parent must provide at least $600 for the child's support during the year. This rule does not apply if the decree or agreement was changed after 1984 to say that the noncustodial parent cannot claim the child as a dependent.

Additional information. For more details, see Pub. 504, Divorced or Separated Individuals.

Specific Instructions

Custodial parent. You may agree to release your claim to the child's exemption for the current tax year or for future years, or both.

● Complete Part I if you agree to release your claim to the child's exemption for the current tax year.

● Complete Part II if you agree to release your claim to the child's exemption for any or all future years. If you do, write the specific future year(s) or "all future years" in the space provided in Part II.

To help ensure future support, you may not want to release your claim to the child's exemption for future years.

Noncustodial parent. Attach this form or similar statement to your tax return for each year you claim the child's exemption. You may claim the exemption only if the other four dependency tests in your tax return instruction booklet are met.

Note: If the custodial parent released his or her claim to the child's exemption for any future year, you must attach a copy of this form or similar statement to your tax return for each future year that you claim the exemption. Keep a copy for your records.

Paperwork Reduction Act Notice. We ask for the information on this form to carry out the Internal Revenue laws of the United States. You are required to give us the information. We need it to ensure that you are complying with these laws and to allow us to figure and collect the right amount of tax.

You are not required to provide the information requested on a form that is subject to the Paperwork Reduction Act unless the form displays a valid OMB control number. Books or records relating to a form or its instructions must be retained as long as their contents may become material in the administration of any Internal Revenue law. Generally, tax returns and return information are confidential, as required by Internal Revenue Code section 6103.

The time needed to complete and file this form will vary depending on individual circumstances. The estimated average time is:

Recordkeeping   .   .   .   .   .   .   7 min.

Learning about the law or
the form   .   .   .   .   5 min.

Preparing the form   .   .   .   .   7 min.

Copying, assembling, and
sending the form to the IRS   .   . 14 min.

If you have comments concerning the accuracy of these time estimates or suggestions for making this form simpler, we would be happy to hear from you. You can write to the Tax Forms Committee, Western Area Distribution Center, Rancho Cordova, CA 95743-0001. Do not send the form to this address. Instead, see the Instructions for Form 1040 or Form 1040A.

Cat. No. 13910F   Form **8332** (Rev. 12-2000)

Form 1040

Department of the Treasury—Internal Revenue Service

U.S. Individual Income Tax Return 2002

(99)   IRS Use Only—Do not write or staple in this space.

For the year Jan. 1–Dec. 31, 2002, or other tax year beginning _____, 2002, ending _____, 20___

OMB No. 1545-0074

Label
(See instructions on page 21.)

Use the IRS label. Otherwise, please print or type.

L A B E L   H E R E

Your first name and initial | Last name | Your social security number

If a joint return, spouse's first name and initial | Last name | Spouse's social security number

Home address (number and street). If you have a P.O. box, see page 21. | Apt. no.

City, town or post office, state, and ZIP code. If you have a foreign address, see page 21.

▲ **Important!** ▲
You must enter your SSN(s) above.

Presidential Election Campaign
(See page 21.)

Note. Checking "Yes" will not change your tax or reduce your refund.
Do you, or your spouse if filing a joint return, want $3 to go to this fund? . . . ▶

You ☐ Yes ☐ No   Spouse ☐ Yes ☐ No

Filing Status

Check only one box.

1 ☐ Single
2 ☐ Married filing jointly (even if only one had income)
3 ☐ Married filing separately. Enter spouse's SSN above and full name here. ▶_____
4 ☐ Head of household (with qualifying person). (See page 21.) If the qualifying person is a child but not your dependent, enter this child's name here. ▶
5 ☐ Qualifying widow(er) with dependent child (year spouse died ▶_____). (See page 21.)

Exemptions

6a ☐ Yourself. If your parent (or someone else) can claim you as a dependent on his or her tax return, do not check box 6a . . . .
b ☐ Spouse . . . .

If more than five dependents, see page 22.

c Dependents:

(1) First name Last name	(2) Dependent's social security number	(3) Dependent's relationship to you	(4)✔ if qualifying child for child tax credit (see page 22)
			☐
			☐
			☐
			☐
			☐

No. of boxes checked on 6a and 6b _____

No. of children on 6c who:
• lived with you _____
• did not live with you due to divorce or separation (see page 22) _____

Dependents on 6c not entered above _____

d Total number of exemptions claimed . . . .

Add numbers on lines above ▶ ☐

Income

Attach Forms W-2 and W-2G here. Also attach Form(s) 1099-R if tax was withheld.

If you did not get a W-2, see page 23.

Enclose, but do not attach, any payment. Also, please use Form 1040-V.

7	Wages, salaries, tips, etc. Attach Form(s) W-2	7
8a	Taxable interest. Attach Schedule B if required	8a
b	Tax-exempt interest. Do not include on line 8a . . . 8b	
9	Ordinary dividends. Attach Schedule B if required	9
10	Taxable refunds, credits, or offsets of state and local income taxes (see page 24) . .	10
11	Alimony received	11
12	Business income or (loss). Attach Schedule C or C-EZ	12
13	Capital gain or (loss). Attach Schedule D if required. If not required, check here ▶ ☐	13
14	Other gains or (losses). Attach Form 4797	14
15a	IRA distributions . . 15a ____ b Taxable amount (see page 25)	15b
16a	Pensions and annuities 16a ____ b Taxable amount (see page 25)	16b
17	Rental real estate, royalties, partnerships, S corporations, trusts, etc. Attach Schedule E	17
18	Farm income or (loss). Attach Schedule F	18
19	Unemployment compensation	19
20a	Social security benefits . 20a ____ b Taxable amount (see page 27)	20b
21	Other income. List type and amount (see page 29) ----------	21
22	Add the amounts in the far right column for lines 7 through 21. This is your total income ▶	22

Adjusted Gross Income

23	Educator expenses (see page 29)	23
24	IRA deduction (see page 29)	24
25	Student loan interest deduction (see page 31)	25
26	Tuition and fees deduction (see page 32)	26
27	Archer MSA deduction. Attach Form 8853	27
28	Moving expenses. Attach Form 3903	28
29	One-half of self-employment tax. Attach Schedule SE .	29
30	Self-employed health insurance deduction (see page 33)	30
31	Self-employed SEP, SIMPLE, and qualified plans . .	31
32	Penalty on early withdrawal of savings	32
33a	Alimony paid b Recipient's SSN ▶ _____	33a

34	Add lines 23 through 33a	34
35	Subtract line 34 from line 22. This is your adjusted gross income . . . . . ▶	35

For Disclosure, Privacy Act, and Paperwork Reduction Act Notice, see page 76.   Cat. No. 11320B   Form **1040** (2002)

Tax Deduction: Specific expenditures that you may deduct from your income before figuring your tax. For example, the interest portion of your home mortgage is a deduction. Note that a tax deduction is not the same as a tax exemption.

The IRS requires that when one married spouse filing separately itemizes his or her deductions, so must the other spouse.

"If I pay the mortgage, I get the deduction."

It's not that simple. In addition to actually making the payments, the home must be your primary residence, and your name must be on the mortgage.

Tax Credit: A percentage of certain expenditures that you may subtract from your tax obligation itself, not just from taxable income. For example, a percentage of what you pay for work-related child care is a credit against income tax.

Deductions

A deduction is an amount you subtract from your taxable income before you figure your tax. Some common examples are interest paid on your home mortgage, certain taxes, and a certain percent of medical and dental costs beyond insurance coverage and medical and dental insurance premiums. You report your deductions on Schedule A—Form 1040 if you itemize your deductions. Follow Schedule A to estimate your itemized deductions, and compare this to the standard deduction in your tax filing status. You will want to use the higher of these.

Certain additional expenses, such as tax preparation, tax advice, and certain accounting and other fees, are deductible to the extent they exceed 2 percent of your adjusted gross income. Some portions of your divorce expenses for attorneys, accountants, or mediator services may be deductible in this category, but you should consult with a professional about this issue and obtain a statement from him or her about the portion of the fee that may be deductible.

If you have few deductions and choose not to itemize or if you are filing the short form tax return (1040 EZ), you may take a "standard deduction." The amount of the standard deduction changes annually. For 2003, the standard deduction for a single filer was $4,750 while that for head of household was $7,000. You can learn the amount of the standard deduction for each filing status for this year or any other by requesting this information from the IRS or your payroll department.

Credits

A tax credit is just what the name implies. You subtract it (give yourself credit) from the amount of tax you would otherwise pay (bottom line on your income tax return). The child care credit is the most significant one for divorcing or separated parents of young children.

The child care credit is a fixed percentage (varying from 20–30 percent for up to two children) of the day care amount for children under age thirteen—or disabled and not able to care for themselves—paid out by parents while they are at work or seeking work. You may claim the credit if you have custody of the child for more than half of the year. Since filing as head of household requires that the child reside with the claiming parent more that half of the year, you should consider coordinating payment of child-care expenses so that the parent who files as head of household for that child also pays the child care expenses and claims that credit. The parent with head of household filing status for a child must be the one to pay for child care of that child. You can't take credit for something you didn't pay.

You can use either the child care credit or a cafeteria (flex) plan but not both. A cafeteria plan allows the employee to pay for child care and family medical expenses from pre-tax dollars that the employer withholds and escrows or holds in trust for the benefit and use of the employee and his or her family. The child care credit effectively does the same thing by returning to you the tax money already paid on dollars used to pay for work-related child care. A cafeteria plan can, like alimony, shift the tax benefits of child care to the non-head-of-household parent.

You will use IRS Form 2441 to claim the child care credit. You can calculate the amount of your credit by using this Child Care Credit Table.

The earned income credit is a special refundable tax credit for certain people who work with earned income generally less than $30,000 per year. The credit reduces the amount of tax you owe. After divorce you need not have children primarily residing with you. However, if any child lives with you for more than half the year, is under age nineteen at the end of the year, or is a full time student and under age twenty-four at the end of the year, the calculation is adjusted to your benefit accordingly. Children of any age who are permanently and totally disabled any time during the year also qualify. To claim the credit and get a refund you must file a tax return even if you did not earn enough money to owe any tax.

If you believe that you may qualify for this credit, go to the local IRS office or call to get the 1040 instruction booklet that includes an earned income credit worksheet.

The child tax credit is up to $1,000 per year for each child under age seventeen. In a divorce situation, this tax credit can only be claimed by the person who uses the dependency exemption for the applicable child. Because this credit becomes less valuable at certain income levels, as does the dependency exemption, it is important that couples carefully look at assigning these benefits to the parent for whom the most tax savings results.

There are two education credits. The Hope Scholarship credit is for each of the first two years of post-secondary education, with a maximum credit of $1,500 per year per student for tuition and related expenses (not meals and lodging). You may claim the

Child Care Credit Income Ranges and Credit Percentages—2003 and Thereafter	
0–$15,000	35%
$15,000–$17,000	34%
$17,000–$19,000	33%
$19,000–$21,000	32%
$21,000–$23,000	31%
$23,000–$25,000	30%
$25,000–$27,000	29%
$27,000–$29,000	28%
$29,000–$31,000	27%
$31,000–$33,000	26%
$33,000–$35,000	25%
$35,000–$37,000	24%
$37,000–$39,000	23%
$39,000–$41,000	22%
$41,000–$43,000	21%
Over $43,000	20%

 For information about the child care credit see IRS Pub. 503, *Child and Dependent Care Expenses* at **www.irs.gov/pub/irs-pdf/p503.pdf**.

"If I pay the day care, I get the child care credit."

It's not that simple. For divorcing couples, in addition to making the payment to the care giver, you must also qualify and file as head of household using the same child for whom you are paying the day care as the basis for your head of household filing status.

 For more information about the earned income credit see IRS Pub. 596, *Earned Income Credit* at **www.irs.gov/pub/irs-pdf/p596.pdf**.

For more information about the child tax credit see IRS Pub. 972, *Child Tax Credit* at **www.irs.gov/pub/irs-pdf/p972.pdf**.

For more information about education credits and other educational tax benefits see IRS Pub. 970, *Tax Benefits for Education* at **www.irs.gov/pub/irs-pdf/p970.pdf**.

In order to estimate how much money to withhold from your paycheck, try the IRS withholding calculator at **www.irs.gov/individuals/article/o,,id=96 196,00.html**.

Lifetime Learning Credit of 20 percent of the first $10,000 for qualified expenses, including educational expenses to find or improve job skills for yourself or your dependent child. The credit applies not only to college students at all levels but also graduate students and working people pursuing job skills training. The credit applies to expenses paid after June 30, 1998, for expenses incurred after that date.

You may only claim one education credit per year per child. Both education credits are phased out for taxpayers with adjusted gross income for single taxpayers between $41,000 and $51,000. For married filing joint taxpayers, the phase-out occurs between $82,000 and $102,000. To claim the credit for a child, the parent must pay the expenses and the student must be eligible to be claimed as a dependency exemption on the parent's tax return.

For more information concerning the technical applications and other aspects of these tax credits, consult with a CPA.

Estimating Your Taxes

Taking into account the tax consequences of your proposed plan is essential to a workable final agreement. You also must determine your net taxable income to use the child support guidelines. As you have seen from the previous sections of this chapter, the tax consequences happen whether you plan for them or not. Misunderstanding or ignoring the tax consequences of your plan can unravel it altogether.

This section shows you how to estimate your taxes. See the tables of the effective federal tax rates prepared by Joseph N. DuCanto, a Chicago attorney. For Connecticut tax rates, use the following formula:

Single and Married Filing Separate—3 percent up to $10,000; 5 percent over $10,000

Head of Household—3 percent up to $16,000; 5 percent over $16,000

Married Filing Joint—3 percent up to $20,000; 5 percent over $20,000

The DuCanto table allows you to estimate your federal taxes by helping you calculate your after-divorce tax rate using the exemptions, deductions, and credits you have agreed to. The left-hand and center columns list taxable income. There are four tax filing statuses, two for married and two for legally separated or divorced people (single and head of household). Each tax filing status has a different standard deduction for those who do not itemize their deductions. These are listed under the filing status heading. The two paired columns under each filing status show actual federal tax payable (left column) and actual (effective) tax rate for each increment in income (right column). The upper corners of the chart show the amount of the dependency exemption, Social Security (FICA), and self-employment taxes.

For Connecticut, find the applicable range for your gross income for your filing status and apply the approximate tax indicated.

UPDATED CALCULATION OF EFFECTIVE FEDERAL TAX RATE (2003) IN PERCENTAGES OF TAXABLE INCOME[1]*

2003 Each Personal or Dependent Exemption = $3,050[4]

2003 FICA Tax- Employee's Portion (7.65%):
- OASDI (Social Security) - 6.2% of Gross Wages to $87,000 (maximum = $5,394.)
- HI (Hospital Insurance) - 1.45% of All Gross Wages
[See reverse for Self-Employment Tax]

MARRIED

TAXABLE INCOME[3]	JOINT (St. Ded: $9,500)[2] FEDERAL TAX	JOINT EFFECTIVE RATE	SEPARATE (St. Ded: $4,750)[2] FEDERAL TAX	SEPARATE EFFECTIVE RATE
1,500	150		150	
1,800	180		180	
2,500	250		250	
3,000	300		300	
5,000	500	10%	500	10%
7,500	750		775	10.33
8,000	800		850	10.63
8,500	850		925	10.88
9,000	900		1,000	11.11
9,500	950		1,075	11.32
10,000	1,000		1,150	11.50
10,500	1,050		1,225	11.67
11,000	1,100		1,300	11.82
11,500	1,150		1,375	11.96
12,000	1,200		1,450	12.08
12,500	1,250		1,525	12.20
13,000	1,300		1,600	12.31
13,500	1,350		1,675	12.41
14,000	1,400		1,750	12.50
14,500	1,475	10.17	1,825	12.59
15,000	1,550	10.33	1,900	12.67
16,000	1,700	10.63	2,050	12.81
17,000	1,850	10.88	2,200	12.94
18,000	2,000	11.11	2,350	13.06
19,000	2,150	11.32	2,500	13.16
20,000	2,300	11.50	2,650	13.25
21,000	2,450	11.67	2,800	13.33
22,000	2,600	11.82	2,950	13.41
23,000	2,750	11.96	3,100	13.48
24,000	2,900	12.08	3,250	13.54
25,000	3,050	12.20	3,400	13.60
26,000	3,200	12.31	3,550	13.65
27,000	3,350	12.41	3,700	13.70
28,000	3,500	12.50	3,850	13.75
29,000	3,650	12.59	4,060	14.00
30,000	3,800	12.67	4,310	14.37
32,000	4,100	12.81	4,810	15.03
34,000	4,400	12.94	5,310	15.62
36,000	4,700	13.06	5,810	16.14
38,000	5,000	13.16	6,310	16.61
40,000	5,300	13.25	6,810	17.03
42,000	5,600	13.33	7,310	17.40
44,000	5,900	13.41	7,810	17.75
46,000	6,200	13.48	8,310	18.07
48,000	6,500	13.54	8,810	18.35
50,000	6,800	13.60	9,310	18.62

JOINT actual tax brackets: 10% $0-14,000; 15% $14,001-56,800.
SEPARATE actual tax brackets: 10% $0-7,000; 15% $7,001-28,400; 25% $28,401-57,325.

SINGLE

TAXABLE INCOME[3]	SINGLE RETURN (St. Ded: $4,750)[2] FEDERAL TAX	SINGLE RETURN EFFECTIVE RATE	HEAD OF HOUSEHOLD (St. Ded: $7,000)[2] FEDERAL TAX	HEAD OF HOUSEHOLD EFFECTIVE RATE
1,500	150		150	
1,800	180		180	
2,500	250		250	
3,000	300		300	
5,000	500	10%	500	
7,500	775	10.33	750	10%
8,000	850	10.63	800	
8,500	925	10.88	850	
9,000	1,000	11.11	900	
9,500	1,075	11.32	950	
10,000	1,150	11.50	1,000	
10,500	1,225	11.67	1,075	10.24
11,000	1,300	11.82	1,150	10.45
11,500	1,375	11.96	1,225	10.65
12,000	1,450	12.08	1,300	10.83
12,500	1,525	12.20	1,375	11.00
13,000	1,600	12.31	1,450	11.15
13,500	1,675	12.41	1,525	11.30
14,000	1,750	12.50	1,600	11.43
14,500	1,825	12.59	1,675	11.55
15,000	1,900	12.67	1,750	11.67
16,000	2,050	12.81	1,900	11.88
17,000	2,200	12.94	2,050	12.06
18,000	2,350	13.06	2,200	12.22
19,000	2,500	13.16	2,350	12.37
20,000	2,650	13.25	2,500	12.50
21,000	2,800	13.33	2,650	12.62
22,000	2,950	13.41	2,800	12.73
23,000	3,100	13.48	2,950	12.83
24,000	3,250	13.54	3,100	12.92
25,000	3,400	13.60	3,250	13.00
26,000	3,550	13.65	3,400	13.08
27,000	3,700	13.70	3,550	13.15
28,000	3,850	13.75	3,700	13.21
29,000	4,060	14.00	3,850	13.28
30,000	4,310	14.37	4,000	13.33
32,000	4,810	15.03	4,300	13.44
34,000	5,310	15.62	4,600	13.53
36,000	5,810	16.14	4,900	13.61
38,000	6,310	16.61	5,200	13.68
40,000	6,810	17.03	5,695	14.24
42,000	7,310	17.40	6,195	14.75
44,000	7,810	17.75	6,695	15.22
46,000	8,310	18.07	7,195	15.64
48,000	8,810	18.35	7,695	16.03
50,000	9,310	18.62	8,195	16.39

SINGLE RETURN actual tax brackets: 10% $0-7,000; 15% $7,001-28,400; 25% $28,401-68,800.
HEAD OF HOUSEHOLD actual tax brackets: 10% $0-10,000; 15% $10,001-38,050; 25% $38,051-98,250.

* Chart has been updated as a result of the passage of the Jobs and Growth Tax Relief Reconciliation Act of 2003 on May 28, 2003.

1. (© 2003, JOSEPH N. DU CANTO.) This chart contains inflation-adjusted tax rates and bracket changes and is applicable only to the calculation of personal income taxes payable for income received in 2003. To obtain taxes payable at a given taxable income, multiply taxable income by the effective rate for the appropriate filing status.
   Example: Taxable Income is $48,000 and the filing status is Married Filing Jointly. $48,000 x 13.54% = $6,499.20 TAXES DUE.

2. The "Standard Deduction" is available to all taxpayers who do not choose to itemize deductions. An additional standard deduction is available to the blind and those over 65. If the person is blind or over 65 and is married, the additional deduction = $950; if single, the additional deduction = $1,150.

3. TAXABLE INCOME is the remaining portion of gross income subject to tax after all allowable deductions (adjustments to income, standard or itemized deductions, exemptions claimed, etc.).

Actual Tax Brackets for 2003 stated in red.

UPDATED CALCULATION OF EFFECTIVE FEDERAL TAX RATE (2003) IN PERCENTAGES OF TAXABLE INCOME[1]*

2003 Each Personal or Dependent Exemption = $3,050[4]
- Itemized deductions reduced by 2% of excess taxable income over $209,250 for joint filers and $104,625 for married filing separately.

2003 Self-Employment Tax(15.3%)
- OASDI (Social Security) - 12.4% of Net Earnings to $87,000 (maximum = $10,788)
- HI (Hospital Insurance) - 2.9% of All Net Earnings
  (See reverse for F.I.C.A.)

TAXABLE INCOME[3]	MARRIED JOINT (St. Ded: $9,500)[2]		MARRIED SEPARATE (St. Ded: $4,750)[2]		TAXABLE INCOME[3]	SINGLE RETURN (St. Ded: $4,750)[2]		HEAD OF HOUSEHOLD (St. Ded: $7,000)[2]	
	FEDERAL TAX	EFFECTIVE RATE	FEDERAL TAX	EFFECTIVE RATE		FEDERAL TAX	EFFECTIVE RATE	FEDERAL TAX	EFFECTIVE RATE
52,000	7,100	13.65	9,810	18.87	52,000	9,810	18.87	8,695	16.72
54,000	7,400	13.70	10,310	19.09	54,000	10,310	19.09	9,195	17.03
56,000	7,700	13.75	10,810	19.30	56,000	10,810	19.30	9,695	17.31
58,000	8,120	14.00	11,330	19.53	58,000	11,310	19.50	10,195	17.58
60,000	8,620	14.37	11,890	19.82	60,000	11,810	19.68	10,695	17.83
62,000	9,120	14.71	12,450	20.08	62,000	12,310	19.85	11,195	18.06
64,000	9,620	15.03	13,010	20.33	64,000	12,810	20.02	11,695	18.27
66,000	10,120	15.33	13,570	20.56	66,000	13,310	20.17	12,195	18.48
68,000	10,620	15.62	14,130	20.78	68,000	13,810	20.31	12,695	18.67
70,000	11,120	15.89	14,690	20.99	70,000	14,346	20.49	13,195	18.85
75,000	12,370	16.49	16,090	21.45	75,000	15,746	20.99	14,445	19.26
80,000	13,620	17.03	17,490	21.86	80,000	17,146	21.43	15,695	19.62
85,000	14,870	17.49	18,890	22.22	85,000	18,546	21.82	16,945	19.94
90,000	16,120	17.91	20,423	22.69	90,000	19,946	22.16	18,195	20.22
95,000	17,370	18.28	22,073	23.23	95,000	21,346	22.47	19,445	20.47
100,000	18,620	18.62	23,723	23.72	100,000	22,746	22.75	20,748	20.75
110,000	21,120	19.20	27,023	24.57	110,000	25,546	23.22	23,548	21.41
120,000	23,781	19.82	30,323	25.27	120,000	28,346	23.62	26,348	21.96
130,000	26,581	20.45	33,623	25.86	130,000	31,146	23.96	29,148	22.42
140,000	29,381	20.99	36,923	26.37	140,000	33,946	24.25	31,948	22.82
150,000	32,181	21.45	40,223	26.82	150,000	37,071	24.71	34,748	23.17
160,000	34,981	21.86	43,603	27.25	160,000	40,371	25.23	37,593	23.50
170,000	37,781	22.22	47,103	27.71	170,000	43,671	25.69	40,893	24.05
180,000	40,846	22.69	50,603	28.11	180,000	46,971	26.10	44,193	24.55
190,000	44,146	23.23	54,103	28.48	190,000	50,271	26.46	47,493	25.00
200,000	47,446	23.72	57,603	28.80	200,000	53,571	26.79	50,793	25.40
225,000	55,696	24.75	66,353	29.49	225,000	61,821	27.48	59,043	26.24
250,000	63,946	25.58	75,103	30.04	250,000	70,071	28.03	67,293	26.92
275,000	72,196	26.25	83,853	30.49	275,000	78,321	28.48	75,543	27.47
300,000	80,446	26.82	92,603	30.87	300,000	86,571	28.86	83,793	27.93
325,000	88,957	27.37	101,353	31.19	325,000	95,082	29.26	92,304	28.40
350,000	97,707	27.92	110,103	31.46	350,000	103,832	29.67	101,054	28.87
375,000	106,457	28.39	118,853	31.69	375,000	112,582	30.02	109,804	29.28
400,000	115,207	28.80	127,603	31.90	400,000	121,332	30.33	118,554	29.64
425,000	123,957	29.17	136,353	32.08	425,000	130,082	30.61	127,304	29.95
450,000	132,707	29.49	145,103	32.25	450,000	138,832	30.85	136,054	30.23
475,000	141,457	29.78	153,853	32.39	475,000	147,582	31.07	144,804	30.48
500,000	150,207	30.04	162,603	32.52	500,000	156,332	31.27	153,554	30.71

Bracket annotations (JOINT): 25% ($56,801–114,650); 28% ($57,326–87,350, Phase Out of Child Credits); 33% ($114,651–174,700, Phase Out of Dependency Exemptions[4]); 35% ($174,701–311,950); $311,951–.

Bracket annotations (SINGLE): 28% ($68,801–143,500, Phase Out of Child Credits[5]); 33% ($143,501–311,950, Phase Out of Dependency Exemptions[4]); 35.0% ($311,951–).

Bracket annotations (HEAD OF HOUSEHOLD): 28% (98,251–159,100, Phase Out of Child Credits[5]); 33% ($159,101–311,950, Phase Out of Dependency Exemptions[4]); 35.0% ($311,951–).

* Chart has been updated as a result of the passage of the Jobs and Growth Tax Relief Reconciliation Act of 2003 on May 28, 2003.

LAW OFFICES:
SCHILLER, DU CANTO AND FLECK
200 N. LA SALLE STREET • CHICAGO, ILLINOIS 60601-1089 • (312) 641-5560
207 E. WESTMINSTER AVENUE • LAKE FOREST, ILLINOIS 60045-1857 • (847) 615-8300
311 S. COUNTY FARM ROAD • WHEATON, ILLINOIS 60187-2438 • (630) 665-5800

4. Personal exemptions are phased out beginning at threshold amounts of $209,250 for joint returns or surviving spouses, $174,400 for heads of households, $139,500 for single taxpayers and $104,6250 for married persons filing separately. The exemption amount is reduced by 2% for each $2,500 ($1,250 for a married person filing separately), or fraction thereof, in excess of the threshold amount.
   Example: Single taxpayer claims himself and has Adjusted Gross Income of $239,500. The amount of his personal exemption that is subject to the phaseout is calculated as follows:

   a. Adjusted gross income ... $239,500
      Threshold Amount ... (139,500)
      Excess amount subject to 2% reduction for each $2,500 ... $100,000
   b. Excess amount divided by phaseout multiple $100,000 ÷ $2,500 = 40; Result multiplied by 2% 40 × 2% = 80%
   c. The $3,050 exemption amount is reduced by $2,440 (80% of $3,050) and the allowable deduction is $610.

5. Child Tax Credit is available for taxpayers with qualifying children, i.e. a child, descendant, stepchild, or eligible foster child who is a U.S. citizen and for whom the taxpayer may claim a dependency exemption and who is less than 17 years old as of the close of the tax year. The amount of the credit is $1,000 per child, and it begins to phase out when the Adjusted Gross Income (AGI) reaches $110,000 for joint filers, $55,000 for marrieds filing separately, and $75,000 for singles including heads of households. Taxpayers who have three or more qualifying children ay also be entitled to an additional credit.

NET INCOME CALCULATION

	HUSBAND	WIFE
1. TAX FILING STATUS		
2. INCOME Employment Other taxable income Alimony[1] Employee retirements contributions[2] ?		
3. ADJUSTED GROSS INCOME[3]		
4. DEDUCTIONS: Standard or excess itemized		
5. EXEMPTIONS		
6. TAXABLE INCOME[4]		
7. FEDERAL TAX[5]		
8. STATE TAX		
9. SOCIAL SECURITY (FICA), MEDICARE, AND/OR OR SELF-EMPLOYMENT TAX[6]		
10. NET DISPOSABLE INCOME[7]		

---

[1] Subtract alimony from the income of the payor; add it to the income of the payee.

[2] Subtract pretax contributions from your income.

[3] Total of section 2.

[4] Subtract your deductions and exemptions from sections 4 and 5 from your adjusted gross income.

[5] See the instructions in the IRS 1040 packet if you want to subtract the earned income credit in this calculation. You can also subtract the child care credit and/or the child credit.

[6] Do not include alimony or other unearned income when calculating this tax.

[7] Subtract the total of lines 7, 8, and 9 from line 6.

INSTRUCTIONS FOR USING THE NET INCOME
CALCULATION FORM

To estimate your future income, gather several years previous tax returns and compare that information to your present pay stubs and other income.

You may use the 10 steps that follow to calculate an estimate of your after-tax incomes under the plan you have worked out so far. If you also calculate your taxes as though you were going to file this last year married filing jointly (or married filing separate and head of household if one of you qualifies), you can contrast these calculations to help you time your final decree (as discussed at the beginning of this chapter). Because many factors can impact the calculation of your net income, you may want to consult a CPA at this time.

1. Determine your likely tax filing status: single or head of household.

2. Add up your likely gross income for the year for each of you, including any alimony you expect to receive. Subtract any alimony you expect to pay. This information could be pulled from your income chart in Chapter 7.

    Subtract your pre-tax contributions to retirement, pension, or other tax-exempt savings plans made from your income (not those made by your employer). You may also subtract cafeteria plan pre-paid estimated day care and/or medical expenses.

3. Your adjusted gross income is the total of your income, with appropriate reductions for alimony and/or nontaxable employee retirement contributions.

4. Subtract either:

    a) The standard deduction for your tax filing status (see the top of each filing status on the DuCanto chart), or

    b) Your likely itemized deductions (see Schedule A of Form 1040 on your previous tax returns). Use the current interest portion of your mortgage and your current property taxes.

5. Subtract the current exemption for yourself and the number of dependent exemptions you have agreed you each will claim (see footnote number 4 on the DuCanto chart).

6. The result from steps 4 and 5 is your taxable income.

7. Find your taxable income on the DuCanto chart (or IRS current tax rate schedule), and write down the amount it shows

you will owe for federal tax. If you qualify for the child care credit and or earned income credit, subtract those amounts from the federal tax amount.

8. Calculate your approximate Connecticut taxes.

9. Figure your Social Security (FICA) or self-employment tax by taking the appropriate percentage (see upper right-hand corner of the DuCanto table) times your earned gross income (step 7). Do not include alimony you expect to receive or other unearned income (interest on investments, for example).

10. Subtract steps 7, 8, and 9 from step 2 to get your estimated net income.

To correct your take-home pay for the rest of the year, give the figures in 2, 7, 8, 9, and 10 to your payroll office or accountant and ask for help to recalculate your W-4. This will adjust your withholding (or estimated tax) now to make your total year-end withholding sufficient to cover your newly calculated taxes. If you are doing tax planning through alimony, you can often increase your current take-home pay if you change your rate of withholding now.

Alimony Recapture and Child-Related Contingency Rules

There are some circumstances under which the IRS may void your alimony arrangement and recapture the deducted payments back into the income of the paying spouse. This not only voids the tax savings back to the beginning but since it is usually discovered later (often in an audit), you could incur interest and penalties as well. These circumstances are contained in two rules:

1. The recapture rule: Alimony must not decrease too fast in the first three years if paid from an income source within payor's control.

2. The related contingency rule: Alimony must not reduce on the "happening of a contingency relating to a child" or a "time which can clearly be associated with [such] a contingency."

RECAPTURE (THE STEEP STAIR-STEP) RULE

The "steep stair-step" rule is designed to prevent "front-end loading"—a large amount of alimony paid in the first year of the divorce and then reduced rapidly within the first three years. Its purpose is to catch divorcing taxpayers who try to use their property settlement as alimony to gain a tax deduction.

The Internal Revenue Code says that $15,000 per year is the cut-off point, so if you plan to pay less than this amount in annual alimony you are in the "safe harbor," as accountants frequently call it. The IRS will examine alimony plans for front-loading for the first three years. So, if you plan any alimony payments of more than $15,000 per year that decrease, don't decrease them rapidly during the first three years.

According to this rule, alimony payments in the first year cannot exceed the payments for the second and third years by more than $15,000. And payments in the second year cannot exceed payments in the third year by more than $15,000. This rule essentially applies to planned excess payments, but prepayments or paying late (for whatever reason) can trigger a recapture if the payment is made in a different calendar year than planned.

To apply this rule, use the following worksheet. This is the form provided by the IRS in Publication 504, Divorced or Separated Individuals.

The term *year* as applied in the formula means "calendar year." Payments made before the divorce (temporary alimony) by a written agreement made into a court order or a court-ordered temporary amount are not included in the recapture calculation. However, if the temporary payments are made by a written agreement that is not made a court order, then those temporary payments are considered in the recapture calculation.

Note that there is no recapture if the reduction of alimony is because of termination of alimony by death or remarriage or if the alimony amount fluctuates by a percentage not in the control of the parties (such as an alimony formula using a percentage of income or business profits).

Temporary payments made before the final divorce, by a written separation agreement which is not made into a court order do count in the alimony considered in this recapture rule. Before-divorce-alimony paid by a written agreement which is made into a court order does not count.

"We have to write up our temporary agreement and take it to the court for the IRS to honor our temporary alimony."

Not quite. The law does not require that you have your temporary agreement made into a court order. You may do so if you want. To be alimony for IRS purposes, it must be by court order or by written agreement.

Worksheet for Recapture of Alimony

Note: Do not enter less than zero on any line.

1. Alimony paid in second year _____

2. Alimony paid in third year _____

3. Floor $15,000

4. Add lines 2 and 3 _____

5. Subtract line 4 from line 1 _____

6. Alimony paid in first year _____

7. Adjusted alimony paid in second year (line 1 less line 5) _____

8. Alimony paid in third year _____

9. Add lines 7 and 8 _____

10. Divide line 9 by 2 _____

11. Floor $15,000

12. Add lines 10 and 11 _____

13. Subtract line 12 from line 6 _____

14. Recaptured alimony. Add lines 5 and 13 _____

Your result is the recaptured alimony, and it is taxed to the person who paid it and deducted from the income of the person who received it in the third post-separation year. Do this calculation for your alimony plan. If your result in step 14 is zero or negative, there will be no recapture under this rule. If your result is positive, adjust the amounts paid under your agreement to avoid recapture.

Any amount paid as temporary alimony before the judgment of divorce, as long as it is by court order, does not have to be counted in this rule. A solution to the problem of high up-front alimony is to pay as much as you can pursuant to your written agreement adopted by the court as a temporary court order before the divorce, where there is no recapture. If you want to start the three-year clock running, begin the payments before the judgment by written agreement and do not have that agreement made into a court order.

THE RELATED CONTINGENCY RULE

As discussed in Chapter 11, the IRS knows that people who are getting divorced try to pay as much as possible to each other in pre-tax-dollars alimony or Section 71 payments.

The IRS tries to restrict child support as alimony by applying the related contingency rule to any reduction in alimony that occurs on or near a date related to a child. There are three circumstances under which the IRS will presume a relationship between the reduction in alimony and children.

- The first one is where the alimony is reduced on the happening of a contingency related to a child. For example, if the separation agreement says that alimony will change when the child reaches a certain age; dies; marries; leaves school, the household, or otherwise emancipates, the IRS would consider the alimony to really be child support.

- The second is if the reduction occurs not more than six months on either side of the date any child reaches eighteen, twenty-one, or the age of emancipation in the state of the child's residence.

- The third is if there are two or more children and two or more reductions in alimony not more than one year before or after the children reach the same chronological age between eighteen and twenty-four.

Example: Mary and Tom have two daughters, Sarah (twelve) and Michele (eighteen). Mary and Tom must be sure that if they reduce alimony one year on either side of when Michele turns twenty that they do not also reduce alimony one year on either side of when Sarah turns twenty.

In any of these circumstances the IRS will presume the reductions are contingencies related to a child and will disallow alimony treatment for the amounts of all reductions and treat these payments retroactively as child support. The IRS will recapture the amount of all such reductions all the way back to the beginning.

Before you throw your hands in the air and give up any hope of an agreement for reducing alimony when your children are leaving the nest, try making the reductions clearly contingent on something that has nothing at all to do with your children. For example: Make the reductions occur regularly over a long period

If your plan calls for a reduction in alimony when any child reaches the age of eighteen, nineteen, twenty-one or majority and/or you plan reductions in maintenance within one year of when your children reach the same age between eighteen and twenty-four, **you must read this section**.

If you are agreeing to alimony *and* have minor children, you should consult with a CPA or divorce attorney and have him or her review your agreement. If on audit the IRS decides your alimony is "disguised" as child support it could disallow the alimony tax treatment.

of time, beginning before any child reaches the "dangerous" age range and continue the payments after that range. Or, make the contingency that triggers the reduction something related to one of you (for example two, four, six, eight, and ten years from the date of the judgment, when the recipient remarries, when the paying spouse retires, or when there is a change in income for either of you). Be sure, however, that these dates do not correspond with a direct child contingency and/or are not within the prohibited child age ranges.

It is possible to rebut the IRS presumption of relatedness of the reductions in alimony with a solid, independent reason for the timing of the reductions. Then, if the reductions just happen to fall in the danger zone, you can plead coincidence, that you did not plan it that way and weren't even thinking about how old your children would be and whether they were nearing emancipation. However, in your tax planning, you should not count on your future ability to persuade the IRS! Overcoming any IRS presumption is very hard to do.

Conclusion

Your first rough look at your tax plan is finished. It will probably not be your final version. Review Chapters 8 through 11 and revise or adjust your tentative agreements according to your tax plan, moving toward reaching your final agreement.

CHAPTER **13**

___

FINISHING UP

FINISHING UP

This chapter is about carrying out all the terms of your separation agreement or court order after a contested trial, including transferring titles to real estate, motor vehicles, stocks, bank accounts, retirements, and other assets. Finishing up also requires paying debts as agreed, which may include a payment by one of you to the other or signing a promissory note and mortgage deed. Notices of changes in either names or addresses are a must.

This chapter also outlines the final steps for finishing a divorce, including information about important legal documents and concepts. You should get legal advice to be sure that you correctly take care of all the final details of your divorce. When the judge incorporates your divorce agreement into your judgment, it becomes an order of the court. As a court order, certain enforcement measures are readily available. If you have problems with enforcement, consult an attorney.

Transfers of Title

If possible, you should have all the forms and documents needed to transfer titles prepared before your uncontested hearing. Sign them along with your separation agreement. This way, you are sure the transfers are signed and avoid the problems associated with trying to find your spouse later to sign. If the transfer will occur after the divorce, your agreement should specify the date the transfers will take place.

Be certain you legally transfer every item. For many items, such as household goods and furniture, transferring ownership is a matter of transferring possession. For other items, like motor vehicles, stocks, bank accounts, and insurance policies, forms are available for you to make these transfers yourself. If any legal documents are needed to transfer certain assets, such as real estate or pensions, you will need to have a lawyer draft and file them for you.

REAL ESTATE

If one spouse is receiving title to what had been jointly owned real estate, a quitclaim deed to the property needs to be prepared and signed by the spouse transferring title. The signature must be properly witnessed and notarized. The quitclaim deed is then recorded in the town clerk's office in the town where the property is located. You may also need a quitclaim deed if you are going to continue to co-own property. In this case, the new deed will speci-

---

Checklist of Titles We Need to Transfer

Directions: With your separation agreement in hand, review it paragraph by paragraph and check each item on the following list which has not yet been transferred according to your agreement. Once the transfer is completed, write the date on the line next to the item.

Real Estate

Check if needed   Date Done

____   Quitclaim Deed   _____

____   Promissory Note   _____

____   Mortgage Deed   _____

Motor Vehicles

____   Title   _____

____   Title   _____

____   Power of Attorney   _____

____   Power of Attorney   _____

Other

____   Stock   _____

____   Stock   _____

____   Bond   _____

____   Bond   _____

____   Bank account   _____

____   Bank account   _____

____   Investment account   _____

____   Investment account   _____

____   IRA   _____

____   IRA   _____

____   401(K) or other savings   _____

____   Pensions   _____

____   Future or current
        pension plan   _____

____   Registered/
        pedigreed pet   _____

____   Membership   _____

____   Ticket Priorities   _____

____   Other   _____

____   _____

____   _____

"We don't need to do all this paperwork after the divorce. We trust each other."

Trust is not enough to cover the possibilities your future may hold. Should either of you become disabled or die or feel pressure from future relationships, things could get very difficult indeed without this paperwork.

If you filed a Notice of *Lis Pendens* at the beginning of the case (*see* p. 102), you should prepare and file a Release of *Lis Pendens* with the quitclaim deed. This document releases the notice to creditors and others that the real estate is part of a disputed court action. You should contact an attorney to obtain advice concerning the preparation and filing of a Release of *Lis Pendens*.

fy the proportion of ownership and survivor agreements that you have made.

Property transferred between spouses as a part of a divorce is exempt from the normal requirements for the payment of real estate conveyance taxes for the state and town. However, to benefit from this exemption, you must complete and file special forms with the town clerk. These forms are also obtained from the town clerk's office.

Use a promissory note to ensure any future installment payments that are part of your property settlement. In addition, to secure the payment, you can use a mortgage deed against real estate or as security on other property. Payments may be regular and frequent, variable in amount, or in one lump sum. There are published forms for promissory notes, but you may want to have a lawyer prepare the notes so they are drafted and filed correctly.

When a promissory note is signed by the person promising to pay, the original should be kept by the person who will receive the payments. When the note is paid in full, the recipient should write "Paid in full" across the face of the original note, sign it, and return the original to the person who paid it, keeping a photocopy for records. Any security, such as a mortgage deed, should then be released.

A mortgage deed is the document that spells out the terms of your promissory note and, when recorded with the town clerk where the property is located, creates a lien against real estate. The real estate thus becomes security for the payment. The real estate must be owned by the person who signs the promissory note and mortgage deed. If there is already a mortgage on the real estate, the new mortgage and mortgage deed become a second mortgage. If there is already a second mortgage on the property, the new mortgage becomes a third, etc.

There are published quitclaim deeds, promissory notes and mortgage forms, each with different enforcement provisions. However, it is highly recommended that a lawyer handle the entire real estate transaction to ensure it is done correctly.

PERSONAL PROPERTY

Items of personal property do not usually have a title. Normally, ownership comes from possession. With the entry of your judgment, your separation agreement controls ownership. You should physically divide your personal property by the time of the divorce or at the time you sign your separation agreement. If one of you will hold some pieces of personal property for the other, clearly state that arrangement in your separation agreement.

Art and other creative works can frequently be a problem if they come into vogue and therefore increase in value after the divorce. If the item does not have a paper title now, you can create one by drafting a bill of sale that describes the item in detail. For example, "12 x 24 watercolor of boat and dock in shades of blue, with six-line original poem in calligraphy on bottom right corner." Create a paper trail for the disposition of your valuable things now and you won't have to locate each other later when you want to sell or transfer them.

MOTOR VEHICLES

It is relatively easy to transfer titles to motor vehicles. The person who keeps the vehicle should obtain the spouse's signature on the title. You may then take the signed title to the Department of Motor Vehicles and request a new title and registration in your name.

If there is a loan on the vehicle, the lender probably holds the title. Typically, lenders do not allow either party to sign off the title until the loan is paid in full. In this case, the releasing spouse signs a form usually available at any office of the Department of Motor Vehicles or from the lender. Take the signed form to the Department of Motor Vehicles in your area; they will issue the proper documentation.

MOTOR VEHICLE INSURANCE

Contact your agent to separate your motor vehicle insurance. You will likely separate one of your cars from the family policy, and your agent will do this for you. If there are only two cars, you will both lose the multi-car discount. Be very clear about who will be insuring your children and the cars they drive.

LIQUID ASSETS: CASH AND BANK ACCOUNTS

Cash is, of course, easy to divide; just count it out. If you have significant amounts, prepare and sign a receipt.

Transferring ownership of bank accounts usually requires one or both of you to prepare a new signature card or to sign other transfer documents the bank provides. Be sure that the bank has the correct Social Security number on each account after the transfer.

Directions: Complete the following checklists as they relate to your situations. Use separate pieces of paper as necessary.

Personal Property Transfer Checklist
We have the following artworks, antiques, and collectibles which have been transferred in writing and in fact as follows:

Item	To Whom	Date Transferred
_____	_____	_____
_____	_____	_____
_____	_____	_____

Motor Vehicle Transfer Checklist
Wife/Husband (or husband and wife) has (have) transferred title or signed power of attorney to husband/wife of:

Vehicle Descrption	Date Transferred
_____	_____

Bank Account Transfer Checklist
Only husband's name appears on the following bank accounts:

Bank	Type of Account	Date Transferred
_____	_____	_____
_____	_____	_____

Only wife's name appears on the following bank accounts:

Bank	Type of Account	Date Transferred
_____	_____	_____
_____	_____	_____

Stocks, Bonds and Securities Transfer Checklist

Stock/Bond	To Whom/Date
_____	_____
_____	_____
_____	_____
_____	_____
_____	_____

Insurance Transfer Checklist

Directions: Fill out the following as you complete each item.

Husband has changed his insurance policies as follows:

Life insurance at _____ (company) now benefits _____.

Life insurance at _____ (company) now benefits _____.

Health insurance at _____ (company) now covers _____.

Car insurance on _____ (vehicles) is in his name only.

Wife has changed her insurance policies as follows:

Life insurance at _____ (company) now benefits _____.

Life insurance at _____ (company) now benefits _____.

Health insurance at _____ (company) now covers _____.

Car insurance on _____ (vehicles) is in her name only.

Non-employee spouse has elected _____ years of COBRA option through _____ and completed the paper work so that coverage for _____ will begin on _____(date).

STOCKS, BONDS, AND OTHER SECURITIES

If you own stocks and bonds through a brokerage account, it is sufficient to simply change the name on the account, or, if you are dividing the contents of the account, open a second account with the same broker and ask that they allocate shares between the two accounts as you agree. As long as you don't sell any of your securities, you will not incur any taxes transferring these securities between you.

If you have the actual stock certificates, you will find a form on the back of the certificate for transferring ownership. Be sure after you fill it out that you sign it in front of the proper authority. The new owner must present the signed certificate to the company so that it can prepare a new certificate and transfer ownership on the books of the company.

If you own bonds and they are not part of an investment account and you do not know how to transfer them, contact the entity that issued the bond (U.S., municipality, private corporation, etc.)

LIFE INSURANCE

Transfer ownership of life insurance by completing forms from the insurance company. Contact your agent or the company directly to obtain the appropriate forms.

Be sure to make any necessary changes in your beneficiary designation required by your agreement. Your designation must be absolutely accurate. You may obtain a copy of your existing beneficiary designation from the insurance company. If your agreement is to continue designating each other for the benefit of the children, be sure your designation does not refer to the other as "wife," "husband," or "spouse" but rather uses full names, as this prevents serious ambiguities if you remarry.

MEDICAL INSURANCE: COBRA

Make certain that if the non-employee spouse is electing the COBRA option to continue his or her medical insurance you prepare all the necessary paperwork before the final judgment. There is a grace period within which a former spouse is covered, usually thirty days from the judgment.

RETIREMENT, PENSIONS, AND PROFIT SHARING

IRAs can be divided by directly transferring all or some of the balance to a similar account in the name of the other spouse. As long as such a transfer is done by one trustee to another (a "qualified rollover") and the money in no way comes directly into your hands, you will avoid withholding, taxes, and penalties. See Chapter 10.

To transfer all or a part of a military retirement, contact: DFAS-CL-L, PO Box 998002, Cleveland, OH 44199-8002. For forms and procedures, call (216)522-5301. Similarly, for Civil Service Retirement System and Federal Employees Retirement System, contact the pension office for their transfer forms and procedures.

For plans covered by E.R.I.S.A. and divisible or transferable by Qualified Domestic Relations Order (QDRO), send a certified copy of the QDRO, previously signed by the judge, to the plan administrator who carries out the transfer described in the order. See Chapter 10 for information about transfers of retirement accounts in general.

Remember that transfers of pensions, profit sharing, and retirement can be legally complex. To ensure the correct transfer, you should have an attorney prepare the documents for the court.

BUSINESS INTERESTS

If your business interest is a corporation, the transaction may involve a simple transfer of stock from one spouse to the other or from both spouses to one spouse. In some cases, however, the division of an interest in a corporation or the value of that corporation is extremely complex and requires a CPA and/or attorney to complete.

For either a partnership or a sole proprietorship, usually no other transfer of ownership is necessary beyond the statement in your separation agreement. In some cases, however, the spouses will continue to share ownership in the business or will need to transfer title to business assets. For these reasons, you should consult with a CPA and/or attorney to assist you in a complete and accurate ownership transfer.

OTHER ASSETS

For other assets, contact the related institution or organization to find out what they require. For pedigreed animals, for example, contact the breed organization. For sports or cultural ticket priorities, contact the ticket office. For frequent flyer miles, contact the airline to see if it permits transfer and if so, how to do it.

Retirement Transfer Checklist

Directions: Complete the following as it relates to your situation. Use separate pieces of paper if necessary:

Retirement	To Whom/Date
_____	_____
_____	_____
_____	_____

Business Interests Transfer Checklist

Directions: Complete the following as it relates to your situation. Use separate pieces of paper if necessary:

Business Interest	To Whom/Date
_____	_____
_____	_____
_____	_____

Notice of Change of Name Checklist

Directions: Check off each of the following for each of you, as needed, as you send or show a conformed copy of your signed judgment along with whatever form they require for a change of name:

Husband	Wife	
_____	_____	State Department of Motor Vehicles Drivers License Office
_____	_____	U. S. Social Security office (to change the name on your Social Security card)
_____	_____	bank
_____	_____	credit union
_____	_____	mortgage company
_____	_____	every creditor and credit card each of you will continue to use
_____	_____	doctor
_____	_____	dentist
_____	_____	children's school
_____	_____	day care
_____	_____	pediatrician
_____	_____	other
_____	_____	

You probably do not need to supply a copy of the signed judgment to most other people who need to know about your change of name, but do not forget to notify them. Some examples of places and people not to forget are:

_____	_____	newspaper and magazine subscriptions
_____	_____	membership organizations
_____	_____	personal correspondents
_____	_____	other
_____	_____	
_____	_____	

DEBTS

As a rule, you don't need to notify creditors about your divorce—or that one of you is now responsible for paying the debt rather than both of you. It's very important, however, to be sure each creditor has the address of the person responsible for paying. If it was a joint debt, you may ask the creditor to remove the non-paying spouse's name from the debt, but the remaining spouse must have sufficient income alone to manage the debt. Remember that the creditor has no obligation to do this. See "Dealing with Debt" in Chapter 10.

Changing Your Name

If one spouse has a former name restored as part of the divorce, make photocopies of the final judgment and give or send one to anyone who needs official notice of the new name. Some entities may require a certified (raised seal) copy. You can obtain this at the clerk of the court's office for $25.

Changing Your Address

You probably agreed fairly early in your separation how to divide the mail. You each did, or should now do, a change of address for any mail sent to each of you individually. But what about mail, magazines, etc., which come addressed to Mr. and Mrs.? Holiday cards will prove particularly difficult if you are not clear about this. Usually, it is best to agree that one of you will receive the joint mail, sort it, and promptly send or deliver any of interest to the other spouse. However, the most innocuous mail can sometimes prove explosive—the catalog from which you disagreed about a large purchase, for example. If you have even the slightest doubt about the volatility of exchanging mail in person, don't. Send it in a large envelope—after leaving a telephone message telling the other spouse that it is coming.

Scheduling Later Events

Your agreement may provide for some transfers of title or payments or changes and stair-steps in your parenting, support, or alimony plans that will take place on a date or event in the future. For example, you may agree to sell the home when the last child emancipates and pay the other spouse his or her interest in the home. You may anticipate changes in your parenting plan, in the support of your children, or of each other. Be sure to schedule all these now and have a system to remind you of the date. If the payout or transfer is tied to the sale of the home, put a note to yourself on the deed or mortgage deed in the house file or safety deposit box. If an event is tied to the tax year, put a note in your tax file. If you relate an event to a child's age, put a note in that child's file.

If your circumstances change after the divorce and you and your spouse can't reach an agreement to change the support or parenting terms, you can consider filing a motion for modification (Form JD-FM-174). However, prior to changing your agreement or filing a motion for modification you should consult with an attorney so that you know you are complying with all legalities.

Checking Your Credit Ratings

Whether or not you requested your credit ratings during the early stages of your negotiations, you should do this now. Finishing your divorce with a positive credit rating is a major step toward financial health in the years to come. Make certain that any corrections to your credit reports include your new name(s) along with your correct addresses. See Chapters 7 and 10 for more about credit.

Making Things Happen: Enforcement

One or both of you may be less than reliable about making promised payments or find yourself unable or unwilling to follow through with transfers of property. You may need to invoke the teeth you included in your agreement, or you may need to seek outside help in getting things back on track. For example, you may need to activate a wage withholding. You may need a court order for something your divorce order (whether by agreement or contested trial) calls for but has not happened.

INTERNAL ENFORCEMENT

If some element of your agreement does not work as planned, look first to the agreement itself. Did you anticipate this event and provide for what was to happen? For example, did you agree that a missed or late payment of alimony means a loss of the tax deductibility? Does a mortgage default mean the other spouse may take back the home? Does unpaid support mean the receiving spouse gets access to a bank account? You may want to revisit the ideas of "teeth" and security detailed in previous chapters.

If you find that your agreement did not anticipate the present problem, try to find the least expensive, least damaging means of fixing it. The more of your agreement you leave intact, the more chance there is that the erring spouse will feel able to honor the

Notice of Change of Address Checklist

Directions: Fill in the following statements according to your agreement:

Husband will notify the following of his change of address, if any:

Wife will notify the following of her change of address, if any:

We will handle the joint mail as follows:

For a copy of the Motion to Modify go to **www.jud.state. ct.us/forms/fm174.pdf**.

rest of the provisions once you resolve the immediate difficulty. As difficult as it may be, try to focus only on the thing that has gone wrong. If you allow your frustrations about the current problems to lead you back into all the old resentments, you are apt to forget the harmony you found when you were able work together.

Security

If you fear that one of you might not be able to comply with the agreement, especially about large ticket items, see if there is some way to secure the action. For example, agree to withhold the transfer of title to an asset until the debt is paid. Record a mortgage deed against real estate. Sometimes you can sign over title to the person who should receive an asset on the payment of certain money but hold the signed paperwork in the file with the attorney or mediator until you receive such payment.

Wage Withholding

Wage withholding can either be an informal arrangement between the employee and his or her employer or a court order to withhold a regular amount of money each payday and forward it to the other spouse. This removes the danger of memory lapse as well as all temptation to spend the money by effectively making someone else responsible for making the payments for you.

Some people set up their own private automatic payment by creating an automatic transfer from the bank or credit union account of the paying spouse to an account of the receiving spouse. Check the cost of this beforehand if you are considering this option.

ENFORCEMENT THROUGH THE COURT

The court will stand in the place of the non-cooperative spouse and transfer the property for him or her by court order. The court can open the door for you to obtain money directly from your spouse's assets and can punish the spouse for non-compliance to make him or her comply. If you need to enforce any part of your divorce judgment through the court, consult an attorney.

Failure to obey the court support orders can result in the suspension of his or her driver's license, professional or occupational license, or recreational license after thirty days.

To avoid these post-divorce court actions, you should transfer title to assets on or before the final uncontested hearing. If you are unable to get your ex-spouse's signature on a title transfer, you can file a motion with the court directing that the title be transferred to you. Again, it is best to get legal advice on these issues.

Reduction to Judgment

When the court incorporates your separation agreement into the divorce judgment, it makes your agreement an order of the court. Everything you promise to do in the agreement is now required by the court and therefore more than a private contract. If one of you fails to keep any agreement about the payment of money, the court may enter another judgment or further orders using the legal means available for collection of judgments, including attachment of wages and/or property. If your ex-spouse fails to convey the actual property to you (for example, keeps the boat or car), you can file what is known as a *replevin action* with the court. These procedures usually require the assistance of a lawyer.

Contempt Citation

A contempt citation is based on the premise that anyone who does not comply with a court order offends the authority of the court. When the court makes your separation agreement an order of the court by incorporating it into the judgment, enforcement by way of a contempt proceeding is available to you. The aggrieved person files a motion stating that the ex-spouse has not done what the court said he or she should do. The court then orders the offending party to appear in court to "show cause," or explain or prove, why he or she should not be held in contempt.

If the court finds that the accused person had the ability to comply with the court order and willfully failed to do so, the court can enter a fine, money judgment, and/or jail sentence. In most cases, the court will suspend the entry of any penalty for a period of time to give the non-complying party a chance to comply. Contempt citations can thus come up for review after review, waiting for a promising party to come through with money or action. A contempt citation usually requires a lawyer to prepare, argue, or defend it. Contempt procedures can be expensive and may not always be satisfactory enforcement methods.

Federal Law Enforcement of Parenting Plans: PKPA and UCCJEA

There are two federal laws that help enforce custody and visitation orders from state to state. The Parental Kidnapping Prevention Act (PKPA) makes it a crime to transfer a child across state lines in violation of a custody order. It permits the FBI and other federal agencies to enforce custody orders in this event.

"Figuratively if not literally, the participants shall come to see themselves as working side by side, attacking the problem, not each other."

Roger Fisher and William Ury, *Getting To Yes.*

"If it ain't broke, don't fix it."

"I'll make him pay through the court. That way if he misses a payment they'll go after him."

Wage withholding payments through the court are not a means of enforcement. The court does not automatically know when payments are not made and therefore does not take action to enforce the order. You must initiate enforcement by filing a request with the court.

The court may, if requested by any party or on its own, order all parties to mediate requests for modification of custody or parenting time.

The Uniform Child Custody Jurisdiction Enforcement Act (UCCJEA) sets guidelines about which state is the right one to make decisions about a given child's custody. This question comes up if the parents live in different states at the time of the divorce or if one parent moves the children to another state after the divorce judgment. This law helps to prevent forum shopping in which a parent moves with the children from state to state until he or she can find one that will give him or her custody or change an old custody order.

Both of these laws are beyond the scope of this book. If you need enforcement under one of these laws, you should consult an attorney.

Title IV D—The Connecticut Child Support Enforcement Program

The IV-D program through the Support Enforcement Services Unit offers a variety of services: establishing and enforcing support orders, establishing paternity, reviewing and adjusting support orders, and providing payment processing services. This program can be particularly helpful if the parent owing the child support lives out of state. See Chapter 9, Child Support.

Using these procedures can be quite slow due to the volume of cases and the necessity of finding and personally serving the person who is not paying. However, if your ex-spouse does not pay support as provided in the temporary orders or final judgment of divorce, this is the least expensive means of collection, especially across state lines. Like contempt citations and garnishments, the technical instructions for this kind of enforcement are beyond the scope of this book. If you need this kind of help, call the office of your local assistant attorney general or a support enforcement office.

Two other ways to collect child support are only available through the IV-D program: income tax offsets and consumer credit reporting. For the Federal and State Income Tax Offset program, the other parent must owe more than $500 if your children have never received public assistance or more than $150 if they have received public assistance. After written notice and time to contest the claim, the other parent's tax refund check will be intercepted. The Consumer Credit Reporting program arranges for unpaid child support of more than $1,000 to be automatically reported to the major credit reporting agencies as an overdue debt on a monthly basis.

Can We Change Our Agreement
After the Court Approves It?

This section reviews the issues relating to changing court divorce orders whether entered by agreement or after a trial. The legal term for this is *modification*. If you are agreeing to the changes, you should write them up, sign them, and file them with the court. To file your modifications with the court to officially modify your old order, you can follow the procedure in Chapter 6 for making an agreement into a court order—but delete the word *temporary* from the example.

If you can't agree to a modification, the person who wants it must file a motion for modification.

If only one of you is asking the court to change the order, you must follow certain rules for the court to do what you want. These rules differ from one area to another, i.e., from property to custody, from child support to alimony. You cannot change some orders because of the law, the way you may have written limitations into your separation agreement, or by the terms of the court order. It is important that you consult with an attorney about the legalities of future modifications *before* you settle your case—and after the divorce if you are considering a modification.

MODIFYING YOUR PROPERTY AND DEBT DIVISION

The court generally cannot change your agreement about property and debts without the agreement of you and your former spouse. In practice, the only grounds for changing a property division without agreement are by showing that the original separation agreement was the result of fraud or duress or mutual mistake. The court generally will not modify or set aside your final division of property and debts even if you made mistakes in your interpretation of the tax consequences or made honest mistakes about the value of assets or the balances of debts. It is therefore a good idea to approach the property and debts portion of your agreement as though chiseled in stone.

MODIFYING YOUR PARENTING PLAN

The court keeps jurisdiction over children and custody arrangements until your children emancipate. You always have the right to ask the court to modify your custody arrangements even if your separation agreement says that a provision relating to your children is "nonmodifiable." You must, however, have sufficient legal grounds, unless you both agree in writing to the change.

Every unpaid installment of child support automatically becomes a judgment enforceable by the spouse who was to receive the payment or by the child being supported.

MODIFYING CHILD SUPPORT

The court keeps jurisdiction over child support until your children emancipate. You always have the right to ask the court to modify child support even if your agreement says that child support is nonmodifiable. You may agree to a review of the support amount annually after exchanging the previous year's tax returns. If you do not want to require this annually, you might provide in your agreement that you will exchange income information more frequently to review child support at the request of either one of you. This means you will always cooperate; neither of you can say no.

If you are considering child support modification, fill in your new incomes on a new child support worksheet. If the child support amount changes by more than 15 percent in either direction, the law gives the court the authority to modify child support. If you have an agreement about modification, file the new worksheet with the court, along with your signed agreement to pay or accept the new amount.

If you seek a modification of your child support agreement but cannot agree to the terms, you will need sufficient grounds to ask the court to change your agreement. The grounds for changing the support amount are "a substantial change of circumstance." In a case utilizing the Child Support Guidelines, the fact that the child support changes by more than 15 percent (up or down) creates a presumption that child support should be modified.

If you change the primary physical custody of your children you will probably need to change the child support accordingly. You can still agree to the approaches to child support suggested in Chapter 9 to avoid having the Child Support Guidelines force you into an unworkable amount for either the paying or receiving parent.

MODIFYING ALIMONY

Modifying or changing alimony probably generates more horror stories among lawyers and divorcing couples than any other aspect of divorce. The misunderstandings are many, and the consequences are sometimes unforeseen and unpleasant. It is vital that you review the chapters on alimony and taxes if you are thinking of modifying your alimony. Because the original alimony provisions of the divorce judgment control whether the amount can be modified in the future, you should consult with an attorney *before* you settle your divorce case so that you fully understand your future rights and responsibilities. If you are considering modification, an attorney will help you to analyze your options and assist in the procedures.

The grounds for asking the court to modify alimony are that there has been "a substantial change of circumstances." If you want the alimony to be nonmodifiable, you must state this clearly in your agreement.

If you and/or your spouse waived your right(s) to alimony in your original agreement then there is probably no hope of modifying alimony now—even if you both agree. The IRS definition of alimony requires that it be under or incident to a divorce or separation instrument. That is generally accepted to mean that it must be agreed to or at least contemplated at the time of the judgment. If you want to leave the door open for alimony later (for a spouse with a chronic illness in remission or an unhealed injury, for example), that spouse must not waive alimony in the final judgment and separation agreement. You could set alimony at $1 per year and, if you choose, state in your agreement the conditions that might give rise to the need for alimony in the future.

A Note About Privacy

If you agree to exchange income tax returns annually to re-evaluate child support, then you will likely learn a great deal more about your former spouse's new spouse's income than anyone may be comfortable with. You might want to agree instead that if either of you re-marries, you will exchange W-2s, 1099s, Schedule Cs (business profit & loss), K-1s, rental profit and loss statements, and corporate tax returns, all concerning the income and businesses of your former spouse only.

APPENDIX A: CONNECTICUT JUDICIAL DISTRICTS

Find the town or city where you or your spouse lives to identify your judicial district.

Town	Judicial District
Andover	Tolland
Ansonia	Ansonia-Milford
Ashford	Windham
Avon	Hartford-New Britain
Barkhamsted	Litchfield
Beacon Falls	Ansonia-Milford
Berlin	Hartford-New Britain
Bethany	New Haven or Ansonia-Milford
Bethel	Danbury
Bethlehem	Litchfield
Bloomfield	Hartford-New Britain
Bolton	Tolland
Bozrah	New London
Branford	New Haven
Bridgeport	Fairfield
Bridgewater	Litchfield
Bristol	Hartford-New Britain
Brookfield	Danbury
Brooklyn	Windham
Burlington	Hartford-New Britain
Canaan	Litchfield
Canterbury	Windham
Canton	Hartford-New Britain
Chaplin	Windham
Cheshire	New Haven
Chester	Middlesex
Clinton	Middlesex
Colchester	New London
Colebrook	Litchfield
Columbia	Tolland
Cornwall	Litchfield or Hartford-New Britain
Coventry	Tolland
Cromwell	Middlesex

Town	Judicial District
Danbury	Danbury
Darien	Stamford-Norwalk or Fairfield
Deep River	Middlesex
Derby	Ansonia-Milford
Durham	Middlesex
Eastford	Windham
East Granby	Hartford-New Britain
East Haddam	Middlesex
East Hampton	Middlesex
East Hartford	Hartford-New Britain
East Haven	New Haven
East Lyme	New London
East Windsor	Hartford-New Britain or Tolland
Easton	Fairfield
Ellington	Tolland
Enfield	Hartford-New Britain or Tolland
Essex	Middlesex
Fairfield	Fairfield
Farmington	Hartford-New Britain
Franklin	New London
Glastonbury	Hartford-New Britain
Goshen	Litchfield
Granby	Hartford-New Britain
Greenwich	Stamford-Norwalk or Fairfield
Griswold	New London
Groton	New London
Guilford	New Haven
Haddam	Middlesex
Hamden	New Haven
Hampton	Windham
Hartford	Hartford-New Britain
Hartland	Litchfield
Harwinton	Litchfield

Town	Judicial District
Hebron	Tolland
Kent	Litchfield
Killingly	Windham
Killingworth	Middlesex
Lebanon	New London
Ledyard	New London
Lisbon	New London
Litchfield	Litchfield
Lyme	New London
Madison	New Haven
Manchester	Hartford-New Britain or Tolland
Mansfield	Tolland
Marlborough	Hartford-New Britain
Meriden	New Haven
Middlebury	Waterbury
Middlefield	Middlesex
Middletown	Middlesex
Milford	Ansonia-Milford or New Haven
Monroe	Fairfield
Montville	New London
Morris	Litchfield
Naugatuck	Waterbury
New Britain	Hartford-New Britain
New Canaan	Stamford-Norwalk or Fairfield
New Fairfield	Danbury
New Hartford	Litchfield
New Haven	New Haven
Newington	Hartford-New Britain
New London	New London
New Milford	Litchfield
Newtown	Danbury
Norfolk	Litchfield
North Branford	New Haven
North Canaan	Litchfield
North Haven	New Haven
North Stonington	New London
Norwalk	Stamford-Norwalk or Fairfield

Town	Judicial District
Norwich	New London
Old Lyme	New London
Old Saybrook	Middlesex
Orange	Ansonia-Milford
Oxford	Ansonia-Milford
Pawcatuck	Norwich
Plainfield	Windham
Plainville	Hartford-New Britain
Plymouth	Hartford-New Britain or Waterbury
Pomfret	Windham
Portland	Middlesex
Preston	New London
Prospect	Waterbury
Putnam	Windham
Redding	Danbury
Ridgefield	Danbury
Rocky Hill	Hartford-New Britain
Roxbury	Litchfield
Salem	New London
Salisbury	Litchfield
Scotland	Windham
Seymour	Ansonia-Milford
Sharon	Litchfield
Shelton	Ansonia-Milford
Sherman	Danbury
Simsbury	Hartford-New Britain
Somers	Tolland
Southbury	Waterbury or Ansonia-Milford
Southington	Hartford-New Britain
South Windsor	Hartford-New Britain or Tolland
Sprague	New London
Stafford	Tolland
Stamford	Stamford-Norwalk or Fairfield
Sterling	Windham
Stonington	New London
Stratford	Fairfield
Suffield	Hartford-New Britain

Town	Judicial District
Thomaston	Litchfield
Thompson	Windham
Tolland	Tolland
Torrington	Litchfield
Trumbull	Fairfield
Union	Tolland
Vernon	Tolland
Voluntown	New London
Wallingford	New Haven
Warren	Litchfield
Washington	Litchfield
Waterbury	Waterbury or Litchfield
Waterford	New London
Watertown	Waterbury
Westbrook	Middlesex
West Hartford	Hartford-New Britain
West Haven	Ansonia-Milford or New Haven
Weston	Stamford-Norwalk or Fairfield
Westport	Stamford-Norwalk or Fairfield
Wethersfield	Hartford-New Britain
Willimantic	Windham
Willington	Tolland
Wilton	Stamford-Norwalk or Fairfield
Winchester	Litchfield
Windham	Windham
Windsor	Hartford-New Britain
Windsor Locks	Hartford-New Britain
Wolcott	Waterbury
Woodbridge	New Haven or Ansonia-Milford
Woodbury	Waterbury or Litchfield
Woodstock	Windham

Judicial District	Court Location	Clerk's Address	Phone
New Haven	New Haven	235 Church Street New Haven, CT 06510	(203)789-7098
New Haven-Meriden	Meriden	54 West Main Street Meriden, CT 06450	(203)238-6666
Hartford-New Britain	Hartford	95 Washington Street Hartford, CT 06106	(860)566-3170
Hartford-New Britain	New Britain	177 Columbus Boulevard New Britain, CT 06051	(860)827-7133
Fairfield	Bridgeport	1061 Main Street Bridgeport, CT 06604	(203)579-6527
New London	New London	70 Huntington Street New London, CT 06320	(860)443-5363
New London	Norwich	One Courthouse Square Norwich, CT 06360	(860)887-3515
Ansonia-Milford	Milford	14 West River Street Milford, CT 06460	(203)877-4293
Waterbury	Waterbury	300 Grand Street Waterbury, CT 06702	(203)596-4023
Middlesex	Middletown	One Court Street Middleton, CT 06457-3374	(860)343-6400
Danbury	Danbury	146 White Street Danbury, CT 06810	(203)797-4400
Litchfield	Litchfield	15 West Street Litchfield, CT 06759	(860)567-0885
Tolland	Rockville	69 Brooklyn Street Rockville, CT 06066	(860)875-6294
Windham	Putnam	155 Church Street Putnam, CT 06260	(860)928-7749
Stamford-Norwalk	Stamford	123 Hoyt Street Stamford, CT 06905	(203)965-5307

APPENDIX B: PARENTING EDUCATION PROGRAMS

Approved by the
State of Connecticut Judicial Branch

Ansonia-Milford Judicial District

1. Griffin Hospital
   Dept. of Psychiatry and Social Services
   130 Division Street
   Derby, CT 06418
   (203)732-7550

2. Catholic Family Services
   203 High Street
   Milford, CT 06460
   (203)874-6270

3. Catholic Family Services
   205 Wakelee Avenue
   Ansonia, CT 06401
   (203)735-7481

Danbury Judicial District

1. Catholic Family Services
   30 Main Street, Suite 503
   Danbury, CT 06810-3004
   (203)743-4412

2. Family Counseling Center
   121 Mount Pleasant Road
   Newtown, CT 06870
   (203)426-8103

Fairfield Judicial District (Bridgeport)

1. Catholic Family Services
   238 Jewett Avenue
   Bridgeport, CT 06606
   (203)372-4301

2. Family Services—Woodfield
   475 Clinton Avenue
   Bridgeport, CT 06605
   (203)368-4291

3. Jewish Family Service
   2370 Park Avenue
   Bridgeport, CT 06604
   (203)366-5438

Hartford Judicial District

1. CT Council of Family Service Agencies
   (To attend a Parenting Education Program
   at one of the following agencies, call
   (860)527-1124 ext. 218.)

   A. Catholic Family Services/Institute for
      the Hispanic Family
      896 Asylum Avenue
      Hartford, CT 06105
      (860)522-8241

   B. Village for Families and Children
      1680 Albany Avenue
      Hartford, CT 06105
      (860)236-4511

   C. Jewish Family Service of
      Greater Hartford
      Crossroads Plaza
      740 Main Street
      West Hartford, CT 06117
      (860)236-1927

2. Pathfinders Advocacy Group
   17 South Highland Street
   West Hartford, CT 06119
   (860)726-1099

3. Community Child Guidance Clinic, Inc.
   317 North Main Street
   Manchester, CT 06040
   (860)643-2101

4. Windsor Parent Education Program
   Yardley Associates, LLP
   Courtyard by Marriott
   One Day Hill Road
   Windsor, CT 06095
   (860)688-1240

5. Enfield Parent Education Program
   Yardley Associates, LLP
   Asnuntuck Community College
   17 Elm Street
   Enfield, CT 06082
   (860)688-8240

Litchfield Judicial District

1. University of Connecticut
   Cooperative Extension System
   1304 Winsted Road
   Torrington, CT 06790
   (888)311-8842

2. CT Council of Family Service Agencies
   (To attend a Parenting Education Program
   at one of the following agencies, call
   (860)482-8561.)

   A. Catholic Family Services
      132 Grove Street
      Torrington, CT 06790
      (860)482-5558

   B. Northwest Center for Family Services
      and Mental Health
      564 Prospect Street
      Torrington, CT 06790
      (860)482-8561

   C. Northwest Center for Family Services
      and Mental Health
      315 Main Street
      Lakeville, CT 06039
      (860)435-2529

3. New Milford Hospital
   Community Mental Health Services
   18 Elm Street
   New Milford, CT 06776
   (860)354-3762

Meriden Judicial District

1. Catholic Family Services
   61 Colony Street
   Meriden, CT 06451
   (203)235-2507

Middlesex Judicial District

1. Hiebel and Roeder Family and
   Child Associates
   300 Plaza Middlesex
   203 Main Street
   Middletown, CT 06457
   (860)347-9911

New Britain Judicial District

1. Wheeler Clinic
   91 Northwest Drive
   Plainville, CT 06062
   (860)793-3533

2. CT Council of Family Service Agencies
   (To attend a Parenting Education Program
   at one of the following agencies, call
   (860)223-9291.)

   A. Catholic Family Services
      90 Franklin Square
      New Britain, CT 06051
      (860)225-3561

   B. Family Service of Central Connecticut
      92 Vine Street
      New Britain, CT 06052
      (860)223-9292

New Haven Judicial District

1. Clinical Associates of Connecticut, PC
   58-60 Boston Street
   Guilford, CT 06437
   (203)458-0661

2. CT Council of Family Service Agencies
   (To attend a Parenting Education Program
   at one of the following agencies, call
   (203)389-5599.)

   A. Catholic Family Services
      478 Orange Street
      New Haven, CT 06511
      (203)787-2207

   B. Family Counseling of Greater
      New Haven
      One Long Wharf Drive, Suite 126
      New Haven, CT 06511
      (203)495-7431

   C. Jewish Family Services of New Haven
      1440 Whalley Avenue
      New Haven, CT 06515
      (203)389-5599

Norwich-New London Judicial District

1. University of Connecticut
   Cooperative Extension System
   562 New London Turnpike
   Norwich, CT 06360
   (888)311-8842

2. Lymes' Youth Services Bureau
   PO Box 589
   59 Lyme Street
   Old Lyme, CT 06371
   (860)434-7208

3. CT Council of Family Service Agencies
   (To attend a Parenting Education Program
   at one of the following agencies, call
   (860)892-7042 ext. 323.)

   A. Big Brothers Big Sisters of South-
      eastern Connecticut
      224 Eastern Point Road
      Groton, CT 06340
      (860)445-2274

   B. Catholic Charities/Catholic Family
      Services
      331 Main Street
      Norwich, CT 06360
      (860)889-8346

   C. United Community & Family Services
      400 Bayonet Street, Suite 103
      New London, CT 06320
      (860)442-4319

   D. United Community & Family Services
      47 East Town Street
      Norwich, CT 06360-2326
      (860)892-7042 ext. 323

Stamford-Norwalk Judicial District

1. CT Council of Family Service Agencies
   (To attend a Parenting Education Program
   at one of the following agencies, call
   (203)324-3167.)

   A. Family Centers, Inc.
      40 Arch Street
      PO Box 7550
      Greenwich, CT 06836-7550
      (203)869-4848

   B. Family Centers, Inc.
      60 Palmer's Hill Road
      Stamford, CT 06902
      (203)324-3167

   C. Catholic Family Services
      30 Myano Lane, Suite 12
      Stamford, CT 06902
      (203)323-1105

   D. Family and Children's Agency
      9 Mott Avenue
      Norwalk, CT 06850
      (203)855-8765

   E. Catholic Family Services
      One Park Street, 3rd Floor
      PO Box 2025
      Norwalk, CT 06852
      (203)750-9711

   F. Jewish Family Service
      111 Prospect Street
      Stamford, CT 06901
      (203)921-4161

Tolland Judicial District

1. Yardley Associates, LLP
   Quality Inn
   100 Hartford Turnpike
   Vernon, CT 06066
   (860)688-1240

2. University of Connecticut
   Human Development Center
   843 Bolton Road, U-117
   Storrs, CT 06269
   (888)311-8842

3. University of Connecticut
   Cooperative Extension Center
   24 Hyde Avenue
   Vernon, CT 06066
   (888)311-8842

Waterbury Judicial District

1. CT Council of Family Service Agencies
   (To attend a Parenting Education Program
   at one of the following agencies, call
   (203)756-8317.)

A. Catholic Family Services
56 Church Street
Waterbury, CT 06702
(203)755-1196

B. Family Services of Greater
Waterbury, Inc
34 Murray Street
Waterbury, CT 06710
(203)756-8317

Windham Judicial District

1. University of Connecticut
Cooperative Extension System
139 Wolf Den Road
Brooklyn, CT 06234
(888)311-8842

2. United Services, Inc.
Sonia Family Support Center
1125 Main Street
Willimantic, CT 06226
(860)774-2020 or
(860)456-2261

BIBLIOGRAPHY

BREAKING APART: A Memoir of Divorce. Swallow, Wendy. New York: Hyperion Publishing, 2001. A memoir of divorce that highlights the stresses and the accomplishments of independence and renewal.

BUYING & SELLING A SMALL BUSINESS. Coltman, Michael M. Seattle: Self-Counsel Press, Inc., 1991. Practical advice for either buying or selling, with a good chapter on valuation methods.

CAUGHT IN THE MIDDLE: Protecting the Children of High-Conflict Divorce. Garrity, Carla B., and Mitchell A. Baris, New York: Lexington Books, MacMillan Publishing Co., 1994. Readable discussion of the on-going effect of high-conflict divorce on children.

CHILD CUSTODY: Building Agreements That Work. Lyster, Mimi. Nolo Press, 1995. Ideal for both the professional mediator and parents, this practical book offers real world solutions to parenting issues with a number of worksheets that may be used with or without professional help in the development of a parenting agreement.

CRAZY TIME: Surviving Divorce. Trafford, Abigail. Harper Perennial, 1992. For the newly separated. The book to read when you feel this can't be happening to you.

CUTTING LOOSE: Why Women Who End Their Marriages Do So Well. Applewhite, Ashton. New York: Harper Collins, 1997. For women contemplating divorce or in the midst of the process, guidelines for moving forward.

DINOSAUR'S DIVORCE: A Guide for Changing Families. Brown, Laurence Krasney, and Marc Tolon Brown. Boston: Little Brown and Co., 1986. *The* book for young children facing divorce. Picture book of likely situations, most encountered after the divorce.

DIVORCE AND NEW BEGINNINGS: Clapp, Genevieve. John Wiley & Sons, 1992. An authoritative guide to recovery and growth, solo parenting, and step families.

FAMILIES APART: Ten Keys to Successful Co-Parenting. Blau, Melinda. Perigee Books, 1994. The book offers practical solutions that give parents a new model of post-divorce relationships. Describes tasks, attitudes, and communications skills that are required to move the family through all the transitions and events that continue to bring parents together in their children's lives.

FIGHTING FOR YOUR MARRIAGE: Positive Steps for Preventing Divorce And Preserving a Lasting Love. Markman, Howard, Scott Stanley, and Susan L. Blumberg. San Fracisco, CA: Jossey-Bass, 1994. Blueprint for how to celebrate and use differences between spouses to enable problem-solving and working communication.

THE FINANCIAL ADVISOR'S GUIDE TO DIVORCE SETTLEMENT: Wilson, Carol Ann, Burr Ridge, IL: Irwin Professional Publishing, 1996. Written for financial planning professionals, this book will also be of interest to those who are looking for detail on a divorce's impact on financial issues.

FROM CONFLICT TO RESOLUTION: Skills and Strategies for Individual, Couple, and Family Therapy. Heitler, Susan M. New York: Norton, 1993. Negotiation and dispute resolution and how to accomplish them. Written for professionals.

GETTING PAST NO: Ury, William. Bantam Books, 1991. This book offers strategies for dealing with someone who is angry, unreasonable, deceitful, or stubborn and does not want to negotiate.

GETTING TO YES: Negotiating Agreement Without Giving In. Fisher, Roger, and William L. Ury. New York: Viking Penguin, 1982; Houghton Mifflin, 1981. Accessible, clear discussion of win-win negotiating for whenever an agreement is needed.

GETTING TOGETHER: Building a Relationship That Gets to Yes. Fischer, Roger, and Scott Brown. New York: Viking Penguin, 1989. Applies the win-win negotiation formula to relationships.

THE GOOD DIVORCE: Keeping Your Family Together When Your Marriage Comes Apart, Ahrons, Constance R. PhD, New York: Harper Collins, 1994. Advocates and anticipates a cultural shift from thinking of divorce as a failure to thinking of it as a natural change of life. Shows how such a change in thinking can help children, especially, to heal.

A GUIDE TO DIVORCE MEDIATION: How to Reach a Fair, Legal Settlement at a Fraction of the Cost. Friedman, Gary J. New York: Workman Publishing, 1993. Story-filled guide to optimum use of mediation.

HEALTHY DIVORCE: Everett, Craig and Sandra Volgy Everett. Jossey-Bass, Inc.; 1994. This book explores ways of confronting such difficult issues as how to tell your children you are getting a divorce, how to plan a separation, and how to cope with your feelings of anger, grief, and abandonment.

LIFE LESSONS: 50 Things I Learned From My Divorce. Joselow, Beth. NYC: Avon, 1994. Fifty pithy sayings which are certain to become classics, such as: Face Problems Squarely and Only When Necessary, Be Prepared, The Law Isn't Always Fair, and It Doesn't Cover Everything. Each is followed by witty, profound, and helpful short discussions.

MOM'S HOUSE, DAD'S HOUSE: Making Shared Custody Work. Ricci, Isolina. New York: MacMillan Publishing Co., 1980. Self-help guide for crafting a shared parenting plan, with sample language, examples, and practical hints.

QUESTIONS FROM DAD: A Very Cool Way to Communicate with Kids. Twilley, Dwight. Charles E. Tuttle Company, Inc., 1994. This book is very useful for long-distance fathers, as it is replete with helpful and practical suggestions and written in an informal, personal, and chatty style.

SPIRITUAL DIVORCE: Divorce As a Catalyst for an Extraordinary Life. Ford, Debbie. Harper, 2001. Based on the tenets of 12-step programs, this book helps individuals understand the life lessons to be learned in the process.

SURVIVAL MANUAL FOR WOMEN IN DIVORCE; SURVIVAL MANUAL FOR MEN IN DIVORCE. Schilling, Edwin III, and Carol Ann Wilson. Dubuque, IA: Kendall Hunt Publishing, 2000. Answers to the most-asked, or should-be-most-asked, questions about financial issues at divorce.

ONWARD

This guidebook has served as a method of bringing you and your family through a life-changing transition on friendly terms. If you have children, you are learning how to work together as parents without having to relate to each other as spouses.

You should feel a sense of pride in bringing your divorce or separation to fruition and be pleased that you can move on with your life in a positive, productive manner.

May your future reflect the strength and confidence that you have gained from negotiating a friendly divorce.